Antitrust Policy in Korea

Seonghoon Jeon

Antitrust Policy in Korea

An Economic Perspective

Springer

Seonghoon Jeon
Department of Economics
Sogang University
Seoul, Korea (Republic of)

ISBN 978-981-95-0631-6 ISBN 978-981-95-0632-3 (eBook)
https://doi.org/10.1007/978-981-95-0632-3

This Springer imprint is published by the registered company Springer Nature Singapore Pte Ltd.
The registered company address is: 152 Beach Road, #21-01/04 Gateway East, Singapore 189721, Singapore

To my grandchildren, Hajoon & Heejun,
with all my love and hope for your bright futures

Foreword

For the last decade or so, antitrust has been "in the air": Around 2015, the European Union's Directorate-General Competition (DGComp) became substantially more aggressive in its enforcement of the EU antitrust (or "competition policy") laws. The UK's Competition and Markets Authority (CMA) stepped up its enforcement efforts as well. And, in the USA, at about the same time, there was growing concern about the rising role of the large digital/platform companies in the US economy and the possibility that antitrust could help address at least some of these concerns—which became a reality in late 2020 with antitrust suits that were filed at the end of the first Trump Administration and with the heightened importance that the Biden Administration gave to antitrust.

In an important sense, this current wave of attention to antitrust followed an earlier, expressly international antitrust wave of the 1980s and 1990s, as many countries' economic policies became more markets-oriented—and those countries' political leaders realized that preserving and encouraging competition was an important way in which this expanded markets-orientation would yield benefits for their economies.

Korea was one of the first countries in this earlier wave. In 1980 Korea's Monopoly Regulation and Fair Trade Act was enacted, followed the next year by the establishment of the Korea Fair Trade Commission (KFTC) to enforce the Act. There is thus over 40 years of experience that can be drawn upon in an assessment of the Korean experience with antitrust.

Prof. Seonghoon Jeon does indeed provide this long-arc assessment in this book. It is no accident that the title is *Antitrust Policy in Korea: An Economic Perspective*. After all, Prof. Jeon has a Ph.D. in Economics from Yale (1991) and has had a long career of teaching economics at Sogang University, as well as serving as an expert witness and testifying in important antitrust cases in Korea (for the KFTC as well as for defendant parties). He also has a long record of public service, which includes serving as a Non-Standing Commissioner of the KFTC during 2009-2012.

Prof. Jeon's economic perspective on Korean antitrust means that he approaches his assessment and insights in terms that will be familiar to most "industrial organization" (IO) economists (and economics-sympathetic lawyers) who are familiar with antitrust more generally. He has three main chapters: on abuse of dominance (or what US antitrust describes as "monopolization"); on mergers; and on cartels (and price-fixing more generally). And within those chapters are terms that will resonate with IO economists as well: exclusive dealing; tying; bundling; foreclosure; natural experiments; merger simulation; leniency programs—to name a few. Within these chapters, Prof. Jeon addresses the relevant economics (and econometrics) and discusses the important Korean antitrust cases in each of the three main areas to which these concepts applied.

Prof. Jeon also has two important chapters—which precede the three just discussed—that address the special issues for Korea in addressing the Korean Chaebols (large multi-market enterprises) and of developing policies that apply to Korea's numerous small and medium-sized enterprises (SMEs). Because these policies are addressed by the KFTC, they are included in this assessment of Korean antitrust policy.

Prof. Jeon provides a useful introduction and overview of Korean antitrust policy in the book's first chapter. And in his concluding chapter he offers his perspective—especially tuned to digital antitrust issues—on antitrust policy generally, and he offers his recommendations as to future directions that Korean antitrust policy should pursue: such as the introduction of private class-action suits, so as to strengthen the deterrence of anti-competitive actions.

In sum, in these seven chapters a reader will learn much about Korean antitrust policy, from the perspective of an experienced and knowledgeable economist. This book offers economists (as well as lawyers) a useful guide to Korea's antitrust experience over these past 40 years and offers important insights for anyone who is interested in comparative international antitrust experiences.

Stern School of Business, New York University, New York, NY, USA
June 2025

Lawrence J. White

Preface

It has been 45 years since the enactment of the Korea Fair Trade Law, formally known as the *Monopoly Regulation and Fair Trade Act*, in 1980. The evolution of antitrust policy in Korea can be assessed from various perspectives. However, the most significant development is arguably the shift toward a more *rationalized and advanced* approach—specifically, the adoption of an effect-based rule-of-reason framework for evaluating the anti-competitive nature and efficiency of business practices, rather than relying on a simplistic, form-based interpretation of statutory language. Over the past two decades, this shift has become increasingly evident, particularly in the active incorporation of economic analysis into antitrust enforcement. While research in industrial organization and antitrust economics had already influenced the field prior to this period, it was in the early 2000s that economists began to participate directly in antitrust cases—submitting economic analyses on behalf of either the competition authority or the defendants.

As an economist specializing in industrial organization, I have been fortunate to play an active role as an expert witness in antitrust cases before the Korea Fair Trade Commission and the courts. Since the early stages of this trend over the past two decades, I have had the opportunity to participate in numerous cases—representing both government agencies and private enterprises. My previous Korean-language publication, *Fair Trade Cases and Economic Analyses* (Jeon, 2020, Park-Young Publishing), was the product of my direct involvement in real antitrust cases. The book selects several major cases in which I participated and presents their key features, along with the economic analyses I submitted to the Korea Fair Trade Commission and the courts in my role as an expert witness.[1]

[1] The book addressed 11 cases: *Moohak-Daesun* in 2003, *Eland Outlets-Carrefour* in 2006, *eBay-G Market* in 2009, and *SK Telecomm and CJ HelloVision* in 2016 in the area of merger; *Posco* in 2001, *Intel* in 2008, *Naver/Daum* in 2014, and *Qualcomm* in 2017 for abuse of market dominance; and *Military Oil Procurement* in 2000, *Graphite Electrodes* in 2002, and *Flour* in 2006 as cartel cases. These cases are also briefly introduced in this book.

What motivated me to write this book was a reflection on the limitations of my previous publication and a desire to address them. While the earlier book offered focused in-depth analyses, its scope was clearly narrow—focusing only on a selection of cases in which I was personally involved. As a result, it excluded other important antitrust cases in Korea that also involved significant economic analysis but fell outside the scope of my direct participation. More importantly, the previous work did not offer a comprehensive overview of antitrust enforcement in Korea, including conventional areas such as abuse of market dominance, mergers, and cartels, as well as uniquely Korean issues like Chaebol antitrust regulations and policies concerning small and medium-sized enterprises (SMEs). In this book, I aim to present a broader and more systematic account of Korean antitrust policy. It covers key areas such as Chaebol and SME-related policies, abuses of market dominance, mergers, and cartels. I also address the underlying economic issues from the perspective of an antitrust economist and examine most of the landmark antitrust cases in Korea—regardless of whether I was personally involved in them.

At a deeper level, this book is driven by my aspiration to leave behind a work that reflects academic neutrality and balanced judgment in the field of antitrust economics before the conclusion of my academic career. As a practitioner—serving as a consulting economist or expert witness—I was often required to advocate for one side, doing my utmost to support it through expert economic analysis. Such partiality, however, is justified by the nature of adversarial proceedings: there are always two opposing parties—plaintiff and defendant—and it is ultimately the Commission or the court that weighs the arguments and determines which is more persuasive. Moreover, a consulting economist can be considered *ex ante* neutral—that is, free to accept or decline a case based on whether they can genuinely support its position, even though they are *ex post* committed once engaged. In contrast, during the five years I spent writing this book, I was not supported by any interested party. I was entirely free to examine each issue on its merits and to adopt positions as I saw fit, without external influence.[2]

The final motivation for writing this book in English is my aspiration to promote broader recognition of Korea's antitrust enforcement within the international antitrust community. Since its establishment in 1981, the Korea Fair Trade Commission (KFTC) has built a relatively long and active history of antitrust enforcement and is well-regarded for its vigorous and sophisticated handling of high-profile cases such as *Microsoft* in 2006, *Qualcomm* in 2017, and *Google* in 2021. [3] Beyond the conventional areas of competition policy—such as abuse of dominance, mergers, and cartels—the KFTC maintains a strong institutional focus on uniquely Korean issues, including Chaebol reform and policies concerning small and medium-sized enterprises (SMEs). Economists have come to play an increasingly influential role in shaping antitrust policy and in guiding decisions by both the Commission and the

[2]This work was supported from the National Research Foundation of Korea's Excellent Scholarly Books Program (NRF-2022S1A6A4046485).

[3]These cases were examined in Chapter 4 of this book.

courts, particularly in cases that require careful economic analysis of competitive effects. Although many Korean antitrust matters are worthy of international attention, there remains a notable lack of English-language literature on Korean competition policy—particularly from an economic perspective. I hope that this book, however modestly, helps fill that gap and contributes to the broader understanding and development of antitrust policy both in Korea and around the world.

I am deeply indebted to many individuals who supported the writing of this book—far too many to name adequately within the confines of this space. Looking back from this culminating stage of my academic career, I wish to pay homage to my mentors, Professors Bengt Holmström and Ki-Jun Jung. They exemplified the scholarly virtues of prudence and steadfastness—qualities I have always admired, though could never fully emulate. More recently, I was especially honored that Professor Lawrence White graciously agreed to write the Foreword to this book—an act of generosity beyond what this work likely deserves. I also owe much to numerous colleagues, fellow economists, and legal practitioners who contributed to the development of this book, whether by collaborating on key materials or by offering insightful feedback on earlier drafts. I would like to express particular appreciation to Professors Yun Jeong Choi, Jinwha Chung, Hayeon Joo, Namhoon Kwon, Han Shik Lee, Jaehyun Nahm, and Sang-Seung Yi; to Drs. Kwangshik Shin and Richard Shin; and to attorneys Chang Sik Hwang, Hwan Jeong, Hongki Kim, Keumseok Oh, Sung Bom Park, and Seongun Yun.

Last but by no means least, I wish to express my heartfelt gratitude to my wife, Meesook, and my children, Yewon and Haesung. Without their unwavering encouragement, patience, and love, I could not have endured the long and at times painful process of writing a book that may ultimately receive little attention or recognition.

Seoul, Korea (Republic of) Seonghoon Jeon

Competing Interests The author has no competing interests to declare that are relevant to the content of this manuscript.

Contents

About the Author

Seonghoon Jeon is an emeritus professor of economics at Sogang University and currently works as an economic advisor in Bae, Kim & Lee LLC (BKL), one of the top three law firms in Korea. Prior to joining BKL, Professor Jeon held the position of the Executive Vice President of Academic Affairs (equivalent to Provost) at Sogang University for two years. From 2009 to 2012, he also served as a non-standing commissioner for the Korea Fair Trade Commission.

Professor Jeon completed his undergraduate studies at Seoul National University in 1982 and received his Ph.D. in Economics from Yale University in 1991. His primary research interests include industrial organization, competition policies, and economic regulation.

Throughout his career, Dr. Jeon has made substantial contributions in both academic research and public policy. He has published numerous papers on theoretical and policy-oriented topics in leading journals such as the *European Economic Review*, *International Journal of Industrial Organization*, *Review of Industrial Organization*, *Applied Economics*, and *Korean Economic Review*. He is also the author of a Korean-language book titled *Fair Trade Cases and Economic Analyses*, which examines major antitrust cases in which he played a key role.

Dr. Jeon currently serves as President of the Korea Competition Forum and previously held the position of President of the Korean Academic Society of Industrial Organization in 2009. Over the past two decades, he has been actively involved in a wide range of antitrust cases in South Korea related to mergers, abuse of dominance, and cartels. He has frequently served as an expert witness, providing economic analysis for defendants, third parties, and the Korea Fair Trade Commission.

Chapter 1
Introduction

This book offers a comprehensive examination of antitrust policy in Korea from an economist's perspective. It covers the fundamental components of the policy, its enforcement history, key economic issues, and significant cases. Topics include the role of chaebols, small and medium-sized enterprises (SMEs), abuses of market dominance, mergers, and cartels.

In this introductory chapter, I present an overview of Korea's antitrust policy, including a brief historical background, its objectives, core components, and distinguishing features. Additionally, I outline the structure of the subsequent chapters and briefly mention related topics that, while relevant, fall outside the scope of this book. Finally, I offer some remarks on the contributions this book makes to the existing body of literature.

1.1 Overview of Antitrust Policy in Korea

The Monopoly Regulation and Fair Trade Act (MRFTA), commonly referred to as the 'Fair Trade Act', was enacted in December 1980 and came into effect in April 1981. Its legislative roots can be traced back to the Price Stabilization and Fair Trade Act of March 1976. During the rapid industrialization of the 1960s under President Park Chung-Hee, structural economic issues began to accumulate. South Korea's export-led growth strategy, implemented in a country with limited domestic demand, inevitably led to high market concentration. By 1974, over 80% of manufacturing industries (1279 out of 1543 product categories) were classified as monopolies or oligopolies.[1] To facilitate industrial policy, the government allowed explicit and implicit cartels through trade associations and imposed entry barriers via competition-restricting laws and regulations. These structural inefficiencies were

[1] Refer to Korea Fair Trade Commission (2011).

S. Jeon, *Antitrust Policy in Korea*, https://doi.org/10.1007/978-981-95-0632-3_1

exacerbated by the inflationary pressures following the 1974 oil shock. The primary objective of the 1976 legislation was to curb price increases rather than to promote competition. As such, it focused on temporary price stabilization and did not address mergers, abuse of market dominance, or cartels. Consequently, there was little to no meaningful antitrust enforcement during this period, and the 'Price Stabilization Act' is not generally regarded as the beginning of Korea's antitrust regime.

The enactment of the 1980 *Fair Trade Act* reflected a growing recognition of the limitations of Korea's growth-centric economic policies. Rising concerns over monopolistic practices and economic concentration led to calls for a more decentralized economic order. Interestingly, the Act was not passed through a regular legislative process but by the *National Security Constitutional Congress*, established after the 1979 military coup led by General Chun Doo-Hwan. While it may seem paradoxical that a law promoting economic decentralization emerged under a military dictatorship, the legislation served to legitimize the new regime's authority. In fact, antitrust laws—often opposed by powerful business interests—are notoriously difficult to pass through democratic legislatures. Without the political upheaval of the time, Korea's adoption of antitrust legislation might have been significantly delayed.

From a global perspective, South Korea was an early adopter of antitrust law relative to its economic development. In 1980, the country ranked 27th in total GDP (US$ 65.4 billion) and 75th in GDP per capita (US$ 1,715).[2] At that time, only a limited number of countries had enacted competition laws[3]—most of them influenced by post-World War II developments such as the Treaty of Paris in 1951 and the Treaty of Rome in1957,[4] which laid the groundwork for European competition policy. A few additional countries followed suit in the 1970s. The global proliferation of competition laws accelerated after the fall of the Berlin Wall in 1989. As Evans and Jenny (2009) describe in "Trustbusting Goes Global," the subsequent two decades saw a surge in the adoption of antitrust regimes, particularly among Eastern European nations transitioning to market economies and EU member states aligning with European competition law. By 2010, 135 jurisdictions had enacted competition laws (Bradford et al. 2018).

Article 1 of the MRFTA clearly articulates the Act's objectives and core provisions:

---

[2]This ranking is based on the website of https://countryeconomy.com.

[3]According to Gutman and Voigt (2014), only 20 countries had enacted competition law before Korea did in 1980.

[4]Japan's *Private Monopoly Prohibition and Fair Trade Act* of 1947 was introduced under US military occupation following World War II. Its primary objective was to dismantle the powerful corporate conglomerates known as *Zaibatsu*, which were believed to have supported Japanese militarism. Similarly, in post-war Germany, the Allied powers imposed antitrust laws in 1958 not only to foster market competition but also to dismantle excessive concentrations of economic power, which were viewed as potential threats to democratic stability. As Motta (2004, p. 10) notes, these early antitrust regimes were as much about political restructuring and economic decentralization as they were about market efficiency.

> The purpose of this Act is to promote fair and free competition, ① to encourage thereby creative enterprising activities, to protect consumers and ② to strive for the balanced development of the national economy, by preventing (i) any abuse of market-dominant positions by enterprises and (ii) any excessive concentration of economic power, and by regulating (iii) undue collaborative acts and (iv) unfair trade practices. *(Numbering added for clarity)*

The Act sets forth two primary goals: ① *to encourage creative entrepreneurial activity and protect consumers* and ② *to promote the balanced development of the national economy*. These objectives closely align with Article 119 of the Constitution of the Republic of Korea, which outlines the foundational principles of the country's economic order:

> (1) The economic order of the Republic of Korea shall be based on a respect for the freedom and creative initiative of enterprises and individuals in economic affairs. (2) The State may regulate and coordinate economic affairs in order to maintain the balanced growth and stability of the national economy, to ensure equitable income distribution, prevent market domination and economic power abuse, and democratize the economy through harmony among economic agents.

Article 119 emphasizes two core principles: *economic freedom* and *economic democratization*. While economic freedom supports entrepreneurial initiative, the concept of economic democratization extends beyond balanced development. It provides a constitutional basis for state intervention to prevent market concentration and promote equitable economic participation. This broader vision laid the groundwork for the enactment of the MRFTA and continues to form Korea's competition policy framework.

The MRFTA incorporates standard antitrust provisions commonly found in other jurisdictions, including regulations on *abuse of market dominance*, *anticompetitive mergers*, and *collusive practices*—collectively referred to as *'conventional competition policies'*. Article 1 of the MRFTA encompasses all three elements, with anticompetitive mergers falling under the broader category of 'excessive concentration of economic power'. The primary objective of these traditional antitrust provisions is *"to encourage thereby creative enterprising activities [and] to protect consumers,"* thereby *promoting competition*. The Korea Fair Trade Commission (KFTC) has actively enforced these conventional policies to enhance market competition. Despite limited resources in terms of staffing and budget, the KFTC was recognized in 2010 as one of the leading competition authorities globally.[5] Since then, it has significantly expanded its institutional capacity, expertise, and enforcement capabilities, aligning its status with Korea's broader economic development.

---

[5] According to Bradford et al. (2018, p. 36), the KFTC ranked 4th in the number of merger control filings in 2010, 1st in the investigation of anticompetitive agreements, 2nd in the implementation of remedies for such agreements, respectively, and 4th in remedies for abuse of dominance. Even as of 2004, Gutman and Voigt (2014, pp. 59–60) awarded Korea a score of 24 out of 30 on their comprehensive competition index, which evaluates factors such as legal scope, available remedies, and private enforcement mechanisms. For comparison, the United States scored 25 points.

In contrast, the MRFTA also includes provisions aimed at achieving the second objective stated in Article 1: *"to strive for the balanced development of the national economy."* These provisions reflect Korea's unique approach to *fostering a sound business ecosystem*. While the definition of such an ecosystem can be subjective, it may be likened to a healthy forest—where large, medium, and small enterprises coexist and thrive together. This vision has led to two distinct regulatory categories under the KFTC: *Chaebol Antitrust Policy*—Targeting the excessive concentration and expansion of large corporate groups (chaebols) and *SMEs Antitrust Policy*—Aimed at promoting fair competition and shared growth between large firms and small and medium-sized enterprises (SMEs).

Throughout this book, I will use the terms *competition policy* and *antitrust* interchangeably in general. However, a nuanced distinction is made when discussing Korea's regulatory framework. *Competition policy* refers specifically to measures that promote market competition (e.g., addressing dominance, mergers, and cartels), while *antitrust* in the Korean context also encompasses broader goals, such as fostering a fair and inclusive business environment.

'Excessive concentration of economic power', i.e., element (ii) in Article 1 of the MRFTA, includes not only anticompetitive mergers but also the excessive expansion of 'chaebols'. 'Unfair trade practices', listed as element (iv) in Article 1 of the Act, covers a wide range of behaviors, including intra-group support among chaebol affiliates and exploitative practices by dominant firms against weaker counterparts. While some unfair trade practices overlap with abuse of dominance in terms of conduct, the legal standard differs. Instead of assessing *market power* in a defined market, the focus is on *relative bargaining power* between transacting firms. When a stronger party (typically a large firm) exploits its superior position to the detriment of a weaker party (usually an SME), such conduct may be deemed unfair—even if the stronger party lacks market dominance in the conventional sense. In many countries, such disputes are resolved through civil litigation. In Korea, however, the KFTC plays a central administrative role in addressing these issues.

What sets Korea apart is the centralized and comprehensive role of the KFTC in regulating large business groups and protecting SMEs. In other countries, such responsibilities are often dispersed across financial, commercial, or civil regulatory bodies. While Korea also has sector-specific laws and agencies—such as the Ministry of SMEs and Startups, which oversees the Framework Act on SMEs—the KFTC remains the primary enforcer of antitrust-related disputes between large and small firms. Moreover, the KFTC administers several special statutes designed to address unfair practices in specific business relationships, such as subcontracting, large retail business, franchising, and agency relationship. These laws provide targeted protections for SMEs in dealings with larger firms, reinforcing the broader goal of economic democratization and balanced development.

In the broader context of Korea's competition regime, ongoing discussions center around the fundamental values that guide its antitrust policy. The first objective stated in Article 1 of the MRFTA—*"to promote fair and free competition and to encourage thereby creative enterprising activities, [and] to protect consumers"*—underscores the importance of efficiency and economic welfare, principles rooted in neoclassical economics. Among the two primary standards of economic welfare—total welfare and consumer surplus—Korea's antitrust policy clearly prioritizes the latter. The emphasis on *"protecting consumers"* extends beyond end users to include all purchasers of goods and services, including intermediaries. Moreover, the assessment of consumer surplus is not confined to short-term price effects; it also considers product quality, variety, innovation, and long-term pricing trends—a multidimensional approach consistent with practices in advanced antitrust jurisdictions. However, antitrust law and policy are not solely about promoting efficiency. They also serve broader societal goals such as protecting small firms, safeguarding economic freedom, and implementing industrial policy. These broader aims are encapsulated in the second objective of Article 1: *"to strive for the balanced development of the national economy."* In Korea, this has translated into two distinctive policy streams: Chaebol Antitrust Policy, which seeks to preserve economic freedom by curbing the concentration of power in large conglomerates and SMEs Antitrust Policy, which aims to protect smaller firms and promote shared growth.

This dual-purpose approach is not unique to Korea. Early US antitrust laws were also motivated by concerns over the concentration of economic and political power. As famously noted, the goal was to counter "the trust power that combined capital gave them by driving out of business the small dealers and worthy men."[6] Similarly, the European Union incorporates SME protection into its competition framework. The EU supports SMEs through favorable state aid policies—such as subsidized loans, R&D assistance, and financial guarantees—and through legal doctrines like the *de minimis* exemption, which shields small-scale agreements from antitrust scrutiny when their market impact is negligible. The philosophical foundation for these broader objectives can be traced to *ordo-liberalism*, a German school of thought that influenced post-war European competition law. Ordo-liberalism, often described as 'disciplined pluralism', holds that: Economic systems should allow all individuals to participate without being overpowered by dominant actors (pluralism), and Economic freedom must be protected through regulation, as unregulated markets can lead to monopolies and cartels that undermine freedom.[7]

To summarize, Korea's antitrust framework can be divided into two main domains: Competition-Promoting Regulations which address abuse of dominance, mergers, and cartels and Ecosystem-Building Regulations which target chaebol dominance and supporting SME growth. What distinguishes Korea is the centralized role of the KFTC in overseeing both domains. In most countries, responsibilities for broader economic fairness are distributed across various agencies and courts. In Korea, however, the KFTC is uniquely empowered to enforce both competition and

---

[6]US v. Trans-Missouri Freight Association 166 U.S. 290, 319 (1897). However, at least since the 1970s, the United States has endorsed the view that competition law should focus narrowly on efficiency, which is typically understood as maximizing consumer welfare. Refer to Bradford et al. (2018, pp. 9–10).

[7]Refer to Motta (2004, p. 16).

ecosystem-oriented policies. This consolidation offers both advantages and challenges. On the one hand, the KFTC can deploy a wide array of policy tools efficiently and respond swiftly to market dynamics. On the other hand, balancing the dual objectives—*"to encourage creative enterprising activities and to protect consumers"* versus *"to strive for balanced development"*—can be difficult. Often, protecting small firms may conflict with preserving competitive processes, and restricting chaebol activities may hinder innovation and efficiency. As the Korean proverb goes, "If you chase two rabbits, you may catch neither." The KFTC's challenge lies in navigating these tensions while maintaining legitimacy and effectiveness in both realms.

1.2 Remaining Chapters of the Book

This book is organized into two parts, comprising five core chapters. The first part explores Korean Specialties, focusing antitrust issues related to Chaebols (large conglomerates) and Small and Medium Enterprises (SMEs). The second part covers Conventional Competition Policies, addressing the foundational pillars of antitrust enforcement such as Market Dominance Abuses, Mergers, and Cartels within the Korean context. Each chapter follows a consistent framework, commencing with an introduction to the Korean policy area and its historical development. Subsequently, the book examines the relevant economic issues and equips readers with the necessary economic tools to analyze the subject matter. Additionally, the book reviews landmark cases that hold legal precedence, carry economic significance, and possess international relevance.

Part I: Korean Specialties

Chapter 2. Chaebol Antitrust Policy in Korea

In this chapter, I will examine the complex structure and behavior of Korean chaebols, focusing on four key dimensions: concentration of economic power, corporate governance, business diversification, and internal transactions. These characteristics have raised persistent concerns from both political and economic standpoints. To address these issues, I will explore the regulatory framework governing chaebols, tracing its historical evolution and institutional rationale. The chapter will also delve into the economic justifications for chaebol-specific regulations. Those include fictitious equity investments, the positive and negative effects of intercorporate shareholding, the risks associated with excessive diversification, and the practice of profit tunneling—where resources are shifted within a corporate group to benefit controlling shareholders at the expense of minority shareholders. To illustrate the practical implications of these regulations, I will present a series of notable case studies involving unfair subsidizing among chaebol affiliates. These cases provide valuable insights into the ownership structures and governance challenges within Korea's largest business groups as well as the enforcement role of the

Korea Fair Trade Commission. Key examples include: the 'Unfair Subsidizing Group Head's Relative' case by *Samsung SDS* in 1999, the 'Quantity-Pushing' case involving *Hyundai Glovis* in 2007, the 'Undue Profit-Deflecting' case of *Hanjin KAL* in 2017, the 'Unfair Collecting Toll' by *Hanwha Solution* in 2020, and the 'Quantity-Pushing and Unfair Subsidizing' case related to *Samsung Wellstory* in 2021.

Chapter 3. SMEs Antitrust Policy in Korea

This chapter begins by examining the growing polarization within Korea's business landscape, highlighting disparities between large corporations and small and medium-sized enterprises (SMEs) across various dimensions. Next, I will explore the distinctive features of Korea's antitrust policy as it pertains to SMEs—features that often diverge from conventional approaches in other countries. This includes a review of the main provisions within MRFTA that address unfair business practices, particularly those arising in transactions between dominant firms and smaller counterparts. In addition to the MRFTA, Korea enacted four specialized statutes that regulate unfair practices in specific business relationships: the Subcontract Act, Large Retail Business Act, Franchise Business Act, and Agency Act. These acts are designed to protect SMEs from exploitative practices in their dealing with larger firms, reflecting Korea's broader commitment to fostering a sound and equitable business ecosystem. The chapter also delves into key economic issues underpinning SMEs antitrust policy. Topics include: the positive and negative effects of vertical constraints, the economic rationale for regulating abuses of superior trade position, the theoretical foundation of the specialized acts, and concerns related to holdup and 'reverse' holdup. To ground these discussions in real-world context, I will examine a series of noteworthy enforcement cases of SMEs-related antitrust issues in Korea: such as the 'Refusal to Deal' case by *Hyundai Oil Bank* in 2004, the 'Minimum Resale Maintenance' involving *TaylorMade/Callaway Golf Korea* in 2009, the 'Exclusive Dealing' case of *Oil Refinery Companies* in 2009, the 'Vertical Restraints' of *Naver/Daum* in 2014, the 'Best Price Guarantee' by *Delivery Hero Korea (Yogiyo)* in 2020, the 'Self Preferencing' of *Naver (Video Contents)* in 2021.

Part II: Conventional Competition Policies

Chapter 4. Market Dominance Abuse Regulation in Korea

This chapter explores the regulatory framework and enforcement practices surrounding the abuse of market dominance in Korea. It begins with a review of the evolution of the Korea Fair Trade Commission's enforcement strategies, highlighting key milestones and shifts in approach over time. Next, I categorize the various forms of abusive conducts as defined under in the MRFTA, providing a structured overview of the legal typologies. These include practices such as exclusive dealing, tying and bundling, predatory pricing, price discrimination, refusal to supply, and other foreclosure strategies that may hinder market competition. A central focus of the chapter is the economic methodology used to assess market dominance and its abuse. I will provide a detailed analysis of tools for market definition—including critical loss analysis, aggregate diversion ratio, time series analysis, and LIFO-LOFI tests—as well as techniques for evaluating market power. These tools form the analytical foundation for identifying and addressing anticompetitive behavior. The chapter also examines the competitive and efficiency effects of typical abusive practices, drawing on both theoretical and empirical perspectives. This includes a discussion of how certain behaviors may simultaneously harm competition while offering potential efficiency gains, necessitating a nuanced case-by-case analysis. To illustrate the practical application of these principles, I will present a series of noteworthy enforcement cases that underscore the importance of economic analysis in decision-making. These include: the 'Refusal of Trade' by *Posco* in 2001, the 'Tying' case involving *Microsoft* in 2006, the 'Restrictions on Advertising in Online Video Content' by *NHN(Naver)* in 2008, the 'Conditional Rebates' by *Intel* in 2008, the 'Discriminatory Royalties and Conditional Rebates' by *Qualcomm* in 2010, the 'Margin Squeeze' by *LGU Plus* in 2015, the 'Business Model involving Licensing and Modem Chipset Supply' of *Qualcomm* in 2017, the 'Charging Unreasonable Prices on Maintenance Software for CT/MRI' by *Siemens* in 2018, the 'Self-Preferencing' of *Naver (Shopping)* in 2021, and the 'Anti-Fragmentation Agreement' of *Google* in 2021. These cases highlight the evolving challenges in regulating dominant firms, particularly in the context of digital markets and global platform competition.

Chapter 5. Merger Regulation in Korea

This chapter begins by outlining the key characteristics of the KFTC's enforcement strategy of merger regulation. Next, I provide a comprehensive overview of the concepts and methodologies, both traditional and modern, that are employed to evaluate the competitive impact of different types of mergers, namely, horizontal, vertical, and conglomerate mergers. The concepts and analytical methods addressed encompass traditional market shares and concentration index, empirical analysis based on 'natural experiments', merger simulation, UPP (Upward Pricing Pressure) for evaluating horizontal merger, as well as vertical arithmetic, bargaining model, vGUPPI (vertical Gross UPP Index), Cournot effect, and elimination of double marginalization for evaluating non-horizontal mergers. These tools reflect the KFTC's adoption of advanced economic analysis, aligning its practices with those of leading global competition authorities. To illustrate the practical application of these methodologies, I will examine a series of noteworthy merger cases in Korea: a horizontal merger between *Hyundai Motor and Kia Car* in 1999, a horizontal merger between *Moohak Soju and Deasun Soju* in 2003, a conglomerate merger between *Hite Beer and Jinro Soju* in 2006, a horizontal merger between *Eland Outlets and Carrefour* in 2006, a horizontal merger between *eBay and G Market* in 2009, a vertical merger between *Microsoft and Nokia* in 2015, a horizontal merger between *SK Telecomm and CJ HelloVision* in 2016, a horizontal merger between *Delivery Hero and Woowa Bro.* in 2021, and a horizontal merger between *Korean Air and Asiana Air* in 2022. These cases offer valuable insights into the competitive effects of mergers, the application of economic tools, and the international dimensions of merger review, particularly when compared with parallel decisions in other jurisdictions.

Chapter 6. Cartel Regulation in Korea

This chapter explores the key features of cartel regulation in Korea, with a particular focus on enforcement strategies, economic rationale, and the role of empirical analysis in assessing harm. The discussion begins with an overview of the core characteristics of Korea's cartel enforcement regime, including the legal framework, investigative procedures, and the KFTC-evolving approach to detection and deterrence. A central component of modern cartel enforcement is the leniency program, which incentivizes cartel participants to self-report and cooperate with authorities. I will examine the economic logic behind leniency programs, highlighting how they disrupt collusive incentives and enhance detection efficiency—an approach widely adopted by competition agencies around the world. The chapter then turns to the estimation of cartel damages, with a focus on two key components: Price overcharges resulting from collusion and Cost pass-through to downstream buyers. To quantify these effects, I will introduce several econometric methods commonly used in antitrust analysis: dummy variable models, forecasting models, difference-in-differences (DID) approaches. These tools are essential for both regulatory enforcement and private damage claims, providing a rigorous basis for assessing the economic impact of collusion. To illustrate the practical application of these methods, I will present a selection of noteworthy cartel cases across various industries in Korea: *Military Oil Procurement* in 2000, *Graphite Electrodes* in 2002, *Flour* in 2006, *Credit Card/VAN* in 2006, *BMW/Lexus Dealers* in 2008, *Ramen* in 2008, *Industrial Explosives* in 2015, and *Compound Feed* in 2015, *LNG Tank* in 2016, *Iron Scrap Purchase* in 2021 and *Public Procurement of Reinforcing Bar* in 2022. These cases are significant not only for their legal outcomes but also for their influence on the development of cartel regulation and the increasing use of economic analysis in KFTC decisions and court rulings. Many of them are closely tied to the quantification of cartel damages, underscoring the growing importance of empirical tools in modern antitrust enforcement.

Chapter 7. Conclusion

In conclusion, this book closes with a discussion of two critical challenges and opportunities for the future of antitrust enforcement in Korea. First, there is a growing need to adapt conventional competition policies to address the rise of big tech and digital platform companies. These firms operate within network economies, leverage vast data advantages, and often pursue winner-takes-all strategies that can entrench market dominance and stifle competition. Traditional tools and frameworks may be insufficient to capture the complexities of digital markets, necessitating new approaches to market definition, dominance assessment, and remedies. Second, Korea's past experiences and recent global developments in antitrust thinking offer valuable insights for shaping a forward-looking enforcement strategy. Lessons drawn from Korea's unique regulatory model—particularly its dual focus on promoting competition and fostering a sound business ecosystem—can inform more nuanced and effective responses to emerging challenges. Integrating these insights with evolving international best practices will be essential for ensuring that Korea's antitrust policy remains both relevant and resilient in the digital age.

Although this book does not focus primarily on institutional design, it is important to briefly introduce the Korea Fair Trade Commission (KFTC)—the sole antitrust enforcement authority in Korea—given its central role in implementing the policies discussed throughout this volume. The KFTC is described as "a ministerial-level central administrative organization under the authority of the Prime Minister and also functions as a quasi-judicial body" (*KFTC website*). The KFTC performs three core functions in enforcing antitrust law: (1) Investigation—It conducts inquiries into potential violations and issues statements of objection (examiner's reports) when problematic conduct is identified; (2) Adjudication—A nine-member commission serves as the decision-making body, operating under a quasi-judicial, adversarial system. Examiners present the case, while respondents defend their actions; (3) Policy and Advocacy—The KFTC also drafts competition policies and reviews existing regulations to identify and eliminate unnecessary restrictions on competition.

The commission is designed to function independently from the secretariat, which handles administrative and investigative tasks. The chairperson and vice chairperson are nominated by the prime minister and appointed by the president. The remaining commissioners are appointed by the president upon recommendation by the chairperson. Commissioners serve 3-year terms, and four of the nine are *non-standing* members—external experts in law and economics—who are expected to enhance the commission's independence from political influence. KFTC decisions are treated as first-instance rulings, and parties may appeal to the Seoul High Court, which functions as the appellate court for antitrust matters. In several high-profile cases, KFTC decisions have been overturned or modified by the judiciary, reflecting the dynamic interaction between administrative and judicial review in Korea's antitrust system. The KFTC also holds exclusive authority to initiate antitrust suits and recommend criminal indictments. Recent amendments to the MRFTA have expanded enforcement channels, allowing private parties to bring certain antitrust claims directly and enabling prosecutors to indict in hardcore cartel cases upon KFTC recommendation.

In addition to its competition-related mandate, the KFTC oversees a range of consumer protection regulations unrelated to competition law. These include oversight of: 'Terms and Conditions', 'Labeling and Advertising', 'Installment Transactions', 'Door-to-Door Sales', 'E-Commerce', 'General Consumer Rights'. However, this book does not address these consumer protection functions, as they fall outside the scope of competition policy and the core themes explored in the preceding chapters.

1.3 Contributions of the Book

This book aims to illuminate the development of antitrust policy in Korea over the past four decades from an economic perspective. Since the enactment of the Monopoly Regulation and Fair Trade Act in 1981, Korea has made significant strides in refining its legal framework, expanding its scope, and strengthening enforcement mechanisms. Particularly in the aftermath of the Asian financial crisis in the late 1990s, the Act has evolved to include a broader range of regulations—especially those targeting the conduct of large corporate groups—and policies promoting the balanced growth of small, medium-sized, and large enterprises.

The KFTC has also adopted advanced policy tools from leading jurisdictions such as the United States and the European Union, increasingly applying the rule of reason and economic analysis in enforcement. These efforts have earned Korea recognition on the global stage, reflecting its growing influence in the international competition policy landscape. Despite this progress, no comprehensive English-language book has yet introduced Korea's antitrust policy to a global audience. This book represents a first attempt to do so, aiming to globalize Korea's antitrust discourse through publication.

The US and the EU have long been the focus of extensive academic and policy literature—ranging from legal analyses to law-and-economics perspectives. Influential works such as *Antitrust Law* by Posner (2001), *Lectures on Antitrust Economics* by Whinston (2006), *Global Antitrust Law and Economics* by Elhauge and Geradin (2007), *EC Competition Law* by Monti (2007), *Cases in European Competition Policy* by Lyons (2009), *The Antitrust Revolution* by Kwaka Jr. and White (2018), and *Antitrust Economics at a Time of Upheaval* by Kwaka Jr. et al. (2023) have shaped global understanding of antitrust enforcement. Japan's experience has also been introduced in *Law and Economics in Japanese Competition Policy* by Arai (2019).

In Korean, many legal scholars and former KFTC officials have published works on the Fair Trade Act, including Kwon et al. (2020), Kim (2022), and Han (2017). I have also contributed to this body of work with *Fair Trade Cases and Economic Analyses* (Jeon 2020), which presents in-depth economic analyses of major antitrust cases. However, a recent, comprehensive English-language book that introduces Korean competition law and policy from both legal and economic perspectives remains absent. Notable precursors include *Competition Law/Policy and Korean Economic Development* by Hur (2006), which offers insights from a policymaker's viewpoint, and a concise overview by Yi and Jung (2007) in journal form. More recently, *Competition Law and Economics: Development Policies and Enforcement Trends in the US and Korea* by Choi and Lee (2020) addresses selected topics but lacks comprehensive coverage.

This book distinguishes itself in two key ways: its comprehensive treatment of all major aspects of Korea's antitrust policy, and its consistent application of a law-and-economics framework.

The contributions of this book to the existing literature and its relevance to antitrust professionals are threefold. First, it introduces the evolution of Korea's competition policy to international scholars, highlighting the KFTC's emergence as a globally recognized enforcement agency. Unique chapters on chaebol and SMEs regulations—distinctive features of Korean antitrust—explore the economic rationale behind these policies. Second, the book equips antitrust practitioners with analytical tools for real-world application, offering methods to assess the competitive effects of abuse of dominance, mergers, and cartels. It discusses 40 landmark cases in Korean antitrust history, over one-third of which involve multinational firms—making it particularly valuable for international practitioners. Third, the book serves as a reference in industrial organization and antitrust economics, offering insights not only for Korea but also for jurisdictions where Korean experiences may inform policy development.

What sets this book apart is its comprehensive economic perspective on Korean antitrust policy, authored by a single economist. While many existing works are authored by legal scholars or former regulators, none have been written in English by an economist. Each main chapter—covering chaebol, SMEs, abuse of dominance, mergers, and cartels—follows a consistent structure that integrates regulatory context, economic analysis, and case studies. Much of the content, beyond standard antitrust tools, may be novel to international experts, while the economic approach may offer fresh perspectives to Korean readers as well.

Cases

US v. Trans-Missouri Freight Association 166 U.S. 290, 319 (1897)

References

Arai K (2019) Law and economics in Japanese competition policy. Springer

Bradford A, Chilton AS, Megaw C, Sokol N (2018) Competition law gone global: Introducing the competition law and enforcement datasets. Journal of Empirical and Legal Studies 16(2): 411–443

Choi JWL, Lee S (2020) Competition law and economics: development policies and enforcement trends in the US and Korea. Edward Elgar Publishing

Elhauge E, Geradin D (2007) Global antitrust law and economics. Foundation Press

Evans D, Jenny F (2009) Trustbusting goes global. In: Evans D, Jenny F (eds) Trustbusters: competition policy authorities speak out. Competition Policy International

Gutman J, Voigt S (2014) Lending a hand to the invisible hand? Assessing the effects of newly enacted competition laws. Unpublished manuscript. University of Hamburg, Institute of Law and Economics, Working Paper

Han C (2017) Fair trade act: the principle of market and law. Korea Competition Federation. [in Korean]

Hur JS (2006) Competition Law/Policy and Korean economic development. Ziumm Press

Jeon S (2020) Fair trade cases and economic analyses. Park Young Publishing. [in Korean]

Kim HB (2022) Theory and practice of fair trade law. Comprehensive Revision, Sam-Il Publishing Company. [in Korean]

Korean Fair Trade Commission (2011) Thirty years history of Korea fair trade commission: Trace of advocating market economy (1981~2010). [in Korean]

Kwaka J Jr, White L (2018) The antitrust revolution, 7th edn. Oxford Press

Kwaka J Jr, Valletti T, White L (2023) Antitrust economics at a time of upheaval: Recent competition policy cases of two continents, edited volume. Competition Policy International

Kwon O, Lee B, Hong D, Hong M, Cho S, Shin Y, Hwang T (2020) Monopoly regulation law. Beop-Mun Press. [in Korean]
Lyons B (2009) Cases in European competition policy, Edited Volume. Cambridge University Press
Monti G (2007) EC competition law. Cambridge University Press
Motta M (2004) Competition policy theory and practice. Cambridge University Press
Posner RA (2001) Antitrust law, 2nd edn. The University of Chicago Press
Whinston MD (2006) Lectures on antitrust economics. The MIT Press
Yi S, Jung Y (2007) A new kid on the block: Korean competition law, policy, and economics. Competition Policy International 3(2):153–183

Part I
Korean Specialties

Chapter 2
Chaebol Antitrust Policy in Korea

The term 'Chaebol' is derived from the Japanese term 'Zaibatsu', both of which are represented by Chinese characters '財閥'. In this context, '財' signifies 'wealth' and '閥' refers to a 'clan'. In South Korea, the general public and media refer to a group of companies controlled by the descendants of the founder as a chaebol. MRFTA (the Act in the following) denotes it as "a business group," which is defined as "a group of companies the business of which is substantially controlled by the same person."[1] Companies which belong to the same business group are called as "affiliates." The chaebol antitrust policy in Korea is characterized by the KFTC's comprehensive and stringent oversight of various restrictions on large business groups. This oversight encompasses the ex ante (pre-emptive) regulations on ownership and governance, as well as the ex post (post-event) regulations targeting moral hazards and tunneling practices. The primary objective of these measures is to curb the "excessive concentration of economic power" stemming from these conglomerates.[2]

In various countries, regulation governing corporate groups are typically established through company or corporate group law. However, it is important to note that these regulations are distinct from competition laws or policies and are not enforced by competition agencies as is the case in Korea. The primary objective of such regulations is to safeguard minority shareholders of controlled affiliates from the potentially harmful actions of majority shareholders within the controlling company who may prioritize their own interests over the profits of the controlled

[1] A Korean business group is typically owned and controlled by multiple family members. For administrative ease, the KFTC designates one person as the head of the group.

[2] The concept of 'ex ante' regulation in this context does not imply that it should be authorized by the regulatory agency before any action is taken, as the term typically suggests. Instead, it signifies that the regulations are designed in such a clear and direct manner that it becomes easy to assess the violations and ensure compliance. On the other hand, 'ex post' regulation should be based on evaluating the effects of related conducts after they have been carried out. Consequently, determining violations and ensuring regulatory compliance in such cases is not a straightforward process.

S. Jeon, *Antitrust Policy in Korea*, https://doi.org/10.1007/978-981-95-0632-3_2

affiliates.[3] In Korea, the concern regarding excessive concentration of economic power extends beyond the protection of minority shareholders. The chaebol antitrust policy in Korea aims to achieve "economic democratization" by fostering a robust business ecosystem.

In this chapter, firstly I will begin with elucidating the key characteristics of Korean chaebols concerning concentration, governance, diversification, and internal trade. These aspects have aroused concerns among the public, both from political and economic standpoints. Moving on, I will provide a comprehensive overview of various regulations that have been implemented to address the concerns surrounding chaebols, as well as delve into their historical background. Furthermore, I will conduct an assessment of the economic justifications behind the regulations imposed on chaebols, focusing on fictitious equity investment such as cross/pyramidal shareholdings, the positive functions of intercorporate shareholding, excessive business diversification, and profit tunneling. Lastly, I will present a selection of chaebol regulations pertaining to unfair subsidizing among affiliated companies. These cases, including *Samsung SDS* in 1999, *Hyundai Glovis* in 2007, *Hanjin KAL* in 2017, *Hanwha Solution* in 2020 and *Samsung Wellstory* in 2021, offer intriguing insights from an economic analysis standpoint and the significance of the related companies and business groups.

2.1 Main Characteristics of Korean Chaebols

As the Act (§1) stipulates, the "excessive concentration of economic power" is one of the main concerns of Korean antitrust policy. The concentration of economic power exists in two aspects: within individual markets and across the entire economy. Korean chaebols have economic powers in both of these dimensions.

2.1.1 Market Concentration

Industries in Korea are highly concentrated. The market concentration is typically measured with CR3, the combined market share of three largest firms. Figure 2.1 shows the recent trend of average market concentration in the mining and manufacturing sector. Roughly saying, the average market share has declined

[3] In Germany, *Konzernrecht* refers to the legal framework governing corporate groups. It is distinct from the Competition Act, which falls under the jurisdiction of the *Bundeskartellamt* (Federal Cartel Office). The dominant motivation of the codification of *Aktiengesetz*, a key legislation concerning with stock corporations and a prominent illustration of *Konzernrecht*, in 1965 is "to protect minority shareholders ('outsider') as well of creditors of controlled corporations from the dangers inherent to the exertion of control by a majority shareholder." Refer to Scheuch (2016).

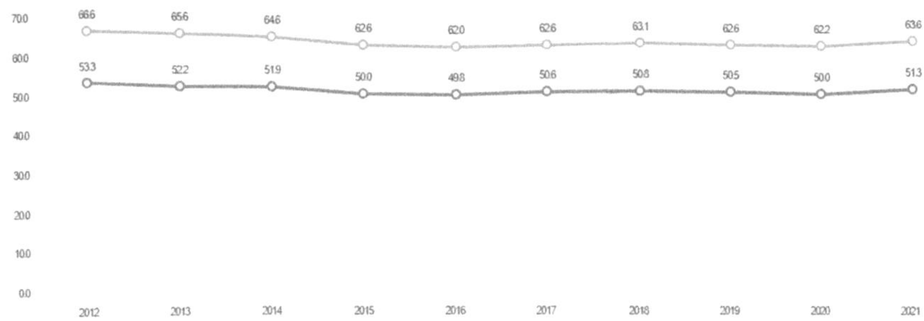

Fig. 2.1 Trend of average market concentration in mining and manufacturing industries. Note: Upper line represents the average CR3 (largest 3-firm concentration ratio) for the product classification in 8 digits according to KSIC (Korea Standard of Industry Classification), while lower line is for the 5-digit classification. The average is weighted with the total shipment of each product. Source: Statistics Bureau, *Annual Survey of Mining and Manufacturing Industries*.

recently slightly, yet it remains fairly concentrated, with CR3 ranging 50% to 60%, depending upon the specific industry classification.

In a relatively small open economy like Korea, it is natural to observe a concentrated market structure to some degree. This is because successful firms are able to attain significant market shares. Furthermore, the government-led export-driven growth strategy in the past emphasized the development of 'national champions' in priority industries. These firms were provided with limited opportunities and resources, consolidating their position as dominant players in the 1960s and 1970s. As a result, Korean chaebols emerged as the main beneficiaries of these policies, establishing themselves as the leading firms in key industries at an early stage.

2.1.2 *General Concentration*

The concentration of economic power in Korea is more conspicuous in the overall economy than within specific markets. Figure 2.2 depicts the recent trend of general concentration which is measured with the shipment shares of large firms in the economy.

The top ten companies in Korea have contributed approximately 25% of total production in the tangible goods sector, although their share has slightly decreased recently. The 100 largest companies have accounted for around 50% of the sector's output, while the 200 largest companies have contributed around 55% over the last 10 years or so. This indicates a significant imbalance among large, medium, and small enterprises in terms of their size and therefore "economic power." Most of the ten largest firms and the majority of the 100 largest firms are part of conglomerates known as chaebols. This highlights the prevalence of high general concentration in

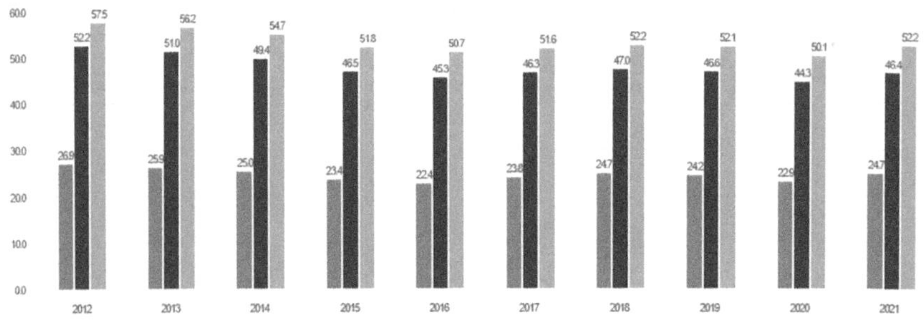

Fig. 2.2 Share of large firms in the economy. Note: Left, middle, and right bars represent the shares of shipments of the 10, 100, and 200 largest firms, respectively, in the mining and manufacturing sector. Source: Statistics Bureau (2024), *Survey of Mining and Manufacturing Industries.*

the Korean economy, which forms the economic backdrop for chaebol and SME policies aimed at establishing 'sound economic ecosystem'.

Both general and market concentration may not be exceptional in Korea. Similar phenomena of higher or lower degrees can be observed in many other countries, However, the peculiarities in Korean chaebols primarily lie in their unique corporate governance structure of ownership and control.

2.1.3 Ownership and Control of Chaebols

The key feature of Korean business groups is that "the same person," which is the terminology of the Act (§2 [11]), substantially controls all the affiliate companies in a business group at the top. The business group is called 'chaebol' when "the same person" is a natural person. In the Korean press, they are incorrectly called the "owner" of chaebol. In this book, I will call the same person "chaebol head" and their (extended) family "chaebol family" or the "controlling family." (When the same person is a legal entity, the business group is not called a chaebol. Mostly, it used to be a public enterprise which is now privatized, but still under the government influence.)

Notice that 'chaebol' is not a legal term in the Act but a casual or journalistic word. The descendants of the chaebol founder control the entire business group, but do not have large shares of their affiliate firms, and in fact, have relatively small shares. However, they exercise a strong influence over the major decision-making processes. Their control is primarily achieved through inter-affiliate shareholding, as demonstrated by Table 2.1, which highlights the chaebol head's strong grip over affiliates despites having only a small ownership stake.

It is noteworthy that the proportion of ownership held by chaebol head has significantly diminished in the past 20 years, decreasing from 2.5% in 1997 to 0.8% in 2023. Similarly, the controlling family's share also experienced a decline, dropping from 3.1% in 2001 to 2.2% in 2023. These outcomes can be

Table 2.1 Ownership structure of ten largest chaebols[a]

	'97	'99	'01	'03	'05	'07	'09	'11	'13	'15	'17	'19	**'21**	**'23**
Chaebol head (family)[b]	**2.5** -	1.8 -	1.3 (3.1)	1.2 (3.5)	1.4 (3.6)	1.3 (3.4)	1.1 (3.3)	1.1 (2.9)	1.0 (3.0)	0.9 (2.7)	0.9 (2.5)	0.9 (2.4)	**0.8 (2.4)**	**0.8 (2.2)**
Affiliate firms	**33.5**	46.6	43.0	42.4	45.3	44.1	45.6	50.3	49.6	50.6	55.5	54.3	**55.2**	**57.5**
Internal share[c]	**42.7**	51.5	46.4	46.2	49.2	47.9	49.3	53.5	52.9	53.6	58.3	56.9	**57.7**	**59.9**

[a]As of May 2023, the list of the ten largest chaebols in terms of total assets includes Samsung, SK, Hyundai Motor, LG, Lotte, Hanwha, GS, Hyundai Heavy Industries, Shinsege, and CJ

Note: [b]The family consists of the head of the chaebol and their close relatives (within 6° of blood kinship and 4° of marriage kinship). (In a recent amendment to the Presidential Enforcement Decree on December 27, 2022, the criteria for defining "close" relatives have been narrowed down to those within a maximum of four degrees of blood kinship and three degrees of marriage kinship. This revision effectively limits the scope of relatives considered to be "close" under the law)

[c]The internal shares include the shares of the head and their family, affiliate firms, and related persons (such as directors and foundations), who are within the control of the chaebol head in group decision-making

Source: KFTC (2024), *Annual White Book of Fair Trade*

attributed to two factors. First, a series of transitions in ownership and control, spanning from the first to the third (and more recently, the fourth for certain chaebols) generation, have taken place over the years. Such transitions typically result in a dispersion of ownership among family members and a dilution of ownership due to inheritance tax obligations.[4] Second, a more fundamental reason could be that the chaebol head's personal financial capacity has been unable to keep pace with the rapid growth of the conglomerate and its affiliated entities.

However, the ownership of shares between affiliates with a business group, known as inter-affiliate shareholding, has significantly increased from 33.5% to 57.5% over time. This growth has not been consistent but rather fluctuates to some extent during the process. These fluctuations can be attributed, in part, to the frequent changes in regulations governing inter-affiliate shareholding, which will be discussed in a later section. Inter-affiliate shareholding takes various forms including cross ($A \leftrightarrow B$), circular ($A \rightarrow B \rightarrow C \rightarrow A$), vertical ($A \rightarrow B \rightarrow C$), and simple ($A \rightarrow B$) shareholding. Here A, B and C represent affiliate firms belonging to the same business group, and the symbol '$\rightarrow$' indicates the holding of shares. In reality, these styles are intermingled and complex, resembling a tangled cobweb. Each style is subject to different regulation within the chaebol framework, as explained in Section 2.2. This differentiation arises because the impact of each style on reinforcing the control rights of affiliate within the chaebol family varies, a topic that will be addressed in Section 2.3.

"Internal" shares refer to the shares that are under the control of a chaebol head, comprising the combined holdings of the family, affiliated companies, and related individuals. The internal shares have experienced significant growth, although not to the same extent as the affiliate shares, as the decrease in chaebol family shares counterbalances the increase in affiliate shares. The crucial role of affiliate firms in the ownership and control of chaebols cannot be emphasized enough. Affiliates also play a vital role in facilitating the expansion and diversification of Korean chaebols' business operations.

La Porta et al. (1999) discovered that the control of business groups by the ultimate owner family through affiliate shareholding was not uncommon. This was observed not only in large publicly traded corporations in advanced countries but also in firms operating in developing nations. These findings contradict the traditional depiction of modern corporations, as described by Berle and Means (1932), which emphasized widespread ownership. However, the unique aspect in Korea is the significant extent of inter-affiliate shareholding and its pivotal role in the ownership–control structure of chaebols.

---

[4] Korea imposes a maximum rate of inheritance tax at 50% for assets exceeding KR₩3 billion. This places it as the second highest rate among OECD countries, just behind Japan's rate of 55%. Furthermore, when considering the extra charge of 10% for the primary shareholder of enterprise succession, Korea's inheritance tax becomes the highest in the OECD.

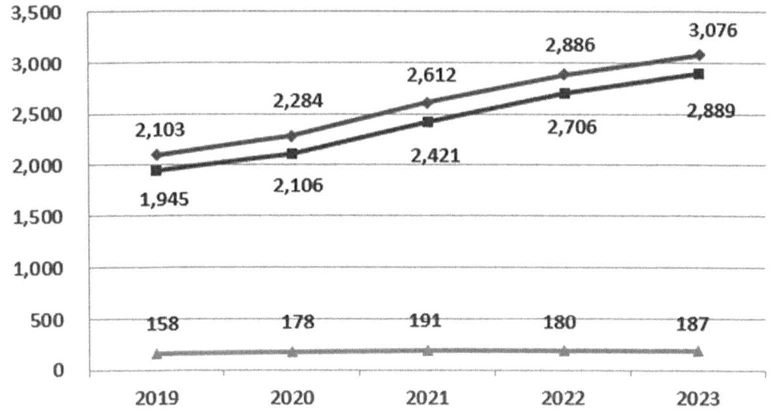

Fig. 2.3 Total number of affiliates in large business groups (total assets more than KR₩5 trillion). Note: Triangle, rectangle, and diamond represent the number of affiliates in large business groups without chaebol heads, the number of those with chaebol heads, and the number of both, respectively. Source: KFTC News Release, "Designation of Large Business Groups Subject to Disclosure," April 26, 2023.

2.1.4 Expansion and Diversification of Chaebols

Over the years, there has been a significant rise in the number of affiliated companies within Korean business conglomerates. This trend is clearly depicted in Fig. 2.3, which highlights the notable and rapid growth of these entities.

Currently, the threshold for business groups to be subject to regulation is set at total assets exceeding KR₩5 trillion. Groups surpassing this threshold face various regulatory measures. Ten business groups have legal entities as their governing heads. These groups were predominantly state enterprises in the past and continue to be influenced by the government even after privatization. Examples include Posco (Pohang Steel Corp), KT (Korea Telecom), and KT&G (Korea Tobacco and Ginseng). The term "chaebols" refers to the 72 business groups led by natural persons who are descendants of the founders.

The primary factor contributing to the growth of affiliates within large business groups over the years is the higher number of new entrants compared to those exiting. This trend is understandable as more business groups meet the required asset size threshold due to the expanding economy. From 2019 to 2023, the total count of large business groups increased from 59 to 82. Simultaneously, the average number of affiliates per group witnessed a slight increase from 35.6 to 37.2 during this period. Thus, the recent surge in the overall number of large business groups can be primarily attributed to new entries into the category of large business groups designated by the Act.

2.1.5 Internal Trade of Large Business Groups

Chaebols frequently engage in internal transactions among their affiliates to support the growth of newly established enterprises. This practice has raised concerns and has consequently led to meticulous monitoring by the KFTC. Table 2.2 below illustrates the proportion of internal transactions among domestic affiliates within the major business conglomerates that are subject to regulation.

All affiliates within various business groups rely on internal trades, which account for 12.2% of their total transactions. Notably, unlisted affiliates have a greater dependence on internal transactions (20.3%) compared to their listed counterparts (7.7%). This contrast between listed and unlisted affiliates is consistent for both business groups with a controlling family (7.8% vs. 20.3%) and those without a controlling family (6.5% vs. 20.0%).

2.2 Key Components of Chaebol Regulation

The regulations pertaining to large business groups under the MRFTA encompass seven key components. These include: (1) Prohibition on Cross Shareholding (§21); (2) Prohibition on Circular Shareholding (§22); (3) Prohibitions on Debt Guarantees for Affiliates (§24); (4) Disenfranchisement of Voting Rights of Finance/Insurance Company and Public Foundation (§25); (5) Restrictions on Holding Company (§18, §19, §20); (6) Disclosure of Material Decision and Information (§26, §27, §28, §29, §35); and (7) Prohibition on Provision of Undue Benefits to Related Parties (§45, §47).

These regulations can be classified into two categories: Category 1—(1 through 4); Category 2—(6 and 7). The business groups subject to Category 1 regulations (referred to as Category 1 chaebols) are known as those "subject to limitations on cross shareholding." These are considerably large business groups, currently

Table 2.2 Internal trade of large business groups (during 2022)

	All affiliates		Listed affiliates		Unlisted affiliates	
	Internal trans. ratio (trillion won)	# of firms	Internal trans. ratio (trillion won)	# of firms	Internal trans. ratio (trillion won)	# of firms
All business groups (82)	12.2% (275.1)	2503	7.7% (110.1)	335	20.3% (164.8)	2168
With controlling family (72)	12.0% (232.9)	2340	7.8% (100.2)	310	20.4% (132.7)	2030
Without controlling family (10)	13.3% (42.2)	163	6.5% (10.2)	25	20.0% (32.0)	138

Source: KFTC (2024), *Annual White Book of Fair Trade*

Table 2.3 Change of designation criterion and numbers of subject business groups and affiliates

Year	1987	1993	2002	2009	2016.4.1.	2016.6.8.	Revision expected[a]
Criterion of total assets (won)	0.4 trillion	30 largest ranking	2 trillion	5 trillion	5 trillion	10 trillion / 5 trillion	0.5% of GDP / 5 trillion
# of business groups	32	30	43	48	65	28 / 53	-
# of affiliates	509	604	704	1137	1736	1118/ 1670	-

Note: [a]Revised on December 2021 and will be implemented in 2024
Source: KFTC News Release, "Improving the designation of large business groups reasonably reflecting the change of economic circumstance," June 8, 2016

possessing total assets exceeding KR₩10 trillion.[5] On the other hand, the business groups subject to Category 2 regulations (referred to as Category 2 chaebols) are termed as those "subject to disclosure." They are relatively large business groups, currently possessing total assets exceeding KR₩5 trillion.[6] Notice that Category 1 chaebols are a subset of Category 2 chaebols. The regulations concerning holding companies (5) are not limited to Category 1 or 2 chaebols but are applicable to all business groups, regardless of their size.

And the nature of regulations of two categories are different in terms of timing of enforcement; i.e., Category 1 as well as holding company regulation is *ex ante* (before any potential issues arise) while Category 2 is *ex post* (after the occurrence of certain events). Both categories of regulations share a common goal of restraining the excessive concentration of economic power. Moreover, Category 2 regulations serve specific purposes individually. Regulation (6) aims to improve the management and governance by introducing public monitoring measures. Regulation (7) focuses on prohibiting the unjustifiable transfer of profits and assets through a practice known as 'tunneling'.[7]

Over time, the nominal size of a business group designated as subject to regulations has enlarged. As the economy grows, it is necessary to adapt to it accordingly. Table 2.3 shows the evolution of the designation and the resulting count of subject business groups and affiliates.

[5]As part of the comprehensive revision of the Act in December 2021, the criterion of Category 1 regulation will change into "the business group which has total assets more than 0.5% of GDP" in order to align with the evolving scale of the whole economy.

[6]The criterion of Category 2 regulation is anticipated to change into a certain percentage of GDP analogously to that of Category 1 regulation.

[7]Johnson et al. (2000) use the term narrowly to refer to "the transfer of assets and profits out of firms for the benefit of those who control them." However, I expand the meaning of tunneling to encompass any conducts of chaebol families that prioritize their own interests over the interests of minority shareholders, whether through financial and real transactions among affiliated entities.

Table 2.4 Top five chaebols

Ranking	Name of business group	Owner	# of affiliates	Total assets of non-finance/insurance companies (trillion won)	Total assets of all companies (trillion won)
1	Samsung	Lee, Jay Yong	63	442.5	893.8
2	SK	Choi, Tae Won	198	327.2	327.3
3	Hyundai Motor	Chung, Mong Ku	60	259.1	342.7
4	LG	Koo, Kwang Mo	63	171.2	171.2
5	Lotte	Shin, Dong Bin	98	129.0	138.7

Source: KFTC News Release, "Designation of 82 business groups subject to disclosure in 2023," April 25, 2023

The MRFTA revision plan in 2016 consisted of three key elements. Firstly, the introduction of two distinct categories of designation was implemented. Previously, all regulations were applicable the business groups with total assets exceeding KR ₩5 trillion. However, the revised plan divided them into Category 1 and Category 2. Secondly, the threshold of Category 1 regulations was increased to KR₩10 trillion, while Category 2 maintained the previous threshold of KR₩5 trillion. Thirdly, public business groups such as Korea Electric Power Corporation, Korea Land and Housing Corporation, etc. were no longer designated as subject to regulations on large business groups. These changes resulted in significant changes in the numbers of business groups and affiliates in 2016 as shown in Table 2.3. Furthermore, through the comprehensive revision of the Act by December 2021, the designation of business groups subject to Category 1 regulations will be more flexible. It will be adjusted in accordance with the growth of the economy, with the criterion indexed to the GDP level at 0.5%.

Among the conglomerates falling under Category 1, a noticeable disparity can be observed between the top five and the remaining entities. Provided below is Table 2.4 showing the key information pertaining to the five most prominent privately owned business conglomerates in the year 2023.

Notice that Samsung is significantly larger, almost one and a half times, than SK and Hyundai Motor. In comparison, SK and Hyundai Motor are almost twice as large as LG and Lotte in terms of their total assets. Therefore, a noticeable imbalance exists among the top 5 chaebols, and the disparity between these top five and other business groups intensifies.

2.2.1 *Prohibition on Cross Shareholding*

Cross shareholding is a direct exchange of shares between two companies; i.e., firm A holds shares of firm B, and firm B holds shares of firm A. This practice is prohibited in principle for business groups with total assets exceeding KR₩10 trillion. The regulation was implemented in 1986 to address the issue of "excessive concentration of economic power." Its main aim is to prohibit the distortion of ownership and control, as chaebol heads can gain control over their affiliates without any new capital investment. For example, the mere exchange of 100 shares between affiliates A and B would only involve a paper work, but the chaebol head's 'internal' shares for both affiliates increase by the same amount. This is the extreme form of expanding the chaebol head's control through artificial capital investment.

Notice that the regulation is applicable only to the affiliates which belong to business groups subject to Category 1 regulation. That is, it does not apply to the affiliates of the smaller business groups with the total assets below KR₩10 trillion. In contrast, Commercial Law prohibits a subsidiary company from owning the shares of the parent company which possesses more than 50% of shares of the subsidiary. This prohibition in Commercial Law applies to the relationship of parent–subsidiary companies regardless of whether they belong to a business group or not. This prohibition, outlined in the Commercial Law, aims to ensure the integrity of capital rather than restricting the concentration of economic power as stipulated in the MRFTA.

At present, there are no instances of cross shareholding among chaebols that are bound by the prohibition except in case of a transition. That is, only those recently included under Category 1 regulations are allowed to have cross shareholding for a limited period of one year.

2.2.2 *Prohibition on Circular Shareholding*

A regulation regarding the practice of circular shareholding was introduced in 2014. The negative implications of circular shareholding have been the subject of intense debate, as it essentially represents an indirect version of cross shareholding. Circular shareholding can be perceived as a combination of holding–company shareholding and cross shareholding. For example, a circular shareholding arrangement such as $A \rightarrow B \rightarrow C \rightarrow A$ can be decomposed of a holding–company's multi-tiers shareholding $A \rightarrow B \rightarrow C$, and (indirect) cross shareholding of $A \rightarrow B\ (C) \rightarrow A$. Hence, if the practice of cross shareholding is deemed inappropriate and should be prohibited, it is logical to also regulate circular shareholding.

However, the chaebols that were impacted strongly opposed the introduction of the prohibition, as it posed a significant challenge for them to completely resolve the issue of circular shareholding. In order to break the cycle of circularity, one of the affiliated companies in the chain would need to either sell the shares involved in the

Table 2.5 Numbers of business groups with circular shareholding and circular links

	2014	2015	2016	2017	2018	2019	2020	2021	2022	2023
Business groups	14	11	8	10	4	4	4	2	4	4
Circular links	483	459	94	282	41	14	21	6	10	10
Δ Circular links	–	−24	−365	+188[a]	−241	−27	+7[a]	−15	4[a]	0

Note: [a]The increases in 2017, 2020, and 2022 are partly because some business groups newly incorporated into Category 2 have many circular links

Source: KFTC News Release, "Analysis and Report of Shareholding of Business Groups Subject to Disclosure in 2023," October 3, 2023

market or to the chaebol head. Selling in the market potentially weakens the chaebol head's control rights, leading to governance risks, and the chaebol head may not be able to afford purchasing the shares due to financial resource limitations. A compromise in policy implementation was reached by prohibiting chaebols solely from "additional shareholding," which could potentially create new circularity or strengthen existing circular relationships.

Despite the allowance of incumbent circular shareholding, its prevalence has considerably decreased following the implementation of the regulation in 2014. Table 2.5 illustrates the progressive decline of this practice.

Notice that the decrease in the number of business groups possessing circular shareholding and the reduction in the number of circular links they had was not a result of legal prohibitions. The data in Table 2.4 pertains to Category 2 business groups, many of which are not bound by the prohibition (i.e., Category 1 regulations). Moreover, it is worth noting that the majority of the circular shareholdings that were eliminated were existing ones that were actually allowed under the law.

Business groups may have had two reasons for their efforts to remove circular shareholding. Above all, the government applied pressure on chaebols to comply with the initiative aimed at curbing the concentration of economic power. Resolving the issue of circular shareholding was a crucial policy agenda for both liberal and progressive governments. Especially, President Moon's left-leaning government, which began in April 2017, exerted a strong drive and pressure in this regard. The significant decrease in 2018 might be due to the government push. In addition to external factors, chaebols themselves may have desired to streamline their governance structure by addressing circularities. Thus, we can argue that the sharp decrease in 2016 was partly driven by internal motivations and partly influenced by external pressure.

Currently, as of 2020, within Category 1 business groups, only Hyundai Motor group are left with four circular links. The following diagram illustrates the interdependence of the affiliates in the Hyundai Motor group through shareholding.

The Chung family (Chung, Mong Ku and his son Chung, Eui Sun) possesses a 7.0% stake in Mobis stocks and a 29.9% stake in Glovis. Mobis operate as the *de facto* parent company within the group, within Hyundai Motor serving as its subsidiary referred to as the child-company of Mobis. Hyundai Motor, in turn, has several subsidiary companies, including Glovis, Kia Car, and Hyundai Steel, which can be referred to as the grandchildren-companies. The Chung family's internal

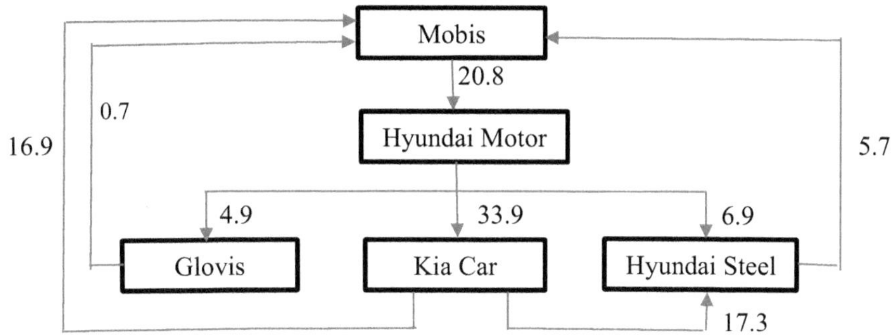

Fig. 2.4 Inter-affiliate shareholding of Hyundai Motor group in 2020. Source: KFTC (2020) "Current Status of Circular Shareholding"

shares of Mobis are 30.3% which comprises Chung's own 7.0% stake and an additional 23.3% stakes from affiliated companies (Kia's 16.9%, H.Steel's 5.7%, and Glovis' 0.7%).

In Fig. 2.4, four circular links can be identified: (1) Mobis → Hyundai Motor → Kia Car → Mobis; (2) Mobis → Hyundai Motor → Hyundai Steel → Mobis; (3) Mobis → Hyundai Motor → Glovis → Mobis; and (4) Mobis → Hyundai Motor → Kia Car → Hyundai Steel → Mobis. In order to eliminate these interdependent links, it is essential to resolve the share ownership of Mobis stocks among affiliates (Kia's 16.9%, Hyundai Steel's 5.7%, and Glovis' 0.7%). This complex situation necessitates the application of Solomon's wisdom and a highly sophisticated financial strategy to find a resolution that does not compromise Chung family's control over the Hyundai Motor group.

In 2019, Samsung group successfully resolved its persistent issue of circular shareholding completely. Back in 2013, Samsung had over 80 circular links of inter-affiliate shareholdings. Over time, the group faced challenges in reducing these links. However, in 2018, it made significant progress by divesting the shares held by Samsung SDI, Samsung Life Insurance, and Electro-Mechanics in Samsung C&T, which served as the *de facto* parent company of Samsung group. This strategic move ultimately eliminated the major complication in its governance structure, as demanded by the KFTC, thereby enhancing transparency within the structure of business group.

2.2.3 *Prohibition on Debt Guarantees for Affiliates*

Affiliates in Category 1 business groups are not allowed to offer debt guarantees for their domestic affiliates. However, this restriction does not apply to finance and insurance companies, as they are involved in providing debt guarantees as part of their operations. The initial implementation of this regulation, in 1992, allowed to provide guarantees up to 200% of their own capital. This limit was subsequently strengthened in 1996, permitting guarantees up to 100%. Finally, in 1998, during the East Asian foreign currency crisis, the regulation evolved to a complete prohibition on providing debt guarantees for affiliates.

During the 1970s and the 1980s, when there was an excess in demand for loanable funds, most financial institutions mandated debt guarantees for managing loans appropriately. This allowed chaebols to exploit inter-affiliate debt guarantees in order to acquire limited financial resources. These practices intensified the concentration of economic power within chaebols and heightened the overall risk of the system. This risk refers to the possibility of one affiliate's failure triggering a chain reaction of negative domino effects on otherwise stable affiliates. Such a scenario actually unfolded with the Daewoo business group, which was one of the top five conglomerates of that era, during a period characterized by a foreign currency crisis.

As stated by the KFTC,[8] all inter-affiliate debt guarantees within Category 1 business groups have been eliminated, with the exception of those occurring in the transitional period following a new designation or under special circumstances.

2.2.4 Disenfranchisement of Voting Rights of Finance/Insurance Company

As per the Act (§25), a provision states that "a member company of a business group subject to limitations on cross shareholding[9] that is engaged in financial business or insurance business shall not exercise its voting rights with respect to shares acquired or held by it in its domestic affiliates." However, there are three exceptions to this rule. The first one applies when "the company acquires or holds shares specifically for the purpose of engaging in financial business or insurance business." The second exception applies when "the company acquires or holds shares by obtaining approval, etc. pursuant to the Insurance Business Act, etc. to efficiently operate and manage insured assets." These two exceptions are considered necessary and valid as they facilitate the smooth operation of financial business or insurance business by allowing the acquisition or holding of such shares.

The third exception holds particular significance, as it pertains to situations where "the general meeting of shareholders of its domestic affiliate (limited to a listed corporation) passes a resolution on any of the following matters: (a) the appointment or dismissal of an executive officer; (b) amendments to the articles of incorporation; (c) the merger of the said affiliate with another company, or the transfer of all or a substantial part of its business (excluding cases where the other company is also an

[8] KFTC, "Analysis and Report on Debt Guarantees of Business Groups Subject to Limitations on Cross Shareholding in 2019," December 2019.

[9] This is Category 1 business group in our terms.

affiliate).[10] In such cases, the total counting of voting shares from all shares of the said affiliate cannot surpass 15% of the overall number of shares issued by the said affiliate, inclusive of the shares to be exercised by the persons and parties associated[11] to the said affiliate."

According to the Banking Act (§16–2), non-financial investments, also known as 'industrial capital', are generally restricted from holding more than 4% of a bank's outstanding voting stocks (15% in cases of a local bank). This regulation is commonly referred to as "the separation of banking and commerce." Despite this restriction, the industrial capital is permitted to possess shares of finance or insurance companies that come with voting rights. For example, Samsung C&T, which is the *de facto* parent company of Samsung group, holds a significant 19.3% of voting shares of Samsung Life Insurance. Similarly, finance or insurance companies are permitted to hold shares of industrial companies. However, the Act on Structural Improvement of Financial Industry (§24) mandates that financial affiliates within the same business group must obtain approval of the Financial Services Commission if they wish to hold more than 20% of voting shares in another company. In the case of an affiliate company within the same business group, the limit is set at 10%. Therefore, it can be observed that while there is some degree of "the separation of financial and industrial capital" in Korea, these regulations are relatively lenient.

The purpose behind the deprivation of voting rights for finance or insurance companies within Category 1 business groups is to supplement the separation of financial and industrial capital, and to restrict on the expansion of control power into unrelated businesses through owning financial affiliates. Nonetheless, the third exception grants leeway to chaebols. It was justified by the need to safeguard the control rights of important domestic businesses against hostile foreign takeover or interference. Particularly, this is necessary when foreign capital holds substantial stakes in key companies that play a crucial role in the Korean economy.

The third exemption to the exclusion of voting rights is both legally binding and highly effective. In case of Samsung business group, as of the end of 2019, two insurance companies, namely, Samsung Life Insurance (8.51%) and Samsung Fire and Marine Insurance (1.49%) together, possess a 10% stake of Samsung Electronics. Consequently, the internal shares of Samsung Electronics amounted to 18.41%, encompassing the contribution of these insurance companies. This signifies that the two insurance companies were granted the authority to utilize only 6.59% of their overall 10% shares in Samsung Electronics for significant decision-making processes like (a), (b), and (c). In this context, the third exception is legally 'binding' in its coercion power. It is also highly 'effective' in terms of usefulness as evidenced by the exercise of exceptional voting rights on 132 occasions between 2012 and 2017

[10]The exclusion in item (c) was introduced during the 2021 comprehensive revision of the Act. This was prompted by the 2015 merger between Cheil Industries and Samsung C&T within Samsung group, which will be discussed further below and in a case study of *Samsung Wellstory* (2021).

[11]"The persons and parties associated" mentioned herein refers to the chaebol head and their close family and parties over whom the head holds sway in significant decision-makings processes, encompassing (a), (b), and (c).

(102 instances for [a]), (23 instances for [b]), and (5 instances for [c]) as reported in a news article.[12]

This regulation began at the time when the MRFTA introduced the restriction of "the excessive concentration of economic power." The Act has recently undergone a comprehensive revision, which has strengthened it in a minor yet significant way. Specifically, a merger and acquisition between affiliated companies is now excluded from the third exception (c). This aims to address a loophole that chaebols may exploit by misusing the exception as a means of tunneling. One such misuse involves approving an unreasonable stock exchange ratio between merging affiliates, favoring the chaebol family. To illustrate, in the recent controversial merger between Samsung C&T and Cheil Industries in 2015, the exchange ratio became a subject of dispute and eventually reached the court. The crux of the issue was that the merger ratio was determined to be advantageous for Cheil Industries, in which the head-to-be of the Samsung group, Jay Y. Lee, the largest shareholder with a 23% stake, held a significant interest.

2.2.5 *Restrictions on Holding Company*

The Act defines a holding company as "a company the main business of which is to control the business activities of a domestic company by holding the shares (including equities) in the domestic company." The Enforcement Decree sets the criteria for a holding company, stating that "the total assets must be at least 500 billion won, and the combined value of shares it holds in its subsidiaries must equal or exceed 50% of its total assets." The restrictions on holding companies apply in all cases, regardless of whether the holding company belongs to a business group of Category 1, 2, or neither.

Despite having different formal objects, the regulations governing holding companies are essentially aimed at limiting "the excessive concentration of economic power," just like the other regulations on large business groups. Initially, when policies were introduced in 1986 to address economic concentration in 1986, the establishment or conversion into a holding company was strictly prohibited. This restriction was in place due to concerns that a holding company's pyramid structure, with parent → child → grandchild, and so forth, could be exploited by chaebol heads with limited capital to create a large business group. However, in the aftermath of the foreign exchange crisis, experts in the business field emphasized the need of holding company structures as an instrument of corporate restructuring. International organization such as the IBRD and OECD also recommended holding companies to enhance transparency of corporate governance and facilitate corporate restructuring. Consequently, taking these suggestions into account, the MRFTA was revised to

[12] http://www.topdaily.kr/news/articleView.html?idxno=70110&replyAll=&reply_sc_order_by=C (July 7, 2020)

Table 2.6 Restrictions on holding company

	(a) Debt	(b) Min. share of subsidiary	(c) Affiliate share	(d) Non-affiliate share	(e) Separation of fin. and indust. Capital
(1) Holding (parent)	Debt ratio less than 200% of total capital	At least 50% (30%) shares of a subsidiary (listed)	No shares of any domestic affiliate other than a subsidiary	No more than 5% shares of any domestic non-affiliate company	No 'general' ('financial')[a] holding company not to hold shares of 'financial' ('general') company
(2) First tier subsidiary (son) of 'general' holding	–	The same as above	The same as above	–	Not to control a financial company as a subsidiary
(3) Second tier subsidiary (grandson) of 'general' holding	–	No shares of domestic affiliates	the same as above	–	–
(4) Third tier subsidiary	–	The same as above	No shares of any domestic affiliate	–	–

Note: [a]A 'financial' holding company is a type of holding company that possesses shares in its subsidiary companies and is involved in either financial or insurance-related business. On the other hand, a 'general' holding company is a holding company that does not fall under the category of a 'financial' holding company

allow the establishment of, and conversion into, a holding company in 1992. Nonetheless, the KFTC also introduced regulations specifically designed to minimize concerns about chaebols or large business groups abusing holding companies in expanding their control rights.[13]

A holding company is subject to several limitations, which are conveniently organized in a matrix displayed in Table 2.6. The rows of the matrix represent different levels of subsidiary companies, while the columns represent different regulatory aspects.

Table 2.6 presents a concise overview of the key provision of holding company regulations in §18 of the Act. And §19 outlines specific limitations imposed on Category 1 business groups aiming to establish a holding company, including by the nullification of debt guarantees between a holding company, its subsidiaries, and

[13]During Japan's post-World War II era, the concept of "Zaibatsu" (similar to "Chaebol" in Chinese characters) underwent dissolution due to the influence of the US General Headquarters. This decision was made in 1947 as a response to the belief that Zaibatsu, which encompassed a holding company structure, had played a role in fueling Japanese militarism. Consequently, the formation of holding companies was strictly prohibited. However, the circumstances changed in Japan, following a similar path to Korea, which led to the authorization of holding companies in 1992.

other domestic affiliates. These restrictions essentially act as a corollary of the prohibitions placed on debt guarantees for the affiliates belonging to Category 1 business groups.

As per the KFTC,[14] there exist 168 holding companies in total, out of which 158 are classified as 'general' holding companies and the remaining 10 are categorized as 'financial' holding companies. Approximately one third of these companies, accounting for 39.5% (66 in number), fall into the small and medium-sized category with the total assets below KR₩500 billion. Similarly, another third of them, comprising 35.3% (59 in number) are classified as large-scale holding companies with the total assets exceeding KR₩1 trillion. Moreover, there are very large-scale holding companies with total assets exceeding KR₩5 trillion, consisting of 10 'general' and 7 'financial' holding companies.

In reality, the majority of large business groups have transitioned into the holding company system. As of June 2022, there exist a total of 29 'converted groups' (28 classified as 'general' and 1 as 'financial'). A business group is considered 'converted' when the combined assets of the holding company system, including the parent company, subsidiaries, second-tier subsidiaries, and third-tier subsidiaries, surpass 50% of the conglomerate's total assets. Notably, SK and LG business conglomerates, ranked 2nd and 4th, respectively, fall under this category of converted business groups. Table 2.7 presents detailed information about the holding companies in these two converted groups.

The SK and LG groups succeeded in converting to the holding company system. Their decision to adopt this corporate governance may be driven by their desires to simplify and enhance transparency within their organization, as well as the government's encouragement in that regard. LG emerged as a frontrunner among major business groups in this endeavor, while Lotte recently followed suit. On the other hand, SK has been steadily working toward transforming their conglomerate for a significant period of time, establishing four holding companies along the way.

The requirement to maintain a holding company's debt ratio at a maximum of 200% (Column (a) in Table 2.6) is comfortably met. This regulation aims to restrict the expansion of control through excessive debt. The minimum shareholding requirement for subsidiary companies within a holding company system (Column (b) in Table 2.6) is reflected in the proportion of shares held. Furthermore, it plays a crucial role in limiting the number of descendant subsidiaries, such as child, grandchild, and great-grandchild companies, and not beyond that level. In reality, one significant obstacle preventing Samsung C&T, the *de facto* holding company in the Samsung group, from being officially recognized as a *de jure* holding company is its remarkably low shareholding in Samsung Electronics. Currently, it only holds 4.61%, which is far below the required minimum of 20% for a listed company.

The central element of a holding company system can be identified as the prohibition of owning any local affiliate apart from subsidiaries. This regulation,

---

[14] KFTC, "Status Analysis and Report of Holding Company Facts Related to Fair Trade Act in 2022," June 28, 2022.

Table 2.7 Holding companies in SK and LG business groups

		SK					LG	
	Holding company	SK Innovation	SK	SK Discovery	SK CFT Holdings	SK Square	LG	LG Holdings
Holding comp. facts	Conversion day	11.01.04	15.08.03	17.12.01	20.01.07	21.11.02	01.04.03	20.05.03
	Total assets (tril. won)	1.85	2.72	1.56	1.45	7.10	9.71	1.44
	Debt ratio	19.4%	72.4%	68.3%	90.5%	2.6%	3.2%	2.0%
	Holding share ratio[a]	78.7%	58.4%	84.6%	99.4%	92.3%	66.2%	89.5%
	Owner share	0.0%	17.4%	0.3%	0.0%	0.0%	15.4%	0.0%
	Family share	0.0%	25.8%	39.3%	0.0%	0.%	23.4%	42.2%
	No. of son comp.	10	23	5	1	12	9	4
	No. of grandson comp.	8	83	5	1	12	43	3
	No. of great-grandson comp.	0	40	0	0	0	7	2
	Asset within hold. Comp. sys. ratio[c]	99.7%					100.0%	
	# of fin. comp.	0					0	

Note: [a]Ratio of Holding Shares: the aggregate value of shares that a holding company holds in its subsidiaries/the total assets held by the holding company (It should exceed 50% in order to be a holding company)
[b]Ratio of Incorporation into Holding Company System: the number of all subsidiaries including grandchild and great-grandchild companies within a holding company system/the number of all affiliates in a business group
[c]Ratio of Assets within Holding Company System: the total assets of all subsidiaries including grandchild and great-grandchild companies within a holding company system/the total assets of all affiliates in a business group
Source: KFTC, "Status Analysis and Report of Holding Company Facts Related to Fair Trade Act in 2022," June 28, 2022.

denoted as Column (c) in Table 2.6, effectively prevents the occurrence of horizontal or circular shareholding within a business group. Instead, it allows for vertical shareholding exclusively within the framework of a holding company system. This approach leads to a more streamlined structure within the business group, enhancing clarity of responsibilities and facilitating restructuring processes. However, as explained before, Hyundai Motor Group faced challenges in fully eliminating four instances of circular shareholding, specifically concerning its conversion into a holding company system. These obstacles were primarily attributed to Mobis as seen in Fig. 2.4, which impeded the progress of the transformation.

Notice that the proportion of incorporation in a holding company system and the proportion of assets within a holding company system may not always be 100%. In the case of Lotte group, this proportion is 68.5%. This means that approximately 1/3 (29 out of 92) of the affiliates in the group operate outside of the Lotte holding system, but are still under the control of the chaebol head. Consequently, a business conglomerate can be divided into two subgroups: one operating within the holding company system and the other operating outside of it. The restriction imposed by Column (c) in Table 2.6 establishes a form of unidirectional firewall preventing the movement of shares from "within" to "outside" the system. The restriction on a holding company's ownership of non-affiliated companies, usually capped at 5% (as stated in Column (d) in Table 2.6), aims to encourage the holding company to focus on its own business area.

The purpose of separating financial and industrial capital (Column (e) in Table 2.6) is to ensure that a 'financial' holding company focuses solely on financial and insurance business, and not to allow it to expand into a 'general' holding company by exploiting the client money in financial subsidiaries through acquiring non-financial subsidiaries and thereby endangering financial security. However, it is possible for a business group with a 'general' (or 'financial') holding company to have a financial (or non-financial) company outside the holding company but within the group. This separation works in both ways at the holding company level (Cell (1)-(e) in Table 2.6), whereas the separation is strictly from 'general' to 'financial' in the first-tier subsidiary level (Cell (2)-(e) in Table 2.6), and not explicitly specified in the lower levels. For example, LG's second-tier subsidiary has one financial company because there are no relevant regulations. These restrictions are in line with the Financial Holding Companies Act, which falls under the jurisdiction of the Financial Services Commission and includes more extensive regulations on the separation of financial activities.

2.2.6 Disclosure of Material Decision and Information

The purpose of the prohibitions on cross and circular shareholding, the disenfranchisement of voting rights of finance or insurance company, and the restrictions on holding company is to improve the structure of corporate ownership and control. The prohibition on providing debt guarantees for affiliates is to ensure equal access to financial resources. The prohibition on granting undue benefits to related parties is to prevent a chaebol from engaging in unfair trade practices known as tunneling. On the other hand, the disclosure of important decision and information intends to facilitate public supervision of a business group by various stakeholders like minority shareholders and creditors. This disclosure also encourages the business group itself to enhance its ownership and control structure and engage in fair trade practices.

The contents subject to disclosure under §26 - §30 of the Act include: (1) Resolutions made by the board of directors regarding large-scale internal trading; (2) Important facts concerning unlisted company; (3) Status updates on business group; and (4) Decisions made regarding public-interest foundation related to the chaebol family; (5) Shareholding status. An affiliate belonging to a business group that falls under Category 2 (with total assets exceeding KR₩5 trillion) must periodically report publicly to DART (Data Analysis, Retrieval and Transfer System of FSS—Financial Supervisory Service), typically on a quarterly basis. This report should cover the following aspects related to the business group: general matters, shareholding, non-holding company affiliates, cross shareholding, circular shareholding, debt guarantees, whether voting rights have been exercised for shares held in domestic affiliates, and transactions with related parties. This reporting requirement was implemented in 2009 following the removal of the limit on inter-affiliate shareholding (discussed in Section 2.3). It was introduced as a measure to compensate for the abolishment of this limit.

In 2000, there was a need to enhance the accountability of the board of directors and the oversight of interested parties, which led to the implementation of a requirement for the public disclosure of resolutions related to significant internal trading. This disclosure encompassed various aspects, including the offering or trading of funds like suspense payments or loans, securities like shares or corporate bonds, assets such as real estate or intangible property rights, and goods or services involving affiliates. Additionally, the disclosure encompassed details such as the purpose, trading counterpart, scale, and terms of the trading.

An unlisted company's essential details encompass various aspects, such as its ownership and corporate governance, including notable shareholders and executive officers. Additionally, it involves alterations in the company's financial structure, such as asset or share acquisitions, donations, provision of security, as well as underwriting of liabilities and exemption from them. Furthermore, it encompasses information regarding the company's management, including the transfer and acquisition of business, mergers and divisions, and the swapping or exchanging of shares.

2.2.7 *Prohibitions on Provision of Undue Benefits to Related Parties*

The regulation is two-fold: (a) The prohibition of unfair trade practices (§45 (1) 9); and (b) The prohibition of providing undue benefits to related parties (§47). The former refers to the prohibition of one of several unfair trade practices (other practices will be discussed in Chap. 3) that apply to any company, regardless of its association with a large business group. On the other hand, the latter is specifically enforced on any affiliate of a business group that falls under the disclosure requirement, specifically, Category 2 group. In practice, the former prohibition on unfair trade practices has primarily been applied to the affiliates of business groups. However, during the implementation of this provision, certain loopholes were discovered. To address this, the KFTC introduced the prohibition on providing undue benefits to related parties in 2013, while also making amendments to the former provision.

The prohibited unfair subsidizing practices stipulated in §45 (1) 9 are: "any of following acts that are likely to hinder fair trade" such as (a) Providing advanced payments, loans, human resources, real estate, securities, goods, services, intangible property rights, etc. for the related party or other company or making a transaction with the related party or other company under substantially advantageous terms; (b) Making a transaction through the related party or other company, acting as an intermediary, that does not play a practical role in the transaction, despite making such transaction with other business entity is substantially advantageous. Inserting a practically unnecessary intermediary in the transaction is referred to as collecting "toll."

In 2003, the Constitutional Court outlined the detrimental effects of unjust subsidizing practices, emphasizing four specific harms; "Firstly, unfair internal trading harms the market function by enabling the survival of inefficient, failing, or marginal company as affiliates. This practice also unfairly excludes independent competitors or restricts the entry of potential competitors in the relevant market. Secondly, continuous unfair internal trading among affiliates, resulting in monopolistic or oligopolistic profits, leads to the concentration of economic power. Thirdly, unfair internal trading dissipates the core competences of a healthy affiliate, transferring them to a failing affiliate and diminishing overall competitiveness. This poses a significant risk to the entire business group's system. Lastly, unfair internal trading hinders the transparency of a company, infringing upon the interests of shareholders, particularly minority shareholders, as well as creditors."[15] Notice that the first statement focuses on an individual market level, the second statement encompasses both an individual market and a business group, the third statement pertains to the business group level, and the fourth statement encompasses the economy as a whole.

The KFTC has faced challenges in establishing the violation of "hindering fair trade," as required by §45 (1) in the Act. This is particularly evident in cases involving the improper transfer of wealth to a chaebol head's successor through the subsidization of a "related party" by an affiliate. One such notable case exemplifying this issue is Samsung SDS's unfair subsidization practice toward its related

[15] Constitutional Court 2001heonga25, July 24 2003.

party.[16] In this specific case, the Supreme Court reached a verdict of not guilty, stating that;[17] "… the Act does not aim to directly regulate the concentration of ownership through abnormal wealth transfers between generations. Furthermore, the negative effects of market concentration resulting from subsidization practices between related parties or affiliates within a business group may not stem directly from the act of subsidization itself. Rather, these effects occur when the subsidized related party or another company obstructs competition in the relevant market it belongs to. … considering that the plaintiff (Samsung SDS)'s conduct in this case facilitated the transfer of wealth between generations, creating a the foundation or the room for the concentration of economic power into the related party only, it cannot be denied that it is not necessary to prove it as a publicly known fact that there are concerns that the related party in the case hinder fair trade in the relevant market through investing the subsidized assets in an affiliate, etc. Hence, the defendant (KFTC)'s argument or proof in the record does not sufficiently substantiate the claim that the conduct in this case hinders fair trade."

The Supreme Court's decision in the aforementioned case appears to have overlooked the comprehensive economic perspective as it pertains to proving the hindrance of fair trade, which was previously mentioned by the Constitutional Court. Subsequently, the KFTC encountered difficulties in demonstrating the hindrance of fair trade in cases where the subsidized is the party affiliated with a business group. Consequently, the supplementary provision §47, known as the "prohibition on provision, etc. of undue benefits to related party," was introduced to facilitate the enforcement of regulations concerning unfair subsidization by affiliates or related parties.

The prohibition on provision of undue benefits to related parties in §47 is imposed on any company of "a business group subject to disclosure" (i.e., Category 2 business group) where "the same person" controlling it is a natural person. Such a company "shall not make any undue benefits attributable to a related party (the same person and their relatives) or to an affiliate whose shares are held by a related party" at least 20%, or to an affiliate whose shares the affiliate prescribed above possesses alone more than 50%.The proscribed acts are: "(i) Making a transaction with the related party or affiliate under terms that are substantially more advantageous than terms that have been applied, or deemed to be applied to transaction between unrelated parties; (ii) Providing the related party of affiliate with a business opportunity that will bring the company substantial benefits, if it conducts such business directly or through any company controlled by it; (iii) Making a transaction of a cash or any other financial instrument with the related party under substantially advantageous terms; (iv) Making a transaction of a certain scale with the related party or affiliate without

[16]The situation revolved around the issuance of Bond with Warrant (BW) by Samsung SDS to Jay Y. Lee, who was the successor of Samsung group at that time. The allegation was that this issuance was done at an exceptionally low price, aiming to transfer controlling shares of Samsun SDS at a discounted rate. While the case also had criminal implications, we will focus solely on the Fair Trade aspect here.

[17]Supreme Court 2001du6364, September 24 2004.

Table 2.8 Comparison between prohibition on unfair subsidizing and prohibition on undue profit-deflecting to group head and relatives[a]

	Unfair subsidizing	Undue profit-deflecting
Related prescript	§45 (1) 9 in the Act	§47 in the Act
Regulatory content	Prohibition on subsidizing **other company** with unfair methods	Prohibition on providing undue benefits for **group head and relatives**
Subsidizing party	Any company	Affiliate of business group with total assets more than KR₩5 trillion
Subsidized party	Related party or other company	(1) Chaebol family or affiliate for which the family has shares above *20% regardless of listed or unlisted* [b] (2) *Affiliate for which the affiliate specified in (1) holds shares more than 50%* [c]
Prohibited conducts	(1) Transaction with terms considerably more advantageous than normal price (2) Transaction through intermediary without practical role in transaction (**Toll**)	(1) Transaction with terms considerably more advantageous than normal price (2) Provision of business opportunity (3) Transaction of cash or financial commodity with considerably advantageous terms (4) Transaction of substantial amount without reasonable consideration or comparison (**Quantity-pushing or funneling of business**)
Safe harbor	Not specified	(1) **Considerably advantageous terms**: the difference with normal terms less than **7%** and annual volume less than **KR₩5 billion** (**KR₩20 billion** for commodity and service) (2) **Considerable amount**: annual volume less than **KR₩20 billion** and less than **12%** of transaction counterpart
Criterion of unfairness	Hindrance of fair trade	Unfairness of accrued benefits

[a]Based on Kim, H.B. (2022, p. 853)
Note: [b]Before the revision in December 2021, 30% for listed and 20% for unlisted.
[c]Added in the revision in December 2021

giving due consideration to its business ability, financial standing, credit rating and technical power, the price terms and conditions of the transaction, etc. or without comparing with other business entities." However, it is possible for the defendant to present a counterargument "if it is inevitable for achieving the objectives of such transactions, in terms of increasing the efficiency of enterprises, confidentiality, and urgency."

Table 2.8 compares the prohibition on unfair subsidizing conducts in §45 (1) 9 with the prohibition on provision of undue benefits to related parties in §47.

As mentioned earlier, one of the reasons why §47 was introduced in addition to §45 (1) 9 in the Act was due to the difficulty in proving the requirement of "hindering unfair trade" in case that the related party was subsidized. Hence, the specific criterion in §47 was abolished and the subsidizing party was narrowed down more specifically to an affiliate belonging to Category 2 group (including Category 1) chaebols, and the subsidized was to its controlling family and the affiliate which they control. This adjustment effectively aligned the additional article with the regulations concerning large business groups, which aim to curb "excessive concentration of economic power." As a result, the burden of proving unfairness could potentially be alleviated by demonstrating the undue amount of benefits obtained by the chaebol family, making it a relatively easier task.

The prohibited contents in two articles overlap to some extent, but they also have distinguishing characteristics. The conduct (1) of §45 (1) 9 in Table 2.8 is identical to the conduct (1) and (3) (which may be redundant since it is included in (i)) of §47 in the table. But the conduct (2) of §45 (1) 9 to prohibit from receiving "toll" and the conduct (4) of §47 to regulate "quantity-pushing or funneling of business" are different. The defensive counterarguments that are allowed such as "efficiency, confidentiality, and urgency" are explicitly stated in §47, and the range of safe harbor is outlined in the KFTC internal guideline. On the other hand, there are no such provisions concerning defenses and the safe harbor in relation to §45 (1) 9. Nonetheless, they are still applicable in practice.

In the recent comprehensive revision of the Act in December 2021, significant changes have been made to the threshold percentages outlined in §47, which determine the subsidized party. Previously, the threshold was set at 30% for listed companies and 20% for unlisted companies. However, under the revised Act, this threshold will now be standardized at 20% for all companies, regardless of their listing status. Additionally, the definition of the subsidized party has been expanded to include subsidiaries in which the chaebol family holds more than 50% of the shares. This means that the range of subsidized affiliates falling under the regulation in §47 has been broadened in two ways. Firstly, by reducing the chaebol family's shareholding percentage to 20% for listed companies, and secondly, by encompassing subsidiaries of an affiliate company where the controlling family holds more than 50% of the shares. These provisions were identified as "the blind spot" in the previous regulations regarding the controlling family's undue profit-deflecting. It is important to note that the revision incorporated in Table 2.8 has been implemented to address and eliminate this blind spot.

Table 2.9 shows the status of internal trade of companies which fall under the regulation on undue profit-deflecting and in the blind spot before the revision.

It should be noted that the number of companies falling outside the scope of regulation (333) are nearly twice as many as those currently regulated (333 vs. 186), and their internal trade volume is three times larger (KR₩27.5 vs. KR₩9.2 trillion). Notably, subsidiaries falling within the blind spot heavily rely on internal trades, accounting for 15.4% of their overall trade activities. These facts serve as the foundation for the recent revision aimed at addressing the blind spot and reducing its impact.

However, despite the revised regulations aimed at simplifying the oversight of unfair subsidization, the KFTC has not achieved satisfactory success in court cases. A recent report presented during a congressional state administration audit reveals

Table 2.9 Status of internal trade of companies under regulation on undue profit-deflecting and in its blind spot (as of December 2018)

	Number of comp.	Ratio (%) of int. trade	Amount (tril. won) of int. trade
Comp. under reg., i.e., listed comp. of chaebol fam. shares ≧ 30% (A)	186	11.2%	9.2
Listed comp. of owner fam. shares 20% ~ 30% (B)	29	8.9%	9.1
Subsidiaries of comp. of chaebol fam. shares ≧ 20% (A + B)	304	15.4%	18.4
Comp. in blind spot total	333	12.4%	27.5

Source: KFTC, "Status of Internal Trade of Business Groups Subject to Disclosure in 2019," News Release, October 14, 2019

that, in the past 5 years since 2015, the KFTC has only fully prevailed in the administrative court in two out of ten cases concerning unfair subsidization.[18] The primary challenge resides in determining the "normal" arm's-length price, which must be deemed acceptable in the court's eyes. This predicament appears to have made the KFTC more cautious when dealing with cases of unfair subsidization. For instance, in a recent incident involving quantity-pushing toward an affiliate of the Hanwha group (currently ranked sixth among business groups), the KFTC itself reached a decision of not guilty. This verdict comes as quite a surprise since the KFTC has previously adopted an aggressive stance of "zero tolerance" toward unfair subsidization practices.

2.3 Economic Logics of Chaebol Regulations

The MRFTA regulates chaebols in various aspects ranging from the *ex ante* prohibition on certain types of inter-affiliate shareholding to the *ex post* regulation on unfair internal transaction and tunneling. The economic arguments on chaebol regulations are diverse and controversial. I will discuss three economic logics on which various regulations were based. Firstly, certain forms of affiliate shareholding can be characterized as 'fictitious' since they lack genuine capital investment. Consequently, these practices are exploited by chaebol owners as a means to extend their control over diverse businesses without utilizing their own financial resources. This abuse of power enables them to expand their influence unchecked. To maintain a balanced argument, I will discuss about some positive functions of intercorporate

[18] Yeonhap News Agency, https://www.yna.co.kr/view/AKR20190930169800002, October 1, 2019.

shareholding. Secondly, it is argued that business diversification, which chaebol heads desire, may be 'excessive' to the point of inefficiency from a national economic perspective, and sometimes even in terms of maximizing the value of companies involved. Such excessive diversification may divert resources from sectors where they could be utilized more productively, potentially harming the overall economy and diminishing the value of the businesses. Lastly, chaebol heads and their families have exhibited opportunistic behavior through moral hazard, commonly referred to as "tunneling." This refers to the practice of siphoning off resources or profits from one company within the chaebol to another, often to the detriment of minority shareholders or other stakeholders. This opportunism poses a significant challenge to fair and transparent business practices. In conclusion, the MRFTA's regulatory framework aims to address these economic logics behind chaebol regulations, targeting fictitious shareholding, excessive diversification, and opportunistic behavior. By curbing these practices, the regulations strive to promote fairness, efficiency, and sustainable growth within the chaebol system.

2.3.1 'Fictitious' Equity Investment

The existing regulation regarding the holding of shares between affiliated companies aims to prevent large business conglomerates from holding shares in certain ways, such as cross shareholding and new circular shareholding. It also establishes a minimum ratio of shareholding that a holding company and its subsidiary must adhere to when controlling lower-level subsidiaries. The various types of inter-affiliate shareholding outlined in the current regulation have one common characteristic: they all involve some degree of fictitious equity investment. By 'fictitious' equity investment, it means that when viewed from the perspective of the entire business group, the investment does not actually result in real equity investment, even though it is accounted for based on the 'nominal' amount of equity invested.

Let us examine a basic form of affiliate shareholding, where affiliate *A* holding affiliate *B*'s equity of worth 100, i.e., $A \xrightarrow{100} B$. In this type of inter-affiliate shareholding, the 'nominal' equity investment and the 'actual' equity investment both amount to 100. When considering *A* and *B* as a whole, there does not exist any 'fictitious' equity investment in this 'simple' form of affiliate shareholding.

Now consider a 'cross' shareholding such as affiliate *A* holding affiliate *B*'s equity worth 100 and *B* holding *A*'s equity worth 50 in return. Denote this as $A \xrightarrow{100} B \xrightarrow{50}$ A. This is the most conspicuous type of inter-affiliate shareholding that involves with fictitious equity investment. In this case, two affiliates exchange equity share documents as far as the amount of 50 is concerned. Hence, combining *A* and *B* together, the 'nominal' equity investment appears to be 150. However, the 'actual' investment is only 50, which *A* invests in *B*. The remaining 100 is considered 'fictitious' investment. In this scenario, the total fictitious equity investment of 100 can be decomposed into each company's share: *A*'s 50 and B's 50. That is,

A re-invests in *B* the amount of 50, which is what *A* received from *B*. And *B* re-invests into *A* the amount of 50, which is what *B* received from *A*. Hence, from the standpoint of each company, the fictitious equity investment can be seen as the portion that an affiliate re-invests into other affiliates using the funds received from others. In other words, the fictitious aspect stems from 're-investment'.

Next, consider a 'multilevel vertical' shareholding[19] such as *A* holding *B*'s equity worth 100 and *B* holding *C*'s equity worth 50, being denoted as $A \xrightarrow{100} B \xrightarrow{50} C$. In this arrangement, *A* invests 100 into *B*, which is 'actual' in that *A* received nothing from other affiliates. On the other hand, *B* re-invests into *C* the amount of 50, which is derived from the investment received from *A*, and therefore, can be considered 'fictitious'. From the standpoint of a business group comprising *A*, *B*, and *C* as a whole, the total nominal investment of 150 is decomposed into a fictitious investment of 50 and an actual investment of 100.

A 'circular' shareholding may be regarded as the combination of a 'multilevel vertical' shareholding and an 'indirect cross' shareholding. Consider an example of *A* investing 100 into *B*'s equities, *B* investing 50 into *C*'s equities and *C* investing 30 back into *A*'s equities. Denote this arrangement as $A \xrightarrow{100} B \xrightarrow{50} C \xrightarrow{30} A$. Here, the equity investment in the direction of $A \rightarrow B \rightarrow C$ represents a 'multilevel vertical' shareholding, while $C \rightarrow A$ is an 'indirect cross' shareholding. In this scenario, *A*'s fictitious amount of re-investment is 30, and *B*'s fictitious amount of re-investment is 50, and *C*'s fictitious amount of re-investment is 30. From the standpoint of a business group of *A*, *B*, and *C* as a whole, the total nominal investment of 180 can be broken down into a fictitious investment of 110 and an actual investment of 70.

Let us consider the marginal effect of each type of affiliate shareholding in terms of the increment of fictitious investment amount starting from the simple type of $A \xrightarrow{100} B$. By adding the cross type of $B \xrightarrow{50} A$ into it, the marginal effect on the nominal investment is 50, while the marginal effect on the fictitious investment is 100. Thus, the marginal fictitious ratio, which is defined by dividing the latter with the former, is 2. Now consider the marginal effect of a multilevel vertical shareholding. From the base of $A \xrightarrow{100} B$, the additional component is $B \xrightarrow{50} C$. The marginal effect on the nominal investment is 50, and the marginal effect on the fictitious investment is 50 as well. Hence, the marginal fictitious ratio is 1. Next, the circular shareholding of $A \xrightarrow{100} B \xrightarrow{50} C \xrightarrow{30} A$ is constructed by adding the indirect cross type of $C \xrightarrow{30} A$ into the multilevel vertical type of $A \xrightarrow{100} B \xrightarrow{50} C$. Here the marginal effect on the nominal investment is 30, and the marginal effect on the fictitious investment is 60. Hence, the marginal fictitious ratio for circular shareholding is 2, which is the same as the ratio of cross shareholding.

[19]The related literature, e.g., La Porta et al. (1999), term it as "pyramidal" shareholding.

As explained in Section 2.2, the MRFTA forbids any instances of cross and new ones of circular shareholding *ex ante*. The rationale may be the significant marginal fictitious ratio of 2 (as illustrated in the above hypothetical example). On the other hand, as Table 2.6 lists, the Act appears to have conflicting views when it comes to limitations on a holding company's affiliate shareholding. On the one hand, the Act mandates that a holding company and its subsidiaries must possess a minimum number of shares in sub-tier subsidiaries. On the other hand, it prohibits any shareholding of affiliates that are not subsidiaries, as well as holding more than 5% shares of non-affiliate companies. This dual stance may aim to strike the balance between two objectives: facilitating effective control and ownership within the holding company system, while preventing excessive expansion through the misuse of 'fictitious' shareholding.

Why is the concept of fictitious equity investment problematic? To begin with, it has the potential to distort accounting information, which is crucial for assessing the financial stability of a company or business group. This distortion can manifest in various ways, such as inflating the capital value, underestimating the debt ratio, and misleading financial investment decisions. While consolidated financial statements and efficient financial markets can partially restore transparency in terms of information, they are not entirely foolproof. Furthermore, fictitious equity investment serves as a tool for expanding control rights across a wide range of businesses. In other words, it acts as a significant barrier that creates a substantial gap between cash flow rights and control rights, as described in finance literature.[20] According to a study by Baek et al. (2004), the value of a firm is negatively affected by the separation between cash flow and control rights, particularly in the context of chaebol ownership.

I will now digress briefly to discuss the previous regulations regarding inter-affiliate shareholding. These regulations aimed to restrict the proportion of equity shares that an affiliate within a large business group could hold in other domestic companies, in relation to the total value of its 'net' assets.[21] This measure was first introduced in the 1986 revision of the MRFTA, as part of the efforts to control the excessive concentration of economic power. However, it was ultimately eliminated in 2009.

In the past, there have been numerous regulatory changes concerning the limit of equity share in relation to net assets. This episode of changes began in 1986 with the introduction of a 40% limit, which was subsequently tightened to 25% in 1994. The

---

[20] Claessens et al. (2000) highlight a significant divergence of control rights from cash flow rights among numerous firms in East Asia.

[21] 'Net' assets refer to the residual value of a company's capital (assets minus debts) once the investment from affiliated equity shareholders has been deducted.

limit was abolished in 1998,[22] only to be reinstated in 1999.[23] Further modifications occurred in 2002, 2004, 2006, and 2007, including loosening regulations on business group coverage, exemptions, and increasing the limit of maximum equity shares of other domestic companies from 25% to 40% of net assets. Finally, in 2009, the limit was abolished once again. While I will not delve into the specifics of the phased-out regulation's history, it is important to discuss the advantages and disadvantages of inter-affiliate shareholding regulations in general. These considerations remain relevant today, despite the removal of the limit on total equity shares.

The primary objective behind setting a limit on the overall quantity of equity shares was to prevent the occurrence of false or deceptive equity investments. The regulation indirectly aimed to control the excessive expansion of a chaebol head's authority over various businesses and mitigate the potential risks associated with hazardous practices such as 'tunneling', which will be addressed later in this discussion. In this subsection, I will assess the relevance of this regulation based on its direct intention, namely, the restriction of fictitious equity investment.

First of all, it is crucial to acknowledge that this policy was destined to fail due to its lack of 'time-consistency', which is an essential requirement for any policy to be effective, as demonstrated by the erratic nature of the revision process. More importantly, it lacks a 'target-oriented' approach. This means that the regulation concerning the restriction on the overall quantity of equity shares does not specifically address the problematic equity investments that contribute to the rise of fictitious investment. Moreover, it fails to differentiate between various types of equity investments, including 'cross', 'circular', 'multi-level vertical', and 'simple' shareholding. We can identify the specific equity shareholding that poses problems in terms of fictitiousness. Consequently, in 2006, I proposed an alternative regulation that focuses on the total amount of 'equity re-investment' rather than the limit on the total quantity of equity shares.[24]

Suppose that a business group consists of n affiliates, and that the cobweb-like inter-affiliate shareholding is represented by $n \times n$ matrix S, where s_{ij} is affiliate j's equity investment to affiliate i.[25] Then the nominal amount of affiliate k's equity

---

[22] During the process of resolving the foreign exchange crisis that commenced in late 1997, there was a discussion regarding the potential hindrance posed by the regulation concerning the ownership of inter-affiliate equity shares. This regulation was thought to impede corporate restructuring, hinder new business ventures, and impede efficient mergers and acquisitions. In response to these arguments, the decision was made to abolish this regulation. Additionally, other regulations pertaining to chaebols, such as the complete prohibition of debt guarantees among affiliated companies, were strengthened to complement this abolishment.

[23] It was claimed that the traditional negative effects caused by chaebols, such as the practice of circular equity investment and extensive business expansion, resurfaced once the regulation on holding inter-affiliate equity shares was abolished. This provided valid grounds for reintroducing the regulation. As a result, the establishment and transformation into a holding company, which had previously been prohibited, were permitted due to the potential benefits the holding company system offers in terms of efficiently restructuring corporate governance and enhancing competitiveness.

[24] See Park et al. (2006).

[25] See Jeon (1994) for the analysis of inter-affiliate shareholding matrix S.

investment in other affiliates in the same group is the sum of k'th column of matrix S, i.e., $\sum_{i=1}^{n} s_{ik}$. On the other hand, the nominal amount of other affiliates' equity investment in affiliate k is the sum of k'th row of matrix S, i.e., $\sum_{j=1}^{n} s_{kj}$. Therefore, the amount of k's 'actual' investment is $\sum_{i=1}^{n} s_{ik} - \sum_{j=1}^{n} s_{kj}$ if the difference is positive, or zero otherwise, that is, $\max\left(\sum_{i=1}^{n} s_{ik} - \sum_{j=1}^{n} s_{kj}, 0\right)$. On the other hand, the amount of k's 'fictitious' investment is the subtraction of its 'actual' investment from nominal investment, i.e., $\sum_{i=1}^{n} s_{ik} - \max\left(\sum_{i=1}^{n} s_{ik} - \sum_{j=1}^{n} s_{kj}, 0\right)$, which is re-arranged as $\min\left(\sum_{i=1}^{n} s_{ik}, \sum_{j=1}^{n} s_{kj}\right)$.[26] We can interpret the representation of k's 'fictitious' investment, which is formulated as $\min\left(\sum_{i=1}^{n} s_{ik}, \sum_{j=1}^{n} s_{kj}\right)$, as the amount which affiliate k reinvests in other affiliates out of what other affiliates invests in k. We may say simply that the fictitious equity investment is 'internal equity re-investment'.

I proposed the limit of total amount of an affiliate's internal equity re-investment in other domestic companies, as an alternative of the regulation at the time (as of 2006) of limiting the total (across the board) amount of equity shares of other domestic companies, into a certain ratio of its total value of 'net' assets. Naturally, the ratio would have been adjusted appropriately into a lower level under the alternative approach. My proposal was not adopted at the time. One of the reasons for this was the practical or legal complications it posed. The act of actively investing in other companies could be seen as a potential violation, whereas receiving investments passively may not be deemed culpable. However, I believe this is not a significant issue since compliance with chaebol regulations should be attributed to the entire business group as a whole, rather than individual affiliates.

In my opinion, my proposal may be a more sensible option compared to the existing regulation, particularly because it is more focused on achieving specific targets. The main objective of my proposal is to reduce the occurrence of fictitious equity investment, which aligns with its intended purpose. After all, the regulation that limited the overall number of equity shares held by domestic companies was abolished in 2009. Presently, the only remaining restrictions are related to cross and circular shareholding, as well as limitations on shareholding by holding companies. Considering the intricate nature of corporate affairs, it might be more appropriate to regulate specific types of shareholding rather than adopting a broad approach that limits intercorporate shareholding in terms of total amount or reinvestment.

---

[26] We can check that $\max(x - y, 0) + \min(x, y) = x$ for any x, y. That is, it holds true that the sum of actual investment and fictitious investment is equal to the total nominal investment.

2.3.2 Positive Functions of Intercorporate Shareholding[27]

Proponents of chaebols put forth various arguments of the positive functions of intercorporate shareholding. In this regard, I will discuss on the two topics, namely, the stabilization of management and the facilitation of new business investment.

The intercorporate affiliates' shares in Korean chaebols serve as a means to safeguard the control right of the whole business group from outside hostile takeovers.[28] The literature on the agency theories of corporate governance in finance presents conflicting perspectives on the role of intercorporate shareholding as stabilizing management. Fama and Jensen (1983) propose that managers, entrenched within the protection of stabilizing shares and immune to potential hostile takeovers in capital market, may not act in the best interest of maximizing the firm value. In other words, the shares held by affiliate companies may undermine the effectiveness of "the market for corporate control" in mitigating the managerial agency problem that arises from the divergent interests between managers, who may pursue personal goals such as laziness, extravagant spending, or excessive expansion of the firm, and the shareholders, who aim to maximize firm value.

On the other hand, if we look at the issue of managerial incentive problem from a long-term perspective, we can see differently that intercorporate shareholding plays a positive role of stabilizing management. That is, if the problem lies in "managerial myopia," where managers focus on boosting stock prices due to takeover market pressures, intercorporate shareholding can potentially provide a protective shield that encourages managers to make more efficient decisions for the long term. Stein (1989) suggests that the root cause of managerial myopia can be attributed to the information asymmetry between managers and investors in the capital market. Due to the limited and incomplete information available regarding managerial investment decisions in the capital market, investors rely on their predictions of the firm's future value based on its current performance. In response to this, managers, who are concerned about how the stock market evaluates the firm's value, may attempt to manipulate market perceptions by prioritizing short-term profit gains at the expense of long-term benefits.[29]

In sum, the effect of intercorporate shareholding on the performance of firms in a business group depends upon the nature of managerial incentive problem. If we are concerned of the usual agency problem of managers pursuing private interests, the entrenchment effect may be negative. On the other hand, if we are concerned about

[27] Subsections 2.3.2 and 2.3.3 are based on Jeon (2002).

[28] As Table 2.1 shows, this phenomenon is particularly evident when considering Korean chaebols, where the ownership stakes held by the head and their families are a mere 0.8% and 2.2%, respectively, as of the year 2021. However, the chaebol heads exercise complete control over the entire conglomerate through the utilization of shares held by inter-corporate affiliate firms, which amount to 57.5%.

[29] According to the efficient market hypothesis, the capital market cannot be easily deceived by managers who try to inflate current profits. Then, managers should live up to such expectations in order to maintain their value and avoid being undervalued in the market.

the managerial myopia, then intercorporate shareholding may play a positive role of motivating management to adopt a long-term perspective.

The argument of affiliates' equity investment helping with starting new business is straightforward, but it is neutral about whether it is positive or negative. It depends upon whether the new business opportunity adds value to both the group and the overall economy. If this is indeed the case, the intercorporate shareholding assumes a constructive role in enhancing efficiency. However, if the new business is to expand monopoly power into a new market, then it may benefit the group while adversely affecting the economy. Moreover, if it is to reduce the owner's risk, which cannot be avoided through portfolio diversification, then it may not have positive impact even for the group. In the subsequent subsection concerning 'excessive' business diversification, I will elaborate on the possible negative consequences at both economy-wide level and even the firm levels.

2.3.3 'Excessive' Business Diversification

Chaebol heads may have a strong inclination to build their own 'empires'. This is a journalistic explanation of their conduct of expanding businesses under control and constructing large business groups. However, we need more sophisticated economics-based explanation about their underlying motivations and objectives. By understanding their economic motives, we can address a crucial question: do they excessively diversify their businesses? In this context, 'excessiveness' can be evaluated based on two criteria. Firstly, whether their diversification is beyond the level to achieve the efficiency of the national economy. Secondly, whether it exceeds the level necessary to maximize the value of individual firms.

The excessiveness of business diversification or conglomerate combination can be assessed in terms of economic efficiency using conventional industrial economics.[30] It can enhance economic efficiency through what is known as the synergy effect. The main source of synergy stems from shared resources, such as R&D investment and entrepreneurial expertise, which can be utilized by firms in a business group. However, business diversification may go beyond the level of exploiting synergy. Chaebols may harm competition by leveraging monopoly power in one market and extending it into another market. There are many ways of leveraging, such as bundling, predation, foreclosure, etc. Antitrust authorities may regulate such anticompetitive practices ex post, but this is not always guaranteed. Furthermore, the harm caused by these practices may be irreversible at the time regulations are implemented.

In the past, there was a factor in industrial policy that encouraged inefficient expansion of businesses, at least until the foreign exchange crisis in the late 1990s. The Korean government provided support to certain strategic industries by offering

[30] Montgomery (1994) surveys the economics of business diversification.

subsidies to a few established companies and placing restrictions on new entrants. The aim of this industrial policy was to prevent duplicative investments in capacity and to control intense competition. However, during times of economic recession and industrial restructuring, the government intervened to rescue struggling large firms in order to prevent a widespread economic shock. This means that the government created barriers to entry and exit during the period of growth driven by government initiatives. In such circumstances, there was a significant advantage for companies that were quick to enter new promising markets, referred to as 'the first mover's advantage'. Chaebols benefited from government support and protection from new competitors during the industry's growth phase, while they shared the losses with the government during the decline phase, thereby ultimately burdening the national economy.

If a chaebol expands its business operations to take advantage of leveraging and being the first mover even after exhausting positive synergy, diversification may be 'excessive' in that it may overshoot the efficient level from the standpoint of national economy. However, even in this case, the individual firms within a group will still benefit at the expense of consumers and excluded firms. Hence, it is a subtler matter whether business diversification may be 'excessive' beyond the optimal level for individual firms within a business group.

The value of a manager's investment in human capital is closely tied to the overall value of the firm they oversee. The risks associated with managerial positions are specific to each individual firm and cannot be reduced through diversification in the capital market. However, business diversification can be employed as a strategy to mitigate these risks. Consequently, managers with control rights may choose to pursue business diversification to minimize the risks associated with their role, which are directly linked to the risks faced by the firm. This approach goes beyond simply maximizing the firm's value. Amihud and Lev (1981) considered this as a component of the agency costs that managers bear.

The issue of excessive business diversification, undertaken to minimize managerial risk, is further compounded by the ownership–control structure within Korean chaebols. Specifically, the head of a business group possesses a small equity stake in several key affiliates and maintains a complex network of substantial inter-affiliate shareholdings, as outlined in Section 2.1. In this particular context, the head of a business group is more inclined to engage in excessive diversification compared to a manager who lacks ownership. The risks faced by a chaebol head are linked to the specific and unique risks associated with the affiliates under their control and ownership, both as a controlling manager and an equity shareholder. Ordinary investors can mitigate the latter risk by diversifying their investment portfolios. However, chaebol heads do not have this option as diversifying their equity investments may lead to a loss or weakening of their control over business group affiliates. While the head's equity ownership to some extent may alleviate this concern, it is insufficient to counterbalance the incentives driving them toward excessive diversification, especially given their limited equity ownership.

Business diversification may not be beneficial for the national economy, even if it leads to increased firm value within a group. This is particularly true when diversification is used to gain monopoly power or exploit barriers to entry and exit that are established through industrial policies. Moreover, if diversification results in a decrease in firm value within a group, it becomes even more inefficient. This inefficiency arises from the unique risks associated with individual firms, which a chaebol head, who serves as both a controlling manager and an equity shareholder, must bear. These risks cannot be mitigated through portfolio diversification; they can only be reduced through business diversification. This is especially relevant in the context of Korea, where many chaebol heads maintain control over their groups by holding small equity shares in key affiliates.

2.3.4 Moral Hazard and 'Tunneling'

In addition to the moral hazard of 'excessive' diversification of business ventures by chaebol heads, one of the most prevalent opportunistic behaviors observed is commonly known as 'tunneling'. According to Johnson et al. (2000a, b), 'tunneling' refers to "the transfer of resources out of a company to its controlling shareholder (who is typically also a top manager)." The term was initially coined "to characterize the expropriation of minority shareholders in Czech Republic (as in removing assets through an underground tunnel)." Tunneling behavior can take various forms, including "outright theft or fraud," "asset sales and contracts such as transfer pricing advantageous to the controlling shareholder, excessive executive compensation, loan guarantees, expropriation of corporate opportunities," and "increasing his share of the firm without transferring any assets through dilutive share issues, minority freeze-outs, insider trading, creeping acquisitions, or other financial transactions that discriminate against minorities."

Under the MRFTA §26 provision, chaebol affiliates that belong to major business conglomerates are mandated to disclose the resolutions made by their board of directors regarding significant internal trading activities. This requirement serves the purpose of monitoring any potentially exploitative actions by the chaebol head. Specifically, as outlined in §45 (1) 9 and §47, these regulations prohibit various forms of tunneling that pose risks, such as unfair subsidizing and unwarranted profit-deflecting. These measures aim to address a broader range of tunneling behavior, which goes beyond what was highlighted by Johnson et al. (2000a, b). They encompass all opportunistic actions taken by chaebol heads or families to undermine competition and negatively impact minority shareholders and consumers.

The noteworthy aspect here pertains to the regulation concerning 'quantity-pushing or funneling of business'. This involves overseeing significant internal transactions that lack reasonable assessment or comparison. This holds true even if the transaction terms, such as transfer prices, align with arms-length dealing and seemingly do not benefit the business group's head. Yoon and Jin (2021) present an intriguing theoretical finding in this regard. They develop a model that depicts a business group with a dominant owner, where two affiliates engage in transactions at market prices, free from transfer price distortions. However, even under these circumstances, a high volume of transactions can exclude competitors in the upstream market and drive up prices, leading to a detrimental impact on competition and reduced consumer benefits. Furthermore, this may serve the controlling shareholder's interests at the expense of minority shareholders in the downstream affiliate. This outcome sheds light on the MRFTA regulation pertaining to large-scale internal transactions.

Many studies have demonstrated the detrimental impacts of the tunneling behavior exhibited by the families of Korean chaebols on the value of firms within their business groups and the interests of minority shareholders. Baek et al. (2004) have revealed that when a firm within a Korean business group undertakes an acquisition, minority shareholders suffer losses while the controlling shareholders reap the benefits, as the acquisition enhances the value of other firms within the group. Baek et al. (2006) have examined the utilization of equity-linked private securities offerings as a means of tunneling among Korean chaebol firms, finding that chaebol issuers involved in intragroup deals manipulate the offering prices to favor their controlling shareholders.[31] More recently, Choi and Cho (2021) have analyzed a sample of Korean public firms from 2011 to 2018, discovering that higher levels of related-party transactions (RPTs) result in a decreased value of cash holdings in terms of their contribution to a firm's stock return. Notably, the negative impact of RPTs is more pronounced in Korean chaebol firms compared to non-chaebol firms.

One of significant implications of law and economics is that legal and institutional environments affect business conduct and economic performance. This influence is particularly evident in the context of tunneling behavior and ownership-control structure. It is widely acknowledged that company laws in civil-law countries, specifically those following the French civil-law system, offer less protection to minority shareholders compared to common-law countries (La Porta et al. 1999). Johnson et al. (2000a, b) note that "In civil-law countries, the expropriation of minority shareholders by the controlling shareholders is often seen as consistent with directors' duties, especially if the controlling shareholder is another firm in the group. Self-dealing transactions are assessed in light of their conformity with statutes, and not on the basis of their fairness to minorities."[32] A similar relationship can be observed between the protection of minority shareholders and ownership concentration. As stated by La Porta et al. (1999), "in countries with poor protection of minority shareholders, losing control involuntarily and thus becoming a minority shareholder may be such a costly proposition in terms of surrendering the private benefits of control that the controlling shareholders would do everything to keep control." This must be one factor that induces Korean chaebol heads with relatively

---

[31] Samsung SDS's issuance of bond with warrants (BWs) in February 1999 stands out as the most significant instance worth discussing. This particular case will be examined more closely in the subsequent Section 3.4.

[32] This may explain the ruling in favor of Samsung SDS in the case of its BWs issuance, as will be discussed later.

small shares to exert efforts to maintain the control of group member firms by means of large inter-affiliate shareholding.

Hence, the influence of the legal system extends beyond the realm of law and impacts economic performance. Johnson et al. (2000a, b) demonstrate that countries with more robust legal institutions that safeguard the rights of minority shareholders experienced less severe financial crises during the period of 1997–1998, as evidenced by lower exchange rate depreciation and stock market decline. In light of the foreign exchange crisis, efforts were made to enhance chaebol regulations through the revisions of MRFTA. These revisions aimed to curb the practice of chaebol heads exploiting their companies for personal gain, while also seeking to enhance the structure of corporate ownership-control. Ultimately, these measures were implemented to foster both financial and economic development.

2.4 Cases of Regulation on Unfair Subsidizing or Undue Profit-Deflecting

In this section, we will explore various instances where regulations have been put in place to address the unfair subsidization of affiliate companies and the unjust diversion of profits toward group heads and their relatives. Such practices are explicitly prohibited by §45 (1) 9 and §47 of the Act. Nevertheless, it is noteworthy that the courts have frequently rendered differing verdicts in similar cases.

2.4.1 Samsung SDS *(1999)*[33]*: Unfair Subsidizing Group Head's Relatives*

Samsung SDS, an unlisted company whose shares were traded in the over-the-counter (OTC) market, issued Bonds with Warrant (BWs) valued at KR₩23 billion through a private placement to Lee, Jay Yong, the son of Chairman Lee, Kun Hee at that time, and several others in 1999. These BWs granted the holders the right to convert them into 2.3 million shares of common stock at a price of KR₩7150 per share after 1 year from the date of issuance. The KFTC determined that Samsung SDS engaged in transactions that offered significantly more favorable terms than the usual market price, resulting in substantial economic gains for the related party. As a result, this action violated §23 (1) 7 [new §45 (1) 9] in the Act as it constituted unfair subsidization.[34]

[33] In this book, the year mentioned in the case is the specific point in time when KFTC made its decision public.

[34] KFTC 1999–212, October 28, 1999. The decision includes a total of 11 instances where unfair subsidization to Samsung group affiliates was involved. We will focus only on *Samsung SDS* case, which holds upmost significance due to its potential influence on the future regulations governing chaebols.

The conversion price was determined based on the valuation method permitted under the inheritance tax regulations, which took into account the 'historical' revenue stream. On the other hand, the KFTC assessed the normal price at KR₩14,566 per share, also in accordance with the inheritance tax rules, but considering the 'future' revenue expectations. Despite being a rather conservative approach, even the KFTC's normal price was significantly lower than the share price of KR₩54,750 on the OTC market at that time. As per the KFTC's decision, this unfair subsidization "enabled substantial gains from stock sales or evaluations following the public offering of the unlisted affiliate, facilitating the transfer of wealth across generations. ... It also bolstered the overall share ratio and control power of the group head or their relatives over Samsung affiliates, establishing an environment conducive to perpetuating and strengthening their fleet-style management. ... Consequently, it raised significant concerns about impeding fair trade in the relevant markets where Samsung affiliates were involved."

However, the KFTC did not prevail in the court. The Appellate Court concluded that "there was a lack of evidence demonstrating the involvement of the related parties in the relevant market. Furthermore, there was no indication of any concerns regarding these parties gaining an advantageous position to eliminate competitors or impede fair trade within the market they operate."[35]

The Supreme Court has come to the same conclusion that dismissed the KFTC decision, albeit with slightly different reasoning. It has determined that the appeal court's reasoning was flawed, as it stated that the subsidized party must be part of the market where harms of competition or concentration of economic power occurred in order to raise the concerns of hindering fair trade. The Supreme Court clarified that it is not necessary for the subsidized party to directly or indirectly participate in the relevant market. However, the judgment states that "it is challenging to conclude that the conduct of the plaintiff [Samsung SDS] in this case, even if it enables the transfer of wealth across generation and creates an environment conducive to concentration of economic power, raises concerns of hindering fair trade. We cannot say that it is not necessary to prove it as a well-known fact that there are concerns of hindering fair trade in the relevant market due to the investment of subsidized assets in affiliate companies by related parties. Therefore, the arguments and proofs presented by the defendant [KFTC]'s as shown in the record alone did not establish that the conduct in this case raised the concerns of hindering unfair trade."[36]

This particular case was also addressed in another judicial court. A non-governmental organization filed a lawsuit against Samsung SDS, contending that the company had evaded the law by selling its BW to Lee, Jay Yong at an unreasonably low price. The organization further accused Samsung SDS of violating the Commercial Law pertaining to the duty of care and the duty of loyalty of directors. In its defense, Samsung SDS justified the pricing of its BWs by claiming that it followed the valuation method permitted by the inheritance tax regulations.

[35] Seoul High Court 2000nu4790, July 3 2001.

[36] Supreme Court 2001du6364, September 24, 2004.

The prosecutors' office ultimately accepted this argument put forth by the defendant. Subsequently, the Constitutional Court upheld the decision made by the prosecutors in 2003 during the appeal proceedings.

Despite Samsung group's successful legal victories in relation to the lawsuits, the consequences that followed were significant and enduring. The case of *Samsung SDS* serves as a clear illustration of 'tunneling', whereby the affiliate's wealth was transferred to the family of the group head, resulting in a concentration of economic power and the unfair expropriation of minority shareholders. Surprisingly, this behavior managed to evade the scrutiny of the Fair Trade Act and Commercial Law. The existing legal framework proved inadequate in identifying and addressing such abnormal tunneling practices, leading the courts to resort to special legal reasoning to grant exemptions.

Following that, the MRFTA underwent revisions aimed at strengthening regulations on chaebols regarding their internal trade practices and unfair subsidization. In 1999, the KFTC introduced §26, which mandated that Category 2 chaebols ("business groups subject to disclosure") publicly reveal the resolutions made by their board of directors pertaining to large-scale internal transactions with or for any related party. This disclosure requirement specifically included the "offering or trading securities, such as shares or corporate bonds." Additionally, in 2004, §27 was introduced, obligating the unlisted affiliates of Category 2 chaebols to disclose material facts in a manner similar to that required of listed companies.

In a significant development, §47 (Prohibition of Provision, etc., of Undue Benefits to Related Parties) was added to §45 (Prohibition of Unfair Trade Practices) in 2013. These two articles, as Table 2.8 compares, differ in terms of regulatory contents, parties involved in subsidizing and being subsidized, and the criteria for determining unfairness. The newly introduced §47 specifically targets the prevention of tunneling behavior by a group head and their relatives. It is notable that the requisite for §47 to apply is "the undue benefits attributable to a related party or an affiliate whose shares are held by a related party" above some prescribed percentage, while that of §45 is "to hinder fair trade." The Supreme Court decision in the *Samsung SDS* case highlighted the difficulty in proving hindrance to fair trade in the relevant market when the subsidized parties were relatives of the group head, especially if they did not invest the subsidized assets in affiliate companies.

The implications of the *Samsung SDS* case extend far beyond antitrust policy in Korea. Despite Samsung group's legal exemption in court, Lee, Jay Yong has not gained public legitimacy as the heir of Samsung group. The anomalous succession procedure exposed in the *Samsung SDS* case has since become a significant stain on his reputation. The subsequent imprisonment of Lee, Jay Yong, not once but twice, for unrelated reasons may be perplexing to foreigners considering Samsung's global success. It is possible that the seemingly indifferent attitude of some Korean individuals toward his imprisonment stems from either his own or Samsung group's original wrongdoing in the succession process. This issue is not limited to Samsung group alone. The prevailing negative sentiment toward chaebols is undoubtedly detrimental to the Korean economy, which heavily relies on these large business conglomerates for rapid growth.

2.4.2 Hyundai Glovis *(2007): Quantity-Pushing*

Glovis, an affiliate of the Hyundai Motor Group, operates as a freight transport agency. It was established in 2001 through investments made by Chung, Mong Ku, the head of the group, who held 40% shares worth KR₩2 billion, and his son Chung, Eui Sun, who held 60% shares worth KR₩3 billion. Within a short span of time, Glovis experienced rapid growth, becoming the second-largest firm in just 2 years and eventually emerging as the largest firm within 4 years in terms of sales in the relevant market. The KFTC reported that between March 2001 and June 2004, four Hyundai affiliates, namely, Hyundai Motor, Kia Car, Hyundai Mobis, and Hyundai Steel, predominantly entrusted Glovis with the transportation of their completed cars, motor parts, and steels. Notably, the terms of trade offered to Glovis were considerably more favorable than the prevailing market prices, thereby constituting unfair trade practices in violation of Section 45 (1) 9.[37]

During the appeal proceedings, the plaintiffs contended that the level of transactions in the freight transport market, amounting to only 6.8%, did not deem to be significant. Moreover, they argued that the deemed "significant" size of the trade itself did not fall under the category of unfair trade practices regulated by the Act. However, the Seoul High Court refuted this argument by highlighting that the level of transactions was indeed substantial. This was evident as Hyundai Motor and Hyundai Steel directed 100% of their transport volume to Glovis, while Kia Car accounted for 82%, and Hyundai Mobis for 80%. Additionally, the court referred to Article 36 (1) of the Enforcement Decree of the Act, which specifies "subsidizing the related party or other company by providing excessive economic gains through providing or transacting with significantly low or high price or *in significant size*" (italic added) as types of unfair trade practices.[38]

The plaintiffs also contended that the defendant [KFTC] failed to compare the normal price in the same or similar market to establish the presence of a "significantly favorable condition." The defendant only mentioned the trade nature, gross profit ratio, and freight transport fare index. Additionally, the plaintiffs argued that Glovis had made significant investments in both human and financial capital to develop an integrated and efficient logistic transportation system to support Hyundai Motor group's operations. However, the Seoul High Court countered these arguments by stating that all the circumstances, including sales, profits, and market shares following the subsidization conduct, demonstrated the existence of unfairness. The court further asserted that the mere necessities in business or trade rationalization did not negate the unfairness or hindrance of fair trade, which are essential elements of unfair subsidizing behavior.[39]

---

[37] KFTC 2007–504, October 24, 2007.

[38] Seoul High Court 2007nu30903, August 19 2007.

[39] The judgment of the Seoul High Court is final since plaintiffs did not appeal to the Supreme Court in this case.

The KFTC has identified five additional cases of unfair subsidization, in addition to the one mentioned. These cases involve Hyundai Motor providing subsidies to Hyundai Mobis and Kia Car, Hyundai Mobis, Glovis, and Hyundai Motor subsidizing Hyundai Card, as well as Hyundai Motor and Kia Car subsidizing Hyundai Hysco, and Kia Car subsidizing Rotem. The decision made by the KFTC was upheld by the appeal court, with the exception of the case involving Hyundai Motor and Kia Car's subsidization of Hyundai Hysco.[40] This particular incident raised controversy as the KFTC claimed that the two motor companies had purchased cold rolled steel sheet from an affiliate at a significantly higher price than the normal market value. The court, however, dismissed the KFTC's decision due to the disputed nature of the subsidized product's price. The KFTC's appeal was also rejected by the Supreme Court.[41] It is worth noting that even with the partial losing, this case still represents a rare instance where the KFTC emerged victorious in addressing unfair subsidization within a business group's affiliates.

The *Glovis* case was somewhat peculiar in that the unfairness of related subsidization claimed by the KFTC was a combination of "*considerably advantageous condition*" and "*significant scale*." At the time of the KFTC decision, the unfair subsidization in §45 (1) 9 in the Act was stipulated as "a transaction with the related party or other company under *significantly advantageous terms*." Notice that the requite for unfairness in the Act was "*significantly* advantageous *terms*," whereas the unfair nature in the KFTC decision was "*considerably* advantageous *condition*." However, the KFTC was unable to specify the 'normal' term of trade for comparison with the actual terms, which the plaintiffs highlighted in their appeal to the court. Unfortunately, the appeal court decision did not provide a clear resolution to this issue. Furthermore, the Act did not originally include "significant scale" as a criterion for unfair trade practices, although it was later added in the Enforcement Decree.

If the Glovis case had been either a "considerably advantageous condition" or a "significant scale" situation, rather than a combination of the two, it is uncertain whether the KFTC would have succeeded in the court. These concerns could have prompted the KFTC to make two revisions to the Act in 2013. Firstly, they changed the adverb of degree before *advantageous* from *significantly* into *considerably*,[42] aiming to expand the scope of unfair practices. More importantly, they introduced a new article §47 in the Act that included a prohibition on quantity-pushing or funneling, "a transaction of a *considerable scale* with the related party or affiliate

[40] KFTC 2007–504, October 24, 2007 and Seoul High Court 2007nu30903, August 9 2007.

[41] Supreme Court 2009du15494, October 25 2012.

[42] Here I have designated the term 'considerably' as a less powerful adverb compared to 'significantly'.

… without comparing with other business entities," as a provision of undue benefits to related parties as well as others (see Table 2.8).

Glovis was an important toehold for Chung Eui Sun to leap into the position of a successor of Hyundai Motor business group. This may be another tunneling case where the group head and his son, who owned Glovis, benefited at the sacrifice of subsidizing entities and their minority shareholders' interests as well as competition in the relevant market. The four Hyundai affiliates, Hyundai Motor, Kia Car, Hyundai Mobis, and Hyundai Steel paid KR₩8.5 billion collectively as penalty surcharges.[43] According to estimations by the KFTC, Chung, Mong Ku and Chung, Eui Sun reaped substantial gains of approximately KR₩1.1 trillion in six years after investing KR₩5 billion to establish Glovis in February 2001.[44] These considerable capital gains likely played a significant role in strengthening Chung, Mong Ku's control power of Hyundai Motor group and building a solid foundation for Chung, Eui Sun's succession basis.

2.4.3 Hanjin KAL *(2017): Undue Profit-Deflecting*

Hanjin is a prominent conglomerate, ranking 15th in terms of its overall assets. Korean Airline (KAL), belongs to this business group. The KFTC conducted an investigation and discovered that KAL had improperly directed profits to two Hanjin affiliates, namely, CyberSky and UniConverse. This action violated §47 (1) and (3) of the Act, which prohibits Category 1 business groups from unjustly deflecting profits to their relatives and affiliated companies that they virtually control. As a result of their findings, the KFTC issued a cease-and-desist order and imposed a total penalty surcharge of KR₩1.43 billion on three affiliated companies.[45] CyberSky operates as an advertising media company, while UniConverse functions as a call center operator. During the period in question, the owner's son and daughters held significant shares in both of these affiliates. The specific actions for which the accused parties are held responsible are as follows: KAL paid higher-than-normal fees and prices to CyberSky for services related to advertising, mail order, and

[43] During the case, it was determined that only the entities providing subsidies were found guilty and were required to pay penalty surcharges. However, following the revision in 2013, both the entities providing subsidies and the entities receiving them became responsible for adhering to the regulations outlined in § 45 (1) 9 and §47, which aim to prevent unfair trade practices benefiting affiliated parties.

[44] Chung, Eui Sun has made approximately KR₩0.6 trillion in capital gains, calculated based on the stock price of Glovis in June 2007 and its selling price in November 2004. See KFTC Decision 2007–504, Oct. 24, 2007 (p. 98). While it can be argued that these capital gains were not solely the result of unfair subsidization, there is also reason to question whether Glovis would have achieved such success without the support of Hyundai Motor business group.

[45] KFTC 2017–009, January 10, 2017.

promotional materials. Additionally, KAL provided financial support to UniConverse for the construction and maintenance of their call center.

The KFTC decision was disapproved by the appellate court.[46] The Seoul High Court provided its judgment based on two primary reasons. Firstly, the KFTC failed to adequately establish the "normal" prices that could be used for comparison with the terms of the transactions under scrutiny. This issue is not unique to this particular case. The court has consistently rejected KFTC decisions pertaining to unfair subsidization in numerous prior cases due to the commission's inability to accurately determine the normal prices. Secondly, the profits gained from the tunneling behavior were deemed too insignificant to raise concerns about the concentration of economic power. This aspect of the judgment is both novel and controversial. The Supreme Court upheld this decision.[47]

This case represents the first implementation of §47 (Undue Profit-Deflecting to Relatives) since the introduction in 2014. As outlined in Table 2.8, the criterion for determining unfairness was lowered to the unfairness of accrued benefits in case of undue profit-deflecting to relatives. This adjustment was made due to the challenges associated with proving the hindrance of unfair trade in cases where subsidies are directed toward individual natural persons such as the chaebol family members, rather than affiliated companies. This issue was previously highlighted in the 1999 *Samsung SDS* case mentioned before. Hence, several legal scholars contend that the mere act of accruing undue benefits through profit-deflecting inherently, i.e., *per se*, proves unfairness under §47, unless there are exceptional circumstances or specific reasons. Furthermore, it is argued that defendants should bear the burden of proving exceptionalities.[48]

Considering that *ex post* regulations concerning chaebols should be grounded in the principle of the rule of reason, the approach of *per se* illegality when regulating the affiliates of Category 1 business groups is not suitable. It is essential to assess the advantages and disadvantages of the relevant conduct in order to make a reasonable evaluation. However, as the purpose of §47 regulation is to curb the tunneling behavior of chaebol families and address the lax enforcement of Commercial Law in protecting minority shareholders, stricter implementation may be warranted.

2.4.4 Hanwha Solution *(2020): Unfair Collecting Toll*

Hanwha is the seventh largest conglomerate in Korea with a total asset value of KR ₩7.17 trillion and 86 affiliated companies as of 2020. Among these affiliates, Hanwha Solution is a chemical company possessing a dominant market share in various chemical products within the country. The KFTC has accused Hanwha

---

46 Seoul High Court 2017nu36153, September 1 2017.

47 Supreme Court 2017du63993, May 12 2022.

48 Lee (2017)

Solution of engaging in unfair subsidizing behavior, violating §45 (1) 9 (Unfair Subsidizing Behavior), on behalf of Han Express, of which the head, Kim, Seung Yun's relatives (his sister and nephew) are major shareholders.[49] The alleged violation encompasses two distinct problematic practices. Firstly, Hanwha Solution has been accused of favoring Han Express by providing them with all the inland transportation of export containers at prices more advantageous than the "normal" rates observed in arms-length independent transactions. Secondly, Hanwha has been found to establish an unnecessary intermediary stage in the transportation of hazardous chemical products like hydrochloric acid and caustic soda, thereby creating a profitable business opportunity for Han Express, which collects tolls for this additional service.

In this case study, I will focus on the second behavior as it represents the first instance of the so-called "toll" that the KFTC addressed through the amendment of §45 (1) 9 in 2014.[50] Hanwha Solution, in its sale of hydrochloric acid and caustic soda either directly or through intermediaries, exclusively provided Han Express with a substantial amount of tank lorry transportation services. This amounted to a value of KR₩152 billion and accounted for 8.4% of the market for transporting hazardous chemical products. Additionally, Hanwha Solution paid considerably higher fees to Han Express, totaling KR₩9.1 billion, during the period from January 2010 to September 2018. In particular, Hanwha Solution altered its transportation arrangement from agency-based to Han Express' intermediation, which constituted approximately 70% of its hydrochloric acid sales. Consequently, Han Express, despite playing only a perfunctory role as an intermediary, profited by appropriating tolls exceeding 20% of the margins. Conversely, Hanwha Solution faced higher transportation costs, while incumbent transporters were relegated to subcontractors for Han Express, resulting in a decrease in their fees.

The arguments put forth by KFTC regarding the hindrance of fair trade in this particular case are fourfold. Firstly, Han Express has gained a competitive edge, leading to a significant increase in their market share from 15–25% to approximately 40% over a span of 8 years. It is important to note that this growth cannot be attributed to Han Express' inherent competitiveness or superior management efficiency. Secondly, Han Express has excluded both existing and potential competitors from accessing business opportunities, resulting in a detrimental impact on fair competition within the market. Furthermore, the implementation of an artificial multilevel transportation scheme has resulted in a decline in overall logistic efficiency. Lastly, the consequences of these actions have led to a concentration of economic power within the hands of the chaebol head and his relatives.

[49] KFTC 2020–314, December 10, 2020.

[50] The KFTC had addressed the issue of tolls even before the revision that explicitly categorized transactions involving intermediaries as unfair subsidization without any practical benefit, successfully winning the court case related to this matter. The relevant references for this are KFTC 2012–288, September. 13, 2012 on "Lotte PSNet's Unfair Subsidizing," Seoul High Court 2012nu30730, July 18 2013, and Supreme Court 2013du17466, February 13 2014.

The Seoul High Court has granted approval to the KFTC decision, along with the imposition of financial penalties on Hanwha Solution and Han Express.[51] This case appears to be encouraging for the KFTC, as it prevailed in the Appellate Court, and the Hanwha's appeal to the Supreme Court was also rejected. This case holds significance as it marks the first instance where the KFTC has addressed the issue of "toll" and the deceptive practice of incorporating an unnecessary intermediary to collect transaction taxes, categorizing it as an unfair form of subsidizing behavior.

2.4.5 Samsung Wellstory *(2021): Quantity-Pushing and Unfair Subsidizing*

The KFTC ruled that five affiliate companies of Samsung group had violated §45 (1) 9 of the Act, which pertains to unfair subsidizing, and imposed penalty surcharges totaling KR₩235 billion, making it the highest amount ever recorded for such cases.[52] As per the KFTC decision, Samsung Electronics, Samsung Display, Samsung Electro-Mechanics, and Samsung SDI, which are four subsidizing companies, directed all of their in-house meal services toward Samsung Wellstory. This subsidized company is a wholly owned subsidiary of Samsung C&T,[53] which serves as the practical holding company for the Samsung group. Furthermore, the contractual terms between Samsung Wellstory and the four subsidizing companies were significantly advantageous, ensuring Samsung Wellstory's substantial profitability. Additionally, the KFTC has indicted Samsung Electronics and Mr. Choi, the former chief of Samsung group's secretarial headquarter known as the "Future Strategy Office." Mr. Choi held responsibility for the decision-making process regarding the conduct in question.[54]

In understanding this case, it is crucial to comprehend Wellstory's position within the governance framework of Samsung group. Specifically, we need to understand how the group head, Lee, J.Y., exerts control over the entire conglomerate through intercorporate shareholding. The subsequent illustration depicts the evolution of

[51] Seoul High Court 2021nu31865, July 12 2023.

[52] KFTC Decision 2021–228, Samsung Wellstory Unfair Subsidizing, August 28, 2021. The penalty surcharges include KR₩101 billion for Samsung Electronics (one of subsidizing companies) and KR₩96 billion for Samsung Wellstory (the subsidized company). The revision of the Act in August 2013 made the subsidized party subject to the regulation as well.

[53] Samsung C&T is a construction and engineering company. It was established in 1938 as the pioneering Samsung company and was initially involved in construction and overseas trading operations.

[54] KFTC's News Release, June 24, 2021 ("Samsung group's quantity pushing for Wellstory's providing inhouse meal services, Sanctioned as unfair subsidizing") and KFTC 2021–228, August 28, 2021. The news release prior to the public disclosure of the KFTC decision made public essential details, including pertinent facts and data, that were redacted in the official decision.

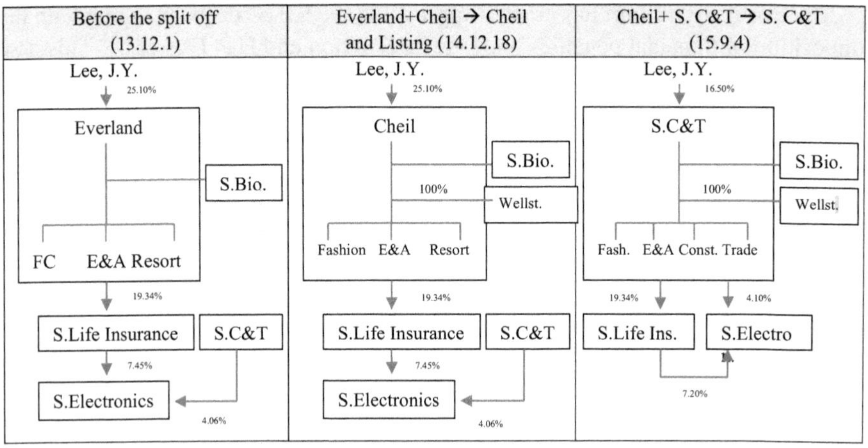

Fig. 2.5 Samsung group and Wellstory. Source: KFTC News Release, "Quantity-pushing of in-house meals into Samsung Wellstory," June 24, 2021

Samsung's governance structure and the role played by Samsung Wellstory throughout the relevant time frame (Fig. 2.5).

Samsung Wellstory was previously a division of Everland called FC (Food Culture). However, on December 1, 2013, it underwent a split and became a wholly owned subsidiary of Everland.[55] Everland then merged with Cheil Industries and the resulting company was named after Cheil Industries, which was listed on December 18, 2014. Subsequently, Cheil Industries merged with Samsung C&T and adopted the name of Samsung C&T on September 4, 2015. The merger between Cheil Industries and Samsung C&T had significant implications for Lee, J.Y.'s control over Samsung Electronics. Previously, Lee had loose and indirect control through Samsung Life Insurance's 7.21% shares, as he did not possess any shares of Samsung C&T. However, following the merger, Lee gained control over Samsung C&T, which played a practical role as the holding company of Samsung group. This allowed him to have a stable share of Samsung Electronics.[56]

[55] The reason for the spin-off was to circumvent the regulations that prevent undue profit-deflecting. The Act was revised on August 13, 2013 (implemented on February 14, 2014), which introduced regulations on excessive profit diversion for the family owning the company and its affiliated entities, where the family holds over 20% shares in an unlisted company (Everland was unlisted at that time). In a comprehensive revision on December 28, 2021, the regulation expanded to include affiliates where the aforementioned affiliate holds over 50% shares and also encompassed profit diversion through quantity-pushing. However, the spin-off in question occurred before this revision. See Table 2.8 for the details on the regulations regarding unfair subsidizing and undue profit-deflecting.

[56] The minority shareholders of Samsung C&T, both domestic and foreign (such as Elliott Management, a foreign private equity fund), raised objections to the merger between Cheil Industries and Samsung C&T. They believed that the merger ratio of 1 (Samsung C&T) to 0.35 (Cheil Industries) was unfair and heavily favored Cheil Industries. Hence, they filed civil damage suits.

Then, why is Samsung Wellstory, a mere in-house meal service company, crucial for the head of Samsung Group? According to the KFTC decision, Samsung Wellstory, a wholly owned subsidiary of Everland → Cheil Industries → Samsung C&T, has been the only cash-cow for the core company under the control of Samsung group. Annually, it generates sales of approximately KR₩1.1 trillion and operating profits of around KR₩100 billion, maintaining a stable performance. These figures are primarily attributed to its internal trade, where it provides meal services exclusively to the captive customers of affiliate companies. This strategic contribution played a pivotal role in justifying the merger between Cheil Industries and Samsung C&T, thereby increasing the value of Cheil Industries. At the time of the merger, Samsung Wellstory accounted for approximately 75% of Cheil Industries' total operating profits. The merged entity required significant funds for share buybacks, addressing appraisal rights, and expanding dividends to address the concerns of minority shareholders from the previous Samsung C&T. To fulfill these requirements, the substantial profits generated by Samsung Wellstory through internal trade were effectively utilized.

The KFTC has accused the Samsung group of engaging in unfair subsidizing practices, citing three main reasons: (1) a significant transaction size,[57] (2) unconventional transaction terms not commonly seen in the relevant business sector, and (3) the absence of competitive bidding. To begin with, the four subsidizing companies exclusively conducted internal trade for their in-house meal services, which accounted for 28.8% of Samsung Wellstory's total sales and constituted 8.5% of the entire in-house meal services market.[58] This internal transaction yielded 72.5% of Samsung Wellstory's operating profits and represented 39.5% of the overall industry of in-house meal services during the relevant period. Furthermore, upon the directive of the group's secretarial headquarters, the four subsidizing affiliates guaranteed profit margins for food material costs, covered consignment fees equivalent to 15% of labor costs, and annually increased the per-meal cost based on CPI and minimum

These disputes have been resolved in Korea. However, Elliott Management took the case to the ISDA court, invoking the Korea–USA FTA. They accused the Korean government of exerting influence on the National Pension Fund, which held the largest 8.9% stake in Samsung C&T, to inadequately approve the merger. After a prolonged five-year dispute, the international arbitration court ruled in June 2023 that the Korean government must pay approximately KR₩130 billion as compensation to Elliott Management. The Korean government intends to appeal this decision, prolonging the legal proceedings.

[57]KFTC filed this case under § 23 (1) 7 (new § 45 (1) 9) of the Act, which pertains to unfair subsidizing. The provision requires the existence of "considerably advantageous condition," and the Enforcement Decree added the transaction with "significant size" in the list for unfair business practices. Through a revision in August 2013, the Act explicitly identified the transaction of a substantial amount without reasonable consideration or comparison (referred to as quantity-pushing or funneling) as one of prohibited conducts under § 23–2 (new §47), specifically addressing undue profit-deflecting. However, Samsung Wellstory, as previously mentioned, was not subject to the regulation of undue profit-deflecting by a split-off decision.

[58]Notice that the court regarded the comparable ratio of 6.8% as "considerable size of transaction in 2007 *Hyundai Glovis* case.

wage. Such contractual terms deviated from standard practices within the relevant industry and were not observed even in Samsung Wellstory's arm's-length dealings. Lastly, the Future Strategy Office obstructed the implementation of competitive bidding for in-house meal services, despite ongoing efforts driven by government pressure in 2014.

Samsung Wellstory has greatly benefited financially from the subsidization of its four affiliates. Through internal transactions of significant size and under considerably advantageous conditions, it was able to achieve an average direct profit ratio of 25.3% over the relevant years.[59] In terms of operating profits, Samsung Wellstory outperformed its competitors by more than three times, with a 15.5% average compared to their 3.1%. The internal meal provision services brought in substantial profits for Samsung Wellstory, enabling the company to adopt an aggressive dividend policy. From 2015 to 2019, it paid the majority of its net incomes, totaling approximately KR₩280 billion, to its parent company, Samsung C&T. With the support of its group affiliates, Samsung Wellstory successfully maintained the largest market share of around 30% from 2013 to 2019. The KFTC argued that Samsung Wellstory, taking advantage of the subsidization, operated aggressively in the external market. It accepted new orders with no operating profits (0%) and renewed orders with negative operating profits (−3%). As a result, independent meal service companies were deprived of opportunities to expand their businesses.

This case evokes a sense of déjà vu of the 2007 *Hyundai Glovis* case. The conducts undertaken bear a striking resemblance to the practices of pushing excessive quantities and engaging unfair subsidization. These actions were primarily aimed at bolstering the profits of an affiliate company within the group, in which the successor of the group head held a significant stake. Consequently, these activities facilitated the smooth transition of group ownership. In the previous *Hyundai Glovis* case, the court endorsed the decision made by the KFTC, ruling that such actions impeded fair trade practices. It remains to be seen how the court will rule in this current case, which is currently awaiting a verdict in the appellate court. Given the nature of legal proceedings, it is expected that it will take a considerable amount of time before a final decision is reached.

Cases

KFTC 1999–212, Samsung SDS Unfair Subsidizing, October 28, 1999
KFTC 2007–504, Hyundai Glovis Unfair Subsidizing, October 24, 2007
KFTC 2017–009, Hanjin KAL Unfair Subsidizing, January 10, 2017
KFTC 2020–314, Hanwha Solution Unfair Subsidizing, December 10, 2020
KFTC 2021–228, Samsung Wellstory Unfair Subsidizing, August 28, 2021
Constitutional Court 2001heonga25, July 24, 2003

[59]The direct profit ratio, which can be calculated by {sales—(food material costs, labor costs, expendables costs)}/sales, is similar to the overall sales profit ratio.

Seoul High Court 2000nu4790, July 3, 2001
Seoul High Court 2007nu30903, August 19, 2007
Seoul High Court 2012nu30730, July 18, 2013
Seoul High Court 2017nu36153, September 1, 2017
Seoul High Court 2021nu31865, July 12, 2023
Supreme Court 2001du6364, September 24, 2004
Supreme Court 2009du15494, October 25, 2012
Supreme Court 2013du17466, February 13, 2014
Supreme Court 2017du63993, May 12, 2022

References

Amihud YA, Lev B (1981) Risk reduction as a managerial motive for conglomerate mergers. Bell J Econ 12(2):605–617

Baek J-S, Kang J-K, Park KS (2004) Corporate governance value: evidence from the Korean financial crisis. J Financ Econ 71(2):265–313

Baek J-S, Kang J-K, Lee I (2006) Business groups and tunneling: evidence from private securities offerings by Korean chaebols. J Financ *61*(5):2415–2449

Berle A, Means G (1932) The modern corporation and private property. Commerce Clearing House

Claessens S, Djankov S, Lang L (2000) The separation of ownership and control in east Asian corporations. J Financ Econ 58:81–112

Choi H, Cho J (2021) Related-party transactions, chaebol affiliations, and the value of cash holding. Sustainability 13(2):699–712

Fama EF, Jensen MC (1983) Separation of ownership and control. J Law Econ 26(2):301–325

Jeon S (1994) A short note on inter-affiliate shareholding matrix. Korean J Ind Organ 3(1) [in Korean]

Jeon S (2002) Policies to limit economic concentration–Focused on regulations in equity investment. In: Current status and polity response in Korean economy 2001–2002. Economic Institute of Sogang University. [in Korean]

Johnson S, Boone P, Breach A, Friedman E (2000a) Corporate governance in the Asian financial crisis. J Financ Econ 58:141–185

Johnson S, La Porta R, de Silanes FL (2000b) Tunneling. Am Econ Rev 90(2):22–27

Kim HB (2022) Theory and practice of fair trade act. Comprehensive Revision, Sam-Il Publishing Co. [in Korean]

La Porta R, de Silanes FL, Shleifer A (1999) Corporate ownership around the world. J Financ 54(2): 471–517

Lee H (2017) The interpretation of 'undue benefits' in 'undue benefit-deflecting to relatives' in KFTA. Chung-Ang University Law J 41(2) [in Korean]

Montgomery C (1994) Corporate diversification. J Econ Perspect 8(3):163–178

Park S, Lee B, Jeon S, Hong M (2006) Studies on improvement of policy to curb economic concentration. Research Project Report to KFTC. [in Korean]

Scheuch A (2016) *Konzernrecht*: an overview of the German regulation of corporate groups and resulting liability issues. European Company Law 13(5):191–198

Statistics Bureau (2024) Survey of mining and manufacturing industries. [in Korean]

Stein J (1989) Efficient capital markets, inefficient firms: a model of myopic corporate behavior. Q J Econ 104:655–669

Yoon K, Jin Y (2021) Related party transactions, agency problem, and exclusive effects. Eur J Law Econ 51:1–30

Chapter 3
SMEs Antitrust Policy in Korea

Antitrust policy for Small and Medium Enterprises (SMEs) is one of the two pillars of Korea's antitrust policy, which aims to "strive for balanced development of the national economy" (MRFTA §1). Both SMEs and Chaebol antitrust policies are the key policy instruments through which the Korea Fair Trade Commission (KFTC) seeks to establish a robust economic system. However, it is crucial to differentiate SMEs 'antitrust' policy from SME 'protection' policy. The latter, enforced by the Ministry of SMEs and Startups (MSS), directly safeguards and supports SMEs. In contrast, the former aims to correct unfair business practices by entities with superior bargaining power, to promote competition, protect SMEs' interests, and ultimately foster a healthy ecosystem.

In this chapter, I will first outline the polarization of enterprises in Korea and present the data that highlight the contrasts between the large firms and SMEs across various aspects. Next, I will explore the unique features of Korean SMEs antitrust policy, which may differ from conventional approaches in other countries. Following this, I will detail the primary elements of unfair business practices which are defined and regulated by the Monopoly Regulation and Fair Trade Act (MRFTA). I will then provide an overview of four specialized laws designed to address unfair business practices specially in the contexts of subcontracting, large retail, franchising, and agency relationships between prominent enterprises and SMEs. Additionally, I will discuss economic issues related to SMEs' antitrust policy, including positive and negative effects of vertical constraints, the economic rationale for regulating abuses of superior trade position, the economic basis for the specialized acts, and the concerns regarding holdup and 'reverse' holdup. Finally, I will examine a selection of noteworthy cases of SMEs' antitrust regulation in Korea, such as the Refusal to Deal by *Hyundai Oil Bank* in 2004, Minimum Resale Maintenance of *TaylorMade/Callaway Golf Korea* in 2009, Exclusive Dealing of *Oil Refinery Companies* in 2009, Vertical Restraints of *Naver/Daum* in 2014, Best Price Guarantee by *Delivery Hero Korea (Yoggiyo)* in 2020, and Self-Preferencing of *Naver (Video Contents)* in 2021.

S. Jeon, *Antitrust Policy in Korea*, https://doi.org/10.1007/978-981-95-0632-3_3

3.1 Polarization of Enterprises in Korea

SMEs play a significant role in the economy of all countries, contributing to a substantial portion of businesses, employment opportunities, and national income.[1] However, there are significant disparities between large corporations and small businesses in various aspects, particularly in the context of Korea. Table 3.1 illustrates the existing polarization of enterprises in Korea.

In the above table, the classification of enterprises is based on their size and assets. Large enterprises are categorized as belonging to Category 1 business groups with total assets exceeding KR₩10 trillion, as of 2019. SMEs (Small and Medium Enterprises) are defined as businesses with average annual sales below a threshold of KR₩40 ~ 150 billion, depending on the nature of the business. Middle Market Enterprises, on the other hand, do not fall under the category of large enterprises or SMEs.[2] According to Table 2.1, the number of large firms, including middle market enterprises, is less than 1% of the total. However, these firms contribute significantly to various aspects of the economy. They account for 34% of the total number of employees, 63% of sales, 75% of operating profits, 79% of assets, and 80% of debts.

The distinct contrast between only a few major corporations and nearly all small and medium-sized businesses in the economy can be affirmed more explicitly through the examination of per firm statistics (Table 3.2).

Table 3.1 Gaps between large, medium, and small enterprises (total)

	Firms (number)	Employees (thousand)	Sales (tril. won)	Oper. Prof. (tril. won)	Assets (tril. won)	Debts (tril. won)
Large Enterprise	2395 (0.3%)	2075 (20.0%)	2366 (47.4%)	126 (57.2%)	8046 (70.7%)	6087 (74.8%)
Middle Market Enterprise	4596 (0.6%)	1440 (13.9%)	761 (15.3%)	39 (17.7%)	926 (8.1%)	434 (5.3%)
Small and Medium Enterprise	745,686 (99.1%)	6859 (66.1%)	1860 (37.3%)	55 (25.0%)	2403 (21.1%)	1618 (19.9%)

Source: Statistics Bureau (2020), "Statistics of Profit Corporations in 2019," Press Release, Jan. 2021

[1] As per the data provided by The World Bank, available at their official website ("Small and Medium Enterprises (SMEs) Finance," https://www.worldbank.org/en/topic/smefinance), it is stated that SMEs play a significant role in the global economy. These SMEs constitute approximately 90% of all businesses and contribute to over 50% of employment opportunities worldwide. Moreover, in emerging economies, formal SMEs contribute around 40% to the Gross Domestic Product (GDP).

[2] In the past, enterprises falling under the category of "Middle Market" were commonly referred to as "Midsized" or "High Potential" Enterprises.

Table 3.2 Gaps between large, medium, and small enterprises (per firm)

	Employees (person)	Sales (bil.won)	Oper. Prof. (bil.won)	Assets (bil.won)	Debts (bil.won)
Large Enterprise	866	987.9	52.6	3359.5	2541.5
Middle Market Enterprise	313	165.6	8.5	201.5	94.4
Small and Medium Enterprise	9	2.5	0.1	3.2	2.2

Table 3.3 Gaps between large, medium, and small enterprises (per employee)

	Sales (mil.won)	Oper. Prof. (mil.won)	Assets (mil.won)	Debts (mil.won)
Large Enterprise	1140	60.7	3877.6	2933.5
Middle Market Enterprise	528	27.1	643.1	301.4
Small and Medium Enterprise	271	8.0	350.3	235.9

SMEs exhibit significantly lower employment rates compared to large enterprises and middle market enterprises. The employment per firm for SMEs stands at a mere 9, accounting for only 1.0% of large enterprises and 2.9% of middle market enterprises. The disparities between larger and smaller firms become more conspicuous when considering their performance. In terms of sales per firm, SMEs lag significantly behind their larger counterparts, representing only 0.3% of the sales of large enterprises and 1.5% of middle market enterprises. The divergence in operating profits per firm is even more pronounced, highlighting the serious discrepancy between SMEs and larger enterprises. Furthermore, the gaps in assets and debts between these two categories are even more substantial.

The polarization among employees can once again be observed through the statistical data in Table 3.3.

The significant variation in operating profits per employee, depending on the size of the company, can result in wage disparities and the division of the labor market. Additionally, the contrast in debts per firm and per employee between large and small companies indicates a concentration of financial resources within larger enterprises.

In order to address the division and fragmentation among businesses and foster a robust business ecosystem, the Korean government extends its support to SMEs through various measures such as direct protection policies, subsidies, loan guarantees, and facilitating entry into the market for small businesses. These policies are implemented by the Ministry of SMEs and Startups (MMS). Conversely, the Korea Fair Trade Commission (KFTC) enforces an antitrust policy for SMEs, aiming to create a level playing field between small and large enterprises. This policy seeks to prevent unfair business practices by larger companies that exploit their dominant bargaining power over small enterprises.

3.2 Specialties of SMEs Antitrust Policy in Korea

The civil law in Korea also addresses unfair trade practices. The Civil Act §104 (Unfair Judicial Act) states that "A juristic act conspicuously lacking in fairness due to strained circumstances, rashness, or the inexperience of the parties involved shall be null and void." However, this articulation on the conditions on unfairness is vague and broad, failing to adequately protect the interests of SMEs and consumers against the exploitative tactics employed by large enterprises. Consequently, the KFTC intervenes in cases of unfair trade practices carried out by large business entities, employing of the administrative measures provided by the MRFTA.

The Act §45 specifically prohibits enterprises from engaging in "unfair trade practices" which include the following actions: (1) "unfairly refusing any transaction," (2) "discriminating against a certain transacting partner," (3) "unfairly excluding competitors," (4) "unfairly coercing customers of competitors to deal with oneself," (5) "unfairly inducing customers of competitors to deal with oneself," (6) "trading with a certain transacting partner by unfairly taking advantage of his/her position in trade," (7) "trading under the terms and conditions which unfairly restrict business activities of a transacting party," (8) "unfairly disrupting business activities of another enterprise," (9) "unfairly subsidizing a person with special interest, or any other companies,"[3] and (10) "an act likely to impair fair trade, other than those listed (above)." Additionally, §46 separately prohibits resale price maintenance in vertical relationship.

This regulation covers a scope of unfair trade practices broader than that which antitrust laws in other countries such as the United States and EU address. The US Sherman Act Sect. 2 (monopolization) and the FTC Act Sect. 5 (unfair methods of competition) along with the Treaty of the Function of the European Union Article 102 primarily focus on the exclusionary behavior of market-dominant firms.[4] However, the Korea MRFTA §45 on prohibiting unfair business practices does not

[3]The prohibition against unfairly subsidizing related parties or affiliate firms applies to all enterprises, irrespective of whether they belong to a large business group. Conversely, §47 addresses the opportunistic behaviors of major chaebols, which involve channeling profits to their family members or affiliated firms. For contrasting details, refer to Table 2.8 in Chap. 2.

[4]Section 5 of the FTC Act also forbids engaging in "unfair or deceptive acts or practices" which "causes, or likely causes, substantial injury to consumers that cannot be reasonably avoided by consumers" or "materially misleads or is likely to mislead consumers." These provisions may encompass certain elements mentioned in §45 of the MRFRA.

require the condition of 'market' dominance for the liability to regulations. On the other hand, the Japan Antimonopoly Act (the Act on Prohibition of Private Monopolization and Maintenance of Fair Trade) §19 also regulates on "unfair methods of trade" which are not confined to market-dominant players, similar to the Korea MRFTA. In this regard, the Korea MRFTA and the Japan Antimonopoly Act bear similarities in their approach.

The German Competition Law (*Gestz gegen Wettbewerbsbeschrankengen*, the Act against Restraints of Competition) includes a similar provision which expands the regulatory scope to cover the abusive conduct of firms that do not hold a market-dominant position. Section 20 targets the behavior of firms with "relative or superior market power" that may not rise to the level of market dominance. It applies to firms on which other businesses as suppliers or purchasers of a certain type of goods or services are "dependent," and particularly in situations where there is a "significant imbalance between the power" of the trading partners. Conversely, Korea MRFTA §45 generally does not assume any such dependence or significant power imbalance. However, §45(1)-6 prohibits transactions with specific trading partner by "unfairly taking advantage of his/her position in trade," which could be interpreted as exploiting "relative or superior market power."

To determine whether an individual act violates §45, it is essential to assess whether the conduct has the potential to harm fair trade. The notion of harming fair trade includes two dimensions: 'restriction of competition' and 'unfairness'. Unfairness can arise from either unfair terms of trade or an unfair method of competition. Therefore, the ten types of unfair trade practices previously enumerated from (1) to (10) are divided into three groups; those associated with (a) restriction of competition; (b) unfair competition method;, and (c) unfair terms of trade. These categories may differ based on the nature of trade practices. Moreover, when determining unfair subsidization, we also consider the criterion of concentration of economic power in addition to restriction of competition. In Section 3.3, I will elaborate on which criterion should be applied to each individual conduct in §45.

It is particularly noteworthy that the unfair trade practices outlined in §45, which defined unfairness based on restrictions to competition as items (1), (2), (3), and (4), overlap with the abuses of market-dominant position described in §5, including 'Refusal to Deal', 'Discrimination', 'Exclusion of Competitors', and 'Binding and Conditional Trade'. These latter abuses pertain specifically to firms with significant market power. However, it is crucial to recognize that the regulations regarding unfair trade practices are not confined to the firms with market power. Thus, many legal scholars consider §5, which addresses the abuses of market dominance, as a special law applicable only to firms with a dominant market position, whereas §45, dealing with unfair trade practices, is viewed as a general law that applies to all firms. This interpretation suggests that the specific law should take precedence in enforcement scenarios where both could apply. Accordingly, the KFTC Guidelines for Assessment of Unfair Trade Practices stipulate that "If the unfair trade practices as described in these guidelines violate the Act §5 (Prohibition on the Abuse of Market Dominance), the Act §5 shall take precedence over these guidelines."

In 2007, the Supreme Court delivered a landmark *en banc* judgment in the case regarding Posco's refusal of trade.[5] The issue at hand was over whether the criterion of unfairness should be evaluated independently, allowing §5 and §45 to be enforced in tandem. The Court clarified that "§3-2 [new §5] (1) 1 of the Fair Trade Act governs abuses of undertaking with market-dominant position, while §23 [new §45] (1) 1 regulates an individual undertaking's refusal of trade, raising concerns of harming competition irrespective of the undertaking's dominance in the relevant market as unfair trade practice. This indicates that the objectives and scopes of a market-dominant undertaking's refusal to trade under Fair Trade Act §3-2 (1) 1 and the refusal of trade as an unfair trade practice under Fair Trade Act §23 (1) 1 are distinct. Therefore, the definition of unfairness in the regulation of a market-dominant undertaking's refusal to trade under Fair Trade Act §3-2 (1) 1 should be assessed and interpreted separately and independently from the definition of unfairness in the refusal to trade as an unfair trade practice under Fair Trade Act §23 (1) 1."[6]

Accordingly, the KFTC has applied §5 and §45 concurrently, whenever applicable, opting to impose the higher surcharge amount for the former. A notable instance of this is the *Microsoft* case in 2006, where the KFTC found Microsoft's budling practice to be in violation of both the provision in §5 (1) 3, which pertains to "unreasonably interfering the business activities of other enterprisers," and the provision in §45 (1) 3, which addresses "unfairly coercing or inducing customers of competitors to deal with one's own business." A surcharge of KR₩33 billion was imposed for the violation under §5. The rational for the KFTC pursuing dual tracks may be attributed to practical considerations. It is more demanding to establishing market dominance and to demonstrate the anticompetitive effects of the alleged abusive behavior, as required in cases under §5. Consequently, the KFTC also charges unfair trade practices, which demand less stringent proof of guilt.

Article 45 (6), which addresses the act of "trading with a certain transacting partner by unfairly taking advantage of his/her position in trade," holds special significance. Unlike §5, which requires 'market dominance', §45 (6) specifies 'trade dominance', as a prerequisite for violation. Furthermore, it lays the general groundwork for regulating specific unfair trade practices under the jurisdiction of the KFTC in four distinct transaction categories between large companies and SMEs: (1) Subcontracting; (2) Large Retail Business; (3) Franchise Business; and (4) Agency. In this context, §45 (6) serves as a foundational clause for these four Special Acts.[7] While §45 (6) generally governs these categories, separate laws have

[5] This case will be discussed in Chap. 4.

[6] This decision was followed by the Supreme Court's later judgment on other types of unfair trade practices such as S-Oil's trade under exclusionary conditions (Supreme Court 2010du25909, April 25 2013) and Hyundai Mobis' exclusion of competitor and trade under exclusionary conditions (Supreme Court 2012du6308, April 10 2014).

[7] Han (2017, p. 315) refers to §45 (6) as the "Grand Father Clause" for four Special Acts.

been enacted to specifically address the considerable volume of trade and unique unfair trade practices in each category between large enterprises and SMEs.

In situations where a contractual relationship is characterized by one-on-one and one-time interactions, private disputes may typically be resolved under the civil law. However, when these interactions expand to one-to-many relationships and extends over prolonged periods, they escalate into matters of public concern. This is particularly true in scenarios such as subcontracting, large-scale retailing, franchise agreements, and agency relations. In these cases, a large enterprise may engage in similar contracts with numerous SMEs, creating ongoing and long-term contractual relationships that significantly impact the public trade system, extending beyond individual private interests.[8] Thus, there is a pressing need for administrative regulations, such as Specific Acts, designed to protect SMEs in these sectors. The KFTC is tasked with the administrative enforcement of these regulations, which are not adequately addressed under general civil law.

In the following section, I will discuss various types of general unfair trade practices as outlined in MRFTA §45. Subsequently, in Section 3.4, I will delve into the specific unfair trade practices governed by the Four Specific Acts.

3.3 Unfair Trade Practices in General

The MRFTA Enforcement Decree establishes a comprehensive framework for identifying and addressing unfair trade practices in accordance with MRFTA §45. Attachment Table 1.2 details the specific categories and standards for such practices. Additionally, the KFTC (2021)'s "Guidelines for Assessment of Unfair Trade Practices" provides a valuable tool for assessing and preventing violations of the Act. These guidelines offer illustrative examples of unfair trade practices, thereby clarifying and defining the various types and criteria associated with such practices, thereby clarifying the various types and criteria associated with such practices. In this section, I will briefly discuss eight specific types of unfair trade practices as outlined by the Enforcement Decree and the Guidelines: (i) refusal to deal, (ii) discrimination, (iii) exclusion of competitor, (iv) unfair luring of competitor's customers, (v) forced trading, (vi) abuses of superior trade position, (vii) binding and conditional trade, (viii) interference with business activities.[9] These practices can be

[8]Refer to Kim (2019, p. 391).

[9]In Chap. 2, I discussed the unfair trade practice of "assisting a person with special interest, or any other companies by conducting any of the following acts" of subsidizing related parties and affiliates within business groups I have omitted the discussion on "an act likely to impair fair trade, other than those listed (above)" as it serves as a preliminary clause for encompassing other unfair trade practices not listed.

classified into three distinct groups based on the criteria for assessing illegality: those restricting competition such as (i), (ii), (iii), (v) a, and (vii); those involving unfair means of competition such as (v) b, c, (iv) and (viii); those featuring unfair terms of trade such as (vi).[10]

In relation to the first category, which concerns restricting competition, a designated "safety zone" exempts certain cases from investigation by the KFTC. In these instances, there is no significant harm to fair trade, as the conduct only poses a minor threat, even if it may technically qualify as an unfair trade practice. Typically, if the combined market share of relevant businesses is below 10% or their total annual sales do not exceed a specific threshold (currently set at KR₩2 billion), the anticompetitive impact on the market is considered minimal. Consequently, the businesses falling within these parameters in such cases will be exempt from further investigation.

Furthermore, in relation to three specific types of unfair trade practices that limit competition—namely (i)-a refusal to deal by a single undertaking, (ii) discrimination, (iii)-a exclusion of competitor by unfair dumping—the assessment primarily focuses on their impact on competition. These practices are deemed illegal when the involved company exerts significant control over a well-defined relevant market, and the practice adversely affects competition more substantially than it promotes efficiency. Specifically, a company is considered to possess significant market control if its market share exceeds 30%, a threshold that is lower than the typical 50% required to establish monopoly power or a dominant market position.

In this section, I will also discuss the vertical restraint known as Resale Price Maintenance (RPM) as well. MRFTA §46 specifically regulates RPM, distinguishing it from regulations on the abuses of market dominance or other unfair trade practices. Other vertical restraints such as exclusive dealing and restrictions of trading territories or parties are addressed under §45 as part of (vii) binding and conditional trade.

3.3.1 Refusal to Deal

There are two types of refusal to deal, either collective or unilateral, the unfairness of which the KFTC investigates.

[10] I will elaborate on (v) a, b, and c in the following.

a. **Collective Refusal to Deal**[11]

It refers to conducts in which an undertaking refuses to engage in a trade or ceases to continue business with *a certain undertaking*, or appreciably restricts the volume or content of goods or services traded. Collective refusal to deal is illegal only if it is implemented jointly with another undertakings in competition *without a justifiable reason.*

If the collective refusal to deal satisfies the requirements of anti-competitive collusion in §40 (1) of the Act, the provisions on unfair collaborative acts shall take priority.

b. **Other Forms of Refusal to Deal**

It refers to conducts in which an undertaking *unfairly* refuses to engage in a trade with a certain undertaking, ceases to continue business with *a certain undertaking* or appreciably restricts the volume or content of goods or services traded.

In this context, the other forms of the refusal to deal are deemed to be a unilateral conduct of a single undertaking, opting not to trade with a particular counterpart. Whether it is a collective or unilateral refusal, it is important to clearly identify the specific business entity that is being refused. Hence, it is not considered illegal to refuse trade with unspecified many entities that do not meet certain criteria based on a reasonable production and sales policy.

Observe the distinction between the criteria for illegality in two types of refusal to deal. Specifically, collective refusal necessitates "without a justifiable reason," whereas unilateral refusal requires "unfairly." According to the Guidelines, in determining whether fair trade is harmed "unfairly," the external characteristics of a conduct are not considered as a primary factor. Rather, the restriction of competition, unfairness, efficiency-enhancing effect, and consumer welfare enhancing effect are considered in parallel. If the negative concerns outweigh the positive factors, the conduct is deemed a violation. The KFTC is responsible for verifying the illegality of a conduct that meets the "unfairly" condition. On the other hand, the conducts committed "without a justifiable reason" (e.g., collective refusal to deal, discrimination in favor of affiliated companies, continuous dumping) are presumed

[11] In the following, the statement in a box is the definition of an individual constituent included in each type according to the Enforcement Decree, and the subsequent explanation is the summary provided by KFTC (2021a, b, c) Guidelines.

to harm fair trade in principle. The party being challenged is tasked with demonstrating the presence of any justifiable reason.[12]

3.3.2 Discrimination

There are four types of discrimination which are subject to the KFTC examination.

a. **Price Discrimination**

> It refers to conducts in which an undertaking sets an appreciably advantageous or disadvantageous price according to the territory or trading party.

The conducts include price discrimination toward *either firms or consumers*. Assessment of illegality is based on the consideration as to *whether the price discrimination restricts competition in a certain relevant market* where the undertaking in question or its counterparty operates. When the anti-competitive effect arises in the market where the undertaking in question operates, it is referred to as a primary line injury to competition. On the other hand, if an undertaking's price competition affects the market where its counterpart operates, it is known as a secondary line injury to competition.

b. **Discrimination of Terms of Trade**

> It refers to conducts in which an undertaking *unfairly* makes an appreciably favorable or unfavorable treatment *for a specific undertaking* through terms and conditions of trade, e.g., quantity and quality of product.

Discrimination of terms of trade refers to the conduct of discriminating through conditions of trade other than price or conditions that directly affect price (e.g., quantity discount), such as discrimination of contents, method of fulfilling contract, terms of payment, etc. It targets a specific undertaking, not including discrimination on consumers. The discriminated undertaking does not need to be specifically identified, and discrimination on all undertakings meeting particular criteria or residing in a particular territory is also deemed discrimination against a specific undertaking.

[12] Supreme Court 2000du833, December 11 2001.

c. **Discrimination in Favor of Affiliates**

It refers to conducts in which an undertaking provides advantageous or disadvantageous terms and conditions of trade, e.g., cost, quantity, and quality, *for the benefit of an affiliate* of the undertaking in question *without a justifiable reason.*

In the assessment of illegality, primary consideration is made as to whether the discrimination leads to *an anti-competitive effect* or results in *a concentration of economic power*. Generally, such discrimination is considered detrimental to fair trade unless the accused party can defend itself with any justifiable reason. However, *if the total market share of the affiliated entity receiving favorable treatment is below 10%*, the anti-competitive effect in the market is considered minimal. In such instances, the undertaking in question shall be in *a safety zone* and be exempt from further investigation.

d. **Collective Discrimination**

It refers to conducts in which undertakings make a collective effort to discriminate *in favor of or against a specific undertaking*, thereby placing the specific undertaking at a considerable advantage or disadvantage.

Unlike illegal concerted practice, collective discrimination can be established independently without agreement. The conducts only include discrimination made against a specific undertaking, and, therefore, do not include discrimination made to a number of unspecified undertakings and consumers. The illegality of collective discrimination is assessed based on the same criteria under the discriminations of price and terms of trade. However, collective discrimination, carried out by multiple undertakings, is more likely to be deemed illegal in comparison to discrimination of price and terms of trade carried out by a single undertaking.

3.3.3 *Exclusion of Competitor*

An undertaking shall not exclude a competitor unfairly by predatory pricing whether in selling or buying.

a. **Unfair Dumping**

It refers to conducts in which an undertaking is *likely to eliminate* a competitor of its own or its affiliate by supplying goods or services *continuously without a justifiable reason*, or *otherwise unfairly*, at a price *appreciably lower than the cost of supply.*

The conducts include unfair dumping on either an undertaking or a consumer. "Likely to exclude the competitor" refers to the possibility of a competitor being eliminated from the market as a result of dumping. It does not necessarily mean that the competitor actually is actually eliminated from the market. Generally, continuous dumping increases the likelihood of excluding a competitor. If the undertaking that engaged in a continuous dumping can provide a valid justification, its reasonableness will be assessed. Regarding temporary dumping, which involves a one-time or short-lived occurrence, the primary consideration is whether the conduct is likely to exclude competitors from the market where the goods or services are traded. The benchmark cost is compared to the dumping price, and this benchmark cost is referred to as "the cost of supply." It is deemed to be the total cost incurred through manufacturing or purchasing.[13]

b. **Predatory Purchasing**

> It refers to conducts in which an undertaking is likely to eliminate a competitor of its own or its affiliate *unfairly* by purchasing goods or services at a price *higher than the usual price.*

The "usual price" refers to the price then employed in the ordinary course of trade between undertakings in the market. The safety zone applies here as well.

3.3.4 *Unfair Luring of Competitor's Customers*

There are three types of unfairly luring of customers of a competitor. Primary consideration in assessing illegality is whether the provision of benefits harms the competitive order by using *unfair means of competition* other than the merit competition based on cost and quality. Since the criteria for assessment of illegality here are not the restriction of competition, there is no safety zone based on market share.

a. **Provision of Unfair Benefits**

> It refers to conducts in which an undertaking provides or offers to provide unfair or excessive benefits in violation of the standard trade practices to lure customers from its competitors.

[13] Hence, this price-cost test based on average total cost may be regarded as being more stringent than the usual one based on average variable cost.

b. **Use of Fraudulent Scheme**

It refers to conducts in which an undertaking lures customers from the competitor by leading them to believe, through ways other than unfair signaling and advertisements according to "act of fairness of signaling and advertisements," that its terms of conditions or goods or services are appreciably better, or that the terms of trade or goods or services of the competitor are appreciably worse, than they actually are, when compared against each other.

c. **Other Unfair Means**

It refers to conducts in which an undertaking lures customers from the competitor by unfairly interfering with trade, inducing the non-observance of an agreement, and hampering conclusion of an agreement between the competitor and its customers.

3.3.5 Forced Trading

An undertaking strengthens its control over the market and limits choices for consumers if it forces its business partners or employees to purchase or sell specific goods or services offered by the undertaking itself or those it designates. Engaging in such conducts is prohibited since it is deemed as using unreasonable means of competition to expand its dominance from one market to another.

a. **Tie-in Sale**

It refers to conducts in which an undertaking unfairly forces the trading counterparty, for which it supplies goods or services, to purchase other goods or services from the undertaking or other designated undertakings against the standard trade practice.

Primary consideration is made as to whether tie-in sale *restricts competition*. To ascertain whether the products or services involved in the tie-in sale can be considered as "different," several factors are taken into account. These factors include whether they are typically traded separately in the market, their commercial use or functional characteristics, consumer recognition, as well as technological trends and product integration in specific cases. A tie-in sale encompasses the sale or lease of goods or services. The actions include making tie-in sales to a business or consumers.

b. **Sales Through Employees**

It refers to conducts in which an undertaking forces staff and executives of its own or of its affiliates to sell or purchase the goods or services from the undertaking or from its affiliates.

Primary consideration is made as to whether the conduct qualifies as use of *unfair means of competition* that harm competitive order. Coercion is not recognized if bonus or incentive is provided for meeting the target as it leaves the staff or executives freedom to choose between foregoing the incentive or achieving the target, or if an undertaking simply urges the staff and executives to meet the target for sales of its goods or services without imposing penalty.

c. **Other Forms of Forced Trading**

It refers to conducts in which an undertaking imposes disadvantage such as *unfair terms of trade* to its counterparty against the standard trade practice, forcing it to trade with the undertaking or other designated undertakings.

Forced trade can take on other forms, even without an established trading relationship between an undertaking and its counterpart. Unlike the abuse of position, which requires a pre-existing relationship, such forced trade can be initiated without any prior connection. This conduct involves compelling an undertaking or consumers to engage in trade against their will.

3.3.6 Abuse of Superior Position in Trade

An undertaking may abuse its superior position and exploit undertakings with an inferior position by imposing penalties, such as forcing them to purchase certain products, or interfering with management decisions. Such conducts are not allowed as they hinder the independent growth of other undertakings and harm fair trade. However, the criteria for unfairness in cases of abuse of the position represents *a version of the unfairness criteria under the Civil Act that is significantly lowered for exceptional cases where an undertaking holds a superior position over the other party*. Therefore, the relative bargaining positions of undertakings should be assessed using stricter criteria than those used to address gaps in negotiation power anticipated by the Civil Act.

The provision on the abuse of the position does not apply to cases in which an undertaking, at the beginning stage of a trade, was able to choose its counterpart on its own and engaged in trade with complete awareness of the agreement's terms, and the participating parties abide by the agreed-upon terms. However, the Act may apply if the undertaking had no choice but to engage in trade with a specific counterparty to start a continuing trade.

In order to establish the superior position of an undertaking, it is crucial to have a *continuing business relationship*. When engaged in a continuous trade, an undertaking usually invests in *specialized capital equipment, human resources, and technologies*. This creates a situation where the undertaking is '*locked in*' in the counterpart, who holds a superior position. For example, an undertaking may be deemed to have a superior position if the counterparty has equipment dedicated to the trade in question. In addition, to determine that an undertaking has a superior position, a party must be dependent on its trade with the other party. Then counterparty may offer *unfair terms of trade*, which the locked-in party is forced to accept in considering the previous investments.[14]

a. **Forced Purchase**

> It refers to conducts in which an undertaking forces its trading counterparty to purchase goods or services against the will of the counterparty.

The forced party is limited to undertakings, and does not include consumers, unless the forced purchase is likely to harm a large number of unspecified consumers, similar violations take place in a continuous and repetitive manner, or the forced purchase is otherwise deemed to be related to the trade order. The goods or services that an undertaking forces to purchase may be either its own or those of another undertaking.

b. **Forced Provision of Benefit**

> It refers to conducts in which an undertaking forces its trading counterparty to provide money, goods, and services or other financial benefits for the welfare of the undertaking in question.

c. **Imposing Sales Target**

> It refers to conducts in which an undertaking sets a sales target on the goods or services it supplies and forces its trading counterparty to meet the target.

[14] Refer to KFTC, "Guidelines for Assessment of Unfair Trade Practices," December 30, 2021.

d. **Imposed Disadvantage**

It refers to conducts in which an undertaking imposes disadvantage to its trading counterparty by setting or changing the terms of trade or in the execution of the trade, through means other than forced purchase, forced provision of benefits, or imposed sales target.

The conducts of imposing disadvantage are either *through setting or changing terms of trade* or *through execution of trade*. The former conduct refers to an undertaking setting or changing the trading condition to the disadvantage of its counterparty, by establishing original conditions or revising existing conditions in a way that places the other party at a disadvantageous position. The terms of trade include all types of restrictive clauses, cost of purchase (at low) or sales (at high), terms of price (including commission fee), method and timing of payment, conditions on returned goods, product inspection method, contract termination conditions, etc. And the latter conduct refers to an undertaking imposing disadvantage by refusing to fulfill the terms of trade or forcing its counterparty to execute certain practices in the trade. Disadvantages can either be imposed in an active or passive way; an undertaking may actively engage in practices that places the counterparty at a disadvantage, or passively refuse to fulfill certain obligations such as covering cost. If the disadvantage takes the form of a financial penalty, the legal responsibilities and the extent of losses must be clearly defined.

e. **Interference with Business Management and Operations**

It refers to conducts in which an undertaking interferes with management and operations of its trading counterparty by imposing restriction on items manufactured, scale of facilities and equipment, quantity of manufacture, and terms of trade, or by giving order or approval for appointment or dismissal of staff and executives.

3.3.7 Binding and Conditional Trade

Conducts are prohibited if they *undermine competition* in the market and compromise consumer welfare. Such conducts include an undertaking restricting other undertakings' freedom to choose business partners (e.g., by forbidding the counterparty from engaging in trade with competitors of its own or its affiliates) and preventing the competitors from entering the market (e.g., by monopolizing the purchase and distribution channels). Similarly, an undertaking is prohibited from placing restrictions on territory or parties of trade for its counterparty that may endow a monopolistic power in the territory or for the parties concerned that ultimately harm competition and consumer welfare.

a. **Exclusive Dealing**

It refers to conducts in which an undertaking engages in trade with another undertaking under the unfair condition that the counterparty refrains from trading with competitors of the undertaking or of its affiliates.

Through exclusive conditions, a manufacturer may prohibit or restrict a retailer from directly trading with or dealing in goods from a competitor. Or a retailer may attempt to oblige a manufacturer to sell or purchase all of its items to or from itself through an exclusive sales or supply agreement. The conducts also include an undertaking preventing its counterparty from ceasing or engaging in trade with its competitor through an exclusive condition.

b. **Restriction of Trading Territory or Trading Party**

It refers to conducts in which an undertaking engages in trade of goods or services with another undertaking under the unfair condition that the trading territory or trading party of the counterparty be restricted.

Restriction of trading territory is referred to as a conduct of restricting the territory in which the counterparty can make sales. Restricted territories can be classified into "responsible territory," where a counterparty is held responsible for sales but may still engage in sales activities outside the area; "open territory," which is a restricted area where multiples parties are allowed to make sales; or "closed territory," which is exclusively allotted to a particular counterparty and prohibits sales outside the designated area. Penalties are applied if the counterparty fails to comply.

Restriction of trading party is when an undertaking limits the customers or business partners of its counterpart. This can occur for instance when a manufacturer or an importer divides the dealers (or sellers) into two groups, designating each group to engage in household or commercial sales only, and does not allow each group to cross territories. Another example is when the undertakings designate specific retailers or wholesalers to certain dealers.

3.3.8 Interference with Business Activities

An undertaking undermines the fair order of competition based on price, quality, and service by interfering with other undertakings' business activities through means such as unfairly using their technologies, pirating labor, or meddling with the formation of business relationships. Such conducts, which make it difficult for the other undertakings to operate business, are considered as using *unfair means to compete in the market*, and are, therefore, prohibited.

a. **Unfair Use of Technology**

It refers to conducts in which an undertaking unfairly uses a specific undertaking's technology to interfere with its business activities, thereby making it difficult for the undertaking to operate business.

b. **Unfair Luring or Recruiting of Manpower**

It refers to conducts of unfairly luring or taking employees from a specific undertaking, thereby making it difficult for the specific undertaking to operate business.

c. **Interference with Business Turnover**

It refers to conducts in which an undertaking unfairly prevents a specific undertaking from changing client or business partner, thereby making it difficult for the specific undertaking to operate business.

d. **Other Interference with Business Activities**

It refers to conducts in which an undertaking unfairly interferes with a specific undertaking's business activities through means other than the unfair use of technology, unfair luring or recruiting of manpower, and interference with business turnover, thereby making it difficult for the undertaking to operate business.

Another specific undertaking is not necessarily limited to a competitor. Also, regardless of the means used, the conducts include all forms of interferences for which the undertaking failed to demonstrate efficiency or other merits.

3.3.9 *Resale Price Maintenance*

MRFTA §46 restricts on RPM as follows: "No enterpriser shall engage in a resale price maintenance: Provided, that this shall not apply where there exist justifiable reasons in terms of the maximum price maintenance preventing the transactions of commodities or services in excess of specified prices." Even if RPM is stipulated separately from unfair business practices in §45, it can be still considered as one of such practices. Other vertical restraints with similar competitive effects such as exclusive dealing and restrictions on trading territory and party are included as unfair business practices. Moreover, the penalty surcharge level is the same for both RPM and unfair business practices (except those related with subsidization of affiliates); i.e., for both violations, the KFTC may impose upon the enterpriser a penalty surcharge not exceeding 4% of the relevant turnover.

Since the consignor may rightfully designate the price at which to sell goods or services to the consignee, consignment sale is not regulated as resale price maintenance even when a specific price is designated. Whether a form of sale is a consignment sale depends on whether the consigner or consignee is the '*de facto* holder of ownership' of the goods and services as well as 'risk taker' of the sales and handling of the goods and services.[15]

a. **Minimum RPM**

> It refers to refers to the act of forcing or setting rules or restrictive conditions on the counterpart enterpriser or enterpriser at the next stage of transaction for compliance with the lowest price when selling (supplying) goods or services.

In principle, the lowest price maintenance is considered illegal as limitations are placed on price competition at distribution stages and infringes upon the autonomy of enterprisers. Nevertheless, there are exceptional circumstances where it is permitted, given there is a valid and justifiable reason, such as enhancing consumer well-being by facilitating competition between brands under certain circumstances of the market. The burden of proof for reasonable justification lies with the enterpriser.

MRFTA §46 reads literally as per se illegality of minimum RPM. However, as stipulated above, the KFTC provides the guidelines for reviewing minimum RPM based on the rule of reason approach. It accommodated a series of the Supreme Court Judgment in 2010 and 2011.[16] Minimum RPM had been illegal per se before those

---

[15] Refer to KFTC, "Guidelines for Assessment of Unfair Trade Practices," December 30, 2021.

[16] Supreme Court 2009du9543, November 25 2010, and Supreme Court 2010du9976, March 10 2011. These decisions based on the rule of reason approach to minimum RPM might be affected by the US Supreme Court decision of *Leegin* in 2007.

cases. Provisional allowance of reasonable justification applied only onto maximum RPM.[17]

b. **Maximum RPM**

It refers the act of a business forcing or setting rules or restrictive conditions for the highest price that must not be exceeded when selling (supplying) goods or services.

Maximum price maintenance is lawful if there is a reasonable justification, such as when competition is triggered and thus improves the welfare of consumers or efficiency and when the benefits of consumers outweigh the negative impact on competition. For example, as part of an exclusive sales contract between a manufacturer and a distributor, the manufacturer sets a maximum price to prevent the distributor from attaining excessive profits. Or a manufacturer sets a maximum price within a certain range to ensure its products are competitive compared to rival offerings. This becomes necessary when the manufacturer has a limited number of distributors, who are prone to collude and increase prices. However, it may be illegal as well. For instance, a manufacturer in a dominant position in the market sets a maximum price to guarantee the profits for distributors and as a result the distributors correspondingly raise prices so that such prices converge around the maximum price.[18]

3.3.10 Summary of Types of Unfair Trade Practice and Criteria of Assessment

Table 3.4 provides a concise overview of various types of unfair trade practice and the criteria of assessing unfairness and illegality as explained above.[19]

Table 3.5 shows the recent record of the KFTC enforcing the regulations on various types of unfair trade practices (Fig. 3.1).

Among the various types of unfair business practices, the most frequently regulated one is 'Abuse of Superior Position in Trade', accounting for 49%, and is followed by 'Unfair Luring of Competitor's Customers' at 15%.

[17] The United States had adopted the per se illegality approach in maximum RPM cases since the Supreme Court Judgment of *Dr. Miles* case in 1911. However, a significant shift occurred, embracing the rule of reason approach, after the *Kahn* decision in 1997.

[18] Refer to KFTC "Guidelines for Review of Resale Price Maintenance, March 12, 2019.

[19] The summary table in the following is based on Kim (2022, pp. 345–346).

Table 3.4 Types of unfair trade practice and criteria of assessment

Types (MRFTA §45, §46)	Sub-types (Enforcement Decree)	Assessment criteria (Enforcement Decree and Guidelines)	(Case Law etc.)
(1) refusal to deal	a. Collective refusal to deal	Without a justifiable reason	**Restriction of competition**
	b. Other forms of refusal to deal	Unfairly	
(2) discrimination	a. Price discrimination	Unfairly	**Restriction of competition**
	b. Discrimination of terms of trade		
	c. Discrimination in favor of affiliates	Without a justifiable reason	**Restriction of competition** + concentration of economic power
	d. Collective discrimination	Unfairly	**Restriction of competition**
(3) exclusion of competitor	a. Unfair dumping	Without a justifiable reason	**Restriction of competition**
	b. Predatory purchasing	Unfairly	
(4) unfair luring of competitor's customers	a. Provision of unfair benefits	Unfairly	Unfair means of competition
	a. Use of fraudulent scheme		
	b. Other unfair means		
(5) forced trading	a. Tie-in sale	Unfairly	**Restriction of competition**
	b. Sales through employees	Unfairly	Unfair means of competition
	a. Other forms of forced trading		
(6) abuse of superior position in trade	a. Forced purchase	–	Unfair terms of trade
	b. Forced provision of benefit		
	c. Imposing sales target		
	d. Imposed disadvantage		
	e. Interference with business management and operation		
(7) binding and conditional trade	a. Exclusive dealing	Unfairly	**Restriction of competition**
	b. Restriction of trading territory or trading party		
(8) interference with business activities	a. Unfair use of technology	Unfairly	Unfair means of competition
	b. Unfair luring or recruiting of manpower		

(continued)

Table 3.4 (continued)

Types (MRFTA §45, §46)	Sub-types (Enforcement Decree)	Assessment criteria (Enforcement Decree and Guidelines)	(Case Law etc.)
	c. Interference with business turnover		
	d. Other interference with business activities		
(9) resale price maintenance	a. Minimum RPM	Without a justifiable reason	**Restriction of competition**
	b. Maximum RPM		

3.4 Unfair Trade Practices in Four Special Acts

The issue of holdup by the parties of superior position in repeated long-term trade relations is a well-known problem, especially in cases like subcontracting, large retailing, franchise, and agency relationships. These situations often involve a large enterprise engaging with multiple smaller entities, resulting in significant bargaining power imbalances during negotiations. To address this, specific acts have been implemented alongside general regulations, such as MRFTA §45, to prevent the abuse of transactional dominance in trade. Unlike spot market transactions, which are less prone to such problems, these long-term trade relationships require additional measures to ensure fairness and protect the interests of all parties involved.

3.4.1 Subcontracting Act

The Subcontracting Act ("Act on Fair Transactions in Subcontracting") was introduced in 1985.[20] Over time, it has been enlarged in coverage and strengthened in terms of punishment steadily. The main objective of this act is "to contribute to the sound development of the national economy by establishing a fair order in subcontract transactions so that the *prime contractor and subcontractor* may complement each other and develop balance on equal terms." (§1 Purpose) Subcontract transactions are such that "a prime contractor entrusts a subcontractor with such tasks as manufacturing, repair, construction, or service" or such that "a prime contractor, who is entrusted with such tasks by another business entity, re-entrusts a subcontractor with what they have been entrusted"[21] (§2 Definitions).

[20]There existed the related guideline since 1982 until the higher-level enforcement of the Act.

[21]One who places an order in a subcontracting transaction is a person who gives a contract to a prime contractor, or a prime contractor in case of re-subcontract.

Table 3.5 KFTC enforcement record of unfair trade practices

(unit: case)

	Refusal to deal	Discrimi-native dealing	Exclusion of competition	Unfair inducing	Unfair transaction coercion	Abuse of business position	Binding and conditional trade	Interference with business activity	Resale price mainte-nance	Total
2018	22	2	6	28	14	104	9	11	10	206
2019	16	4	1	24	3	94	7	11	12	172
2020	18	1	1	19	4	71	6	20	8	148
2021	11	2	0	31	6	63	5	15	8	141
2022	8	4	1	16	3	43	1	6	14	96
2023	9	2	1	12	8	49	3	7	11	102
Total	84 (9.7%)	15 (1.7%)	10 (1.2%)	130 (15.0%)	38 (4.4%)	424 (49.0%)	31 (3.6%)	70 (8.1%)	63 (7.3%)	865 (100%)

[a]KFTC (2023) *Annual Statistics*

Excluded are ‘others’ that cannot be classified as one of the types in Table 3.4 and ‘unfair subsidization’, which is categorized as one type of unfair trade practice in the Act, but is treated as chaebol regulation in this book

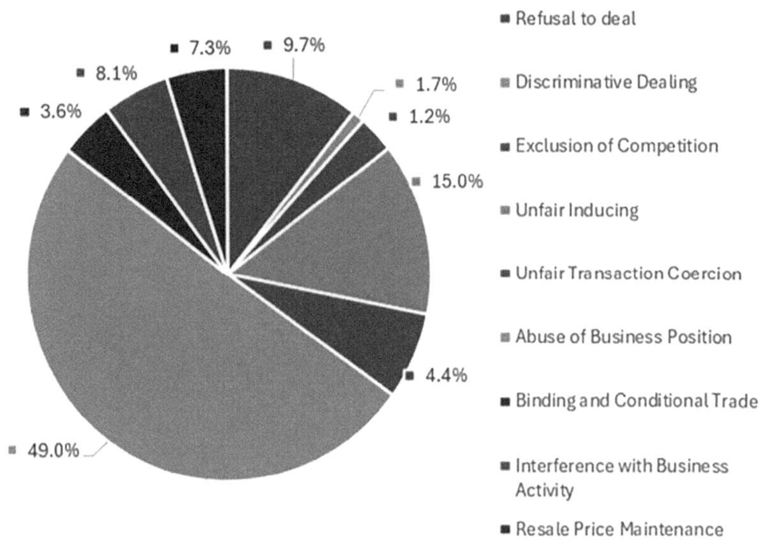

Fig. 3.1 KFTC enforcement shares of unfair trade practices. * Based on the last row of Table 3.11

The Subcontracting Act considers the size of contracting parties as a determining factor for their trade position. It confines prime contractors to ones above a certain size threshold, while subcontractors to ones below a lower size threshold. This size classification serves as a proxy variable in assessing the trade dynamics between the parties involved. There are generally three categories of subcontracting relationships outlined in the Act: between (1) a large-sized prime contractor with an SME subcontractor; (2) an SME prime contractor with a smaller SME contractor; and (3) an affiliate of a large business group with a mid-sized subcontractor. Notice that in case of the second type, subcontracting transactions between an SME and an SME, even a subcontracting relationship between two comparable SMEs with almost equal bargaining position, may be subject to the regulations in the Act.

The Subcontracting Act is very comprehensive in that it specifies 10 requirements and 14 explicit prohibitions that a prime contractor must adhere to. Moreover, it encompasses all aspects of the contracting process, including pre-contracting, during contracting, and post-contracting stages. To provide a concise overview, Table 3.6 presents the obligations or prohibitions imposed on a primary contractor as stipulated in the Act, categorized by the corresponding contracting stage.[22]

[22]The summary table in the following is based on Han et al. (2020, p. 84).

Table 3.6 Requirements and prohibitions onto prime contractor in the act

Contract stage	Interim stage	Payment stage	Whole process
• Issuance and retention of documents • Presumption of entrustment[a] • Prohibition against unfair special agreements • **Prohibition against fixing unreasonable subcontract consideration**	• Prohibition of compelling purchase of goods, etc. • Opening local letters of credit • **Prohibition of unreasonable cancellation of entrustment** • Inspection and notification of inspection results • **Prohibition of unreasonable return of goods** • **Prohibition against reduction of consideration** • Prohibition of unfair requests for economic profits • Guarantees for payment of consideration[b]	• Payment of subcontract consideration[c] • Payment in advance[d] • Prohibition of unfair requests for settlement of purchase price, etc. • Payment of refund of customs duties, etc. • Adjustment of subcontract consideration due to change in design, etc. • Adjustment of subcontract consideration due to fluctuation in supply costs • Prohibition against unreasonable payment in substitutes	• Prohibition of request to provide technical data • **Prohibition of abuse of acquired technical data** • Prohibition of unreasonable intervention of management • **Prohibition on retaliatory measures** • Prohibition of evasion of the act

[a] In case that a prime contractor fails to send the reply to a subcontractor's request on confirmation of the details of subcontract within 15 days, it is presumed that entrustment is made as notified by the subcontractor

[b] In return, a subcontractor should provide a guarantee for performance of a relevant contract

[c] Within 60 days from the date of receipt of subject matter

[d] Where a prime contractor receives an advance payment from the person placing an order, they shall pay an advance payment to the subcontractor within 15 days

In case of violating the requirements or prohibitions as listed above in Table 3.6, KFTC may impose upon the prime contractor a penalty surcharge *not exceeding double the subcontract consideration* as well as corrective measures to stop the violation, to delete or modify special terms and conditions, or to take other measures necessary for preventing a recurrence of the violation or rectifying it. The basic rule of calculating surcharges is to multiply two times of the subcontract consideration by the 'ratio of law violation', and then to determine a certain percentage of the product according to the seriousness of violation. The ratio of law violation is defined as the ratio of the relevant amount of law violation divided by the subtraction consideration. Hence, it is simplified as a certain percentage of two times of the relevant amount of law violation.

The victim of a prime contractor's violation of any provisions in the Act may pursue a civil lawsuit to seek the compensation for any injuries or losses incurred as a result. In Korea, the general principle of civil law pertaining to compensation for torts is based on actual compensatory damages. However, *punitive damages* have been introduced specifically for violations of certain provisions in the subcontracting act. That is, if a prime contractor inflicts an injury or loss upon an individual by violating any of the six provisions bolded in Table 3.6—*Prohibition against Fixing Unreasonable Subcontract Consideration, Prohibition of Unreasonable Cancellation of Entrustment, Prohibition of Unreasonable Return of Goods, Prohibition against Reduction of Consideration, Prohibition of Abuse of Acquired Technical Data,* and *Prohibition on Retaliatory Measures*—they shall be held liable for compensating the injured party. The compensation shall *not exceed three times the amount of the injury or loss* suffered by the affected person.[23] On the other hand, for other violations, the principle of actual compensatory damages will apply.

In addition, the burden of proof in the civil lawsuit for damage recovery in case of violations of the subcontracting act lies with the defendant, who is the prime contractor involved in the case. This means that the prime contractor will not be exempt for the liability of damage compensation unless it can be proven that the injury or loss was not the result of their intentional actions or negligence.

The KFTC has the exclusive right to allege violations of the MRFTA in general. However, in case of violating several provisions in the Act, the Prosecutor General, the Chairperson of the Board of Audit and Inspection, or the Minster of SMEs and Startups may request the KFTC to initiate criminal proceedings. This request is specifically applicable in situations where there are serious concerns regarding the disruption of a fair subcontracting system, potential social repercussions, or harm caused to subcontractors.

The disputes around subcontract relationship are basically civil matters. In most countries, except for Korea and Japan, the conflicts are resolved through legal proceedings in civil courts, without any involvement from government administrative bodies. The rationale behind the stringent implementation of the Subcontract Act in Korea may be based on concerns regarding the concentration of economic power and the uneven growth of large and small enterprises, which have been significant issues. However, it is crucial to exercise caution regarding the potential drawbacks of the current act, such as the meticulous specification and the severe punishment to the extent that the current act may result in the social costs due to the abuse of administrative measures and the possibility of ‘reverse’ holdup by subcontractors.[24]

[23]It is different from the treble damage recovery in the United States in that the liability is not fixed in, but up to, three times the injury or loss.

[24]The remark on the possibility of ‘reverse’ hold-up problem was made by Han et al. (2020, p. 534).

3.4.2 Large Retail Business Act

The Large Retail Business Act ("Fair Transactions in Large Retail Business Act") was introduced in 2012.[25] It is "to contribute to the balanced national economic growth by maintaining fair transactional order in the large retail business and by enabling large retailing business entities, suppliers, or sales floor tenants to thrive on an equal footing, fostering a mutually beneficial relationship among them." (§1 Purpose) The large retail business entities, who source goods used by consumers from multiple business entities and sell them, are defined by the size either in terms of annual retail sales (currently at least KR₩100 billion) or in terms of the total area of sales floors (currently at least 3000 m^2) (§2 Definitions).

They include large department stores, discount marts and TV home shopping mall. The Act may not apply to open market platforms which have neither direct sales to consumer nor physical retail space and not to complex shopping malls and premium outlets focused on leasing to tenants. Nonetheless, given the increasing convergence between various offline and online retail business models, there are apprehensions regarding the potential imbalance in regulating large retailers based solely on their apparent format, which could ultimately distort the competitive landscape within the retail industry.[26]

There are three types of transactions between a large retail business entity and suppliers: (a) direct purchase; (b) purchase under a special contract; and (c) consignment sale. The term "direct purchase" refers to a transaction whereby the large retail business entity acquires goods from a supplier and assumes responsibility for selling any unsold items among the purchased goods. On the other hand, "purchase under a special contract" pertains to a transaction where the retail business entity procures goods on credit from a supplier, with the condition that they can return unsold items among the purchased goods. They then pay a sales amount after deducting a specific margin or a predetermined amount from the profit generated by the sale of said goods. Lastly, "consignment sale" involves the retail business entity selling goods provided by a supplier under its own name and subsequently paying the supplier the proceeds from the sales, while subtracting a predetermined fee or charge. (§2 Definitions)

The Large Retail Business Act is highly comprehensive and detailed. It outlines 4 specific requirements and 11 prohibitions that all large retailers must adhere to. Additionally, it encompasses every stage of the transaction process, ranging from before to during and after. Interestingly, the structure and content of this Act bear a striking resemblance to the Subcontracting Act. Below is a table summarizing the various obligations imposed on large retailers as specified in the Act, categorized by the stage of the transaction.

[25] There existed the related guideline since 1985 until the higher-level implementation of the Act.

[26] Refer to Oh et al. (2017, pp. 22–23).

Table 3.7 Requirements and prohibitions onto large retailer in the act

Contract stage	Interim stage	Payment stage	Whole process
• Delivery and retention of documents[a] • Prohibition of requiring suppliers to prepare for goods before document delivery • Presumption of contracting[b]	• Prohibition of refusal or delay of receipt of goods • **Prohibition of unreasonable return of goods** • Prohibition of unjustly shifting burden of sales promotional expenses[c] • **Prohibition against using employees by suppliers** • Prohibition of unfair requests for economic profits • Compensation for costs of equipment for sales floor • Prohibition against giving unreasonable disadvantages	• **Prohibition of reduction in payments of goods** • Payment of proceeds from sales[d]	• **Prohibition of forcing exclusive dealing** • Prohibition of request for management information[e] • **Prohibition on retaliatory measures**

[a]Enforcement Decree of the Act specifies the matters to be stated in contract documents as follows: (a) Transaction type, transaction item, and transaction period; (b) Method of delivery, place, and date of delivery; (c) Quantity of the goods provided or prepared for sale by suppliers: (d) Means of payment for goods and date of the payment; (e) Terms and conditions for returning goods; (f) Sales floor rent (limited to sales floor tenants), sales revenue, or handling charges to be deducted by large retail business entities from the sales of goods (limited to purchase under a special contract or consignment sales), and the expenses additionally borne by suppliers, other than sales revenue or handling charges; (g) Conditions of the dispatch of employees; (h) Matters of contracts concerning provision of sales incentives; (i) Floors, location and size of the sales floors

[b]In case that a large retailing entity fails to send the reply to a supplier's request on confirmation of the details of contract within 15 days, it is presumed that the contract is made as notified by the supplier

[c]The ratio of sharing sales promotion expenses shall be determined according to the ratio of expected profits among related parties from the event

[d]Within 40 days from the monthly closing date

[e]Concerning the supply terms for the goods which suppliers supply to other business entities, the lease terms for opening a sales floor in other business entities' stores, and the equivalent information listed above

In case of violating the requirements or prohibitions as listed above in Table 3.7, the KFTC may levy on the large retailing entity a penalty surcharge *not exceeding the amount of supplied goods or annual rent*. Additionally, corrective measures may be imposed to prevent recurrence of such violation or rectifying it, including the removal or modification of special terms and conditions.

Despite the general principle of compensating actual damage incurred in Korean civil law, *punitive damages* were introduced for the violation of some provisions in the Large Retail Business Act. That is, if a large retailing entity inflicts an injury or loss upon a person by violating four specific provisions bolded in Table 3.7—*Prohibition of Reduction in Payment of Goods, Prohibition of Unreasonable Return of Goods, Prohibition against Using Employees by Suppliers,* and *Prohibition on Retaliatory Measures*—it shall be liable to compensate the injured party for their loss or harm *to the extent not exceeding three times the injury or loss* inflicted. On the contrary, the principle of actual compensatory damages applies for other violations. Moreover, the burden of proof in the civil lawsuit for damage recovery in case of violations of the Act lies with the defendant, the involved large retailing entity. And in case of violating *Prohibition of Forcing Exclusive Dealing*, the KFTC should accuse the violator and file criminal charges if there are serious concerns of disrupting the transactional order in the large retail business sector.

The Large Retail Business Act is to establish a fair transactional order in the vertical relationship of large retailers and small suppliers or sales floor tenants. It is said that the Act, as a special act for comprehensively regulating unfair practices in the retailing business, has no precedent in the world.[27] Relatedly, there is another act regarding large retailing business known as the Retail Industry Development Act, which was enacted in 1997 under the jurisdiction of Ministry of Trade, Industry and Energy. Initially, this act was to enhance the structure and efficiency of retail business, and consequently benefiting consumers. The government provided increased support to the retail industry and reduced regulations during its introduction. However, since 2010, the focus of this Act has shifted toward regulating large retail business entities such as department stores and discount marts, as well as protecting small traditional businesses like local groceries.[28] When comparing the Large Retail Business Act with the Retail Industry Development Act, the former primarily aims to promote fair transactions within the vertical relationship of retail business, while the latter focuses on facilitating competition in the horizontal aspects of the industry.

---

[27] Refer to Ji (2012, p. 90).

[28] Among the noteworthy regulations are the limits on the entry of large discount marts and SSMs (super supermarkets) within the area of traditional business protection and the prohibition of their operation in very early in the morning (currently 0 to 10 a.m.) and several days in a month (currently two weekend days). Many economists have questioned the effectiveness of such regulations in protecting small traditional businesses in terms of local employment opportunities and sales for small enterprises. For further insights, refer to Choi and Jeong (2016) and Kwon and Chun (2016). Furthermore, the emergence of online shopping businesses and the subsequent decline of brick-and-mortar stores has transformed the retail industry's competitive landscape. The competition has shifted from a traditional 'large vs. small' paradigm to an 'online vs. offline' dynamic. Consequently, the justification for implementing regulations aimed at large offline retailers has become less convincing.

3.4.3 Franchise Business Act

The Franchise Business Act ("Act on Fair Transactions in Franchise Business") was introduced in 2002. Its main objective is "to contribute to the promotion of the welfare of consumers and the sound growth of the national economy by establishing a fair trade order for franchise business and ensuring that franchisers and franchisees can grow together in a mutually beneficial and balanced manner on an equal footing." (§1 Purpose) The term "franchise business" refers to an ongoing business relationship where a franchiser grants its franchisees the right to use its own trademarks, service marks, trade names, signs, or any other business marks in selling goods (including raw materials and auxiliary materials) or services in accordance with certain quality standards or business methods. The franchiser also provides supports, trainings, and control to its franchisees in managing business activities. In turn for the use of business marks and the support and training provided, franchisees are required to pay franchise fees to their franchiser. (§2 Definitions)

The Franchise Business Act is also very comprehensive and has a similar structure with other special acts for fair transactions. It specifies many obligations which a franchiser should comply with. Moreover, it covers all the stages before, during, and after transaction. The table in the following summarizes the requirements and prohibition imposed onto a franchiser in the Act with each stage of the transaction.

A franchiser should avoid opening direct retail store in the immediate geographical area where a franchisee operates, or establishing a franchise store that offers similar products or services as the franchisee. Similarly, the franchisee should refrain from engaging in the same type of business as the franchisor while the franchise agreement is in effect. This follows *the doctrine of ancillary restraints*, which considers agreements that may appear to be highly anticompetitive acceptable if they are subordinate and collateral to a separate legitimate transaction, as an integral part of an arrangement with redeeming competitive virtues.[29]

If the franchisers fail to comply with the requirements or prohibitions as listed above in Table 3.8, the KFTC may levy a penalty surcharge *not exceeding an amount of 2% of relevant sales*. as well as corrective measures to stop the violation, to delete or modify special terms and conditions, or to take other measures necessary for preventing recurrence of such violation or rectifying such violation.

Despite the conventional principle of compensatory damage in Korean civil law, *punitive damages* were introduced for the violation of some provisions in the Act.

[29]This doctrine can be traced back to Judge William Taft's decision in *US v. Addyston Pipe, and Steel Co.*, 85 F.271 (sixth Cir. 1899). According to Judge Taft, "No conventional restraint of trade can be enforced unless the covenant embodying it is merely ancillary to the main purpose of a lawful contract and necessary to protect the covenantee in the full enjoyment of the legitimate fruits of the contract, or to protect him from the dangers of an unjust use of those fruits by the other party." Refer to Werden (2007).

Table 3.8 Requirements and prohibitions onto franchisers in the act

Contract stage	Interim stage	Whole process
• Registration of information disclosure[a] • Deposit of franchise fees[b] • Duty to provide information disclosure statements[c] • **Prohibition on providing false or exaggerated information**	• **Prohibition on unfair trade practices**[d] • Prohibition of unfair pressure to improve store environments • Prohibition of unfair restriction of business hours • Prohibition of violation of sales areas[e] • Notification of execution details of advertising and promotional expenses[f]	• **Prohibition of retaliatory measures** • Renewal of franchise agreement[g] • Limitations on termination of franchise agreement

[a]It contains matters in regard to the following items: (1) the general status of a franchiser; (2) the current status of the franchise business of a franchiser (including matters concerning sales of its franchisees); (3) the relevant fact where a franchiser or its executive officer were involved with criminal charges and civil lawsuits as well as fair trade violations

[b]Each franchiser shall require its franchisees to deposit franchise fees before entering into an agreement, which means any consideration that the franchisee pays to the franchiser in order to obtain a franchise license, as a security for the payment of obligations or damages incurred in connection with the purchase price for commodities, etc. supplied by the franchiser, as the price for fixture, facilities, or commodities supplied or a rent for real estate provided by the franchiser at the time a franchise license is granted in order to start a franchise business, and for the use of business marks licensed under an agreement with the franchiser, support for and training on business activities, etc.

[c]This includes the document stating the current status of neighboring franchisees up to 10

[d]This includes: (1) suspending or refusing the supply of commodities or services or business assistance; (2) Imposing unfair restraints or limitations on the prices of commodities or services; (3) putting a franchisee at an unfair disadvantage by abusing its position in transactions; (4) unreasonably imposing obligations to compensate for damage on a franchisee, imposing an excessive penalty; (5) inducing franchisees of a competing franchiser to conduct transactions with the franchiser

[e]No franchiser shall open a direct retail store or a franchise store of its owned store or its affiliated company of the same type of business as that of a franchisee within the sales area for the franchisee during the period of franchise agreement, unless there is a valid reason for doing so

[f]In case where the franchiser organizes advertising and promotional events, and if the franchisee has to bear some or all of the associated costs, the franchiser shall notify the franchisee about the execution details and allow the franchisee to peruse the details if requested

[g]Upon request by a franchisee to renew their franchise agreement within 180 to 90 days prior to its expiration date, the franchiser is prohibited from rejecting this request without valid reasons for a period of up to 10 years

That is, if a franchiser inflicts an injury or loss to an individual by violating three provisions bolded in Table 3.8—*Prohibition on Providing False or Exaggerated Information, Prohibition on Unfair Trade Practices (Suspending or refusing the supply of commodities or services or business assistance),* and *Prohibition on Retaliatory Measures*—they will be held accountable for compensating the affected person. The compensation amount shall *not exceed three times the injury or loss* inflicted upon the individual. Moreover, the burden of proof in the civil lawsuit of damage recovery in case of violations of the Act lies with the defendant, who is the franchisor involved in the case. And in case of violating *Prohibition on Providing False or Exaggerated Information*, the KFTC should accuse the violator and file a criminal charge.

3.4.4 Agency Act

The Agency Act ("Act on Fair Transactions in Agency") was enacted in 2015, marking it as the most recent addition among four special acts. It is "contribute to the sound growth of the national economy by establishing a fair trading order for agency transactions and by ensuring the mutually complementary and balanced growth of suppliers and agencies on equal grounds." (§1 Purpose) The term "agency transactions" means transactions conducted between a supplier and an agency for the resale or consignment sale of goods or services[30] which are provided on a repetitive basis through a contractual agreement with a fixed duration. (§2 Definitions)

The Agency Act bears a resemblance to other specialized acts, although it is comparatively less complex. The subsequent table provides a comprehensive overview of the obligations and restrictions placed upon a supplier under the Act, categorized by the various stages of the transaction.

The majority of the restrictions in the Act, as in Table 3.9, are basically the same as the prohibitions of Abuse of Superior Position in Trade stipulated in MRFTA §45 such as Forced Purchase, Forced Provision of Benefit, Imposing Sales Target, Imposed Disadvantage, and Interference with Business Management and Operation. The new inclusion such as Refusal or Evasion of Requests for Confirmation of Details of Order Placed is to prevent suppliers from excessively supplying goods to an agency beyond the ordered amount (so-called quantity-pushing), which frequently occurred in agency transactions. Basically, the Act reiterates and clarifies the relevant provisions found MRFTA §45 within the special context of agency transactions. In this regard, there was raised the controversy over the redundancy of this special act, with certain lawmakers suggesting that the adaptions made to the MRFTA may be sufficient.[31]

---

[30]The resale means 'buying' and 'selling' and the resale agencies possess the ownership of purchased commodities and assume all the risk of agency business. The consignment sales in the Commercial Code are such that a consigner possesses the ownership of consigned commodities and determines the sales price. However, the consignment sales in the Act include all other types of sales through agencies as well as the narrow sense of consignment sale. It is notable that services are not resalable by the nature. Hence the 'services' in the Act may be interpreted as the rights to consume services, which are resalable, rather than the services themselves.

[31]The enactment of the Act was incidental. In 2013, an accident of flagrant abuse of an agency by a supplier in the milk industry led to the suicide of an agency employee. This incident sparked a widespread societal concern known as "A's domineering B" phenomenon in contractual relationship between parties A and B. The hasty enactment might be somewhat influenced by this incident.

Table 3.9 Requirements and prohibitions onto suppliers in the act

Contract stage	Interim stage	Whole process
• Duty to prepare agency transaction contract[a]	• **Prohibition on forced purchases** • **Prohibition on forced provision of economic benefits**[b] • Prohibition on compulsion of meeting sales targets • Prohibition on imposing disadvantage • Prohibition on interference with management activities[c] • Prohibition on refusal or evasion of requests for confirmation of details of order placed	• Prohibition of retaliation

[a]The contract should specify: (1) the forms, items, and period of transactions; (2) the methods, places, and dates and time of delivery; (3) the means and timing to pay price of goods; (4) the conditions for return of goods; (5) the transfer of business; (6) the grounds and procedures for termination of the contract; (7) the payment of sales incentives; (8) other matters regarding the rights and obligations of the parties to the agency transaction

[b]The prohibited conducts include compelling an agency to bear: (1) the costs, human resources, etc. for a sales promotional event of the supplier; (2) the labor costs for the supplier's worker; (3) donations or sponsorship

[c]The management interference is such as requiring an agent: (1) to obtain the consent from the supplier in appointing or dismissing executive officers or employees; (2) to provide information about business secrets; (3) to comply with the supplier's instruction regarding operational decisions

If the requirements or prohibitions as listed above in Table 3.9 are violated, the KFTC may impose a penalty surcharge upon the suppliers to the extent *not exceeding the amount associated with the violation of the Act* as well as necessary corrective measures. The penalty surcharge appears to be smaller compared to those prescribed in other special acts as well as unfair trade practices under the MRFTA. The upper limits of penalty surcharges in Subcontracting Act, Large Retail Business Act, Franchise Business Act, and Unfair Trade Practices are double the subcontract consideration, the amount of supplied goods or annual rent, the amount of 2% of relevant sales, and the amount of 2% of relevant sales, respectively.

If a franchiser inflicts an injury or loss upon an individual by violating the provisions bolded in Table 3.9—*Prohibition on Forced Purchase* and *Prohibition on Forced Provision of Economic Benefits*—they shall be liable to compensate the injured party *to the extent not exceeding three times the injury or loss* suffered the person. Moreover, the burden of proof in the civil suit of damage recovery in case of violations of the Act is on the defendant, who is the franchiser involved. And in case of violating the above two prohibitions, the KFTC is obliged to accuse the violator and file criminal charges against them.

The four special Acts on Fair Transactions in Subcontracting, Large Retail Business, Franchise Business, and Agency are rather unique in Korean antitrust policy. Japan's special act on subcontracting, which predated Korea's Subcontracting Act, has narrower coverage and impose weaker punishment in terms of penalty surcharge and criminal indictments.[32] The United States, on the other hand, initially adopted the FTC Franchise Rule in 1978 with a substantial revision taking place in 2007. However, this rule solely focuses on pre-sale disclosure and does not prohibit abusive practices by franchisers, such as unjust termination, no renewal, restrictions on transferring a franchisee's interests, encroachment, etc. Instead, the regulation of such misconducts in industries like automotive, beer, wine, farm equipment, and construction equipment falls under state-level statutes.[33] To the best of my knowledge, there are no other special acts, such as the Acts on Large Retail Business and Agency, in other countries, which have the comprehensive coverage and the stringent enforcement as observed in Korea.[34]

The purpose of these acts is to safeguard SMEs that find themselves in a disadvantaged position in A–B relations. Over all, they would be beneficial in leveling playing fields for A and B and building up a more equitable business eco-world. But we should be careful that too many restrictions may inadvertently lead to the misuse of administrative measures and a phenomenon known as 'reverse holdup' by party B. This could result in the undesirable outcome of shrinking beneficial transactions that the special Acts seek to promote.

3.5 Economic Issues in SMEs Antitrust Policy

The SMEs Antitrust Policy in Korea covers a vast array of activities conducted by companies operating in various market structures. Certain unfair trade practices are deemed illegal by the "unfairness" of competition method. They include 'Unfair Luring of Competitor's Customers', and 'Interference with 'Business Activities' in Table 3.4. In evaluating the illegality of such conducts, a form-based approach may

[32] The subcontract act, translated as "Act against Delay in Payment of Subcontract Proceeds, etc. to Subcontractors," was enacted in Japan as early as in 1956. It requires a prime contractor (so called parental entrepreneur) to deliver a written document to a subcontractor, and specifies the 11 prohibited conducts of a prime contractor to safeguard a subcontractor's interests. Even if Japan's subcontract act was a precedent of the Korean one in terms of formal structure, the coverage in the former seems to be narrower and the specification less concrete than the latter. Especially, the punishment in case of violation is limited to recommendation, and there is no further imposition of penalty surcharges if the prime contractor accepts the JFTC recommendation.

[33] Refer to Pitegoff and Garner (2014, pp. 185–187).

[34] Kim, Y. J and W. Lee (2016) mention that they do not find the special agency act to protect agents as comparable as that in Korea. They mention that Belgium, Australia, and the United States have implemented some special laws to protect dealers. For example, in the majority of the US states, the relationship between a manufacturer and a dealer is subject to Article 2 of the Uniform Commercial Code. This particular article pertains to contracts for the sales of goods. (For further information, refer to "Selling Through Dealers–Antitrust Guidelines for Manufactures" https://www.thompsonhine.com/publications/selling-through-dealers-antitrust-guidelines-for-manufacturers). However, note that a thorough search for all the special acts in other countries have not been conducted.

be employed instead of an effect-based one relying on economic analyses. I will skip economic discussions on those practices. Some unfair trade practices, such as 'Refusal to Deal', 'Discrimination', 'Exclusion of Competitor', and 'Forced Trading' in Table 3.4 overlap with abuses of market dominance. I will address them in the subsequent relevant chapter.

In this subsection, I will focus on two economic issues on SMEs' antitrust policy: (a) Vertical Restraints and (b) Abuses of Superior Trade Position. Vertical restraints such as Exclusive Dealing, Exclusive Territories (these two conducts are grouped in 'Binding and Conditional Trade' in Table 3.4) and Resale Price Maintenance are well-established topics in the field of industrial organization economics. I will discuss the basic economic reasoning behind their negative impact on competition versus their potential to enhance efficiency. The regulations on the Abuse of Superior Trade Position hold a unique position in Korean antitrust policy, and they serve as the foundation for four distinct acts on Subcontracting, Large Retail Business, Franchise, and Agency transactions. I will endeavor to find the economic rationale of these regulations in situations involving one dominant party engaged in long-term relationships with multiple partners. These relationships often require specific investments, making the dominant party more prone to engaging in opportunistic behaviors. Additionally, I will explore the possibility of 'reverse' holdup, where party B exploits its position in the A-B relationship.

3.5.1 *Anticompetitive vs. Efficiency Effects of Vertical Restraints*

Vertical restraints have long been recognized for their detrimental impact on competition, and their nature appears to be quite clear-cut. Illustrated in the diagram below are two instances of such restraints, illustrating the vertical relationship between manufacturers and retailers.

In an exclusive dealing restraint on the left side of Fig. 3.2, manufacturer 1 requires a retailer to deal with them exclusively. This may result in limiting *inter-brand* competition between M1 and M2. On the other hand, in an exclusive territory restraint on the right side of the above figure, the manufacturer divides territories or customer groups, permitting only R1 and R2 to operate within one specific region or with one particular group. This arrangement may raise concerns about restricting *intra-brand* competition between R1 and R2.

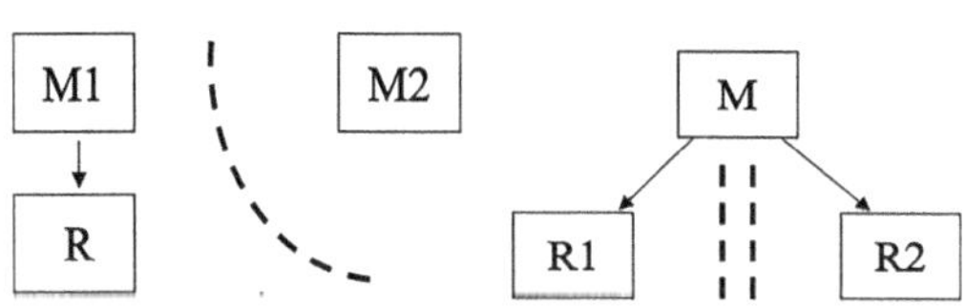

Fig. 3.2 Exclusive dealing vs. exclusive territories

Minimum RPM, which places a lower floor on retail price, evidently leads to an increase in the final price, consequently resulting in a negative impact on consumer welfare. Two alternative reasons for the implementation of minimum RPM can be identified, both of which are rooted in the facilitation of cartels. The first explanation suggests that minimum RPM is introduced to enforce *retailer cartels*. Retailers assign the responsibility of monitoring and enforcing the cartel to manufacturers, compelling them to refuse selling intermediate goods to non-compliant retailers. However, this raises concerns about the retailers' ability to exert sufficient bargaining power to persuade manufacturers to act as enforcers on their behalf.[35] Another explanation for the existence of minimum RPM is that it may be employed to strengthen *manufacturer cartels*. By imposing a lower limit on retail prices, manufacturers are unable to boost sales by reducing wholesale prices, thereby benefiting from cheating on collusion.

Maximum RPM sets up an upper ceiling above which retail prices cannot be raised. Generally, this has the pro-competitive effect of lowering consumer prices. However, there is an exception when the maximum price is set at a monopoly level, and it serves the role of a focal point for retailers to set their prices. Thus, antitrust scrutiny is warranted only when the maximum RPM price exceeds the competitive level.

The economic justifications for vertical restraints are varied and extensive. The initial controversy surrounding the presumption of anticompetitive behavior in exclusive contracts, as critiqued by the Chicago school, has paved the way for the development of economic trends that support the use of vertical restraints for the purpose of enhancing efficiency.

Telser (1960) is often recognized as a pioneer in explaining the efficiency of vertical constraints such as exclusive territories and minimum resale price maintenance (RPM). Let's consider a scenario in which retailer *A* invests money in sales efforts for a manufacturer's new or less frequently purchased products. They provide special pre-sale services like demonstrations and additional staff, and set a higher price to cover these promotional expenses. On the other hand, retailer *B* does not make any such sales efforts and offers a lower price than *A*. In this situation, many customers would choose to visit retailer A's store to gather all the necessary information about the products, but ultimately make their purchase from retailer B at a reduced price. Consequently, the competing retailer's "free riding" behavior weakens the neighboring retailer's motivation to engage in promotional activities. According to Telser, implementing either exclusive territories or minimum RPM at the retail price helps counteract the issue of free riding. These mechanisms ensure that retailers are adequately compensated for their sales expenses and are not discouraged from making promotional efforts.

Marvel (1982) presented an analogous argument for justifying exclusive dealing in terms of enhancing a manufacturer's incentives of advertising and investment in a

[35] Williamson (1987, p. 136) raised a question about "whether dealers are often in a position to impose restrictive term on unwilling manufacturers."

dealer's outlet. Now suppose that a manufacturer supports a retailer by providing training for their staff, improving store environments, or spends on advertising his brand, which attracts more customers. Then the retailer may take advantage of this by persuading customers to purchase other brand products that offer a higher margin. This kind of opportunistic behavior by the retailer will diminish the manufacturer's incentives to investment or advertising further. However, an exclusive dealing contract prevents the retailer from switching customers to other brands, which in turn encourages the manufacturer to continue investing in advertising or other promotional activities.

On the other hand, when the price ceiling is set at a competitive level, maximum RPM can eliminate the inefficiency caused by the well-known problem of double marginalization. This problem arises when market power exists in both the manufacturing and retail stages. In such cases, a manufacturer sets a wholesale price higher than the competitive level, at which their marginal revenue equals marginal cost. Similarly, a retailer charges a retail price higher than the level that maximizes the aggregate profits of a vertically integrated firm involved in both manufacturing and retailing, considering the wholesale price as their marginal cost and applying the principle of marginalization. Vertical integration resolves the issue of double marginalization by internalizing the vertical externalities arising from the retailer's price reduction, which directly affects the wholesaler's profits. This represents a rare economic scenario in which both firms and consumers benefit, leading to a Pareto improvement. If the price ceiling is appropriately set, maximum RPM can achieve the same efficient outcome as vertical integration in terms of lower retail prices.

3.5.2 Economic Rationale of Regulation on Abuses of Superior Trade Position and the Special Acts

The abuse of superior position in trade is most likely to occur in long-term relationship between undertakings, where one party is required to make substantial investments in order to maintain the relationship. In the event of switching to another partner, this party is expected to endure considerable losses due to complications associated with changing equipment and other factors.[36] To safeguard the interests of the investing party, regulations are implemented to address the typical types of unfair practices in Table 3.4, such as 'Forced Purchase', 'Forced Provision of Benefit', 'Imposing Sales Target', 'Imposed Disadvantage', and 'Interference with Business Management and Operation', and all those enlisted in Table 3.6 to Table 3.9 in contexts of the four special Acts. These regulations aim to protect the

[36]Various terms have been used for 'specific investments' such as 'specific assets', 'relation-specific investments', 'transaction-specific investments', 'firm-specific investments', and 'idiosyncratic investments' as well as 'reliance investments' in legal literature.

party that makes specific investment in long-term business relationships and is vulnerable to the opportunistic behavior of another party in superior trade position.

The economic basis for these regulations can be traced back to the long tradition of 'transaction cost economics', and which were pioneered and advanced by Coase (1937), Williamson (1975), and Klein et al. (1979), to name just a few. According to Williamson (1979, p. 239), "the three critical dimensions for characterizing transactions are (i) uncertainty, (ii) the frequency with which transactions occur, and (iii) the degree to which durable transaction-specific investments are incurred." It is assumed that the parties involved in a contract are limited by (iv) bounded rationality and (v) opportunism. Given the transaction characteristics and behavioral assumptions, the contracts that govern long-term relationship are inevitably incomplete. Consequently, once a specific investment is made,[37] there is a genuine possibility of opportunistic behavior aimed at appropriating 'quasi rents'.

Given the conditions of (i) uncertainty and iv) bounded rationality, transaction-cost economics highlights an important antitrust implication. Specifically, it suggests that the combination of (ii) the long-term relationship in frequent transactions and (iii) relation-specific investments is likely to lead (v) the opportunism of holdup. To address this issue, firms may choose to employ either 'internal' governance through vertical integration or 'contractual' governance through vertical restraints. These mechanisms aim to protect specific investments and mitigate the holdup problem.[38] However, the firm cannot expand boundlessly since the transaction costs innate in the allocation mechanism of internal control would ultimately outweigh the costs associated with market-based transactions. Additionally, they may not always result in mutually beneficial terms and provisions for both parties involved in asymmetric trade relationships and contract bargaining.

In such circumstances, alternative governance mechanisms come into play. 'Institutional' governance, such as antitrust regulations, can intervene to substitute for internal or contractual governance. These regulations serve to regulate and oversee trade relationships, ensuring fair practices and preventing anti-competitive behavior. Overall, transaction-cost economics highlights the challenges posed by uncertainty and bounded rationality in business interactions. It emphasizes the need for effective governance mechanisms that balance the protection of investments with the prevention of opportunistic behavior.

The business relationships subject to the special acts on subcontracting, large retain business, franchise business, and agency are characterized by long-term commitments and necessitate various types of specific investments from both parties involved. Notably, there are three types of investments that are specific to these

[37]This notion is also found in KFTC "Guidelines for Assessment of Unfair Trade Practices" in 2021.

[38]Using the terminology of Williamson (1975), the 'internal' governance may correspond to a 'hierarchy', while the 'contractual' governance can be described as a 'hybrid' incorporating elements of both market and hierarchy.

relationships: site specificity, physical asset specificity, and human asset specificity. For instance, a subcontractor may locate a specialized plant in close proximity to a prime contractor in order to economize inventory or transportation costs. Similarly, a sale floor tenant may lease a spot in a large retailer's store. A subcontractor may acquire a specialized equipment to manufacture the subcontracted product, even though its value in alternative uses may be significantly lower.[39] A tenant on a sales floor, a franchisee, or an agent may invest in assets that are specific to the brand and outlet requirements set by the franchiser or supplier, such as outdoor advertisements and store interiors.[40]

In the aforementioned example, the relation-specificity may be symmetrical in that a prime contractor, a large retailer, a franchiser, or a supplier may make own specific investments as such or provide subsidies to encourage the counter-party's specific investments. And both parties involved in the relationship make specific human-capital investments which are developed through a learning-by-doing process. Williamson (1979, p. 240) specially notes that "Human-capital investments that are transaction-specific commonly occur as well. Specialized training and learning-by-doing economies in production operations are illustrations. Except when these investments are transferable to alternative suppliers at low cost, which is rare, the benefit of set-up costs can be realized only so long as the relationship between the buyer and seller of intermediate product is maintained."[41]

In subcontracting, large retail business, franchise business, and agency, all share a common feature: 1-to-N relationship. This means that a large retailer procures goods from multiple sellers, a franchiser allows numerous franchisees to utilize its trademarks and business licenses, and a manufacturer makes agency contracts with several resellers. Within these 1-to-N relationships, there naturally arise a discrepancy in bargaining power between the two trading parties, with one party holding a superior position. In such monopolistic circumstances, the dominant party (A) in the superior position tends to take advantage of their power and appropriate the quasi-rents that result from the relation-specific investments made by the competitive party (B) in the inferior position within the relevant trade. While it is possible to argue the

[39] Klein et al. (1979) noted a most conspicuous example of physical asset specificity in General Motors and Fisher Body relationship. After carmakers began making standardized coaches out of steel, coachmakers invested much in the specific assets such as required dies. Klein et al. argued that one of the reasons why GM eventually integrated with Fisher Body might be to mitigate the holdup problem due to relation-specific dies. However, Miwa and Ramseyer (2000) found less evidence of large-scale relation-specific investments than the theory suggested, particularly of physical-asset specificity in automobile subcontracting relationships in Japan.

[40] According to a report by KFTC (2021a, b, c), a sales floor tenant in an outlet, a department store, and a large mart spent KR₩52 million, KR₩50 million, and KR₩14 million, respectively, in changing interiors, on one-time average.

[41] Williamson also mentions, "Additional transaction-specific savings can accrue at the interface between supplier and buyer as contracts are successively adapted to unfolding events, and as periodic contract-renewal agreements are reached. Familiarity here permits communication economies to be realized: specialized language develops as experience accumulates and nuances are signaled and received in a sensitive way. Both institutional and personal trust relations evolve."

opposite viewpoint and express concerns about party *B*'s opportunistic behavior, this issue is generally less significant than the former. Unless the governance of the market, hybrid or hierarchy, effectively addresses the problem of party *A*'s holdup and adequately protects party *B*'s relation-specific investments, which contribute the value of the business relation, the government regulations are warranted as a form of institutional governance. This provides the rationale behind the regulations founded in special Acts related to this matter.

3.5.3 Possibility of 'Reverse' Holdup

The concept of a 'reverse' holdup is often mentioned in discussions about patent licensing. Typically, when the owner of Standard Essential Patents (SEPs) incorporates their patents into industry standards, they charge royalties that go beyond the Fair, Reasonable, and Non-Discriminatory (FRAND) terms. This allows them to take advantage of the licensee's investments in the technology and their post-incorporation lock-in status. On the other hand, the 'reverse' patent holdup occurs when the licensee threatens to take the patent dispute to court in order to pay royalties that are below the FRAND level. This approach considers the patent holder's upfront R&D costs, which are sunk.[42]

Han et al. (2020, p. 534) discuss the potential occurrence of a phenomenon known as 'reverse' hold-up within subcontracting arrangements. They note that the regulations in the Subcontracting Act in Korea are highly detailed and impose severe penalties, which may inadvertently create opportunities for subcontractors to exploit these rules and engage in opportunistic behavior that harms the overall integrity of subcontracting businesses. The occurrence of reverse holdup is not limited to subcontracting relationships alone. Similar to the Subcontracting Act, other special acts also impose strict restrictions, providing excessive protection to one party, which can potentially lead to the misuse of these regulations for personal gain. However, as will be discussed in the following paragraphs, several distinct features may increase the likelihood of reverse holdup occurring within subcontracting relationships.

To begin with, the primary contractor typically avoids working with numerous subcontractors. For instance, most assemblers prefer to obtain necessary parts from a limited number of suppliers. This approach allows them to establish long-term relationships that are tightly integrated and helps them avoid various setup costs associated with specific relationships. Consequently, the concept of sole sourcing or parallel sourcing in original equipment manufacturers (OEMs) extends to the relationship between the primary contractor and subcontractors. Therefore, it is reasonable to assume that the competition among subcontractors and the 1-to-N

[42] Refer to Lemley and Shapiro (2007) for the patent holdup, and to Kieff and Layne-Farrar (2013) for the reverse holdup.

relationship are less prominent in subcontracting compared to large-scale retailing, franchising, and agency relationships. Given their relatively equal standing in the trade, subcontractors are more inclined to engage in fair negotiations with the primary contractor.

Furthermore, apart from the limited number of subcontractors engaged in business transactions with a main contractor, the categorization of subcontracting relationships outlined in the Act could potentially enhance the relative bargaining power of subcontractors compared to other business relationships governed by specific laws. As previously mentioned, the Act places strict obligations on an SME main contractor, which is only marginally larger than or equal in size to an SME subcontractor. According to the report by KFTC (2021), 83% of the prime contractors surveyed were SMEs.[43] Therefore, it cannot be assumed that a main contractor significantly larger than an SME subcontractor holds a superior position in trading.

Finally, it is crucial to acknowledge that subcontracting practices are widespread across various industries.[44] Consequently, specific investments in these practices vary, and their significance in enhancing the value of the relationship depends on the industry's nature. It is anticipated that in certain industries, the investments made by prime contractors contribute significantly to the overall trade surplus, similar to the investments made by subcontractors. According to Lee et al. (2009, p. 1234), "In some cases, general contractors guarantee their subcontractor partners continuous work and invest in a closer relationship with these subcontractors by providing training and even managerial support. These kinds of investments are valuable only so long as they maintain the partnership relationship. Therefore, the partnership relationship is highly asset-specific." They remarked further that "In construction projects with high degree of uncertainty, there is a greater potential for subcontractors to demonstrate opportunistic behavior, such as lowering the quality of the subcontracted work by reducing resource input in order to maximize their profits."[45]

The Subcontracting Act restricts the prime contractor from 'Unreasonable Cancellation of Entrustment' and 'Reduction of Consideration'. It also introduces punitive damages for violations, which can be up to three times the amount of injury or loss. As a result, subcontractors are more likely to engage in opportunistic behavior, such as reducing their efforts and compromising the quality of subcontracted work. This is particularly true when their underperformance cannot be easily verified by a third party. This implies that 'excessive' protection of subcontractors, who may not necessarily be in a weaker position in the trade, can

[43] In the investigation conducted by KFTC (2021a, b, c) on subcontracting practices, half of the 10,000 samples were chosen from the top segment of sales volume distribution, while the other half was selected randomly.

[44] The sample report from KFTC (2021a, b, c) comprises a group of prime contractors, consisting of 7000 manufacturers, 2500 service providers, and 500 construction business entities.

[45] Richardson and Roumasset (1995, p. 75) also noted it in case of sole sourcing that "if the buyer has made specific investments in the sole supplier and faces switching costs, then the buyer may not have a credible threat to switch." If the switching cost exceeds the cost of low supplier performance, the supplier may behave opportunistically and increase his or her profits without causing the buyer to switch.

lead to a reverse holdup problem. This problem undermines the long-term relationships between prime contractors and subcontractors, as well as the necessary investments made to enhance the value of trade. Having said that, I cannot emphasize enough that I do not intend to undervalue the importance of the Subcontracting Act and other similar legislation in ensuring a fair balance between both parties and fostering a healthy ecosystem for the growth of large and small firms. My intention is simply to draw attention to the potential risks associated with excessive regulations or 'false' positives in the implementation of the Subcontracting Act, as well as in regulating unfair trade practices in general.

3.6 Cases of Regulation on Unfair Trade Practices

In this section, I select several cases of unfair trade practices, and discuss the economic issues involved.

3.6.1 Hyundai Oil Bank *(2004)*[46]*: Refusal to Deal*

In 1999, Hyundai Oil Bank (an oil refinery company) combined with Hanwha Energy (another oil refinery company) and Hanwha Energy Plaza (a gas retailing company) in the wake of the industrial restructuring that took place during the East Asian economic crisis. Hanwha Energy, renamed as Incheon Refinery, faced financial difficulties and underwent a reorganization procedure. In 2001, it became independent from Hyundai Oil Bank. At the same time, Hanwha Energy Plaza, which had been responsible for purchasing petroleum products exclusively from Hanwha Energy and supplying them to its own gas stations as well as other independently owned stations, was merged with Hyundai Oil Bank. However, a problem arose when Hyundai Oil Bank refused to renew the sales agency contract with Incheon Refinery in 2002, a contract that had been in place since the two companies were separated. In response to this refusal, Incheon Refinery filed a complaint with the KFTC, claiming that Hyundai Oil Bank was engaging in unfair business practices. However, the KFTC determined that Hyundai Oil Bank had not violated any laws or regulations regarding unfair trade practices. Incheon Refinery resisted the KFTC's decision in two routes—one by challenging the constitutionality of the KFTC's decision in the Constitutional Court[47] and another by seeking the maintenance of the sales agency contract through litigation in the Civil Court.

[46] Year 2004 is when the Constitutional Court Judgment was made. In this case, the KFTC did not announced its decision since the KFTC made a non-guilt decision.

[47] The non-guilt decision either by the prosecutor or the KFTC may be appealed to in the Constitutional Court as being unconstitutional.

Interestingly, the judgments rendered by these two courts were contrary, as will be explained below.

According to the ruling of the Constitutional Court in 2004,[48] the relevant conduct in question is the unilateral refusal to deal, which is explicitly prohibited by §45 of the Act as a type of unfair trade practice. Several factors were taken into consideration during the evaluation: there was intense competition due to an excess supply of petroleum products at that time; the structure of the retailing service was inflexible due to exclusive agreements between refineries and gas stations; the refinery industry was dominated by three major companies, including Hyundai Oil Bank; Incheon Refinery heavily relied on Hyundai Oil Bank's sales network, with 55% of its domestic sales being made to the latter; the concerned conduct posed significant operational losses for Incheon Refinery as it faced difficulties in finding alternative outlets. Taking all these factors into account, the act of refusing to deal in this case should be deemed as unfair business conduct, as it substantially excludes trading partners from transaction opportunities and hinders the normal course of business, thereby undermining fair trade principles. Conversely, the necessity of such conduct for Hyundai Oil Bank's business did not appear to outweigh the evident negative impact on competition. Despite this, the KFTC upheld its previous decision of non-guilt.

On the other hand, in 2008, the Supreme Court made a ruling quite different from that of the Constitutional Court.[49] In the case of Incheon Refinery, it experienced an increase in operating profits following the termination of the contract. Moreover, it gained court approval for its reorganization plan by asserting that it could achieve sustained profitability through the expansion of its sales retailing network. This implies that the damages incurred from the refusal to renew the contract did not significantly hinder Incheon Refinery's ability to manage its regular business operations. Additionally, Hyundai Oil Bank justified the termination of the contract as a self-defense strategy to overcome a management crisis at that time. The company faced various financial difficulties, resulting in the CEO's resignation. By replacing the export of petroleum products, which accounted for 60% of domestic prices due to oversupply, with supplying its affiliate gas stations, Hyundai Oil Bank aimed to alleviate the management crisis and sustain its business activities. Considering these circumstances, the Court concluded that the decision to not renew the contract may not be deemed as an overall unfair conduct.

[48] Constitutional Court 2002hyeonma496, June 2 2004.

[49] Supreme Court 2004da39238, February 14 2008.

3.6.2 TaylorMade/Callaway Golf Korea *(2009): Minimum Resale Price Maintenance*

TaylorMade/Callaway cases are those in which the Supreme Court confirmed the principle that the minimum RPM should be judged by *the rule of reason.*[50] TaylorMade/Callaway Golf Korea, the exclusive importers of the US-brand golf products, required dealers not to sell their products below specified price levels. They enforced this policy by penalizing any dealers who violated it, thereby withholding further supply to them between 2005 and 2008. The KFTC decided in 2009 that such minimum RPM should be *per se* illegal under the MRFTA,[51] and the Appeal Court upheld this decision.[52]

However, the Supreme Court has determined that the Appeal Court needs to reassess these cases involving minimum RPM by the rule of reason, despite this appearing to contradict the provisions in the MRFTA. The Supreme Court's ruling states that "even if minimum RPM may appear to restrict competition within a particular brand, it can be allowed in exceptional cases if there are valid reasons that would enhance competition between brands in the relevant market and ultimately benefit consumers. These justifiable reasons may include promoting competition among retailers based on factors other than price, offering a wider range of products for consumers to choose from, and facilitating the entry of new retailers into the market. The burden of proof in this regard might be on defendants considering the relevant provisions."[53]

Seoul High Court, which took the case, reversed and remanded by the Supreme Court, reviewing the justifiable reasons forwarded by the appellants, upheld the appeal court judgment that the minimum RPM by TaylorMade/Callaway Golf Korea is illegal.[54] After a series of the legal disputes, the KFTC revised the guideline for reviewing resale maintenance in 2016. They adopted the rule-of-reason principle to evaluate both maximum and minimum RPM. In the United States,the *Leegin* decision of 2007 overturned the *Dr. Miles* decision of 1911, which had deemed

[50]TaylorMade in Supreme Court 2010du9976, March 10 2011, and Callaway Golf in Supreme Court 2010du13753, July 27 2011.

[51]Notwithstanding, the KFTC considered the defendants' arguments for the necessity of the rule of reason criterion and the pro-competitive justification of minimum RPM on the ground of eliminating the free-riding incentives of price-cutting dealers and promoting inter-brand competition. However, the KFTC countered these arguments by stating that the pro-competitive benefits were not convincing since golf product dealers were not operating exclusively. See KFTC 2009–034 and 2009–036, January 1, 2009.

[52]Seoul High Court 2009nu5482, April 21 2010, and Seoul High Court 2009nu12956, June 9 2010.

[53]Supreme Court 2010du9976, March 10 2011, and Supreme Court 2010du13753, July 27 2011.

[54]Seoul High Court 2011nu10777, April 29 2012, and Seoul High Court 2011nu24141, April 29 2012

per se illegality for vertical price restraints, including minimum RPM. The *Leegin* decision established that such restraints should be assessed based on the rule of reason.[55]

3.6.3 Oil Refinery Companies *(2009): Exclusive Dealing and Imposed Disadvantage*

Since 1998, four oil refinery companies, namely, SK Energy (including SK Networks), GS Caltex, Hyundai Oil Bank, and S-Oil, have required all self-owned gas stations to enter purchase agreements in exchange for using their respective oil brand names. To ensure compliance, these companies applied temporary prices when gas stations placed orders for oils and settled the final prices at a later time after the oils were supplied. In 2009, the KFTC determined that these practices violated §23 [new §45] (Prohibition of Unfair Trade Practices) of the Act. Specifically, they were found to have engaged in (5) [new (7)] Binding and Conditional Trade—Exclusive Dealing and (4) [new (6)] Abuse of Superior Position in Trade—Imposed Disadvantage. As a result, the KFTC issued a cease-and-desist order to prohibit these practices, although no penalty surcharges were imposed.[56]

Out of the four companies mentioned, only S-Oil, which had the smallest portion of the market (approximately 13%), appealed to the court against the decision made by the KFTC. S-Oil argued that the agreements were made voluntarily and that its own foreclosure rate was as low as 2.71% when evaluated individually and properly. Therefore, it believed that there was no significant restriction on competition. S-Oil also highlighted the potential positive impact of exclusive dealing in fostering competition between different brands, which could outweigh any negative effects on competition. Moreover, S-Oil emphasized that the price settlement after delivery involved adjusting the predetermined price based on market conditions, ensuring that gas stations were not disadvantaged in any way.

---

[55] *Leegin Creative Leather Products, Inc. v. PSKS, Inc.* (2007). *Dr. Miles Medical Co. v. John D. Park and Sons* (1911). In the *Leegin* ruling, the Supreme Court clearly elucidated the potential benefit of implementing minimum RPM as follows: "Absent vertical price restraints, the retail services that enhance Interbrand competition might be underprovided. This is because discounting retailers can free ride on retailers who furnish services and then capture some for the increased demand those services generate."

[56] KFTC 2009–050, February 3 2009. The KFTC has revisited its policy regarding exclusive agreements between oil refineries and gas stations, as well as the long-standing practice of gas stations only selling one brand of oil. As a result, KFTC has decided not to impose any penalty surcharges in this particular case. Previously, the KFTC discouraged gas stations from offering multiple brands of oil in order to encourage proper advertising and prevent the dilution of oil quality through mixing with other products. However, starting from 2008, KFTC began regulating all purchase agreements to address violations of the unfair trade practice of exclusive dealing.

The decision of the KFTC on the first act of exclusive dealing was approved by the Appellate Court, although they disagreed on the second act of imposed disadvantage.[57] The Supreme Court upheld the judgment made by the appellate court.[58] The Court clarified that the evaluation of the "unfairness" of exclusive dealing, as an unfair trade practice under §23 [new §45] of the Act, should be approached differently than when assessing it as an abuse of market-dominant position under §5. Specifically, the evaluation should primarily focus on whether the conduct is likely to exclude actual and potential competitors. However, it should also consider whether "the conduct of exclusive dealing is likely to hinder or raise concerns about restricting the freedom of the counterpart company in choosing trade partners." In other words, the criteria for determining the unfairness of exclusive dealing encompasses not only the restraint of competition but also the freedom to choose trading partners. This suggests that the weight given to the former is diminished in cases of unfair trade practice compared to the emphasis placed on the anti-competitive effects in the relevant market in cases of market dominance abuse.

When evaluating the impact of exclusive dealing on competition, a noteworthy aspect in this particular case was the question of whether the foreclosure rate should be analyzed in isolation, specifically focusing on S-Oil's individual rate, or if it should be considered in conjunction with the contribution of all four companies involved, as suggested by the EC (2000) guidelines on vertical restraints.[59] S-Oil argued that the cumulative effect criterion was not explicitly stated in the guidelines provided by the KFTC, and therefore only the stand-alone evaluation should be applied. However, the Court expressed its opinion that regardless of the evaluation method used, whether cumulative or stand-alone, a comprehensive assessment of factors such as the structure of the relevant market and the behavior of market participants should be taken into account. Based on such an assessment, S-Oil's exclusive dealing practices were deemed likely to raise concerns regarding the foreclosure of potential competitors and the restriction of competition within the relevant market. Additionally, the Court concluded that the potential benefits in terms of efficiency enhancement were insufficient to outweigh the anti-competitive effects.

The Court, however, did not give its approval to the KFTC's allegation against S-Oil for unfairly imposing disadvantages on gas stations through post-delivery adjustments of oil prices. In recognizing S-Oil's dominant position in trading with

---

[57] Seoul High Court 2009nu6959, October 21 2010.

[58] Supreme Court 2010du25909, April 25 2013.

[59] "2.1. Single branding/ (142) .... foreclosure may however occur for potential entrants when number of major suppliers enter into non-compete contracts with a significant number of buyers on the relevant market (cumulative effect situation)." The US Court took the cumulative foreclosing effect into account in 1953 *Motion Picture* case (FTC v. Motion Picture Advertising Service Co., 344 U.S. 392 1953).

its own gas stations, the Court took into account factors such as the significant difference in size, the reliance of gas stations on S-Oil's brand oil, and the challenges involved in switching to alternative suppliers. Nevertheless, the Court's ruling states that the practice of adjusting prices after delivery, which primarily reflects market competition in a favorable manner, does not actually harm gas stations. The Court concluded that "such conduct of the plaintiff (S-Oil) is not considered as raising the concerns of undermining trade fairness by imposing disadvantages such as forced purchase, forced provision of benefit, imposing sales target, etc., to the extent that it determines or change the terms of transaction by abusing the superior position in trading."

3.6.4 Naver/Daum *(2014): Vertical Restraints*

While KFTC investigated whether various conducts of Internet portals and advertising platforms in the relevant markets could be considered abuses of dominance and unfair trade practices, Naver and Daum applied, and KFTC accepted, a consent decree in 2014.[60][61] Among the concerned five conducts, I will focus on the vertical restraint policy implemented by advertising platforms, which restricts advertising agencies from transferring advertisers within a platform.[62][63] In terms of click numbers in 2013, Naver and Daum held dominant positions in the Korean Internet service market, capturing approximately 50% and 20%, respectively.[64] It is presumed that their market shares in the online advertising market were also quite similar. Naver separates its online advertising management business, known as Naver Business Platform (NBP), from its portal businesses which include Internet search and keyword advertising, while Daum Communication integrates both of these businesses.

[60] KFTC 2014–103 and 2014–104, May 8 2014.

[61] The introduction of the consent decree in Korea took place in 2011. Any business entity that is being investigated or examined can seek the consent decree for all accusations, excluding cases of unfairly concerted conduct and prosecutable violations of MRFTA.

[62] Here are some other questionable practices: (i) Combining specialized search results (e.g., shopping, real estate, movies, books, music, etc.) with general search results on platforms (Naver and Daum) (ii) Promoting certain products through keyword advertising without clearly differentiating them from organic search results (Naver and Daum) (iii) Giving priority to NBP (Naver) in forming advertising partnerships with media platforms for network keyword advertising, (iv) Supporting an affiliate by sending personnel resources (Naver).

[63] In the case at hand, the author, acting as a project manager for Naver, presented an expert witness report containing economic analyses during the KFTC examination phase. Drawing upon Jeon (2020, Chap. 7), this subsection is grounded on the primary arguments put forth in the aforementioned report.

[64] During that period, Google trailed behind the other two competitors as the third player in the market, holding a market share of under 5%.

NBP and Daum Communication utilized keyword advertising systems known as 'Click Choice' and 'Daum Clicks', respectively. These systems implemented a restriction on the number or size of 'incumbent' advertisers that could be transferred to their agents who were responsible for selling and managing their keyword advertising. This limitation was based on the sales volume of the previous quarter. Since 2011, they have prohibited any further transfer of advertisers that exceeded this limit. The term 'incumbent' advertisers refer to those who advertise through agencies or independently using advertising systems. The act of transporting refers to an agent acquiring the agency rights of incumbent advertisers from another agent and assuming control over their management. The restrictions imposed by NBP and Daum Communication on the transportation of incumbent advertisers by advertising agents can be classified as vertical restrictions on downstream undertakings by upstream platform enterprises.

The KFTC suspected that the NBP might be engaged in actions that violate the rules against both market dominance abuses (§5) and unfair trade practices, particularly by unreasonably interfering with the business activities of other enterprises (§45), and that Daum Communication might be in violation of the prohibition on unfair trade practice by unreasonably interfering with the business activities of other enterprises (§45) only. The reason for KFTC's differential treatment of these two firms might be attributed to the difficulty in proving Daum Communication's dominance in the relevant market.

KFTC's argument might be based on the traditional notion that vertical restraints hinder competition within a brand, that is, specifically in the context of ad platforms limiting competition among agents vying for incumbent advertisers within an ad platform. However, the pricing of keyword advertising is determined through advertisers' bidding,[65] and agents' margins are fixed at 15% of advertising revenues. Therefore, the vertical restriction on transporting does not impact downstream prices or directly affect well-being of agents and advertisers. Furthermore, given the circumstances, the arguments against vertical restraints, such as facilitating platform cartels or excluding their competitors, are not convincing.

Alternatively, the vertical restraint can address the issue of one agent free-riding on the efforts of another in recruiting and managing new advertisers. It also tackles the inefficiency caused by an agent poaching an existing advertiser from another on the advertising platform. The process of recruiting a new advertiser is more expensive for an agent compared to transferring an existing one. This is because attracting a new advertiser involves significant setup costs such as selecting keywords, designing advertisements, and building bidding strategies. On the other hand, an agent can

[65] The mechanism of keyword bidding is a variant of second price auction. The price per click of n-th place is determined by the next bidder's rank index, which is the product of bid amount and quality index assigned algorithmically by the ad platform reflecting the quality of advertising contents, divided by his own quality index: i.e., $PPP(n) = RI(n+1)/QI(n) = Bid(n+1)*Q(n+1)/Q(n)$.

leverage previous investments in these efforts and save on expenses when transporting an incumbent advertiser. Assuming both scenarios yield a 15% profit margin on advertising revenues, it is more favorable for an agent to transport an incumbent advertiser rather than recruit a new one. However, if agents engage in a competition to poach each other's incumbent advertisers instead of recruiting new ones, it will negatively impact the ad platform's sales and profits in keyword search advertising. Implementing a limit on an agent's ability to transfer incumbent advertisers can help mitigate the issue of free-riding and the resulting inefficiency caused by vertical externality.

The case may be compared with the related cases in the United States and EC. The US FTC (January 3, 2013) and the EC (April 25, 2013) issued the statements acknowledging that Google had agreed to cease imposing obligations that hinder advertisers from managing search campaigns on competing advertising platforms. The primary concerns raised in the United States and EC revolved around contractual restrictions on the transferability of online search advertising campaigns between Google's Adwords and competing search advertising platforms. These concerns were resolved by Google's commitments to rectify the problematic practice.

However, the practices employed by Naver/Daum and Google differ significantly in terms of their impact on competition. Naver/Daum imposed restrictions on the transferability of advertisers within their advertising platform, while Google imposed restrictions on the mobility of advertisers across its Adwords platform and competing advertising platforms offered by rivals. The anticompetitive effects of Naver/Daum's approach are not as obvious as those of Google's, particularly when it comes to excluding competing ad platforms. The latter may also have some justifiable reasons for implementing such vertical restraints. However, it appears that the usual efficiency justifications put forth by the latter are less convincing than those put forth by the former. In this regard, therefore, I have reservations about the outcome of Naver/Daum's vertical restraints being resolved through a consent decree, which avoided the judgment of their illegality. It might be interesting to see KFTC's decision based on the rule of reason by comparing their anti-competitive with pro-competitive effects.

3.6.5 Delivery Hero Korea—Yoggiyo *(2020): Best Price Guarantee*

Yoggiyo (YGY) is a delivery app brand operated by Delivery Hero Korea (DHK), a local branch of Germany-based Delivery Hero GmbH (DH). A delivery app is a food ordering marketplace that facilitates transactions between final consumers and restaurants offering home delivery services. In Korea, there are three major delivery app services that collectively hold more than 90% of the market share, with YGY being the second largest. YGY introduced a policy known as "Best Price Guarantee

(BPG)" or "Most Favored Nation (MFN)," which involved reimbursing consumers 300% of the price difference between YGY and competitive apps or direct call order (up to a maximum KR₩5000). This policy aims to prevent delivery restaurants from selling their products at a higher price on YGY and terminated their delivery intermediation contracts if they violated this rule. The policy was implemented from June 2013 to February 2017.

KFTC (2020) determined that YGY had violated the Act §45, which prohibits unfair trade practice, by abusing its superior bargaining power and unreasonably interfering with the business activities of other enterprises, particularly their ability to independently set prices. As a result, the KFTC imposed a penalty surcharge of approximately KR₩0.5 billion and issued an injunction order.[66] KFTC's argument was centered on the belief that the "Best Price Guarantee" (BPG) policy implemented by YGY would primarily boost YGY's sales rather than benefiting the delivery restaurants. They contended that it might shift the channel through which consumers placed food order, potentially increasing the costs for restaurants due to YGY's commission fees.

The defendant attempted to justify the policy by suggesting that it could address the issue of free-riding by delivery restaurants. These restaurants benefited from advertising on YGY and could then attract consumers to place direct call orders. However, the KFTC did not give significant consideration to this possibility, as most consumers using delivery apps would unlikely go through the inconvenience of directly calling restaurants, especially for relatively inexpensive food deliveries. Additionally, the standard Most Favored Customer (MFC) clause typically guarantees the lowest price of goods a company sells directly, while the BPG in question aimed to make the price of goods sold by others the lowest.

The case concluded with the KFTC's decision since the defendant did not appeal to the administrative court.[67] The KFTC forwarded the accusation against the defendant to the prosecutorial office at the request of the Ministry of SMEs and Startups, rather than making its own decision to do so. But in the subsequent criminal suit found DHK in September 2022, the first court found DHK not guilty. The reason for this verdict was the absence of clear evidence demonstrating the defendant's recognition or intention to unfairly interfere with the business activities of others. It may appear somewhat unusual that the KFTC did not bring the case under Act §5, which addresses the abuse of market dominance. DHK could be presumed to have a market-dominant position, considering that CR3 (Concentration Ration of the top 3 firms) exceeded 90%, and YGY was the second largest player in the market with a market share not significantly behind the leader. Occasionally, in

[66] KFTC 2020–215, August 24 2020.

[67] The appellate suit should be initiated within 1 month following the KFTC decision. Incidentally, the KFTC was in process of reviewing the merger of Delivery Hero-Woowa Bros., which will be discussed in Chap. 5, during the period.

such cases, the KFTC has applied violation of both market dominance abuse and unfair business practice concurrently. However, in this particular case, it might have been challenging for the KFTC to prove the anticompetitive effects in the relevant market to the extent that the Supreme Court, as established in the 2007 *Posco* case, requires.

3.6.6 Naver—Video Contents *(2021): Self-Preferencing*

Naver was accused of manipulating its algorithm for searching video contents to favor its own video services, such as Naver TV, over its competitors in terms of search result rankings starting from August 2017. There were two specific concerns: firstly, Naver allegedly failed to provide proper information about the key attributes used to evaluate content relevance with search queries for competing video service providers while clearly explaining them to its own division. Second, it was alleged that Naver gave additional ranking points only to certain categories of its own video content, affecting the exposure ranking of search results. In response of these allegations, the KFTC in 2021 concluded that Naver had violated Act §45, which pertains to unfair trade practice. They found Naver guilty of abusing its superior bargaining power and unfairly luring customers away from competitors. As a result, the KFTC imposed a penalty surcharge of KR₩0.2 billion and issued an injunction order.[68] However, Seoul High Court, in 2023, did not accept KFTC's first accusation but acknowledged only the second one.[69]

This case is connected to the *Naver—Shopping* case,[70] which will be discussed in Chap. 4 regarding market dominance. The alleged conduct in both cases involves "Self-Preferencing" through the manipulation of search algorithms to favor Naver's own services over competitors, albeit in different contexts. However, the KFTC primarily addressed the *Naver—Shopping* case under Act §5 (abuse of market dominance) by interfering with competitors' businesses through unfairly discriminatory trade conditions. In contrast, this case was addressed solely under Act §45 (unfair trade practice) for unfairly luring competitors' customers. It is worth noting that Naver held a dominant position in Internet search, with nearly 90% market share in terms of search query volume in 2017. Therefore, there shouldn't be any difficulty in proving market dominance rather than bargaining power dominance. Additionally, the KFTC applied both clauses in Act §45 (unfair trade conduct) in the *Naver—Shopping* case, encompassing both unfair discrimination in trade conditions and unfair luring of competitors' customers for the same type of self-preferencing

[68] KFTC 2021–021, January 25 2021.

[69] Seoul High Court 2021nu35218, February 9 2023.

[70] KFTC 2021–027, January 27 2021.

conduct. However, in this case, the KFTC accused Naver only of unfair trade practice of luring competitors' customers.

This distinction may arise from the court's requirement for the KFTC to provide evidence of the extent of anticompetitive effects. The KFTC may face a higher burden of proof in cases involving market dominance compared to those categorized as unfair trade practice. Furthermore, within the realm of unfair trade practices, the burden of proof may be higher for discrimination cases compared to cases involving unfair luring. The differentiation between market dominance abuse and unfair business practice was established following the significant *Posco* case in 2007. Meanwhile, the variance in the treatment of discrimination and unfair luring may be elucidated by referencing Table 3.4 in this chapter. Discrimination's unfairness has been assessed based on the criterion of 'restriction of competition', while unfair luring is evaluated through the lens of 'unfair means of competition'.

Cases

KFTC 2009–050, *oil refinery companies* refusal to trade, February 3, 2009
KFTC 2014–103 and 2014–104, *Naver/Daum* advertising platforms consent decree, may 8, 2014
KFTC 2020–215, *delivery hero Korea–Yoggiyo*: best Price guarantee, august 24, 2020
KFTC 2021–021, *Naver–video contents* self Preferencing unfair trade practice, January 25, 2021
KFTC 2021–027, *Naver–shopping* self Preferencing market dominance abuse, January 27, 2021
Constitutional Court 2002hyenma496, June 2, 2004
Seoul High Court 2009nu5482, April 21, 2010
Seoul High Court 2009nu12956, June 9, 2010
Seoul High Court 2009nu6959, October 21, 2010
Seoul High Court 2011nu10777, April 29, 2012
Seoul High Court 2011nu24141, April 29, 2012
Seoul High Court 2021nu35218, February 9, 2023
Supreme Court 2000du833, December 11, 2001
Supreme Court 2004da39238, February 14, 2008
Supreme Court 2009du9543, November 25, 2010
Supreme Court 2010du9976, March 10, 2011
Supreme Court 2010du1375, July 14, 2011
Supreme Court 2010du25909, April 25, 2013
Supreme Court 2012du6308, April 10, 2014
Addyston Pipe & Steel Co., 85 F.271 (6th Cir. 1899)
Dr. Miles Medical Co. v. John D. Park & Sons. (Supreme 1911)
FTC v. Motion Picture Advertising Service Co, 344 US 392, 153 (Supreme 1953)
Leegin Creative Leather Products, Inc. v. PSKS, Inc. (Supreme 2007)

References

Coase R (1937) The nature of the firm. Economica 4:386–405
Choi YJ, Jeong J (2016) Effects of the sunday shopping restriction in Korea. Contemp Econ Policy 34(1):203–215

Han C (2017) Fair trade act: the principle of market and law. Korea Competition Federation. [in Korean]

Han C, Yoon & Yang Competition Group (2020) Subcontracting act: a practical guide for Enterprise business. Korea Competition Federation. [in Korean]

Jeon S (2020) Fair trade cases and economic analyses. Park Young Publishing. [in Korean]

Ji CH (2012) The background and significance of large retail business act. Competition Journal. [in Korean]

Kieff KS, Layne-Farrar A (2013) Incentive effects from different approaches to holdup mitigation surrounding patent remedies and standard-setting organizations. J Compet Law Econ 9:1091–1123

Kim HB (2022) Theory and practice of fair trade act. Comprehensive Revision, Sam-Il Publishing Co. [in Korean]

Klein B, Crawford R, Alchian A (1979) Vertical integration, appropriable rents, and the competitive contracting process. J Law Econ 21:297–326

Korea Fair Trade Commission (2021a) Guidelines for assessment of unfair trade practices. December 30, 2021. [in Korean]

Korea Fair Trade Commission (2021b) Report on large retailers' practices. December 9, 2021. [in Korean]

Korea Fair Trade Commission (2021c) Report on subcontracting practices. December 16, 2021. [in Korean]

Kwon E, Chun H (2016) The effect of super supermarket on the entry and exit of retail stores in Korea. Stud Econ 64(3):5–32. [in Korean]

Lee H, Seo J, Park M, Ryu H, Kwon H (2009) Transaction-cost-based selection of appropriate general contractor-subcontractor relationship type. J Const Engin and Manag 135:1232–1240

Lemley M, Shapiro C (2007) Patent holdup and royalty stacking. Texas Law Rev 85:2172–2173

Marvel HP (1982) Exclusive dealing. J Law Econ 25(1):1–26

Miwa Y, Ramseyer JM (2000) Rethinking relation-specific investment: subcontracting in the Japanese automobile industry. Mich L Rev 98:2636–2667

Oh KS, BKL Competition Group (2017) Large retail business act: theory and practice. Publishing Co., Park-Young. [in Korean]

Pitegoff TM, Garner WM (2014) Franchise relationship laws. In: Barkoff RM, Selden AC (eds) Fundamentals of franchising, 2nd edn. American Bar Association

Richardson J, Roumasset J (1995) Sole sourcing, competitive sourcing, parallel sourcing: mechanisms for supplier performance. Manag Decis Econ 16:71–84

Telser LG (1960) Why should manufacturers want fair trade? J Law Econ 3:86–105

Weiden GJ (2007) The ancillary restraints doctrine after *Dagher*. The Sedona Conference Journal 8: 17–27

Williamson O (1975) Market and hierarchies: analysis and antitrust implications. Free Press

Williamson O (1979) Transaction-cost economics: the governance of contractual relations. J Law Econ 22:233–269

Williamson O (1987) Antitrust economics: mergers, contracting, and strategic behavior. Basil Blackwell

Part II
Conventional Competition Policies

Chapter 4
Market Dominance Abuse Regulation in Korea

Regulation against the abuse of market dominance is a key component of conventional antitrust policies worldwide. This enforcement is grounded in the 'rule of reason' principle, which prohibits conduct by a dominant market player if its anticompetitive effects outweigh its efficiency benefits.[1] In Korea, this principle is similarly applied, albeit with some unique developments in its enforcement. While abusive practices might resemble the unfair business practices discussed previously, proving antitrust violations in the context of market dominance requires more stringent evidence.

In this chapter, I will first examine how the KFTC's enforcement actions against abuses of market dominance have evolved. Following that, I will discuss the economic foundations for defining markets and evaluating market power, which serve as the starting points for analyzing abuses of market dominance. Subsequently, I will delve into the general economic issues surrounding competition and the efficiency effects of typical abusive conduct, which are central topics in industrial organization. This discussion will include exclusive dealing, tying and bundling, predatory pricing, price discrimination, refusal to supply, and other foreclosing behaviors. Finally, I will analyze several significant cases of market dominance abuse in Korea, including: *Posco*'s refusal to trade in 2001, *Microsoft*'s tying practices in 2006, *NHN (Naver)*'s advertising restrictions in online video content in 2008, *Intel*'s conditional rebates in 2008, *Qualcomm*'s discriminatory royalties in 2010, *LGU Plus*' margin squeeze in 2015, *Qualcomm*'s licensing and modem chipset supply business model in 2017, *Siemens*' maintenance software fees in 2018, *Naver—Shopping*'s self-preferencing in 2021, and *Google*'s antifragmentation agreement. These cases offer valuable insights into the importance of economic analysis in making reasoned decisions on the abuses of market

[1] Antitrust law does not consider the mere possession of monopoly power illegal if it results from "superior skill, foresight, or industry," as established in *U.S v. Grinnell Corp.*, 384 U. 563 (1966).

S. Jeon, *Antitrust Policy in Korea*, https://doi.org/10.1007/978-981-95-0632-3_4

dominance and provide a basis for evaluating KFTC's decisions in comparison with those of other antitrust agencies such as in the United States, the EU, Japan, and China.

4.1 Main Features of Regulation on Market Dominance Abuses in Korea

4.1.1 Market-Dominant Position

The subject of regulation concerning the abuse of market dominance is defined as a "market-dominating enterprise" by MRFTA §2, which describes it as "any enterprise capable of individually or collectively with other enterprises determining, maintaining, or changing the prices, quantity, quality of goods or services, or other terms and conditions of business as a supplier or customer in a specific business area." MRFTA §4 outlines the criteria for presuming market dominance: a single enterprise holding a market share of 50% or more, or three enterprises collectively holding 75% or more, excluding any with less than a 10% market share and enterprises whose sales or purchases are below KR₩4 billion. According to the Enforcement Decree §4, the relevant enterprise and its affiliated companies are considered a single enterprise. This delineation includes 'single dominance', where a single entity can independently set business terms, unaffected by competitors, customers, or consumers, and 'collective dominance', where two or three entities can jointly influence market conditions. However, market share alone does not determine market dominance. Other factors, such as barriers to entry, the relative size of competitors, the potential for collusion, the presence of substitute goods and adjacent markets, the ability to foreclose the market, and resource power, must also be considered (KFTC [2021] Guidelines).

Section 2 of the US Sherman Act prohibits any person from "monopolizing, or attempting to monopolize, any part of the trade or commerce among the several States, or with foreign nations." The US courts have not established a precise market share threshold for inferring monopoly power. However, Judge Hand, in the landmark 1945 *Alcoa* case, suggested that a market share of 90% "is enough to constitute a monopoly; it is doubtful whether sixty or sixty-four percent would be enough; and certainly, thirty-three percent is not." This guideline was quickly affirmed by the Supreme Court in the 1946 *American Tobacco* Case. Since then, a market share exceeding two-thirds has been considered sufficient to create a rebuttable presumption of monopoly power, whereas a market share of more than 50% is generally required to establish such a presumption. For 'attempted' monopolization, a lesser market share may still indicate a dangerous probability of achieving monopoly power.[2]

In the EU, market dominance is associated with 'significant market power' (SMP). Market power is often measured using the Lerner Index in economics, defined as the ratio of the price-cost margin to price. However, market power does not automatically imply market dominance, as any firm in a market, except in a scenario of perfect competition, possesses some degree of market power by this definition.[3] To hold a dominant market position, an entity must have enough market power to substantially increase prices above competitive levels for a significant period and act independently of competitors, customers, and consumers to a noticeable extent. EC (2005) discussion paper suggests that single dominance is very likely when an enterprise holds 40% or more of the market share, especially if its rivals have significantly smaller shares. Dominance is more probable in the market share range of 40% to 50% than below 40%, though firms with market shares under 40% could still be considered dominant. However, entities with market shares of no more than 25% are unlikely to be deemed dominant in their market. For collective dominance to be recognized, two or more enterprises must act together in a specific market as a collective entity capable of adopting a common market policy. The establishment of such a collective entity necessitates identifying economic links, such as cooperation agreements, ownership interests, and other legal connections. EC (2008) guidance, which focuses solely on single dominance, posits that dominance is unlikely if an enterprise's market share is below 40% in the relevant market.[4]

Broadly speaking, the concept of a market-dominant position in the MRFTA, as defined by a CR1 greater than 50% or CR3 greater than 75%, aligns with the notion of significant market power in the EU. Both frameworks generally require a market share of 40% or more and encompass both collective and single dominance.

---

[2] Attempted monopolization involves three key elements: (a) anticompetitive conduct, (b) a specific intent to monopolize, and (c) a dangerous probability of achieving monopoly power, as outlined in the US DOJ's (2008) report on single-firm conduct. The DOJ retracted this report in 2009 due to controversy over the standards for exclusionary conduct, with the main criticism being that "the report advocated hesitancy in the face of potential abuses by monopoly firms," according to a DOJ press release from 2009. Rosch, the FTC chairman in 2009, remarked that "despite the withdrawal, I think the Report is still relevant," critiquing what he saw as "an overly lenient approach to enforcement." He highlighted issues such as the disproportionality test, which requires that anticompetitive harm outweigh procompetitive effects, and the establishment of a broad safe harbor, as problematic. In this section, I will refer only to parts of the Report that do not pertain to the controversially weakened enforcement of Section 2 of the Sherman Act.

[3] For instance, in a market characterized by product differentiation, a firm's individual demand curve slopes downward due to consumer loyalty to its product, enabling the firm to set its price above marginal cost and exercise some degree of market power. However, this does not necessarily indicate that the firm holds a dominant position in the market.

[4] However, the Guidance Paper (Para. 14) clarified that "there may be specific cases below that threshold where competitors are not in a position to constrain effectively the conduct of a dominant undertaking, for example where they face serious capacity limitations. Such cases may also deserve attention on the part of Commission."

However, the basis for collective dominance within Korean antitrust law remains unclear. It appears to hinge on the concept of a 'shared monopoly' among two or three firms whose combined market share exceeds 75%, excluding any minor firm with less than a 10% share. In a concentrated oligopolistic market, major firms can jointly exercise monopoly power through tacit agreements or conscious parallelism, taking into account oligopolistic interactions. In the EU, for collective dominance to be recognized, the entities must act in concert as a 'collective entity', and some form of 'economic links' must be established. Such a provision is absent from Korean legislation, including Acts, Decrees, and Guidelines. One related aspect is the method of calculating a company's market share, which includes the shares of its affiliated companies. While affiliation within a business group represents an important form of economic link, this requirement does not directly address collective dominance. Furthermore, the approach seems somewhat strained, as it mandates the aggregation of affiliated companies' shares, regardless of whether they operate within the same relevant market.

On the other hand, the concept of monopoly power in US antitrust law is more stringent than that of market dominance in Korea and the EU. It encompasses not only the ability to raise prices above those in a competitive market but also "the power to control prices or exclude competition." To demonstrate monopoly power, a significant degree of market power is required, as stated by US DOJ (2008, p. 21). However, when assessing 'attempted' monopolization, a lesser degree of monopoly power suffices. It is noteworthy that certain types of unfair trade practices in Korean antitrust law, focusing on anticompetitive effects—such as refusal to deal by a single entity, discrimination, and exclusion of competitors through unfair pricing—may be analogous to attempted monopolization under US antitrust law. As highlighted in the previous chapter, an entity with a market share of 30% or higher, which is below the typical 50% threshold for a market-dominant position, falls under the scope of this regulation.

I examine a case that illustrates peculiarities in determining market dominance by the KFTC and the judiciary. The KFTC, in 2007, found that Interpark Gmarket, the second-largest firm with a combined market share of 39.5% (including its affiliate's share of 5.5% and its own 34.0%), held a market-dominant position in the relevant market of open market operations.[5] Auction, the market leader, had a share of 51.9%, while the third-largest competitor held only 3.5%. The KFTC mechanically applied the criterion for presuming market dominance—CR3 greater than 75%—to Interpark Gmarket's case without discussing whether it exhibited single or collective dominance. Both the Seoul High Court and the Supreme Court affirmed the KFTC's decision.[6] However, it remains unclear whether the second player could independently determine, maintain, or alter business terms without considering the market leader. Moreover, the KFTC did not provide evidence of economic links between

[5]KFTC 2007-555, December 18, 2007.

[6]Seoul High Court 2008nu2851, August 20, 2008 and Supreme Court 2008du16322, June 10, 2011.

Interpark Gmarket and Auction. Arguably, it would have been more suitable for the KFTC to approach this case as an instance of unfair trade practices rather than abuse of market dominance.

4.1.2 *Types of Abusive Conducts*

The types of abusive conduct outlined in the Act, Enforcement Decree, and Guidelines[7] are summarized in the table below.

The initial two paragraphs of the Act detail 'exploitative' abuses, as listed under items 1 and 2 in Table 4.1. Conversely, the third, fourth, and the beginning of the fifth paragraphs address 'exclusionary' abuses, identified as items 3, 4, and the first part of 5. The latter portion of the fifth paragraph potentially covers both exploitative and exclusionary abuses. The table below elucidates each category of abusive conduct as defined by the Decree and Guidelines.

It is widely recognized that US antitrust laws focus exclusively on regulating exclusionary abuses, but not exploitative abuses. This approach stems from the belief that high prices and profits earned by a monopolist, who has achieved its position through "superior skill, foresight, or industry," should be considered legitimate. The rationale is that penalizing such success could dampen the dynamic incentives for innovation. Conversely, the EU addresses both exploitative and exclusionary practices within its regulatory framework. Article 102 of the Treaty on the Functioning of the European Union (TFEU), previously known as Article 82 of the Treaty of the European Community, outlines examples of abusive conduct in a non-exhaustive manner. These include "(a) directly or indirectly imposing unfair purchase or selling prices or other unfair trading conditions, (b) limiting production, markets, or technical development to the detriment of consumers, (c) applying dissimilar conditions to equivalent transactions with other trading parties, thereby placing them at a competitive disadvantage, and (d) making the conclusion of contracts contingent on the acceptance by the other parties of supplementary obligations which, either by their nature or according to commercial usage, have no relation to the subject of such contracts." The behaviors described in (a) and (b) bear a resemblance to the first two paragraphs of Article 5 in the MRFTA.

As outlined in Table 4.2, the Enforcement Decree specifies that exploitative abuses are confined to scenarios where "the prices of goods or services are significantly increased or decreased without justifiable reasons, contrary to changes in supply and demand, and the costs necessary to provide these goods or services," and where "the supply of goods or services is substantially reduced without legitimate grounds, considering recent market trends or despite a shortage in distribution channels. "Essentially, the KFTC targets not the excessive 'level' of prices or output but the irregular 'change' in them. This approach is relatively cautious compared to

[7] Korea Presidential Decree in 2021 and KFTC Guidelines in 2021.

Table 4.1 Types of abusive conducts

Act §3-2 (1)	Enforcement Decree	Guidelines	Numbering
1. Charging unreasonable price			1
2. Controlling sale unreasonably			2
3. Interfering with the business activities of other enterprisers	(1) Obstructing the purchase of raw materials		3(1)
	(2) Employing the essential workers of other enterprises		3(2)
	(3) Denying access to the use of essential factors		3(3)
	(4) Other conducts specified in Guidelines	(1) Refusing to deal	3(4)i)
		(2) Offering unreasonable condition	3(4)ii)
		(3) Discriminating price	3(4)iii)
		(4) Forcing disadvantageous deal	3(4)iv)
		(5) Collecting a loan at once	3(4)v)
		(6) Hampering the execution of required procedures	3(4)vi)
		(7) Exercising intellectual property right unfairly	3(4)vii)
4. Impeding the participation of new competitors	(1) Exclusive dealing		4(1)
	(2) Acquiring essential rights		4(2)
	(3) Denying access to the use of essential factors		4(3)
	(4) Other conducts specified in Guidelines	(1) Refusing to deal	4(4)i)
		(2) Hampering the execution of required procedures	4(4)ii)
		(3) Controlling essential raw materials	4(4)iii)
		(4) Using intellectual property right unfairly	4(4)iv)
5. (former part) Excluding competitive enterprisers	(1) Predatory pricing		5a(1)
	(2) Trading with exclusive condition		5a(2)
5. (latter part) Undermining the interests of consumers			5b

Table 4.2 Explanation of abusive conducts

Specific type	Explanation
1. Charging unreasonable price	Prices of goods or services being sharply raised or moderately brought down without justifiable grounds in contrast to changes in their supply and demand, and costs necessary to supply the goods or services
2. Controlling sale unreasonably	The supply of goods or services being sharply reduced without justifiable grounds in the light of recent market trends or despite a short supply in distribution channels
3(1). Obstructing the purchase of raw materials	Sharply increasing the purchase of raw materials beyond the necessary level or forcing or encouraging the raw material supplier not to supply raw materials to other enterprises
3(2). Employing the essential workers of other enterprises	Employing the workers essential for the business activities of other enterprises by offering the workers excessive economic interests in the light of the normal practices
3(3). Denying the access to the use of essential factors	Refusing, discontinuing, or limiting the use of or access to essential factors necessary for the other enterprise to produce, supply, and sell the goods and services without a justifiable reason
3(4)(i). Refusing to deal	Unfairly limiting the amount or content of goods or services traded significantly or refusing to engage in business with a specific enterprise
3(4)(ii). Offering unreasonable condition	Providing trading terms that are unreasonable compared to standard industry practices.
3(4)(iii). Discriminating price	Unfairly discriminating price or the trading conditions compared to those offered to its own or other trading partners
3(4)(iv). Forcing disadvantageous deal	Unfairly forcing deal or action that puts a trading partner at a disadvantage
3(4)(v) Collecting a loan at once	Collecting a loan all at once without a justifiable reason after lending business funds to a trading counterpart
3(4)(vi) Hampering the execution of required procedures	Interfering with other enterprisers' execution of procedures (permits, recommendations, etc., from related agencies or organizations) necessary for their ongoing business activities by unfair means
3(4)(vii) Exercising intellectual property right unfairly	Interfering with the business operations of other enterprises through the unfair use of administrative or legal procedures, such as patent infringement lawsuits, patent invalidation trials related to intellectual property rights
4(1). Exclusive dealing	Entering into an exclusive trading contract with a distribution enterprise without a valid justification
4(2). Acquiring essential rights	Acquiring the necessary rights for the ongoing business operation of another enterprise without a valid justification
4(3). Denying access to the use of essential factors	Denying or limiting access to critical resources needed for the production, supply, and sale of goods or services by a new competitor without a valid justification
4(4)(i). Refusing to deal	Refusing or decreasing the sale or purchase of goods to a business that is either attempting to engage in trade or is

(continued)

Table 4.2 (continued)

Specific type	Explanation
	already trading with a new competitor without a valid justification
4(4)(ii). Hampering the execution of required procedures	Obstructing the ability of other businesses to complete the necessary procedures (such as obtaining permits or recommendations from relevant agencies or organizations) required to enter a market through unfair tactics
4(4)(iii). Controlling essential raw materials	Unfairly manipulating the supply and demand of essential raw materials (including parts and materials) needed for manufacturing goods to create barriers that hinder a competitor's entry into the market
4(4)(iv). Using intellectual property right unfairly	Using administrative or legal procedures, such as filing patent infringement lawsuits or initiating patent invalidation trials related to intellectual property rights, in an unfair manner to obstruct the business activities of other enterprises
5a(1). Predatory pricing	Unfairly excluding a competitor by providing goods or services at a lower price than the normal market price or purchasing goods or services at a higher price than the normal trading price
5a(2). Trading with exclusive condition	Engaging in unfair trading practices with a trading partner under the condition that they do not engage in trade with a competitor
5b. Undermining the interests of consumers	No further explanation

EU case law, which has established that "charging a price which is excessive because it bears no reasonable relation to the economic value of the product constitutes an abuse."[8] Nevertheless, instances of exploitative abuses are quite rare in Korea, as they are in the EU, with virtually no recent cases. This tendency underscores a global consensus that sector-specific regulatory authorities, operating ex ante, are better suited for addressing issues related to price or quantity controls than competition agencies working ex post.

Antitrust authorities in most developed countries prioritize addressing exclusionary practices when regulating the abuse of market dominance. As illustrated in Table 4.1, the Act outlines ten types of exclusionary practices against 'actual' competitors, as specified in the third paragraph of §5, along with relevant sections in the Enforcement Decree and Guidelines. Additionally, seven types of exclusionary practices against 'potential' competitors are delineated in the fourth paragraph and related sections, while two types of practices affecting both actual and potential competitors are described in the initial part of the fifth paragraph and its corresponding clauses. Altogether, these provisions enumerate a total of 19 types

[8]Refer to EU Court of the First Instance (1978). The court considers factors such as the product's production costs, prices of comparable products in the same and other markets, and the profit margins earned by the company when determining whether prices are excessive.

of exclusionary practices. In contrast, Article 102 of the Treaty on the Functioning of the European Union (TFEU) cites only two instances of exclusionary conduct, specifically, discrimination and contractual obligations as mentioned in points (c) and (d) above. The US Sherman Act does not detail specific behaviors that constitute illegal monopolization. Moreover, US case law characterizes such conduct in a highly abstract manner, describing it as "the willful acquisition or maintenance of that [monopoly] power, distinguished from growth or development resulting from a superior product, business acumen, or historical accident."[9]

Reflecting on the standard categorizations of market dominance abuses developed by antitrust experts and enforcement agencies, the 17 types of abusive conduct detailed in the Act, as well as in related provisions of the Enforcement Decree and the Guidelines as presented in Table 4.1, appear overly detailed and somewhat redundant. Typically, dominant market abuses can be grouped into broader categories such as exclusive dealing, tying and bundling, predatory pricing, discrimination, refusal to supply, and other foreclosing behaviors.[10] The table below reorganizes the content of Table 4.1 according to these common classifications.

The Act §5 distinguishes between exclusionary conducts aimed at incumbent enterprises and those targeting new entrants. However, many of these conducts share similar characteristics, as they may affect both incumbents and entrants in their practices. Therefore, provisions 3(3) and 4(3), 3(4)(i) and 4(4)(i), 3(4)(vi) and 4(4)(ii), 3(4)(vi) and 4(4)(ii), and 3(4)(vii) and 4(4)(iv) are grouped together in Table 4.3.

In my classification of various types of abuse under Korean antitrust policy, I categorize a significant number under the umbrella of 'exclusive dealing'. This category includes the specific practice referred to as exclusive dealing in clause 4(1). Broadly defined, exclusive dealing encompasses all contracts and practices that obligate upstream input suppliers to provide all or a substantial portion of the essential factors for producing related goods or services, or require downstream buyers to purchase all or a significant part of the products offered by a dominant firm, with the aim of excluding competitors. The more narrowly defined exclusive dealing mentioned in clause 4(1) refers specifically to entering into an exclusive trading agreement with downstream distributors. The other practices identified in Table 4.3 as exclusive dealing are understood in the broader sense of the term as described above. For instance, 'offering unreasonable conditions' in clause 3(4)(ii) can be interpreted as utilizing methods other than contractual agreements to effectively enforce exclusive dealing. The terms 'tying and bundling', 'predation', 'discrimination', and 'refusal to supply' are used in their traditional senses. The three practices

[9] *U.S v. Grinnell Corp.*, 384 U. 563 (1966).

[10] In its Guidance, EC (2008) identified common types of abuses, including exclusive dealing, tying and bundling, predation, refusal to supply, and margin squeeze. US DOJ (2008) report on single-firm conduct covers various topics, including price predation, tying, bundled discounts, single-product loyalty discounts, unilateral and unconditional refusals to deal with rivals, and exclusive dealing. It's worth noting that bundled discounts are related to bundling, and single-product loyalty discounts are frequently employed as a form of exclusive contract.

Table 4.3 Re-classification of abusive conducts

Typical classification	Type of abuses in Korea antitrust policy
Exclusive dealing	3(1) obstructing the purchase of raw materials
	3(2) employing the essential workers of other enterprises
	3(4)(ii) offering unreasonable condition
	4(1) exclusive dealing
	4(2) acquiring essential rights
	4(4)(iii) controlling essential raw materials
	5f(2) trading with exclusive condition
Tying and bundling	3(4)(iv) forcing disadvantageous deal
Predation	5f(1) predatory pricing
Discrimination	3(4)(iii) discriminating price
Refusal to supply	3(3) & 4(3) denying the access to the use of essential factors
	3(4)(i) & 4(4)(i) refusing to deal
Other foreclosing conducts	3(4)(v) collecting a loan at once
	3(4)(vi) & 4(4)(ii) hampering the execution of required procedures
	3(4)(vii) & 4(4)(iv) using intellectual property right unfairly

categorized under ‘other foreclosing conducts’ in Table 4.3 are quite specific and do not align neatly with conventional definitions of exclusionary practices.

Conversely, the latter part of the fifth item in Article 5(1) of the MRFTA broadly categorizes practices that ‘undermine the interests of consumers’ as potential abuses of market dominance. These are seen as exploitative behaviors distinct from ‘charging an unreasonable price’ and ‘controlling sales unreasonably’, as outlined in Table 4.1. Some defendants have contested this broad interpretation, arguing that such an expansive definition of prohibitions may infringe upon the void-for-vagueness principle rooted in civil law tradition, potentially rendering it unconstitutional. The Supreme Court, in 2010, addressed these concerns by stating, “The abusive practices of market-dominant undertakings that undermine the interests of consumers are too varied and subject to change to be explicitly enumerated one by one using legislative techniques. ... It is possible, however, to elucidate them through systematic and comprehensive interpretations of the various types of abusive practices of market-dominant undertakings specified in Article 5(1). Moreover, the market-dominant entity, being the respondent in such cases, may be able to foresee the practices subject to regulation more accurately than the general public. Given these considerations, the provision does not violate the void-for-vagueness principle that stems from the rule of law.”[11]

[11] Supreme Court 2009du1983 May 27, 2010.

4.1.3 Standards for Evaluating Abusive Conducts

When comparing market dominance abuses with unfair trade practices, significant overlaps are observed. Most market dominance abuses identified in categories such as exclusive dealing, tying and bundling, predation, discrimination, and refusal to supply, as listed in Table 4.3, correspond to unfair trade practices. These practices are assessed based on criteria related to competition restriction or unfair trade terms, as outlined in Table 3.1. However, as highlighted in Chap. 3, the Supreme Court delineated the distinction between market dominance abuses and unfair trade practices in the landmark *Posco* refusal of trade case in 2007. The Court stated, "While §3-2(1) [§5 in the revised version] of the Fair Trade Act governs the abuses of a market-dominant position, §23(1) [§45(1) in the revised version] separately addresses instances where an individual enterprise unfairly refuses trade, raising competition concerns irrespective of the enterprise's dominance in the relevant market, as an unfair trade practice. This indicates that the objectives and scopes of regulating a market-dominant firm's refusal of trade under Fair Trade Act §3-2 (1) and the regulation of refusal of trade as an unfair trade practice under Fair Trade Act §23(1) are distinct. Consequently, the interpretation of unfairness in the context of a market-dominant firm's refusal to trade under Fair Trade Act §3-2 (1) must be conducted separately and independently from the interpretation of unfairness in the context of refusal of trade as an unfair trade practice under Fair Trade Act §23(1)."[12]

Furthermore, the Supreme Court's decision in the *Posco* case set a precedent for assessing the unfairness of a market-dominant firm's refusal to trade, a standard that is broadly applicable to all types of market dominance abuses. The decision articulates that "the unfairness of trade refusal by a market-dominant enterprise, as described in §3-2(1) of the MRFTA, must be interpreted in alignment with the legislative objective of promoting competition in monopolistic and oligopolistic markets. Consequently, it is not adequate to recognize unfairness solely based on the harm to a specific enterprise. Unfairness may be established when, among other considerations, the market-dominant enterprise's refusal to trade is deemed an action taken with *the intention and purpose* of maintaining or enhancing its market monopoly, that is, with the aim of artificially influencing market order by limiting free competition [*subjective requirement*]. Additionally, the act must objectively have the potential to *result in the effect of restricting competition* [*objective requirement*]." (Italics and parentheses have been added for emphasis and clarification.)

The *Posco* decision further elaborated on the subjective and objective criteria for demonstrating the unfairness of market dominance abuses, stating: "Thus, the plaintiff [KFTC], in claiming that the act of trade refusal by a market-dominant firm constitutes an abuse of dominant position, must establish that the refusal to trade—characterized by concerns of potentially restrictive effects on competition, such as increases in commodity prices, reductions in output, hindrances to

[12] Supreme Court 2002du6826, November 22, 2007.

innovation, a decrease in the number of viable competitors, and a reduction in diversity—was carried out with the specific intention and purpose to produce such effects. If it can be shown that the trade refusal indeed led to actual adverse outcomes in the market, it may reasonably be inferred that the act was carried out with the requisite intention and concern for restricting competition. In the absence of such direct evidence, the determination of whether the refusal to trade, with its potential to restrict competition, was motivated by such intention and purpose must consider all relevant factors, including the process and motivation behind the refusal, the manner in which it was executed, the characteristics of the relevant market, the extent of harm inflicted on trading partners, and the impact on market prices, output, innovation, and diversity." This implies that demonstrating the actual effects of competition restriction can suffice to infer both the subjective and objective requirements. This approach underscores the importance of effect-based analysis and highlights the critical role of economic assessment in such cases.

The KFTC 2021 Guidelines incorporate the principles set forth in the *Posco* decision for assessing the anticompetitive effects of exclusionary abusive conduct. These guidelines specify that direct impacts on competition, such as price increases, output reductions, limitations on the diversity of commodities and services, and hindrances to innovation, will be considered. Additionally, they will evaluate the potential for foreclosure and the increase of rivals' costs, which could lead to these effects.

The Supreme Court also established the criteria for assessing exploitative abuses as detailed in the latter portion of the fifth item in the MRFTA §5(1), identifying practices that 'undermine the interests of consumers considerably' as potential abuses of market dominance. In a decision regarding the termination of a group contract by certain companies in the cable broadcasting industry, the Supreme Court elucidated, "The objective of regulating abuses by market-dominant firms extends beyond merely safeguarding the interests of individual consumers directly impacted by the act. It encompasses protecting the broader consumer interests that prevail in a competitive market from the realization of excessive monopolistic profits by a dominant market player, as well as fostering competition in monopolistic and oligopolistic markets. Accordingly, in assessing the unfairness of actions that significantly undermine consumer interests, it is critical to specifically consider whether there are indications that the act was driven by the market-dominant entity's intent and purpose to realize excessive monopolistic profits [*subjective requirement*], and whether the act resulted in, or there is a risk of, significantly harming consumer interests in the relevant market, taking into account factors such as the nature of the product, the conduct's character, its duration, and the market's structure and characteristics [*objective requirement*]."[13] (Parentheses have been added for clarity.) Thus, the evaluation of unfairness in diminishing consumer interests should concentrate on both the exploitative intent and its effects. This ruling articulates a distinct legal framework for addressing the unfairness of exploitative abuses that harm

[13] Supreme Court 2009du1983, May 27, 2010.

consumer interests, differentiating it from the approach to exclusionary abuses as established in the *Posco* decision.

Instances of market dominance abuse are infrequent due to the strict criteria for violating the law. However, the consequences for a firm found guilty of such abuse are substantial, as it may be required to alter business strategies that were pivotal in establishing or preserving its monopolistic position, in addition to facing significant penalty surcharges. The KFTC is authorized to levy penalty surcharges on a market-dominant entity engaged in abusive practices, amounting to up to 6% of the relevant sales.[14] Table 4.4 below illustrates the annual trend in the KFTC's enforcement actions against the abuse of market dominance.

It is noteworthy that the record for 2007 is exceptionally high. This anomaly suggests that the KFTC aggressively pursued enforcement against numerous cases, which may have been more aptly classified as unfair trade practices, specifically during that year. Several of these cases did not succeed in court, particularly because they were assessed using the standards established by the Supreme Court in the 2007 *Posco* decision. The subsequent decline in the number of KFTC enforcement actions concerning market dominance abuses reflects a more cautious approach, aligning with the evaluative criteria set forth in the *Posco* decision.

4.2 Market Definition and Market Power

Defining a relevant market for the purpose of antitrust enforcement involves identifying the actual or potential competitors that exert competitive constraints on the concerned business entities, preventing them from acting independently of competitive pressures. Typically, this is the initial step in all regulations aimed at promoting competition.[15] In this section, I will introduce the fundamental concepts and tools for defining the relevant market and discuss some challenges encountered in measuring market power through indices of market shares and concentration ratios.

[14] With the comprehensive revision of the MRFTA in 2021, the maximum penalty surcharge for engaging in abuses of market dominance was increased from 3% to 6% of the relevant sales over the period during which the abusive conduct occurred.

[15] The US DOJ and FTC merger guidelines suggest that it is not always necessary to begin with market definition when conducting a merger review. They mention that "Some of the analytical tools used by the Agencies to assess competitive effects do not rely on market definition."

Table 4.4 KFTC enforcement record on regulating market dominance abuses

Year	Fincing complaints with the prosecution		Corrective order		Corrective recommentation	Request for correction	Warning	Voluntary correction	Total
		Surcharge		Surcharge					
1981–1999	3	3	16	2	4	0	5	0	28
2000	0	0	0	0	0	0	0	0	0
2001	0	0	3	2	0	0	1		4
2002	0	0	0	0	0	0	0	0	0
2003	0	0	1	0	0	0	0	0	1
2004	0	0	0	0	0	0	0	0	0
2005	0	0	0	0	0	0	0	0	0
2006	0	0	2	1	0	0	0	0	2
2007	0	0	37	25	0	0	1	0	38
2008	0	0	3	1	0	0	1	1	5
2009	0	0	2	2	0	0	0	0	2
2010	2	1	3	2	0	0	2	0	7
2011	0	0	0	0	0	0	0	0	0
2012	0	0	1	1	0	0	0	0	1
2013	0	0	0	0	0	0	0	0	0
2014	0	0	0	0	0	0	0	0	0

2015	1	1	3	3	0	0	1	0	5
2016	0	0	0	0	0	0	0	0	0
2017	0	0	3	1	0	0	1	0	4
2018	0	0	1	1	0	0	0	0	1
2019	1	1	1	1	0	0	0	0	2
2020	0	0	1	1	0	0	0	0	1
2021	0	0	3	3	0	0	0	0	3
2022	0	0	0	0	0	0	0	0	0
2023	1	1	2	2	0	0	0	0	3
Total	**8**	**8**	**82**	**48**	**4**	**0**	**12**	**1**	**107**
Ratio	**7.5%**		**76.6%**		**3.7%**	**0.0%**	**11.2%**	**0.9%**	**100%**

Source: KFTC Annual Statistics

4.2.1 Basic Concept and Various Methods of Market Definition

The MRFTA §2 defines the relevant market as "the range of transactions where there exist or may exist competitive relations in terms of objects, stages, or regions of trade," and KFTC guidelines of market dominance abuse and merger regulation elaborate it as "the set of products or the entire geographic area to which a representative consumer can switch their purchases in response to a small but significant and non-transitory increase in prices of specific products or regions while keeping other prices constant."

The principle aligns with the SSNIP (small but significant and non-transitory increase in price) test, which serves as the basis for market definition by antitrust enforcement agencies in the United States, the EU, and many other countries.[16] According to the horizontal merger guideline in the US DOJ and FTC (2010), these agencies utilize the hypothetical monopoly test, which requires determining whether "a hypothetical profit-maximizing firm, not subject to price regulation, that was the only present and future seller of those products ("hypothetical monopolist") likely would impose at least a small but significant and non-transitory increase in price ("SSNIP") on at least one product in the market, including at least one product sold by one of the merging firms." Similarly, EC (1997) notice outlines the question to be addressed as follows: "whether the parties' customers would switch to readily available substitutes or to suppliers located elsewhere in response to a hypothetical small (in the range 5%–10%), permanent relative price increase in the products and areas being considered. If substitution would be enough to make the price increase unprofitable because of the resulting loss of sales, additional substitutes and areas are included in the relevant market. This would be done until the set of products and geographic areas is such that small, permanent increases in relative prices would be profitable."

There appears to be a subtle difference between market definition in Korea and that in the United States. In Korea, a market is defined from a consumer's perspective as the largest range where they can switch purchases in response to SSNIP (referred to as the 'representative consumer version'). In contrast, in the United States, it is defined from a producer's perspective as the smallest range where they can make profits by SSNIP (referred to as the 'hypothetical monopolist version'). However, in practice, such an apparent difference does not matter, as KFTC employs the same tools to implement the SSNIP test in defining the relevant market as is done in the United States and the European Union.

Caution should be exercised when selecting a benchmark price, which is the starting point in the SSNIP test. This issue was highlighted by the well-known cellophane fallacy in the 1956 *du Pont* case, where the Supreme Court included all flexible packaging materials (including greaseproof paper, glassine, waxed paper,

[16] For the SSNIP test in historical context, refer to Werden (2003).

foil, Pliofilm, as well as cellophane) in the relevant market. Many antitrust economists argued that the decision made an error by expanding the market to include weak substitutes, starting from the then-prevailing monopolistic price when considering consumers' responses to price increases. They suggested that the market might have been confined to cellophane alone if the price increase from the lower competitive level had been appropriately considered. Subsequently, it became conventional to consider price adjustment toward a competitive level in cases of market dominance abuses where the past exercise of monopoly power is a concern. On the other hand, it is acceptable to start from the prevailing price in the SSNIP test when the issue at hand is the potential future exercise of monopoly power after a proposed merger.

Another subtlety involves determining the appropriate size of a 'small but significant' increase in price in the SSNIP test. US DOJ and FTC (2010) guidelines typically recommend to use "a SSNIP of 5% of the price paid by customers for the products or services to which the merging firms contribute value" (underline added),[17] but they also note that the proper SSNIP size "depends upon the nature of the industry and the merging firms' positions in it." It is important to emphasize the benchmark price should reflect the value added by the concerned undertaking. In the context of mergers in the retailing industry, it has been suggested that an appropriate SSNIP size is often 1% to 2% of sale prices, rather than the higher range of 5% to10%.[18] This can be seen as a rule of thumb indicating that retailers typically add about 20% of vale to the prices of commodities they sell. However, the nature of industry may sometimes require to consider a SSNIP size greater than 10%. For example, in a merger between two local soju companies, Moohak and Daesun, as discussed in Chap. 5, the presence of two distinct consumer groups, one loyal to local brand and the other sensitive to price changes, enabled local soju companies to profit from a substantial price increase, even if small price increases were unprofitable. In such case, it may be warranted to take a high SSNIP size into account. There have also been court cases in the United States, where market conditions made it necessary to consider a SSNIP size of 20% to 25% in a hospital merger.[19]

4.2.1.1 Critical Loss Analysis

The SSNIP test serves as a conceptual framework for market definition within competition policy, while critical loss analysis offers a practical approach for its application in real-world cases. Since its introduction by Harris and Simons in 1989,

---

[17]EC (1997) considers "a hypotheticall small (in the range 5%~10%)" price increase.

[18]See Harris and Jorde (1983): "In the high-volume grocery business ... net income typically represents 0.5% of sales, so a 5% increase in price would represent a 1000% increase in profit ... Surely, a sizable number of competitors not now in the market would enter in profits were running at that exorbitant level."

[19]US v. Mercy Health Services, US District Court, October 27, 1995.

critical loss analysis has been employed in numerous US antitrust cases. Enforcement agencies such as the UK's Office of Fair Trading (OFT), the US DOJ, and the US FTC explicitly recognize the method as a valuable tool in their market definition guidelines. In Korea, Jeon (2004) introduced critical loss analysis through an economic analysis of the geographic market definition pertinent to the *Moohak–Daesun* merger. The Seoul High Court, referencing Jeon's analysis, validated it as "an effective and appropriate method for defining the relevant geographic market through the systematic application of the 'SSNIP' method to practical cases."[20] Following this, Jeon et al. (2005) employed the method once more in defining the product market relevant to the *Hite–Jinro* merger, with the KFTC affirming their approach in 2006.[21]

The concept behind critical loss analysis is straightforward. The profitability of a price increase hinges on the magnitude of the subsequent loss in sales. The 'critical loss for an X-% price increase' is determined as the maximum percentage loss of sales volume that would still allow for no loss in profit following an X-% price increase. Alternatively, critical loss represents the smallest percentage loss of sales volume that would lead to a decrease in profits. Therefore, if the actual loss in sales is greater (lesser) than the critical loss, the price increase will result in a decrease (increase) in profits.[22] The table below provides a summary of how critical loss analysis is utilized in defining the market.[23]

If the actual sales loss following a SSNIP is less than the critical loss associated with that SSNIP, then a hypothetical monopolist could realize higher profits through such a price increase. This suggests that the relevant market is appropriately defined without the need for further expansion, as there are no closely substitutable products or regions to which consumers could switch in response to the SSNIP. Conversely, if the actual sales loss following a SSNIP exceeds the critical loss, then a hypothetical monopolist would not achieve higher profits by implementing such a price increase. This indicates that the relevant market needs to be expanded to encompass the next closest substitutes. The process of market definition using critical loss analysis begins by considering a set of products and regions where anticompetitive concerns are highlighted. The actual sales loss is then compared to the critical loss iteratively until no further expansion is necessary—when the actual loss is less than the critical loss. Therefore, the relevant market is defined as the smallest market within which a hypothetical monopolist could increase profits through a SSNIP.

---

[20] Seoul High Court 2003u2252, October 14, 2004.

[21] KFTC 2006-009, January 24, 2006. The merger cases of *Moohak–Daesun* and *Hite–Jinro* will be addressed in Chap. 5.

[22] It's worth noting that I have chosen to use a breakeven version of critical loss rather than a profit-maximization version. The breakeven version is commonly employed in practical applications due to its simplicity and because it is not dependent on the shape of the demand curve.

[23] If we reinterpret sales loss due to a price change as the price elasticity of demand, then critical loss analysis can be seen as critical elasticity analysis. This perspective frames the analysis in terms of elasticity rather than absolute sales loss.

Table 4.5 Framework of critical loss analysis

Actual Sales Loss (AL) after SSNIP < Critical Sales Loss (CL) for SSNIP
⇒ Profitability of SSNIP by A Hypothetical Monopolist
No Further Market Expansion

We have a simple relationship between the critical loss for a SNNIP level X and the price-cost margin M as follows: $CL = \frac{X}{X+M}$.[24] Critical loss corresponding to X-% price increase depends on the magnitude of X. The larger the price increase is, the greater the sales loss a hypothetical monopolist can tolerate without experiencing a loss in profits. Another crucial factor is the price-cost margin, $M = \frac{P-C}{P}$, where P represents unit price and C stands for marginal or incremental costs. In cases with high price-cost margins, each lost sale results in a relatively significant reduction in profits. Hence a high margin rate implies a lower level of critical loss.[25]

In the application of critical loss analysis, as illustrated in Table 4.5, the Critical Loss (CL) is typically calculated using margin data derived from the accounting records of the relevant firms. Meanwhile, Actual Loss (AL) is estimated either econometrically, using actual demand data, or through survey data on consumer responses to price increases. It is important to note that CL and AL are estimated independently in the conventional approach to critical loss analysis. However, given the intrinsic connection between CL and AL under the premise of a firm's profit maximization, the traditional method of critical loss analysis has been critiqued for overlooking this interrelationship, potentially leading to inaccurate market definitions. As a response to these criticisms, the concept of the aggregate diversion ratio emerged in the early 2000s as an alternative metric to critical loss. This concept aims to more accurately reflect the dynamics between CL and AL by considering the degree to which sales diverted from one product due to a price increase are captured by other products within the same market.

4.2.1.2 Aggregate Diversion Ratio

Katz and Shapiro (2003) and O'Brien and Wickelgren (2003), referred to KSOW (Katz-Shapiro-O'Brien-Wickelgren) in the following, highlighted the issue

[24]This formula is straightforwardly derived from the breakeven condition for a price increase. See Church and Ware (2000).

[25]When interpreting the significance of high profit margins, it is important to exercise caution and be mindful of the well-known "Cellophane Fallacy." This fallacy arises when current high profit margins result from either monopoly power or collusion among market players. In such cases, using the basic formula for critical loss analysis might lead to an erroneous expansion of the market definition. Therefore, it becomes necessary to adjust the initial pricing used for calculating profit margins to a counterfactual competitive price, in order to obtain a more accurate assessment.

of critical loss analysis and proposed an alternative method to address the concerns.[26] The profit maximizing condition for a firm implies the following relationship, which is commonly known as the Lerner equation:

$$M = \frac{P - MC}{P} = \frac{1}{E_f} \tag{4.1}$$

where E_f represents the elasticity of individual demand that a firm faces. That is, a firm's profit margin tends to be smaller when it faces high demand elasticity. This reflects the idea that a firm cannot easily raise prices when consumers have readily available alternatives, which leads to a more elastic demand. The greater the actual sales loss (AL) a firm experiences due to a price increase, the higher its demand elasticity. Therefore, a relationship between demand elasticity E_f and actual loss AL can be expressed as follows:

$$AL = (1 - D)XE_f \tag{4.2}$$

where D is the aggregate diversion ratio, which is defined as the ratio of purchases diverted to other products withing a candidate market relative to the total decrease in sales of a product due to a price increase by X, and this decrease can be approximated by XE.[27] Here, a 'candidate' market refers to a group of products (or regions) that are being assessed under the SSNIP test to determine if the group is the appropriate relevant market or not. When you plug Eq. (4.1) into Eq. (4.2), we have

$$AL = (1 - D)X\frac{1}{M}. \tag{4.3}$$

Taking into account the critical loss formula, $CL = \frac{X}{X+M}$, and reformulating the condition of market definition within the framework of critical loss analysis presented in Table 4.5, we obtain:[28]

$$AL < CL \Leftrightarrow D > CL. \tag{4.4}$$

The relationship described by KSOW suggests that if the hypothetical monopoly firm in a candidate market can achieve an $X\%$ Small but Significant and

---

[26]Prior to KSWO, Langenfeld and Li (2001) and Danger and Frech III (2001) had conducted research in a similar domain. Subsequently, Farrell and Shapiro (2008) proposed directions for enhancing critical loss analysis, drawing upon insights from the controversies surrounding it.

[27]In the context of linear demand functions, when a price increase of $X\%$ occurs, the total reduction in sales can be precisely calculated as XE_f, the product of the considered price increase and the own price demand elasticity. For non-linear demand functions, this relationship holds as an approximation.

[28]The derivation is straightforward. Using Eq. (4.3) and the relationship of $CL = \frac{X}{X+M}$, we have $AL < CL \Leftrightarrow (1 - D)X\frac{1}{M} < \frac{X}{M+X} \Leftrightarrow 1 - \frac{M}{M+X} < D \Leftrightarrow CL < D$.

Non-transitory Increase in Price (SSNIP), it can increase its profits, provided that the aggregate diversion ratio exceeds the critical loss ratio. This concept is logical because when a larger portion of sales within the candidate market remains unaffected by the price increase of a product, the actual revenue loss incurred by the firm is smaller. Consequently, the potential for increasing profits becomes greater.

The practical critique of critical loss analysis is that it may lead to an overly broad market definition, particularly in industries characterized by high margins. A larger margin ratio results in a smaller critical loss, increasing the likelihood that the actual loss exceeds the critical loss. This suggests a need to expand the relevant market. However, according to the Lerner condition Eq. (4.1), a high margin ratio also inversely affects the actual loss, a factor that traditional critical loss analysis fails to adequately consider. Conversely, the KSOW reformulation could result in a narrower market definition in high-margin industries. This occurs because the criteria for ceasing further market definition become easier to meet when the margin ratio is high. This adjustment addresses the original methodology's oversight by more accurately reflecting the impact of profitability on market dynamics.

The reformulation of critical loss analysis by KSOW has its errors and limitations. The critical loss analysis presented in Table 4.5 adopts a uniform price increase across all products within a candidate market, employing what is referred to as the 'uniform SSNIP test'. In contrast, Katz and Shapiro (2003) propose a test utilizing the aggregate diversion ratio Eq. (4.4) that considers the price increase of a single product within a candidate market, termed the 'stand-alone SSNIP test'. However, Daljord et al. (2007) demonstrated that the accurate reformulation for the case of a stand-alone SSNIP test is not captured by Eq. (4.4) but should be articulated as follows:[29]

$$AL < CL \Leftrightarrow D > \frac{X}{M}. \tag{4.5}$$

It should be noted that the criteria set by $D > \frac{X}{M}$ in Eq. (4.5) are stricter than those set by$D > CL$ in Eq. (4.4), given that $CL = \frac{X}{M+X} < \frac{X}{M}$. Erroneously applying Eq. (4.4) leads to narrower market definition than applying Eq. (4.5) correctly.

On the other hand, O'Brien and Wickelgren (2003) developed the reformulation in Eq. (4.4) within the context of a uniform SSNIP test. However, Coate and Simons (2009) argue that Eq. (4.4) has limitations even in this context. For Eq. (4.1) to be valid under a uniform SSNIP test, it must be assumed that the portion of sales diverted to other products within a candidate market, in the event of a price increase for one product, remains unchanged when the prices of all products within the candidate market increase uniformly. That is to say, the retention rate R, defined as the portion of sales diverted to other products within a candidate market in case of a price increase for one product, stays the same even when there is a uniform price

[29] Equation (4.5) assumes symmetry between two firms. In cases of asymmetry, the reformulation should be modified to: $\lambda D > X/M$ where $\lambda = (p_2 - c_2)/(p_1 - c_1)$.

increase across all products with the candidate market. Equation (4.1) presupposes the assumption of $R = 1$, which is obviously too restrictive. For instance, consider a candidate market comprising German luxury cars such as Benz, BMW, and Audi. Assume that if the price of a Benz increases by 5%, the decrease in demand for the product shifts by 1/3 each to BMW, Audi, and other luxury cars outside of the candidate market, respectively. Then the aggregate diversion ratio is 2/3. However, if the prices of all three products—Benz, BMW, and Audi—increase simultaneously by 5%, it is unrealistic to expect that the sales diverted into BMW and Audi would remain the same as if only the price of Benz had increased by 5%. In an extreme scenario, it is conceivable that all sales previously diverted internally shift away to other luxury brands such as Lexus, implying R = 0. According to Coate and Simons (2009), a corrected reformulation of Eq. (4.4) is:

$$AL < CL \Leftrightarrow D \cdot R > CL (0 \leq R \leq 1) \tag{4.6}$$

which serves as a warning that a straightforward application of the KSOW reformulation without duly considering the retention rate could potentially result in a narrow market definition.

Equations (4.5) and (4.6) highlight intrinsic criticisms of the KSOW approach. The fundamental defenses of standard critical loss analysis primarily challenge the relevance of the Lerner equation Eq. (4.1). Firstly, and somewhat bluntly, some antitrust scholars, such as Scheffman and Simons (2003), question the practical applicability of the profit maximization condition Equation (4.1), which underpins the type of criticism associated with KSOW, suggesting that firms may not always choose price and output to maximize their profits, possibly due to bounded rationality or agency problems. However, the majority of economists uphold profit maximization as the core hypothesis for explaining the behavior of, and interactions among, firms. Secondly, and more palatable to economists, are the realistic scenarios where the simple Lerner condition of Eq. (4.1) does not apply, even when firms are attempting to maximize profits. Firms often produce multiple products that may be complements or substitutes for each other and consider the spillover effects on the demands of other products when setting the price of one product. Additionally, firms must take into account factors such as reputation, consumer loyalty, network effects, learning effects, etc. in a comprehensive manner. Moreover, in oligopolistic markets, firms must strategize, anticipating competitors' responses. These considerations suggest that Eq. (4.1) may not always be relevant. Therefore, proponents of critical loss analysis argue that Actual Loss (AL) should not be deduced solely by the inverse relationship between margin and elasticity, as suggested by Eq. (4.1). Instead, they recommend that AL should be directly determined by estimating the demand function econometrically or from survey data.

4.2.1.3 Time Series Analysis

Market definition through the analysis of time series of commodity prices has been a significant area of research in empirical industrial economics since Stigler and Sherwin (1985) examined the correlation coefficient of regional product prices. Werden and Froeb (1993) introduced alternative tools for market definition, such as the speed of price adjustment, Granger causality, and cointegration tests.[30] The underlying principle is that for a group of commodities to constitute a market, their prices must either be equal or move in unison. Therefore, the extent to which two prices move together can be used to determine whether the respective goods belong to the same market.

However, there are some limitations to defining markets through price tests. Werden and Froeb (1993) highlighted that price correlation might overstate the actual relationship between two products. For instance, due to shared costs or inflation, prices might rise and fall simultaneously, leading to a high correlation between two products that includes a "spurious" component and overestimates the true relationship. Furthermore, the factors causing price interdependence may not relate to those that influence market power. One method to address the issue of exaggerated correlations due to common drivers is to eliminate the spurious component by controlling for various common explanatory variables of the two prices, such as GDP, costs, foreign exchange rate, etc. This involves using a 'partial' correlation coefficient between prices, calculated after adjusting for all common drivers and trend factors. A practical challenge in defining markets with price correlation is the absence of a benchmark level of correlation, akin to the 'critical' loss concept. Werden and Froeb (1993), serving as antitrust economists at the US DOJ, estimated various correlations of prices (nominal, real, differential, log transformation) between sugar and High Fructose Corn Syrup (HFCS) ranging from 0.41 to 0.72, and 'hinted' that HFCS and sugar may represent separate markets in the merger case of ADM and Nabisco. However, they did not definitively conclude the significance of that magnitude of correlation as evidence of separate market definition.[31]

Despite these limits, time series analyses, when executed with care, remain a valuable complementary tool for market definition. Furthermore, recent advancements in time series analysis techniques that go beyond simple price correlations,

---

[30]Rodriguez and Williams (2001) utilized price correlation and cointegration techniques to define markets for world oils and gasoline across three western states in the United States. Wu and Wu (1997) conducted an analysis of price correlation to delineate markets for glass and metal utensils. Forni (2004) conducted tests for the stationariness of price differentials as a method of defining regional milk markets in Italy. Additionally, Böckers and Heimeshoff (2014) explored the level of competition and integration in European electricity markets through the analysis of price time series data.

[31] *U.S. v. Archer-Daniels-Midland Co.* Werden and Froeb (1993, p. 346) state that "We suspect that Stigler and Sherwin would view these correlations as too low to establish that sugar is in the relevant market for HFCS, but we just do not know."

such as Granger causality and cointegration, have been employed for the purpose of market definition. Granger causality, for instance, assesses whether the lags of one variable, as well as its own lags, contribute to improving predictions of another variable. Denote one own variable as X_t, and the other variable as Y_t. Granger (1969) posited that if $Y_{t-1}, Y_{t-2}, \ldots, Y_{t-p}$ are useful in prediction of X_t, it suggests causality. Conversely, the absence of such predictability may indicate exogeneity between the two variables. The simple model and the null hypothesis of the Granger causality test are as follows:

$$\ln(P_{it}) = c_i + \sum_{k=1}^{p} \alpha_{ik} \ln(P_{i,t-k}) + \sum_{k=1}^{p} \beta_{ik} \ln\left(P_{j,t-k}\right) + u_{it} \tag{4.7}$$

$$H_0: \quad \beta_1 = \beta_2 = \cdots = \beta_p = 0.$$

The null hypothesis H_0 is that P_j "Granger does not cause" P_i. If we can reject the null hypothesis and find that P_j "Granger causes" P_i, then we may interpret it as indicating that variables i and j are closely related, suggesting that two products belong to the same market. It is advisable to use prices adjusted for common drivers in conducting the test to eliminate any spuriousness.

Cointegration exists when a linear combination of two variables is stationary, even though each variable individually exhibits a unit root.[32] Engle and Granger (1987) identified "prices of the same commodity in different markets or close substitutes in the same market" as instances of time series that exhibit cointegration. Therefore, if two prices are cointegrated, it may be interpreted that they belong to the same market. Cointegration analysis offers the advantage of considering the long-run equilibrium relationship between commodity prices, an aspect not captured by contemporaneous correlation.

4.2.1.4 LIFO-LOFI

Regional trade flows serve as a significant basis for defining geographic markets. EC (1997) highlighted the "current geographic pattern of purchases" and "trade flows/ pattern of shipments" as initial evidence to consider in geographic market delineation. Elzinga and Hogarty (1973) proposed the indices of LIFO (Little In From Outside) and LOFI (Little Out From Inside) for this purpose. LIFO is defined as the 'Amount Produced and Consumed in A Region/Total Amount Consumed in the Region', whereas LOFI is defined as the 'Amount Produced and Consumed in A Region/Total Amount Produced in the Region'. In essence, LIFO quantifies the share of total consumption within a region that is met by regional producers, with the remaining demand satisfied from external sources. Conversely, LOFI

[32] I won't elaborate on the technical details of time series analysis here. For a deeper understanding of concepts such as stationariness, unit root, and cointegration tests, see Wooldridge (2006).

calculates the share of total production within a region that is consumed by regional customers, with the surplus production distributed for consumption in other regions. The LIFO-LOFI analysis, also known as the Elzinga-Hogarty (E-H) test, is employed to determine whether both ratios exceed 75%, a threshold indicating that a candidate area constitutes the relevant geographic market.[33,34]

Exercising caution is necessary when defining a geographic market using the LIFO-LOFI analysis and the Elzinga-Hogarty (E-H) test, as some economists have highlighted an inherent expansionary bias within the test. This concern emerged notably during a series of hospital mergers in the United States during the 1990s. Of approximately 900 cases, the US DOJ and the FTC blocked seven, but courts subsequently overturned all seven decisions. Throughout these proceedings, the E-H test played a pivotal role. Courts accepted defense arguments that the relevant geographic market should be expanded to areas where LIFO and LOFI ratios meet or exceed 75% or 90%. Particularly in cases where the anticompetitive effects of merged hospitals were evaluated ex post, there has been criticism that courts excessively broadened the geographic market definition based on the E-H test. It has been noted that even Kenneth Elzinga, one of the test's creators, acknowledged the limitations of the E-H test in assessing mergers between hospitals, given the highly differentiated nature of their services.[35]

Capps et al. (2001) labeled the inherent bias toward expanding a geographic market in the Elzinga-Hogarty (E-H) test as the "Silent Majority Fallacy." They argue that even if a minority of patients travel to a hospital outside a given region, and this minority is substantial, there may not be a direct correlation between the market experiences of travelers and non-travelers post-merger. This discrepancy arises if the two groups exhibit fundamentally different demand behaviors, possibly due to differences in their preferences for travel or their need for local versus non-local services. Consequently, the presence of a minority willing to travel does not necessarily mean that local firms lack market power over the majority of consumers who prefer not to travel. This implies that in scenarios where consumer preferences vary due to factors like proximity to family and friends, or where hospital services are differentiated by specialties in treating serious illnesses, a hypothetical monopolist hospital could still exercise market power over the majority of patients who are less inclined to travel, even if 30% to 40% of patients are willing to seek care outside their local area. Therefore, the market definition should not be unnecessarily broadened.

The SSNIP test serves as a conceptual framework for market definition, rather than a mandatory or always feasible tool for defining a relevant market. Among the analytical tools discussed, critical loss analysis and the aggregate diversion ratio test

---

[33] The definitions and criteria of LIFO and LOFI can be confusing because they appear contrary to their literal meanings. For example, when both ratios are high, the terms "little in" and "little out" may seem to be accurate.

[34] Some people argue that a more stringent critical threshold of 90% should be implemented.

[35] See Dranove and Sfekas (2009).

align closely with the SSNIP test framework. In contrast, time series and LIFO-LOFI analyses are not directly related to the SSNIP test. Furthermore, a market can be defined without resorting to such formal analyses. KFTC (2021) guidelines outline the criteria for determining a relevant market as follows: "The decision on whether a specific good or service belongs to the same trading field is based on (i) the similarity of functions and use of goods or services, (ii) the buyer's recognition of the possibility of substituting goods or services and the related form of purchase, (iii) the seller's recognition of the possibility of substituting goods or services and the related form of management decision-making, (iv) the Korea Criteria Industry Code announced by the Commissioner of the Korea National Statistical Office, among others."[36]

4.2.2 Market Share and Market Power

Market power refers to a firm's ability to elevate prices above the competitive level or marginal cost. Consequently, the Lerner index, denoted by M in Eq. (4.1), serves as the ideal measure of a firm's market power. Nonetheless, accurately measuring a firm's marginal cost (MC) or estimating the demand elasticity E_f that a firm confronts can be challenging. Therefore, market share is frequently utilized as a practical surrogate for assessing market power. The connection between market share and market power can be elucidated by the following relationship:

$$E_f = \frac{E_D + (1 - s)E_R}{s} \tag{4.8}$$

where E_D is the elasticity of market demand, E_R is the elasticity of supply response of fringe firms to the price set by a dominant firm, and s represents the market share of a dominant firm. Equation (4.8) is derived from the model of single dominant firm with competing fringe suppliers, with which Landes and Posner (1981) addressed the issue of market power in antitrust cases.[37]

Plugging Eq. (4.8) into Eq. (4.1), we obtain:

[36] Additionally several other factors are considered when defining a geographic market. These include: (v) the business capacity (production capacity and the scope of sales network) of the seller and characteristics of goods or services (decomposability, possibility of degeneration, damageability); (vi) transportation cost; and (vii) feasibility of changing purchasing area in terms of time, economic considerations, and legal constraints.

[37] Equation (4.8) is derived by using the definition of a dominant firm's demand as $q^f = Q_D - S_R$ where q^f, Q_D, and S_R represents the dominant firm's output, industry output, and supply response of fringe firms, respectively, and by reformulating the firm's demand elasticity with industry demand elasticity and supply response elasticity.

$$\frac{P - MC}{P} = \frac{s}{E_D + (1 - s)E_R}. \tag{4.9}$$

The larger a firm's market share s, the greater its market power as defined by Lerner index M, assuming constant elasticity of market demand and elasticity of supply response from fringe firms. However, it is important to note that market share is not the sole determinant of market power. It also depends on the elasticity of market demand E_D and the elasticity of supply response from fringe firms E_R. This underscores the necessity for accurately defining the relevant market and thoroughly considering competitive restraints due to supply subsititution and potential entrants to ensure that market share accurately reflects market power. For instance, excluding a close demand substitute from the market definition would increase the elasticity of market demand, leading to a lower estimation of market power despite a large market share. Similarly, failing to account for supply substitution and potential entrants would increase the elasticity of supply response, yielding a similar reduction in perceived market power.

In an oligopolistic model of Cournot quantity competition, Cowling and Waterson (1976) established the following relationship:

$$\frac{P - MC}{P} = \frac{(1 + v)H}{E_D} \tag{4.10}$$

where H represents the Hirshman-Herfindal Index (HHI) and v measures the extent of concerted conduct among firms in the market. It is noteworthy that the margin in Eq. (4.10) represents an industry average, whereas the margin in Eq. (4.9) pertains to a specific relevant firm. H is a measure of market concentration, defined as the sum of the market shares of individual firms.[38] v represents the degree of interdependence among firms in the market. More precisely, it quantifies the extent to which competitors are expected to adjust their outputs in response to one firm's output, a concept referred to as 'conjectural variation' in theoretical literature.[39] Equation (4.10) illustrates a fundamental Structure-Conduct-Performance (S-C-P) relationship in industrial organization economics; if the market is more concentrated (H is higher), and firms engage more in collusive behavior (v is larger), then the market performance deteriorates, i.e., Lerner index M is greater.

Equation (4.9) serves as the foundation for using the market share of a dominant firm as an indicator of single dominance, while Eq. (4.10) provides the basis for

---

[38] In case of identical firms, $H = 1/N$. This indicates that a market characterized by H consists of $1/H$ firms of the same size. For example, if all firms are of equal size and H is 0.2, then there are 5 (=1/0.2) firms present in the market.

[39] In a scenario characterized by intense price competition, $v = -1$, indicating that other firms are expected to offset any decrease in one firm's output. In Cournot competition, $v = 0$, meaning that firms consider the output levels of their competitors as given and do not adjust their output in response to changes in another firm's output. Conversely, if $v > 0$, it suggests that firms in the market are behaving in a coordinated manner, aligning their actions to some degree.

suggesting that a high level of market concentration, as measured by HHI or the CR3, implies collective dominance. Employing parameters such as market share or market concentration represents a structural approach to evaluating market power. Alternatively, market power can be inferred by observing firms' pricing behavior, which can be described as a conduct approach. For instance, if retail prices vary across regions or over time in response to the level of competition, the price premium in a monopolistic region or period over the minimum competitive level can be considered a measure of market power, as indicated by the Lerner index M or at least its lower bound.[40] A similar principle can be applied in the case of price differentiation. If a firm charges different prices for the same product, the price differential may be interpreted as the lower bound of the Lerner index .

In this context, it is noteworthy that Richard Schmalensee, serving as an expert witness for Microsoft, utilized the conduct approach to assess market power during the US *Microsoft* case in 1998. Countering the structural approach that calculated Microsoft's market share in the Intel-compatible PC operating system market to be as high as 90%, he posited that Microsoft did not exhibit typical monopolistic behavior. "Working backward from an estimate of the demand elasticity for personal computers, he calculated that the monopoly price for Windows should have been at least 16 times higher than the price actually charged." Conversely, economists on the opposing side, such as Franklin Fisher, rebutted Schmalensee's argument by suggesting that "Microsoft's pricing was in line with long-term monopoly pricing once factors that incentivized Microsoft to moderate its prices were considered. These factors included the benefits of expanding its installed base, boosting demand for complementary products, and minimizing software piracy."[41]

4.3 Economic Arguments on Abusive Conducts

Exploitative abusive conducts are nominally subject to antitrust regulation in Korea; however, in practice, they are virtually unregulated by the KFTC. The cautious approach to enforcing price or quantity regulations on dominant firms stems from concerns that such actions may dampen innovation and dynamic competition *for* the market (as opposed to competition *within* the market), which antitrust policy aims to promote. Additionally, there is a belief that antitrust enforcement agencies lack the specialized knowledge and capabilities that industry-specific regulatory authorities possess for such regulation. In the following discussion, I will concentrate on exclusionary abusive conducts, briefly examining the anticompetitive effects and

[40] This approach was adopted in the 1997 US *Staples* case. FTC v. Staples, Inc., 970 F.Supp. 1066 (D.D.C. 1997).

[41] See Gibert and Katz (2001).

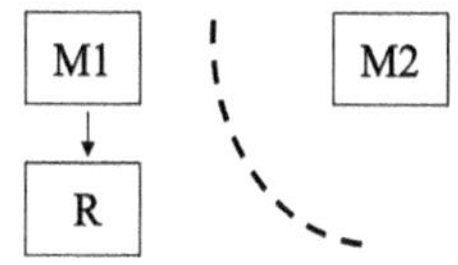

Fig. 4.1 Exclusive dealing

efficiency-enhancing effects associated with typical exclusionary behaviors as categorized in Table 4.3.[42]

4.3.1 *Exclusive Dealing*

The anticompetitive effects of exclusive dealing arrangements appear to be straightforward. Figure 4.1 illustrates exclusive dealing within the vertical relationship between manufacturers and retailers.

Manufacturer 1 forces a retailer to exclusively deal with them. This may result in a restriction of *inter-brand* competition between manufacturer 1 M_1 and manufacturer M_2. This represents a classic argument against exclusive dealing.

Conversely, Marvel (1982) offered some justification for exclusive dealing by highlighting its potential to enhance a manufacturer's incentives for advertising and investing in a dealer's outlet. Consider a scenario where a manufacturer supports a retailer by training staff, improving store environments, or spending on advertising for their brand, which attracts more customers. There is a risk that the retailer might then steer these customers toward purchasing other brands that offer a higher margin. Such opportunistic behavior by the retailer could diminish the manufacturer's incentives to invest or advertise. An exclusive dealing contract prevents the retailer from redirecting customers to other brands, thus encouraging the manufacturer to invest and advertise.

Economic discourse surrounding exclusive dealing has evolved considerably since the Chicago School's critique of the traditional anticompetitive assumptions associated with these contracts. Bork (1978, p. 306) succinctly encapsulates the core concept as follows: "It cannot charge the retailer that full amount in money and then charge it again in exclusivity that the retailer does not wish to grant. ... [T]he reason is not barring entry, but rather pursuing a more rational objective, such as securing the specialized selling efforts of the outlet."

Whinston (2006, pp. 137–139) explain the Chicago school's attack on the notion that exclusive contracts are inherently anticompetitive by presenting a simple model of a sequential exclusive contracting game involving three players, an incumbent seller *I*, a buyer *B*, and a potential entrant *E*. The game unfolds in the following manner: "First, *I* can offer *B* an exclusive contract along with a payment *t* in return for *B* signing the contract. Second, *B* decides whether to accept the contract. Third,

[42]For a thorough exploration on the economics of exclusionary conducts, see Fumagalli et al. (2018).

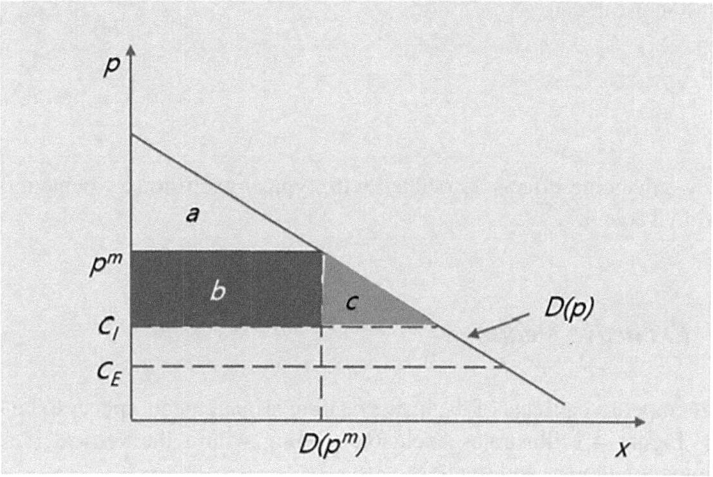

Fig. 4.2 The Chicago School argument: Figure from Whinston (2006, p. 139)

after observing whether B has signed an exclusive contract, E decides whether to enter (and incur the entry cost f). Finally, whichever firms are in the market name prices to B, who then chooses from whom and how much to purchase." In this scenario, it is assumed that E is more efficient than I in terms of unit cost ($c_E < c_I$), and that E would enter in the absence of an exclusive contract due to the entry cost, which adds an element of interest to the model (Fig. 4.2).

Ravel backward as usual in solving sequential games. At the last stage, E in case of entry sets the price at c_I and makes profits of $(c_I - c_E)D(c_I) > f$. Then B would accept I's exclusivity offer only if payment t is greater than the surplus at $p = c_I$, which is represented by the sum of areas a, b, and c. However, I can make monopoly profits as much as b, which fall short of the payment of $a + b + c$ to be made to B in return for exclusivity. That is, in order for an incumbent seller to induce a buyer to accept their offer, the incumbent should compensate the buyer with a payment more than what they can gain from monopoly-maintaining exclusivity. This is essentially what Bork meant with his statement; "It cannot charge the retailer that full amount in money and then charge it again in exclusivity that the retailer does not wish to grant."[43]

[43]Whinston (2006, pp. 144–151) extends this basic model with a single buyer into a model with multiple buyers to show that anticompetitive exclusive dealing contract which excludes an efficient entrant may be feasible. When there are multiple buyers, according to Whinston, "the contract signed by any one buyer can have a negative externality on all other buyers by reducing the likelihood of entry. (The protection of competition is, in a sense, a public good.) Intuitively, in such circumstances, the incumbent may find it worthwhile to induce a particular buyer or a subset of buyers to sign because by doing so he can monopolize *other* buyers without paying them anything." Refer to Rasmussen et al. (1991) and Segal and Whinston (2000a, b) for the formal theoretical models. These examples highlight the achievements in post-Chicago industrial organization that

Whinston (2006, pp. 144–151) extends this basic model with a single buyer into a model with multiple buyers to show that anticompetitive exclusive dealing contract which excludes an efficient entrant may be feasible. When there are multiple buyers, according to Whinston, "the contract signed by any one buyer can have a negative externality on all other buyers by reducing the likelihood of entry. (The protection of competition is, in a sense, a public good.) Intuitively, in such circumstances, the incumbent may find it worthwhile to induce a particular buyer or a subset of buyers to sign because by doing so he can monopolize *other* buyers without paying them anything." Refer to Rasmussen et al. (1991) and Segal and Whinston (2000a) for the formal theoretical models. These examples highlight the achievements in post-Chicago industrial organization that utilize game theory to explain strategic behaviors driven by either anticompetitive or efficiency motives.

Segal and Whinston (2000a, b) have developed a game theoretic model to analyze exclusive dealing contracts that enhance efficiency. They have incorporated essential elements of transaction cost economics, such as relation-specific investment, incomplete contracts, and holdup, into their formal model. Their main findings can be summarized as follows. Either the buyer or the seller makes investments that are specific to their relationship. These investments increase the value of trade within their partnership but come at the expense of reducing its external value. Examples of such investments include advertising, training, or the seller's interior investments in the buyer's outlet, as well as royalty investments made by the buyer on behalf of the seller. These investments cannot be fully specified in a contract due to limitations in rationality or verifiability. Consequently, these investments are not considered during the ex-post bargaining stage because of their relationship-specific nature. This phenomenon is commonly referred to as holdup. Ex ante, anticipating opportunistic behavior, the incentives for making these investments are diminished in advance. Vertical integration can resolve this problem. However, if integration is not feasible, an exclusive dealing contract that eliminates the option of external trade can increase the value of these relationship-specific investments within the partnership.[44]

4.3.2 Tying and Bundling

Tying refers to the mandatory purchase of a tied product when acquiring a tying product, and the quantity of the tied product can vary based on the customer's preference. While bundling is often grouped together with tying, it typically involves

---

utilize game theory to explain strategic behaviors drive by either anticompetitive or efficiency motives.

[44]Whinston (2006, pp. 178–188) provides a more detailed introduction of the model in Segal and Whinston (2000a, b) and their results.

linking two products in a one-to-one fashion.[45] Despite the disparity in their outward appearance, the economic consequences of tying and bundling, whether they are anticompetitive or geared toward enhancing efficiency, can be fundamentally analyzed in a similar manner. As such, I will discuss them jointly.

Traditional anticompetitive arguments against tying or bundling are based on the leverage theory. This theory posits that a firm with monopoly power in the market for a tying product can extend its monopoly power to another, competitive market for a tied product by leveraging its position in the tying product's market. As a result, competition diminishes and social welfare suffers. The leverage theory was widely accepted by courts and competition agencies until the first half of the twentieth century. However, it later faced criticism from the Chicago School. This critique introduced the 'One Monopoly Rent Theory', which contends that a monopolist of a tying product cannot increase the sales of a tied product without forgoing monopoly rent in the market for the tying product. Essentially, tying or bundling can redistribute monopoly rent but cannot expand it. Chicago School economists further argued that the primary objective of tying or bundling might be to enhance efficiency rather than to extend monopoly power.

Post-Chicago economists have sought to address Chicago School critiques through two main approaches: one involves developing theoretical models to demonstrate that there are industrial scenarios in which a monopolistic firm uses tying and bundling to expand its monopolistic power, and the other aims to explain the motives behind tying and bundling in terms of increasing profits and efficiencies, beyond just anticompetitive purposes. An influential work in the first category is by Whinston (1990). The core concept is that a monopolistic firm of one product may have the incentive to tie another product facing potential competition in order to exclude entrants through tying, especially when two conditions are satisfied: (a) there are separate demands for the tied product, and (b) the market for the tied product is oligopolistic with economies of scale arising from fixed entry costs. Under these circumstances, tying could deter other competitors from entering the tied product market, as they would not be able to achieve a scale of production that allows for profitable entry.

The *Microsoft* case spurred an interesting evolution in theoretical models that incorporated dynamic competition and identified the motivation behind tying and bundling as not only protecting a monopolistic position in the tying product market but also extending it into the tied product market. Notable contributions include Carlton and Waldman (2002), Choi and Stefanadis (2001), among others. A common thread among these models is that the two products are perfect complements, and there are potential entrants in both markets, mirroring the market dynamics observed in the Microsoft case. While the specifics of each model vary, a key conclusion is that an incumbent monopolist can use tying to delay early entrance

[45] There are two types of bundling: 'mixed' bundling, where the individual components are available for purchase separately, and 'pure' bundling, where only the combined package of multiple components can be purchased.

in one market and make sequential entry into another market more difficult and costly.

The concept of efficiency enhancement through tying and bundling has a long history. It is recognized that the usage of a consumable tied product (e.g., printer cartridge) can serve as a good indicator of consumer preference for a durable tying product (e.g., printer), making tying a viable method for second-degree price discrimination in the presence of imperfect information about consumer characteristics. Stigler (1968) presented a compelling finding that bundling could achieve the same effect as price discrimination. This concept was further developed by Adams and Yellen (1976), who posited that pure bundling could more effectively exploit consumer surplus by pooling consumers' varying willingness to pay, especially when consumer preferences for two products are negatively correlated. McAfee et al. (1989) expanded upon this result, showing its applicability even when the correlation of consumer preferences is not negative. Price discrimination in itself is not a violation of antitrust law. The reason is that firms with market power may adopt price discrimination as a strategy for profit maximization, and such discrimination can potentially expand the market, enhancing social welfare while also increasing profits.

There are several additional rationales for bundling. Firms may mandate that buyers of durable goods use their own replacement parts to ensure the products function correctly and to uphold their reputation. Additionally, bundling can serve as a strategy for circumventing price regulation on certain products. It can also lead to cost savings for both consumers and suppliers. Consumers benefit from reduced search costs when making package purchases, while suppliers can save on packaging and distribution costs through joint production and bundled sales. Bundling for these reasons is not associated with anticompetitive effects; instead, it contributes to efficiency enhancement.

A model by Amelio and Jullien (2012) stands out for providing a business rationale within the context of platform industries. Platform enterprises operating in a two-sided market often offer some products on one side for free. They may even consider subsidizing consumers by implementing negative pricing strategies, with the expectation of recouping these expenses through increased profits on the other side of the market. However, such subsidization efforts can be undermined by consumers' opportunistic behavior, such as accepting the subsidies without engaging in further consumption. In this scenario, bundling multiple products that hold value for consumers and setting appropriate prices can effectively lead to negative pricing for some products within the bundle. Amelio and Jullien demonstrated that such bundling strategies can enhance consumer surplus as well as the profits of a monopolistic platform. In a duopolistic setting, the outcomes can vary based on the magnitude of network effects and the nature of competition. Nonetheless, social welfare tends to increase as the network effect becomes more pronounced.

4.3.3 Predatory Pricing

Price predation has long been one of the most contentious topics among antitrust economists. It is commonly observed that dominant firms with monopolistic power may aggressively reduce prices to suppress weaker competitors or to expel them from the market. However, economists have found it challenging to rigorously justify a predatory pricing strategy aimed at excluding actual or potential competitors. Indeed, when assuming rational economic agents operating with perfect information, modeling predation in a coherent manner proves to be difficult.

For an incumbent dominant firm to engage in predatory pricing, it must sustain losses by setting prices below cost until the competitor is eliminated. These losses are expected to be recouped through subsequent monopoly pricing and profits. Given that the sales volume of the dominant firm exceeds that of the competitor, its losses will be proportionately larger as well. Even if below-cost pricing successfully ousts an existing competitor, potential competitors might be deterred from entering the market after observing the price hike to monopoly levels intended for recoupment. Furthermore, rational consumers, foreseeing higher monopoly prices following the competitor's exit, may forego the temporary benefits of lower prices during the predation period and choose to support the higher-priced competitor instead.[46]

When faced with an actual entrant, the predatory strategy of below-cost pricing by a dominant incumbent proves profitable only if it deters future potential entrants who are intimidated by the incumbent's aggressive stance. Otherwise, it would be more rational for the incumbent to accommodate the new entrant and share the market in an oligopolistic competition setting. Essentially, predation is only viable if entrants believe that the incumbent might indeed carry out the threat of predation in response to future entries. However, the assumption of rational economic agents, a cornerstone of game theory, suggests that entrants should not yield to the 'incredible' threat of predation, as acting on such a threat does not align with the incumbent's own interests.[47] This encapsulates the logical progression of arguments against predation that follow the Chicago School tradition.[48]

The traditional notion that an incumbent monopolist may engage in predatory behavior against early entrants to maintain a reputation for aggressiveness and deter future entries has persisted within the antitrust community. Selton (1978) subjected this reputation argument to game theory analysis. Imagine a monopolist facing a

[46]Certainly, consumers might exhibit myopic behavior or opportunistically free-ride on others' loyalty to a brand. Posner (2001, pp. 207–208) provided an insightful commentary on rational purchasing behavior from the buyer's perspective and its implications for the success of predatory strategies.

[47]This is the requirement of sequential rationality in game theory.

[48]Another argument, presented by McGee (1958), suggests that merger would present a less costly alternative to predation. However, this argument lacks practical relevance today, as mergers leading to monopoly are prohibited under antitrust law.

series of sequential entries across his N chain stores. Working backwards from the final N-th stage, the incumbent monopolist opts to accommodate rather than predate upon the N-th entrant. Given this, the incumbent has no incentive to predate upon the $(N - 1)$-th entrant, as the reputation gained would not be useful in deterring the subsequent N-th entrant. This logic extends forward to the first stage; knowing that predatory actions against the first entrant will not influence outcomes in the following $(N - 1)$ stages, the incumbent's optimal strategy is also to accommodate the first entrant. This outcome, known as Selten's "Chain Store Paradox," arises as a logical consequence of sequential rationality.

Since the 1980s, the emergence of new theoretical industrial organization has led to several attempts to resolve Selten's paradox and to account for predatory behavior with models that are theoretically consistent and feature sequentially rational equilibrium.[49] By introducing uncertainties regarding the incumbent's type—for example, an innate tendency toward predation ("craziness or insanity") or a cost advantage over entrants—predatory actions by the 'sane' or 'high-cost' incumbent in the early stages of finite-period entry games can be theoretically justified.[50] The rationale is to maintain a reputation for toughness or efficiency, thereby keeping later entrants wary of facing a tough type of incumbent. Thus, for the reputation-based theory of predation to be effective, there must be incompleteness and asymmetry of information, where entrants are unaware of the true nature of the incumbent's characteristics, while the incumbent has self-awareness.

A simpler way to explain predation involves introducing a different kind of asymmetry between the incumbent and entrants in terms of financial resources to withstand losses during predatory periods. This concept is known as the 'deep pocket' or 'long purse' theory, suggesting the incumbent possesses substantial financial resources that entrants lack.[51] Here, it is assumed that the capital market is incomplete, preventing entrants from securing the funds needed to survive the predatory period. Therefore, some form of incompleteness and asymmetry is a crucial element in theoretical models that seek to explain predation.

Despite its controversial nature, predation is considered practically significant by many antitrust experts and is now theoretically justified as leading to anticompetitive exclusion. However, most antitrust experts advocate for a cautious approach to addressing price predation, emphasizing the importance of price-cost and recoupment tests. This caution is due to the serious social costs associated with false positive regulation, which can stifle competition based on merit.

---

[49] Among them are Kreps and Wilson (1982) and Milgrom and Roberts (1982)

[50] In game theory, the uncertainty regarding a player's type is referred to as 'incomplete' information, which is distinct from 'imperfect' information that pertains to a lack of knowledge about another player's previous moves. It is important to note that a wide range of outcomes, including predation, can occur in the equilibria of 'infinitely' repeated games, even when perfect information is available. This phenomenon is widely recognized as the folk theorem.

[51] Motta (2004, pp. 433–441) offers a succinct discussion of several "deep pocket" models, ranging from simple to sophisticated.

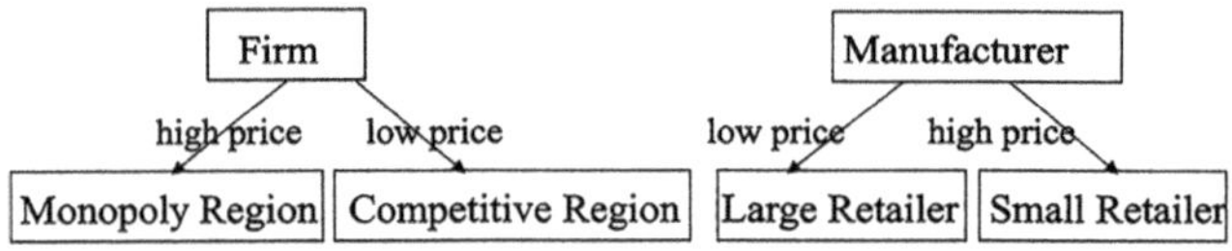

Fig. 4.3 Primary vs. secondary line injuries

4.3.4 Price Discrimination

Price discrimination can lead to two types of anticompetitive effects: primary-line injuries and secondary-line injuries.[52] Primary-line injuries refer to the harm caused to rival firms, while secondary-line injuries concern the harm inflicted on disfavored customers through discriminatory pricing practices. The KFTC Guidelines on unfair trade practices distinguish between these two by focusing on "the anticompetitiveness in the market where the undertaking operates" and "the anticompetitiveness in the market where the trading partner operates." The following figure provides examples of both types of injuries.

The left example in Fig. 4.3 illustrates primary-line injuries, where a firm adopts a strategy of charging high prices in regions where it holds a monopoly and low prices in competitive regions to undermine rivals. This approach, which merges price discrimination with predatory pricing, aims to eliminate competition from the market. This tactic was notably deemed unlawful in the historic case of Standard Oil in 1911.[53] The right example in Fig. 4.3 demonstrates secondary-line injuries, depicting a scenario where a manufacturer offers lower prices to a large retailer while charging a higher price to a small retailer. A pertinent case is the *Morton Salt* case of 1948, where the respondent engaged in quantity discount sales to wholesalers and retailers. The US FTC determined that the respondent had engaged in price discrimination among different purchasers of identical grades and qualities of products, contravening Section 2 of the Clayton Act as amended by the Robinson-Patman Act. The US Supreme Court affirmed the issuance of a cease-and-desist order against the respondent.[54]

Primary-line injuries are considered anticompetitive in a manner similar to predatory pricing. Conversely, secondary-line injuries have been a subject of debate, as they may not necessarily restrain competition but could still harm competitors. Numerous antitrust scholars have criticized the Robinson-Patman Act of 1936, which amended Section 2 of the Clayton Act to prohibit price discrimination, arguing that it was designed more to protect small businesses than to promote

[52] See Church and Ware (2000, pp. 177~178).

[53] *Standard Oil Co. of New Jersey v. United States*, 221 U.S. 1 (1911).

[54] *FTC v. Morton Salt Co.*, 334 U.S. 37 (1948).

economic efficiency.[55] However, price discrimination that results in secondary-line injuries becomes problematic when it amplifies anticompetitiveness, especially when combined with other abusive practices. For instance, in the 1911 *Standard Oil* case, it was reported that Standard Oil negotiated substantial discounts on rail fares for transporting its products and also secured rebates on the transportation fares of its competitors by threatening to build its own oil pipelines. This compelled railroad companies to engage in discriminatory pricing that resulted in secondary-line injuries, with Standard Oil benefitting from such price discrimination. When coupled with predatory pricing—a form of primary-line injury—these practices reinforced Standard Oil's monopoly by driving competitors out of the oil refining industry.

Price discrimination stands as a fascinating subject within industrial organization economics, exploring its various methods and impacts.[56] Theoretically, price discrimination (PD) is categorized into three types: first-degree (perfect), second-degree (menu pricing), and third-degree (group pricing). In first-degree PD, assuming perfect information about consumers' characteristics, a monopolistic firm is able to capture all consumer surplus by tailoring prices to each consumer's willingness to pay. Setting aside concerns of exploitativeness, first-degree PD unequivocally enhances efficiency by broadening the market and increasing the overall social surplus. Under conditions of imperfect information about consumer characteristics, firms may resort to second-degree PD, which involves offering a range of price-quantity options for consumers to select according to their preferences. This process enables consumers to self-select based on their preferences, a mechanism often referred to as 'self-selection'. This form of menu pricing is commonly seen in the mobile communication and data service sectors. The efficiency benefits of second-degree PD fundamentally mirror those of first-degree PD, albeit to a lesser degree with respect to market expansion. Consequently, exclusionary effects are not typically associated with either first-degree or second-degree PD.

Contrary to first and second-degree price discrimination (PD), third-degree PD does not invariably lead to market expansion and thus may not always enhance efficiency. Moreover, it can result in anticompetitive effects, including primary-line and secondary-line injuries, as depicted in Fig. 4.3. Third-degree PD involves segmenting markets based on observable characteristics of markets or customers, such as region, size, period, age, gender, etc. The examples provided in Fig. 4.3 demonstrate price differentiation based on region and size, which could potentially have exclusionary effects. Nevertheless, it's important to note that third-degree PD can also lead to efficiency-enhancing effects through market expansion. For instance, a bookseller might not cater to markets in low-income countries at a uniform price. However, by practicing price discrimination based on countries, the bookseller can make the market in low-income countries accessible by setting lower prices, while maintaining higher prices in high-income countries. This

[55] Viscusi et al. (2000, pp. 284~292).

[56] See Pepall et al. (2014).

differentiation in third-degree PD from first and second-degree PDs lies in its potential to not always result in market expansion, a characteristic inherent to the latter. Therefore, when evaluating the practices of third-degree PD, it is crucial to carefully weigh its anticompetitive effects against its efficiency-enhancing impacts.

4.3.5 *Refusal to Supply*

The antitrust regulation concerning 'refusal to supply' traces its origins back to the 1912 *Terminal Railroad Association* case in the United States, where the Supreme Court deemed it a violation of antitrust laws to deny a competitor access to a facility essential for market entry or competition.[57] The 'essential facility doctrine' was further elucidated in the 1983 *MCI* case. In this case, the US Appeals Court found it unlawful for the local telecommunications monopolist AT&T to refuse interconnection of its local network to competing long-distance carriers like MCI. The court outlined necessary conditions for a refusal to deal to constitute a violation of Section 2 of the Sherman Act: (1) control of the essential facility by a monopolist; (2) a competitor's inability, in practical or reasonable terms, to duplicate the essential facility; (3) the denial of the facility's use to a competitor; and (4) the feasibility of providing the facility.[58] However, these conditions have proven to be stringent and controversial, making the doctrine challenging to apply in subsequent cases.

The critique from the Chicago School also played a significant role in discussions on the refusal to supply. The underlying logic is akin to the 'One Monopoly Rent Theory' applied to tying and bundling scenarios.[59] Consider a situation where an incumbent monopolist in the upstream input market operates an affiliate and faces a potential or actual competitor in the downstream market, which is at least as efficient as its own affiliate. By refusing to supply the input to the downstream competitor, the upstream monopolist could seemingly extend its monopoly power into the downstream market. However, according to the Chicago School critique, the upstream monopolist lacks the incentive to engage in such behavior. Instead, the monopolist could achieve greater benefits by entering into a contract with the downstream competitor that includes: (a) supplying the more efficient competitor with the necessary inputs (effectively sidelining the downstream affiliate), and (b) capturing all the rents from the competitor through a lump-sum payment for the input supply. This arrangement, effectively substituting the affiliate with a more efficient rival, would result in increased profits for the incumbent.

The Chicago School's critique regarding the incentive for refusal to supply has elicited numerous counterarguments. First, vertically integrated firms that supply

[57] *U.S. v. Terminal R.R. Ass'n*, 224 U.S. 383 (1912).

[58] *MCI Communications v AT&T*, 708 F.2d 1081 (1983).

[59] I referred to Fumaglli et al. (2018, pp. 470~490) for an exploration of the Chicago school critique and the subsequent counterarguments.

inputs of an essential nature are often subject to sector-specific regulation in network services such as telecommunications, gas, electricity, and the Internet. Integrated dominant entities may only charge input prices or access fees to their downstream competitors with regulatory agency approval. Thus, the constraints imposed by sector-specific regulation prevent the incumbent from extracting the full monopoly rents from the downstream competitor, making refusal to supply a more attractive strategy. Second, it is challenging for the incumbent to credibly commit to not competing with the rival by sidelining its affiliate in the downstream market. Consequently, the rival may be reluctant to pay the full rent, wary of the incumbent's potential for opportunistic behavior and the likelihood of ensuing competition.

Third, consider a scenario where a vertically integrated firm competes with rivals in both the upstream and downstream markets. In such cases, the incumbent may be incentivized not to supply the input to the downstream competitor as a strategy to "raise rivals' costs." If the incumbent withholds the input supply, the downstream competitor would have to seek the input from an upstream rival, potentially increasing the upstream rival's market power and leading to higher input prices for the downstream competitor. This scenario allows the vertically integrated incumbent to benefit from increasing the costs incurred by its rivals. Lastly, by introducing a dynamic structure into the competition both downstream and upstream, we can apply the dynamic leverage theory, which Carlton and Waldman (2002) developed in the context of Microsoft's tying practices, to the refusal to supply. Imagine that entering the downstream market in period 1 is essential for (or facilitates) entry into the upstream market in period 2. By refusing to supply the input to the downstream competitor, the incumbent could safeguard its monopolistic position in the upstream market, leveraging its control over input supply to influence competitive dynamics across both markets.

Many antitrust experts advocate for a cautious approach toward the refusal to supply. Various justifications for refusal include stock shortages, limited capacity, concerns over quality degradation, and reputation considerations. Additionally, refusal to supply can serve as a tool to enforce vertical restraints, such as resale price maintenance and exclusive territories, which have previously been explained to have efficiency effects. Beyond the efficiencies directly associated with refusal to supply, there are significant concerns regarding the dynamic inefficiencies that could arise from intervening in the practice of trade refusal. Specifically, such regulatory intervention could dampen firms' incentives to innovate or invest in the related market. This is because it might encourage other parties to free ride on the technologies or infrastructure developed by the investing firm, thereby having a chilling effect on the overall dynamism and competitive vigor of the market.

4.3.6 *Frame of Market Foreclosure*

Most exclusionary abuses, aside from price-based strategies like predation and discrimination, can be categorized under market foreclosure. The figures below

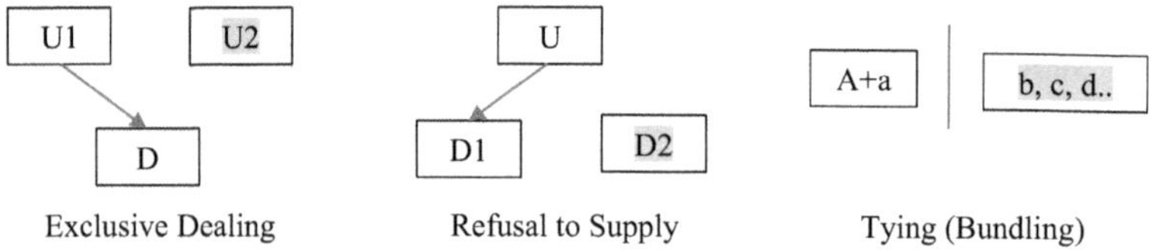

Fig. 4.4 Framework of market foreclusure

illustrate how exclusive dealing, refusal to supply, and tying (as well as bundling) act to foreclose competitors from the relevant market.

Exclusive dealing, depicted on the left, illustrates a vertical foreclosure of upstream competitors, whereas the refusal to supply, shown in the middle, demonstrates a vertical foreclosure of downstream competitors. Conversely, tying (or bundling), represented on the right, constitutes a form of horizontal foreclosure in the market for complementary products.

Generally, the anticompetitive effects of exclusionary abuses can be analyzed in terms of Raising Rivals' Costs (RRC). All the foreclosing conducts illustrated in Fig. 4.4 increase the costs for competitors (U2, D2, and b, c, d) in selling their products, securing necessary inputs, and bundling their offerings with main products. RRC, to some extent, causes harm to competitors. However, not all RRC actions fall under the abuse of dominance according to antitrust laws. For antitrust liability to be established, the impact must extend beyond harm to individual competitors to affect market competition as a whole. This is only considered plausible when the entity involved, such as D, U, and A, holds a dominant position in the relevant market.

Price-based exclusion can also be explained using the RRC framework. A firm with monopsony power might compel a seller to offer significant discounts to itself, thereby gaining a competitive edge over rivals. This constitutes the secondary-line injury of price discrimination. In the case of *Standard Oil*, it is reported that Rockefeller explicitly secured rebates on competitors' fares for railroad oil transportation, representing an extreme form of RRC. Conditional rebates or loyalty rebates, often linked with exclusive dealing contracts, are considered forms of price-based exclusionary conduct. Their impact, which I will discuss later in the context of the Intel case, involves lowering the 'effective' price that a competitor must offer to break the loyalty condition to a level akin to dumping. This is categorized as RRC in terms of opportunity cost.

Various tactics fall under the umbrella of RRC: some may appear neutral but can become anticompetitive when applied excessively, some are ambiguous in their competitive impact, and others are overtly and straightforwardly anticompetitive. An incumbent with significant financial resources might escalate marketing and R&D expenditures to increase the costs for financially weaker competitors. As noted by Williamson (1968), the 1965 *Pennington* case involved a dominant firm in the coal-mining industry with capital-intensive technology increasing workers' wages to raise labor costs for labor-intensive competitors.[60] Another strategy involves lobbying for government regulations that impose stricter safety standards, which are less costly for the lobbying firm to comply with than for its competitors. Some RRC strategies are quite clear in their anticompetitive nature. For instance, in the *Qualcomm I* case, which I will explore as an example of dominance abuse, Qualcomm charged handset manufacturers discriminatory royalties for licensing its CDMA technologies based on whether they used its own modem chips. The *Qualcomm II* case presents a subtler scenario—Qualcomm imposed what has been referred to as the "Qualcomm tax" on mobile handset OEMs, amounting to about 5% of the handset value, irrespective of the modem chips used. The KFTC and the US FTC have argued that this tactic ultimately led to increased costs for Qualcomm's modem chip competitors.

The analytical framework for RRC was proposed by Salop and Sheffman (1983, 1987) and further developed into a principal tool for antitrust analysis through the works of Kranttenmaker and Salop (1986), Scheffman (1992), and others. They identified the prerequisites for RRC tactics to exert an anticompetitive effect leading to market foreclosure: (1) dominance in the main market; (2) potential for foreclosure and actual extension of dominance into a subsidiary market; (3) low elasticities of demand in the relevant markets;[61] (4) absence of countervailing efficiencies; and (5) maturity of the relevant markets. Absent any of these necessary conditions, RRC strategies would not necessarily raise concerns about diminishing competition and reducing consumer welfare.

The KFTC 2021 Guidelines advise considering both foreclosure and Raising Rivals' Costs (RRC) when assessing the impact of market dominance abuse on competition restraint. They note that foreclosure and RRC, by diminishing the number of effective competitors and curbing competitive pressure on a dominant enterprise, can lead to anticompetitive effects such as price increases or output reductions, constraints on the diversity of goods and services, and detrimental impacts on innovation. In assessing the extent of the foreclosure effect, factors such as the degree of access denial or difficulty a competitor faces due to the conduct in question, the significance of the foreclosure effect on the growth and new entry of actual and potential competitors, trends in market share changes, and the reputational impact in dealings with other enterprises are thoroughly evaluated. When evaluating the RRC effect, the focus is primarily on whether the conduct in question obstructs a competitor from accessing efficient distribution and supply channels, hinders the acquisition of adequate resources for production and distribution, or creates artificial entry barriers. The evaluation also considers whether overcoming such obstacles would incur significant costs and time.

---

[60] *United Mine Workers v. Pennington*, 381 U.S. 657 (1965).

[61] This condition is necessary to ensure that a price increase does not lead to a reduction in profits.

4.4 Cases of Regulation on Market Dominance Abuses in Korea

In this section, I will examine several cases of dominance abuse that are significant in terms of legal precedents, economic analyses, and international comparisons. I will detail the main decisions made by the KFTC and the courts, discuss the related economic issues, and, where possible, compare these cases with similar instances in other countries.

4.4.1 Posco *(2001): Refusal of Trade*[62]

In 2001, the KFTC ruled that Posco, the dominant firm in the hot rolled coil market, had obstructed a competitor's business by refusing to supply hot rolled coils to Hysco.[63] Hot rolled coils are an essential input for producing cold rolled steels. However, in 2007, the Supreme Court overturned and remanded the appellate court decision that had supported the KFTC's stance.[64] This en banc decision became a landmark precedent for subsequent cases by establishing the standard for evaluating exclusionary abuses of market dominance and distinguishing it from the standard for evaluating unfair trade practices that restrain competition.

Posco operates as an integrated mill, encompassing all stages of iron making and rolling, whereas Hysco, an affiliate of Hyundai Motor Group, is solely a rolling enterprise without blast or electric furnace facilities. The KFTC and the Seoul High Court, which hears appeals on KFTC decisions, identified the relevant market as the production of hot rolled coils in Korea and recognized Posco's market dominance, with a 79.8% supply share of hot rolled coils in Korea as of 2000. According to their rulings, Posco refused to supply hot rolled coils—an essential input—to Hysco, a new entrant in the downstream market of cold rolled steels. This action, leveraging its dominance in the hot rolled coils market, was seen as obstructing a competitor's business operations and an attempt to maintain its own dominance. It was argued that such conduct not only harmed competition and consumer welfare but also constituted an unfair abuse of market dominance. This abuse lessened competition by imposing increased costs and disadvantageous conditions on Hysco for importing hot rolled coils, as well as trade instability to the extent that it hindered Hysco's function as an effective competitor in the relevant market.

---

[62]The year mentioned corresponds to when the KFTC issued its decision on the case. This notation will be consistently applied in the subsequent cases.

[63]KFTC 2001-068, April 12, 2001.

[64]Seoul High Court 2001nu5370, August 27, 2002, and Supreme Court 2002du6826, November 22, 2007. The decision was made by a majority of ten Supreme Court Judges, with three Judges expressing dissenting opinions.

The Supreme Court acknowledged the relevant market as cold-rolled steels in Korea and Posco's dominant position therein, in line with the decisions by the KFTC and the Appellate Court. However, it overturned their judgment on the unfairness of trade refusal by introducing the 'Posco standard', which outlines *subjective* and *objective* requirements for proving abuses of market dominance. The Court clarified that "the assessment of trade refusal as an abuse by a market-dominant entity under §3-2 (§5 in the revised version) 1(3) of the MRFTA must align with the law's purpose to 'promote competition in monopolistic and oligopolistic markets'. Therefore, the mere harm to a specific entity is insufficient for deeming an action unfair. Unfairness is recognized when, among other factors, the market-dominant entity's refusal to trade is intended to maintain or strengthen its market monopoly, thereby artificially disrupting market order by limiting free competition [*subjective requirement*]. Additionally, the action must objectively have the potential to restrain competition [*objective requirement*]." (Parentheses are added for clarification.)

The Supreme Court, while considering the market circumstances both prior to and subsequent to the alleged act of trade refusal, determined that the disadvantages reported by Hysco due to this act, as suggested by the KFTC and the appellate court, "were not significant enough to be deemed as raising concerns of competition restraint at the time of the trade refusal." More specifically, the Court justified its decision by stating: "Based on the evidence presented to the appellate court, despite the trade refusal by Posco [the plaintiff], Hysco [the intervenor] continued to produce and sell cold-rolled steels by importing the necessary hot rolled coils from Japan. After completing its cold-rolled steel plant in 2001 and commencing normal operations, Hysco not only generated net profits but also maintained its business activities as a producer and seller of cold-rolled steels in a standard manner."

Jeon and Lee (2005) presented an expert witness report to the Supreme Court on behalf of Posco, addressing the geographic market pertinent to this case. Utilizing methodologies such as critical loss analysis and time series analyses, including price correlation and the Granger Causality test as discussed in Sect. 4.3, they concluded that the relevant geographic market should encompass East Asian countries, namely, Japan, China, and Russia.[65] The Supreme Court, however, did not agree with this definition of the geographic market as proposed in the expert witness report. Nonetheless, in its assessment of the unfairness of the disputed conduct in terms of market competition harm, the Court noted that Hysco encountered no issues in substituting its purchases to Japan and in generating profits from its normal business operations. This observation suggests that Japanese steel manufacturers and Posco were effectively in competition, indicating that East Asia, including Japan, could be considered within the relevant geographic market.

It can be contended that the Supreme Court's evaluation of unfairness is not aligned with its definition of the geographic market as limited to domestic

[65]For the estimation of demands and actual losses, they employed the Deaton and Muellbauer (1980)'s Almost Ideal Demand System (AIDS) model. For detailed analyses, refer to Jeon (2020, Chap. 5).

boundaries. Specifically, while the Court determined that Posco's refusal to trade did not raise concerns of anticompetitive effects due to the possibility of substituting purchases with imports from Japan, it simultaneously restricted the geographic market to the domestic sphere. This restriction could imply that overseas steel manufacturers, including those from Japan, were not considered actual competitors to Posco. Consequently, the Supreme Court might have needed to reassess Posco's dominance in the market across East Asian countries before evaluating the unfairness of the conduct in question. Despite this reflection, the significance of the *Posco* decision in establishing the standards for assessing the unfairness of market dominance actions—based on their harmful effects on market-level competition, distinct from the less stringent standards for unfair trade practices focused on harm to competitors—cannot be overstated.

4.4.2 Microsoft *(2006): Tying*

The Microsoft case of tying is widely regarded as one of the most high-profile antitrust cases of the twenty-first century, both internationally and in Korea. In 2006, the KFTC found Microsoft guilty under MRFTA §3-2 for abusing its dominant position by interfering with competitors' businesses and under §23 for engaging in unfair business practices by coercively (a) tying Windows Media Services (WMS) to its Windows server operating system (OS); (b) Windows Media Player (WMP); and (c) its messenger programs to the Windows PC OS. The KFTC ordered various remedies to rectify these illegal conducts and imposed penalty surcharges totaling approximately KR₩35 billion.[66] The KFTC's corrective measures targeted all cited issues, requiring Microsoft to offer the WMS program separately from the Windows server OS, provide versions of WMP and its messenger that are both separated and integrated from the Windows PC OS, with the stipulation that it operates an online media/messenger center where PC users can download competitors' products. Microsoft appealed the KFTC decision immediately, but the lawsuit concluded with Microsoft withdrawing its appeal just before the Seoul High Court was set to issue its judgment on October 10, 2007, thus ending the case without a court ruling.

The KFTC charged that Microsoft held a dominant market position in the 'domestic PC server OS' and 'worldwide Intel-compatible PC OS markets (primary markets), and used this dominance to extend its influence into the 'domestic' markets of 'media server programming', 'streaming media player', and 'personal messenger' (subsidiary markets), thereby reinforcing its dominance in the primary markets. The main arguments against Microsoft's practices echoed those in related Microsoft

---

[66]KFTC 2006-042, February 24, 2006. The KFTC's investigation into issue (c) was initiated following a complaint from Daum Communications in 2001. The investigations into issues (a) and (b) commenced on the KFTC's own initiative, while RealNetworks filed a complaint regarding the same matters in 2004.

cases in the United States and the EU, focusing on issues such as the distinctiveness of the tying and tied products, the 'ubiquity' of Microsoft's application software, the network and 'tipping' effects in the subsidiary markets, and the 'applications barrier to entry' in the primary markets. By reinforcing these phenomena, Microsoft's tying practices could undermine its competitors in the subsidiary markets while maintaining or enhancing its market power in the primary markets.

The antitrust history of Microsoft in the United States spans over a decade and unfolds across four distinct stages.[67] The initial phase commenced with the FTC investigating Microsoft's exclusionary licensing practices, including the 'per processor' contracts,[68] in 1990. This phase concluded in 1993 when the Commission reached a deadlock with a 2-2 vote. Following this, the DOJ initiated the second stage of investigation, culminating in a consent decree with Microsoft, which an appellate court approved in 1995.[69] The third stage began in 1997 when the DOJ filed a lawsuit alleging Microsoft had violated the consent decree's provisions regarding the bundling or integrating of products. Judge Jackson mandated that Microsoft should offer its Windows 95 operating system and Internet Explorer as separate products. However, this order was overturned by an appeals court, which ruled that Windows 95 and IE provided computer users with functionalities that were not available through separate programs in 1988.[70]

In the final (fourth) stage of the litigation, the US DOJ, 20 states, and the District of Columbia filed a lawsuit against Microsoft, accusing the company of monopolizing the personal computer operating systems (PC OSs) and browser markets through exclusionary and predatory practices, including the tying of Internet Explorer (IE) to the operating system in 1998. Judge Jackson ruled that Microsoft had violated the Sherman Act and approved the government's proposed remedies in 2000. These remedies included conduct restrictions to limit various exclusive contracts and a structural breakup of Microsoft into two separate entities: one for OS and another for applications. Although the appellate court upheld the monopolization claim, it reversed other district court findings and, expressing reservations about the proposed structural breakup, remanded the case back to the district court to identify a suitable remedy in 2001. Subsequently, in 2002, the DOJ and Microsoft reached a settlement agreement.[71] The focus in the last stage of the Microsoft case centered on the company's efforts to protect and maintain its operating system monopoly. "MS

[67] I referred to Gilbert (1999), Gibert and Katz (2001) and Rubinfeld (2014) for the history of battles between US antitrust agencies and MS, the court rulings, and the debates surrounding the economic issues involved.

[68] Under the 'per-processor' contract, OEMs paid Microsoft licensing fees for the Windows PC OS, not for each copy of MS OS software, but for each computer system sold that utilized an Intel microprocessor, regardless of whether the system was sold with Microsoft OS software installed.

[69] *U.S. v. Microsoft*, 1995-2 Trade Cases para. 71 (D.D.C. 1995).

[70] *U.S. v. Microsoft*, Court of Appeals for the District of Columbia Circuit, No. 97-5343, June 23, 1988.

[71] *U.S. v. Microsoft*, 253 F.3d 34 (D.C. Cir., 2001) (*en banc*). *US v. MS*, 231 F. Supp. 2e 1443d 34 (D.D.C. 2002).

and the government considered Internet browsers combined with the Java language and server-based applications to be particularly pontent sources of potential competition to Windows. ... Java did this by providing a "middle ware" layer of software between applications programs and the underlying OS system. Natscape was a threat to MS because its Navigator browser was a distribution vehicle for Java that could further its acceptance as a language for application programs that was independent of the underlying OS."[72] Thus, the expansion of the Navigator browser could potentially weaken Microsoft's monopoly power by circumventing the 'applications barrier to entry' into the PC OS market.

Following an exhaustive investigation initiated by a complaint from Sun Microsystems in 1998, the European Commission determined that Microsoft's practices of bundling its personal computer operating system (PC OS) with Windows Media Player (WMP) and failing to disclose workgroup server information constituted an abuse of a dominant position under Article 82 of the Treaty establishing the European Community (TEC). Consequently, in 2004, the Commission imposed a record fine of €497 million. As part of the behavioral remedies, the Commission required Microsoft to unbundle its PC OS from WMP and to disclose server interface documentation, enabling non-Microsoft workgroup servers to achieve full interoperability with Windows PCs and servers.[73] The Court of First Instance upheld the Commission's decision in 2007, and Microsoft opted not to pursue any further appeals. Notably, the Commission's argument for foreclosure in the server case highlighted the critical role of interoperability between PC server OS and application programs in overcoming the applications barrier to entry into the PC OS market, drawing a parallel to the role of Internet browsers in conjunction with the Java programming language. The argument was that "increasing numbers of applications could be delivered through servers and the need for a sophisticated and expensive OS on the PC client would erode. ... a server operating system could even more credibly expose a rich set of APIs to application program developers than Netscape in conjunction with Java."[74]

The KFTC's 2006 decision in the Microsoft case drew on precedents set in the United States and the EU. However, the case also introduced novel aspects, such as the tying of Windows Media Services (WMS) to the Windows server operating system (OS) and the bundling of its messenger programs with the Windows PC OS. More significantly, the extensive investigation period and the extraordinary seven rounds of commission hearings that debated various issues between July 13 and October 26, 2005, provided a crucial impetus for the KFTC to elevate its capability in assessing abuse of market dominance cases to a global standard. The experience gained from the Microsoft case significantly bolstered the KFTC's competence and confidence, enabling it to independently tackle major cases involving multinational corporations, such as *Intel* (2008), *Qualcomm I* (2009), and

[72] The quotation is from Gibert and Katz (2001, p. 27).

[73] See Kuhn and Van Reenen (2009) for the *Microsoft* case in the EU.

[74] The quotation is from Kuhn and Van Reenen (2009, p. 62).

Qualcomm II (2017), beyond the scope of antitrust enforcement actions in other countries.

4.4.3 NHN [Naver] *(2008): Restriction of Advertisements in Online Video Contents*

In 2008, the KFTC found NHN (now known as Naver) in violation of the MRFTA §3-2(1), for abusing its dominant position by interfering with competitors' businesses.[75] This interference involved imposing disadvantageous deals on video-streaming content providers on the Internet, for which NHN was subjected to corrective orders and surcharges. The KFTC alleged that NHN held a dominant position in the domestic market for Internet portal service users and exploited this position to undermine competition in the online advertising and video content markets. This was achieved by enforcing a restrictive trade condition on video content providers (CPs), such as Pandora TV, dictating that they could not feature advertisements in their video content services displayed in NHN's search results without NHN's consent, during the period from April 2006 to March 2007. The Seoul High Court, in 2009, rejected the KFTC's decision, challenging the entirety of its reasoning, including the definition of the relevant market, the method of evaluating market dominance, and the unfairness of the conduct in question.[76] Subsequently, the Supreme Court, in 2014, upheld the appellate court's judgment, agreeing with its conclusions.[77]

The KFTC delineated the relevant product market as the user side of Internet portal services, offering Internet users a bundled service encompassing 1S (Internet search) and 4C (Communication, including email and messenger; Community, such as online cafés and blogs; electronic Commerce; and Content, including news, entertainment, and information). The KFTC excluded entities that provided only components of the 1S-4C bundle from being considered market participants. As of the end of 2006, the top three firms held market shares of 48.5% (Naver), 16.7% (Daum), and 15.6% (SK Communications) in terms of 'sales'.[78] The cumulative market share exceeded 75%, leading to the presumption that Naver occupied a dominant market position. The KFTC (2008, p. 21) straightforwardly posited that the concerned prohibition on advertising could impede the growth of video content

[75] KFTC 2008-251, August 28, 2008. This decision addressed the issue of NHN unfairly subsidizing its affiliate under §23 (1) 7). But I will focus only on the abuse of dominance aspect of the case.

[76] Seoul High Court 2008nu27102, October 8, 2009.

[77] Supreme Court 2009du20366, November 13, 2014.

[78] The KFTC clearly dismissed the use of UV (unique visitors) or ADT (average duration time) as metrics for measuring market shares, citing their variability depending on the method of aggregation, as well as differing times and periods.

providers in the video content service market and sustain and amplify NHN's dominance in the online advertising market.

Jeon and You (2008) argued that in cases involving abuse of dominance, the analysis should begin with "the specific business related to the concerned conduct" and then assess the extent to which the market could be expanded.[79] They proposed that the appropriate relevant markets in this instance are the "video content link service" market, where market dominance should be assessed, and the "video content provision service" market, which could be affected by the abusive conduct in terms of anticompetitive effects. Video content link services are offered by both Internet portals or general search service providers, like Naver, and specialized vertical search providers, such as Pandora TV. As of March 2008, Naver's market share, based on 'page views' in the video content link service market, was less than 10%, which is too small for NHN (Naver) to be considered dominant in the relevant market. Furthermore, during the period of the concerned conduct, Pandora TV held a significant market share in the video content provision market, with 34.2% of page views, indicating its substantial presence.

The Supreme Court's opinion aligned closely with the arguments presented by the defendant, highlighting the necessity to assess whether NHN held a dominant position and misused it within the specific market for intermediating between its users and video content providers, rather than in the broader Internet portal services market. It was deemed inappropriate to determine market power based on the total sales of Internet portals for the purposes of this particular market. Furthermore, while NHN's actions in restricting advertisements might harm video content providers, they do not result in the anticompetitive effects required for a finding of dominance abuse, as established by the *Posco* decision in 2007. Notably, the Court's refusal to endorse the KFTC's market definition in this instance is significant, given the courts' usual deference to the KFTC's expertise in defining markets, which often involves technical considerations.

4.4.4 Intel *(2008): Conditional Rebates*

Intel offered rebates to PC Original Equipment Manufacturers (OEMs) such as Samsung Electronics and Sambo Computer, contingent upon them either not purchasing Central Processing Units (CPUs) from its competitor AMD or procuring more than a specified proportion of their CPU needs from Intel. These conditions applied to Samsung from the third quarter of 2002 to the second quarter of 2005, and to Sambo from the fourth quarter of 2003 to the second quarter of 2005. In 2008, the KFTC issued a cease-and-desist order against Intel. This order forbade Intel from

[79]The definition of Internet portal services and the 1S-4C bundle appears to stem from an *ex ante* and comprehensive approach, likely more suitable for merger evaluations. Conversely, an *ex post* and specific approach might be more pertinent when assessing abuses of market dominance.

offering such exclusionary conditional rebates and from obstructing AMD's efforts to launch new products, and imposed a fine of KR₩26 billion.[80] Intel promptly appealed the decision to the Seoul High Court, which upheld the KFTC's ruling.[81] Intel chose not to pursue further appeals to the Supreme Court, thereby concluding the case. The litigation intensely debated the 'effective price-cost test' for an 'as efficient' competitor, a methodology recommended by the EC for evaluating conditional rebates. This dispute between the defendant and the KFTC centered around the application of this test to assess the legality of Intel's rebate practices.[82]

Conditional rebates are payments made *ex post for all units* purchased on the condition that a customer acquires more than a specified threshold or a required proportion of their total purchases from a supplier within a certain time frame. Due to their retrospective nature, these rebates are also known as retroactive rebates, or loyalty rebates, reflecting their role in encouraging customers to meet the stipulated purchase requirements. Given their potential to exclude competition when employed by a dominant firm, EC (2005) proposed a methodology in its Discussion Paper for assessing their exclusionary impact. This test is more rigorous than the safe harbor criteria applied to traditional predatory pricing analyses. Subsequent revisions by OECD (2008) and further elaborations in EC (2008)'s Guidance Paper retained the core principles of the 2005 EC proposal. The test involves an 'effective' price-cost comparison for a hypothetical 'as efficient competitor' (AEC), aimed at determining whether such a competitor could compete effectively under the conditions imposed by the dominant firm's rebate scheme. This approach underscores the heightened scrutiny applied to the examination of conditional rebates and their potential to undermine competitive market dynamics.

where

P = Average price of a dominant firm[83]

P_E = Effective price of a competitor (a competitor's unit price of selling the commercially viable share to a customer in match with a dominant firm's conditional rebates)

ΔR = Dominant firm's conditional rebates with exclusionary purpose (the difference. between total rebates and default rebates provided unconditionally regardless of exclusive conditions)[84]

Q_D = Total demands of a customer

---

[80] KFTC 2008-295, November 5, 2008.

[81] Seoul High Court 2008nu35462, Jume 19, 2013.

[82] In the case involving Intel and the KFTC, a notable disagreement was about the definition of the relevant geographic market. The KFTC defined it as 'domestic direct OEM sales', whereas Intel argued for a broader scope, including 'all worldwide sales, both direct and indirect'. However, the primary focus here is on the effective price-cost safe harbor test, which is a key aspect in evaluating Intel's pricing strategies.

[83] P does not apply conditional rebates that are contingent upon exclusivity condition, but does account for default rebates awarded irrespective of fulfilling any exclusivity criteria.

[84] Total rebates consist of those awarded upon meeting specific exclusivity conditions and those granted unconditionally by default.

Table 4.6 AEC effective price–cost test

Conditional rebates are considered within the safe harbor, indicating no possibility of exclusionary effects if $P_E = P - \frac{\Delta R}{Q_D CVS} \geq$ Average Cost of a Dominant Firm

CVS = Commercially viable share of a competitor for the customer (that a competitor could. achieve if it is allowed to contest with the dominant firm without exclusive abuses)[85]

The EC's safe harbor test involves comparing the effective price P_E with the average cost of the sales relevant to the alleged abuse by the dominant firm denoted by Q_D CVS. If the effective price exceeds the properly measured average cost (AC), a competitor that is (a) as efficient as the dominant firm and (b) willing to match competition, can set its price below the effective price and still maintain a commercially viable share. Thus, if a competitor fails to secure a commercially viable share (CVS) under these conditions, it may be due to one of two reasons: either the competitor is less efficient than the dominant firm, or it chose not to match the dominant firm's rebates. In essence, the loss of a commercially viable share by the competitor is not attributed to the exclusionary potential of conditional rebates but rather to merit-based price competition between the two firms. It is important to reiterate that the As Efficient Competitor (AEC) test has been recognized globally as a standard for assessing the aggressive pricing policies of dominant entities in competition policy.[86]

The KFTC's position on the safe harbor test for conditional rebates, as illustrated in Table 4.6, appears ambiguous. The KFTC attempted to demonstrate that Intel's rebates could potentially exclude its competitor by applying the AEC test, while also noting that conducting such an analysis is not essential for establishing the unfairness or illegality of Intel's conditional rebates. In evaluating the conditional rebates for Samsung, the KFTC posited that AMD's commercially viable share (CVS) was 3% and that Intel's default rebates, provided to AMD unconditionally, were 1.15%. This assumption was based on an incident where Intel's rebates for Samsung were reduced to 1.15% of its total purchases from AMD, following Samsung's decision to procure 3% of its total CPU demands from AMD in the first quarter of 2002. Consequently, the KFTC argued that the effective price became negative.

That is, the reduction in rebates that Samsung had to accept for not meeting the exclusivity condition can be represented by $\Delta R = R - (T - 0.03P\,Q_D) \times 0.0115$ (R = actual rebates during the relevant period, T = actual total purchase amount in that period). Employing the notation in Table 4.6, the KFTC's analysis amounts to:

[85] EC (2008) guidance paper refers to it as "the relevant sale."

[86] In the United States., since the 1993 *Brook Group* case (*Brooke Group Ltd. vs. Brown & Williamson Tobacco Corp.*, 509 U.S. 209), a price is considered predatory if it falls below an appropriate measure of the defendant's (dominant firm's) cost. EC (2008) and OECD (2008) confirmed the AEC test which stipulates that dominant firm's own costs should serve as the benchmark for this assessment.

$$P_E = P - \frac{R - (T - 0.03PQ_D) \times 0.0115}{0.0115Q_D} < 0 \qquad (4.11)$$

This implies that even if AMD offered its products to Samsung at no cost, it would still be unable to compete with Intel.

On the contrary, Jeon (2007, 2008) argued that AMD's CVS for Samsung could be as high as 12.9%, based on the observation that Samsung, after starting to use AMD CPU in the first quarter of 2002, increased its purchases from AMD to 12.9% in the second quarter of the same year.[87] This increase to 12.9% effectively 'revealed' the CVS (commercially viable share) or the MSS (market segment share) at which Samsung was not dependent on Intel for its CPU supply, allowing AMD to effectively compete with Intel. Jeon suggested that the CVS must be at least 9.3%, reflecting the average competitive conditions in 2002 since Q1 2002—3% in Q1, 12.9% in Q2 and 12.0% in Q3, with an average of 9.3%. By substituting 12.9% or 9.3% for 3% as CVS in Eq. (4.11), then P_E exceeds the appropriate measure of AC.[88]

Another aspect of concern in this case involved Intel's conditional rebates to Sambo Computer, which were contingent upon Sambo not using AMD CPUs for PCs sold through the home shopping channel and maintaining partial exclusivity (70%) for PCs sold domestically. The KFTC did not apply the safe harbor test of the AEC effective price-cost analysis for Sambo, as it had done in the case of Samsung. The conditions attached to Intel's rebates for Sambo were not as stringent as those for Samsung, and the partial exclusivity requirement was not binding in practice. Consequently, it can be deduced that these rebates are 'safe' with respect to the potential for excluding AMD. Jeon (2007, 2008) attempted to apply the test under very conservative assumptions and concluded that the rebates were incapable of excluding the competitor.

The Intel case was not unique to the KFTC. Competition authorities in Japan, the United States and the EU had been investigating Intel's conditional rebates following complaints from AMD since around 2000, and they rendered decisions regarding the illegality or required remedies of Intel's practices. The Japan Fair Trade Commission (JFTC) made an early decision in 2005. It recommended that Intel should stop providing rebates to PC Original Equipment Manufacturers (OEMs) contingent upon them exclusively using Intel CPUs or installing them in more than 90% of their Market Segment Share (MSS) or a specified amount. JFTC (2005) cited the reduction in the domestic market share of AMD and Transmeta from 24% in 2003 to 11% in 2004 as evidence of the anticompetitive effect of Intel's practices, without

[87] Jeon (2007, 2008) provided an expert witness report to the KFTC on behalf of Intel. In response, the KFTC 2008 decision scrutinized Jeon's analyses for potential flaws.

[88] The KFTC and the defendant showed a disagreement regarding the proper measure of AC—the former preferred to ATC, the latter to AVC. However, if CVS was estimated as12.9% or 9.3%, the choice of either cost measure did not affect the test result materially.

conducting an AEC effective price-cost test analysis. The JFTC and Intel eventually reached a consent decree, with Intel agreeing to accept the recommendations.

The US competition agency was cautious in its decision on the Intel case. The US FTC, in 2009, invoked Section 5 of the FTC Act to file a complaint against Intel for anticompetitive practices. These practices included the secretive redesign of compiler software aimed at impairing the performance of competitors' CPUs and efforts to extend its monopolistic position into the graphics processing unit (GPU) market, which was emerging as a potential competitive threat by diminishing the reliance on CPUs.[89] Interestingly, unlike other regulatory bodies, the FTC's complaint did not address Intel's conditional rebates or the interference with the launch of competitors' new products as abusive practices.[90] On August 4, 2010, as detailed in a press release, the FTC and Intel reached a consent decree that required Intel to cease the practices in question.

On May 13, 2009, the EC declared its decision regarding Intel's abuse of its dominant position, finding that Intel contravened Article 82 of the EC Treaty. This violation involved awarding exclusivity-conditioned rebates and payments, termed as 'price-based exclusion', to PC Original Equipment Manufacturers (OEMs) and retailers such as Acer, Dell, HP, Lenovo, NEC, and MSH (Media Saturn Holding), and engaging in 'naked restraints' by interfering with their installation of AMD CPUs in PCs during the period from October 2002 to December 2007. The EC imposed substantial fines amounting to €1.06 billion, more than doubling the fines levied in the Microsoft case in 2004, which were €0.494 billion. In its comprehensive analysis, the EC (2009, pp. 302–453) endeavored to apply the AEC effective price-cost test, as illustrated in Table 4.6, and determined that Intel's rebates did not qualify for a safe harbor. However, the EC also exercised caution in affirming the necessity of such a test for proving the illegality of conditional rebates, stating: "It should also be highlighted that the as efficient competitor analysis is one way of examining the capability of harming competition in the present context. However, it should not be regarded as a necessary or absolute test." Prior to this analysis, the EC (2009, pp. 276–279) underscored that Intel's rebates were categorized as fidelity rebates, which have been recognized as an abuse of dominant position since the 1979 *Hoffmann-La Roche* case law.

---

[89] FTC Act Section 5 governs a broad spectrum of "unfair methods of competition, and deceptive acts and practices in commerce." However, the provision for treble damage recovery for violations under the Sherman Act is not applicable in this context. This suggests that while FTC Act Section 5 extends its regulatory reach, it does so with potentially less severe punitive measures compared to the Sherman Act.

[90] One reason why the FTC did not file a complaint regarding conditional rebates could be attributed to the US standard for single-product conditional rebates. This standard dictates that rebates should be allocated across all units rather than just the contestable units when calculating the effective price. This approach aligns with the traditional predatory pricing criterion, as noted in OECD (2008). Consequently, the effective price calculated under this US standard would be higher than that of the EC test, making it more challenging to demonstrate the potential for excluding a competitor. However, in the context of multiproduct loyalty rebates, where all rebates are allocated to the contestable product, the standards of the United States and the EU converge.

The EU General Court (GC) on June 12, 2014, fully upheld the EC's decision regarding Intel's practices. However, the EU Court of Justice (CJ) on September 6, 2017, overturned this judgment and remanded the case back to the GC.[91] The GC's judgment was notably conservative, treating exclusivity rebates like those offered by Intel as inherently anticompetitive and quasi per se illegal, without recognizing the necessity of conducting an AEC test. Conversely, the CJ noted that "while the Commission emphasised that the rebates at issue were by their very nature capable of restricting competition, it nevertheless carried out an in-depth examination of the circumstances of the case in its decision, which led it to conclude that an as efficient competitor would have had to offer prices which would not have been viable and that, accordingly, the rebate scheme at issue was capable of foreclosing such a competitor. The AEC test therefore played an important role in the Commission's assessment of whether the rebate scheme at issue was capable of having foreclosure effects on as efficient competitors. The Court therefore holds that the General Court was required to examine all of Intel's arguments concerning that test (such as, inter alia, the errors allegedly committed by the Commission as regards that test), which the General Court failed to do. The Court therefore sets aside the judgment of the General Court as a result of that failure in its analysis of whether the rebates at issue were capable of restricting competition. The Court refers the case back to the General Court so that it may examine, in the light of the arguments."

The judgment by the EU Court of Justice in the Intel case holds significant implications, regardless of the General Court's final decision on the remanded judgment concerning the legality of Intel's conduct. Broadly speaking, it affirmed the rule of reason approach in determining exclusionary dominance abuses and underscored the importance of economic analysis in assessing their anticompetitive effects. Specifically, regarding the As Efficient Competitor (AEC) effective price-cost test for conditional rebates, the judgment validated the significance of such analyses, despite the challenges in estimating relevant parameters like the commercially viable share (CVS), default rebates, and appropriate average costs.

4.4.5 Qualcomm I *(2009): Discriminatory Royalties and Conditional Rebates*

In 2009, the KFTC filed a complaint against Qualcomm, alleging two forms of misconduct. Firstly, Qualcomm was accused of discriminating against domestic handset Original Equipment Manufacturers (OEMs) such as LG Electronics, Samsung Electronics, and Pantech Curitel by charging them unfairly high royalties for patents related to the CDMA mobile communication standard between April 2004 and July 2009. Secondly, Qualcomm was charged with providing rebates to these companies on the condition that they purchase modem and RF chips for

[91] Intel appealed to the Supreme Court in the EU, whereas it did not pursue such an appeal in Korea.

CDMA2000 handsets in excess of certain ratios or amounts during the period from July 2000 to July 2009. The KFTC found Qualcomm guilty under Section 3-2 (1) of the KMRFTA for abusing its dominant position. This abuse was manifested in two ways: unfairly interfering with competitors' businesses by discriminatory practices and excluding competitors by coercing trading partners not to deal with them. As a result, the KFTC ordered Qualcomm to cease and desist these practices and imposed a fine of KR₩273.2 billion—the largest amount ever levied for the abuse of market dominance.[92] The Seoul High Court, in 2013, upheld the entirety of the KFTC's decision. Later, the Supreme Court, in 2019, affirmed most of the KFTC's rulings but remanded a portion back to the appellate court for further consideration.[93]

In the following discussion, I will highlight some intriguing aspects of this case. Qualcomm was an integrated enterprise, holding a monopolistic stance in both the upstream market for CDMA mobile communication technology and the downstream market for CDMA2000 handset components, such as modem and RF chips that utilized this technology. Controversially, the KFTC delineated the relevant geographic market for both CDMA technology and chips as 'domestic' instead of 'worldwide'. The KFTC's approach to defining the geographic markets for products of multinational firms—products characterized by minimal transportation costs and low cultural and linguistic barriers, such as software and processor chips—has not been consistent. For example, the market for PC operating systems was categorized as worldwide in the 2006 *Microsoft* case, while the market for CPUs was considered domestic in the 2008 *Intel* case.[94] In contrast, these markets were recognized as worldwide in related cases in the United States and the EU. It was not until the 2017 *Qualcomm II* case that the KFTC aligned with the global standard of defining such markets for globally distributed software or chips as 'worldwide'. As we will explore later, the variance in geographic market definitions between the *Qualcomm I* and *Qualcomm II* cases bears significant implications for the regional scope within which corrective orders should be enforced.

The 2009 *Qualcomm I* case can be seen as an extension of the 2008 *Intel* case. In addition to addressing concerns of discriminatory royalty charges, the Qualcomm case expanded the scope to include both single- and multiproduct conditional

---

[92] KFTC 2009-281, December 30, 2009. KFTC accused Qualcomm's agreements with handphone OEMs of imposing royalties on expired patents as unfair business conducts also, even though Qualcomm did not actually collect the royalties.

[93] Seoul High Court 2010nu3932, June 19, 2013. Supreme Court 2013du14726, January 13, 2019.

[94] In the *Intel* and *Qualcomm I* cases, the KFTC justified its definition of the domestic market on the basis that multinational monopolistic firms engage in direct sales to buyers through regional divisions. The KFTC argued that buyers are unable to switch their purchases to alternative regions overseas due to the companies' segmentation policies, even if there is a significant price increase (as determined by the SSNIP test) in one region. This rationale is problematic as it suggests a mechanical approach to defining the geographic market as domestic simply because the firm in question is a multinational entity with regionally segmented operations. Moreover, this reasoning appears to overlook the theoretical nature of the 'hypothetical monopolist' SSNIP test, which is designed to consider market conditions beyond actual regulatory and practical constraints.

royalties, whereas the Intel case was confined to single-product conditional royalties. Conditional royalties inherently promote loyalty through ex post retroactive payments that are applied to all units once certain conditions are met. The specific conditions are often customized for individual trading partners. The rebate system employed by Qualcomm was notably complex and tailored to each OEM. Fundamentally, these rebates were contingent upon reaching a certain quantity and ratio of each OEM's total purchases of Qualcomm's modem chips and RF chips (known as single-product conditional rebates), as well as upon the proportions of each OEM's aggregate procurement of Qualcomm's modem chips and RF chips combined (termed multiproduct conditional rebates). Additionally, the structure of Qualcomm's rebates was progressive.

In the United States, multiproduct conditional rebates are scrutinized more stringently than single-product ones. US courts have applied the price-cost test, commonly used for predatory pricing, to single-product conditional rebates.[95] This means such rebates are considered lawful if the average price of all units sold, after accounting for the rebates, remains above the appropriate measure of cost. In contrast, multiproduct conditional rebates have been deemed inherently guilty of monopolization without recourse to the price-cost test in some court decisions,[96] although these have not reached the Supreme Court and thus lack the status of precedent. The US Antitrust Modernization Commission (2007) criticized the decision in *LePage's* case and suggested a "safe harbor" test for bundled or multiproduct conditional rebates. To be considered illegal under Article 2 of the Sherman Act, the test requires that "after allocating all discounts and rebates attributable to the entire bundle of products to the competitive product, the defendant sold the competitive product below its incremental cost." Conversely, EC (2008) guidance recommended applying the same principle to both single- and multiproduct conditional rebates. This principle dictates that the effective price of the contestable part or product, after all rebates have been allocated, should fall below a proper measure of cost to potentially exclude a competitor. Therefore, the EC guidance adopts stricter criteria for conditional rebates, whether single or multiproduct, compared to traditional predatory pricing. In the *Qualcomm I* case, the KFTC did not perform an effective price-cost test as it had previously in the *Intel* case. Qualcomm presented an economic analysis purporting that its conditional rebates could not exclude an as-efficient competitor. However, the appellate court found this assertion inconclusive since, according to the analysis—even by the defendant's own admission—the 'effective prices' of modem chips fell below the average total costs or long-run average incremental costs across several ranges.

Two aspects of the Supreme Court's decision in Qualcomm I merit attention. Firstly, the Court recognized errors in the KFTC's demonstration of the anticompetitive nature of conditional rebates concerning RF chips 'in part' and thus ruled that the surcharges related to RF chip rebates should be annulled 'in their entirety'.

---

95 *Concord Boat vs. Brunswick* 207 F.3d 1039, (8th Cir. 2000).

96 *LePage's v. 3M*, 324 F.3d 141 (3rd Cir. 2003).

More significantly, from an economist's standpoint, the Supreme Court expressed that "there is no prerequisite for the KFTC to validate, as a precondition of unfairness, that a hypothetical or actual competitor equally as efficient as the dominant market firm could match the rebates in terms of prices and costs via retrospective accounting and economic analyses." However, it endorsed the application of such economic analyses by firms to substantiate the actual constraining power or unfairness of conditional rebates and to augment the decisiveness of the ruling. Additionally, the Court noted that firms typically have access to cost-related data fundamental for economic analyses and, therefore, "...they are able to challenge the *prima facie* reasonable evidence provided by the KFTC of the actual constraining power or unfairness of conditional rebates by demonstrating the dependability of the foundational data, analytical methodologies, etc." In essence, the Supreme Court has acknowledged the potential for defendants to argue based on the As-Efficient-Competitor (AEC) effective price-cost test in cases concerning conditional rebates. This represents a significant advancement in the role of economic analysis in antitrust litigation.

4.4.6 **LGU Plus** *(2015): Margin Squeeze*

Enterprise Messaging Service (EMS) facilitates the transmission of text messages from a company's computer system to users' mobile devices via telecommunication networks. This service is extensively used by financial institutions, public agencies, retail centers, hospitals, and various other entities. LGU Plus, as a vertically integrated provider, offers both the upstream mobile communication service and the downstream EMS, holding a presumed dominant position in both sectors. In 2015, the KFTC concluded that LGU Plus had exploited its dominant market status to marginalize competitors in the domestic EMS market from June 2010 to September 2014. The KFTC imposed a penalty surcharge of KR₩4.5 billion and issued a cease-and-desist order. LGU Plus was charged with contravening Section 5 of the Act and Section 9 of the Decree through predatory pricing practices. Specifically, the KFTC accused LGU Plus of "unfairly excluding competitors by offering goods or services at prices lower than the normal trading price or by purchasing at higher prices."[97]

The KFTC and the courts have jointly acknowledged the following facts in the case concerning LGU Plus. The company held dominant positions in both the upstream and downstream markets relevant to the case. Among the three companies providing mobile communication services, LGU Plus has consistently maintained a market share of around 20%. In the EMS market, LGU Plus was the largest player, with a market share of 46% and a three-firm concentration ratio of 79% in 2013. It charged corporate clients for messaging services at a per-unit price that was lower

[97] KFTC 2015-049, February 23, 2015.

than the average cost of transporting services (KR₩9.2 per unit since November 2011) across the three mobile communication providers.

The KFTC and the appellate court employed the standard of predatory pricing to assess the alleged abusive conduct in this case. The Decree's below-cost test references a nebulous "normal trading price."[98] According to the KFTC's decision, it is suggested that the lowest bound of this normal trading price should be, at a minimum, above the per-unit usage price of mobile transporting service, which is indispensable for providing a text messaging service. However, the Seoul High Court did not endorse this assumption, mandating that the KFTC should substantiate its claim with "investigation and consideration of a realistic trading price established in the market." While the KFTC proposed that a rise in the defendant's market share and a decline in competitors' shares could indicate anticompetitive behavior, the Seoul High Court dismissed this claim. The court highlighted the decline in prices and the expansion of the market for the relevant product. Moreover, when applying the recoupment criterion of predatory pricing, the court observed that "it might not be feasible for LGU Plus to recoup the losses incurred post-competition exclusion." The court's reasoning included the presence of formidable competitors like SKT and KT, both larger and also vertically integrated, akin to LGU Plus, and the potential for reentry of ousted competitors into the market.[99] Therefore, the Seoul High Court overturned the decision of the KFTC.

The case experienced a significant reversal when the Supreme Court, in 2021, overturned and remanded the lower court's judgment.[100] The Supreme Court explicitly addressed the concept of a "margin squeeze," which occurs when a vertically integrated firm narrows the gap between the upstream 'wholesale' price of an input and the downstream 'retail' price of the final product.[101] The Court recognized margin squeeze as a form of abusive conduct, constituting "unfair exclusion of competitors by supplying goods or services at a lower price or purchasing at a higher price than the normal trading price." The "normal trading price" was interpreted as the price that would generally prevail in the absence of market-dominant position abuse. Accordingly, the normal trading price of EMS was inferred to be "at least higher than the purchase price of transporting service, which is a crucial input for the plaintiff's competitors in the enterprise messaging service market"—aligning with the KFTC's decision. Consequently, a negative margin could suggest the potential exclusion of efficient competitors. Unlike the Seoul High Court, the Supreme Court did not take into account the recoupment criterion typically associated with predatory pricing.

[98] The normal trading price is not explicitly specified as average variable cost or average total cost.

[99] Seoul High Court 2015nu38278, January 31, 2018.

[100] Supreme Court 2018du3770, June 30, 2021.

[101] The KFTC and the Seoul High Court did not explicitly reference the term "margin squeeze." Instead, they approached the case within the broader framework of predatory pricing. This approach may stem from the fact that neither the Decree nor the KFTC guidelines specifically categorize margin squeeze as a form of market dominance abuse.

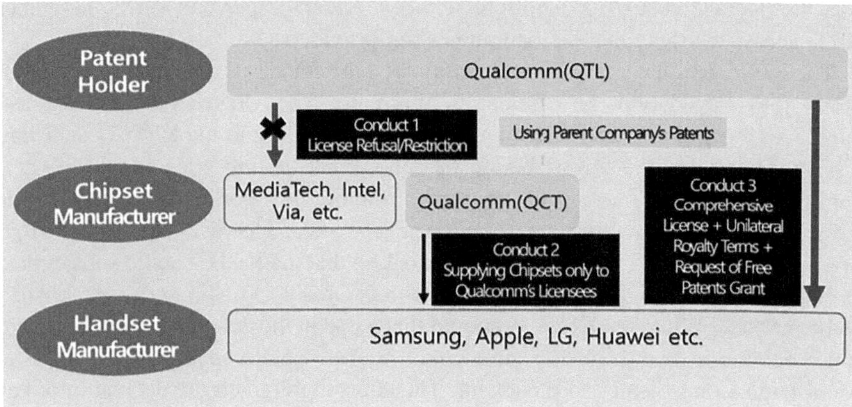

Fig. 4.5 Qualcomm's business model: Figure from KFTC (2017, p. 39)

4.4.7 **Qualcomm II** *(2017): Raising Rivals' Costs by Licensing and Modem Chip Supply Business Model*

In 2007, the KFTC issued an injunction against Qualcomm for engaging in competitive restraints within mobile communication patent licensing and modem chip supply, imposing a record fine of KR₩1.03 billion.[102] The specific anticompetitive behaviors cited by the KFTC were: (a) refusing or limiting the licensing of mobile communications Standard Essential Patents (SEPs) to competing modem chip manufacturers (Conduct 1); (b) obligating mobile handset OEMs to license Qualcomm's patents as a prerequisite for acquiring Qualcomm's modem chips (Conduct 2); and (c) enforcing restrictive licensing terms on handset OEMs, including comprehensive portfolio licensing, unilaterally determined royalty terms, and the demand for the grant of free patents (Conduct 3). Figure 4.5 illustrates Qualcomm's business model, incorporating the three contentious practices highlighted by the KFTC.

QTL (Qualcomm Technology Licensing) refers to the division responsible for patent licensing business and QCT (Qualcomm CDMA Technologies) is that of modem chipsets business.

The KFTC delineated the relevant product markets as 'Qualcomm's complete set of CDMA, WCDMA, and LTE Standard Essential Patents (SEPs) licenses, specific to each standard' and 'modem chipsets for CDMA, WCDMA, and LTE SEPs, specific to each standard', and it identified the geographic scope as 'worldwide'. Qualcomm held dominant positions in both of these markets. The KFTC underscored that Qualcomm's monopolistic status in the licensing market was acquired through standardization processes and its commitment to FRAND (Fair, Reasonable, and Non-Discriminatory) licensing terms. As a vertically integrated

[102] KFTC 2017-025, January 20, 2017.

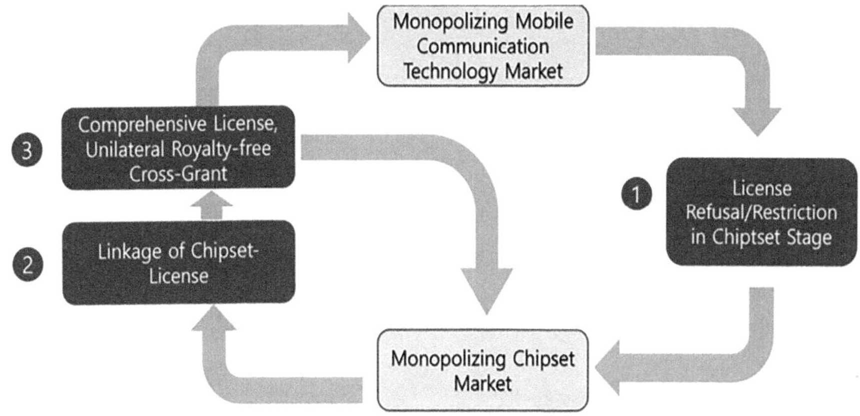

Fig. 4.6 Cycling structure of Qualcomm's business model: Figure from KFTC (2017, p. 41)

firm operating both in the upstream license market and the downstream chipset market, Qualcomm also wielded dual market power. According to the KFTC's decision (p. 39), the three contentious practices of Qualcomm "were structurally inter-related, cyclically reinforcing one another," illustrating the structure as follows (Fig. 4.6):

According to the KFTC's press release (December 28, 2016, pp. 7–8), Qualcomm's alleged strategy for market dominance was multifaceted: It aimed "i) to **monopolize the chipset market** by refusing/restricting licensing to chipset competitors and thereby constructing disadvantageous conditions for competitors' competition, to **avoid the FRAND commitment restraint** and bolster the **bargaining power** in license market by leveraging its market power in the chipset domain, including restricting chipset supply when handset manufacturers did not agree to and comply with licensing agreement, ii) to exploit the enhanced power obtained in this manner to **impose various onerous terms** on handset manufacturers, such as enforcing unilateral license conditions and demanding the grant of free patents, and iii) then to use these again as a tool (referred to as a 'patent umbrella') to give its own chipsets a competitive edge over its competitors and to create **a self-reinforcing cycle** that maintains and amplifies its monopoly power in both the **chipset market** and **licence market**."

The KFTC invoked §3-2 (1) of the MRFTA, which pertains to the abuse of a dominant market position, to address Conducts 1, 2, and 3 by Qualcomm. It alleged that Qualcomm interfered with competitors' businesses. Additionally, § 23 (1), related to unfair business practices, was applied concurrently to Conducts 2 and 3, where Qualcomm was accused of unfairly exploiting its trading position. It is significant to note that the KFTC's cease-and-desist order, which mandates revisions to the licensing contracts to rectify these conducts, was intended to apply to all enterprises, both domestic and international, that impact the domestic markets. In essence, this includes all manufacturers or sellers providing modem chipsets and

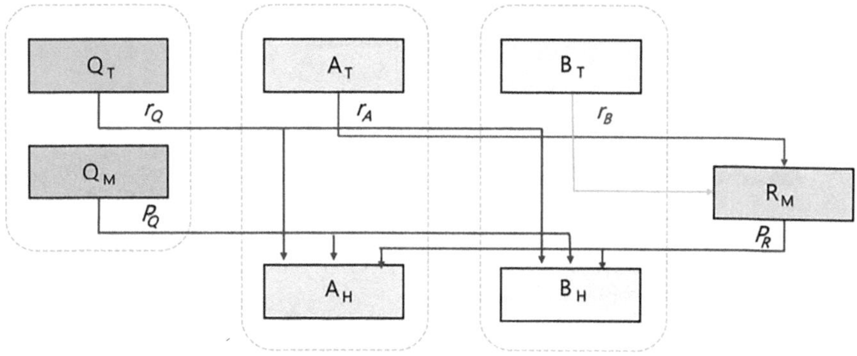

Fig. 4.7 RRC model of 'patent umbrella'

handsets within the domestic market, regardless of whether they are based in Korea or abroad. This broad scope of the remedy logically follows from the worldwide market definition used in this case. This approach stands in stark contrast to the previous *Qualcomm I* case, where the geographic market was defined as domestic, and the remedies were limited to interactions with domestic handset manufacturers.

Jeon (2016) submitted an economic analysis to the KFTC regarding the anticompetitive effects of Qualcomm's business model, both in terms of its individual components and as a whole, and proposed suitable remedies on behalf of an interested party. The majority of the arguments presented aligned with the conclusions of the KFTC decision. The refusal to license in Conduct 1 was seen to increase the costs for Qualcomm's competitors by exposing them to the risk of patent infringement lawsuits, despite Qualcomm's so-called 'forbearance policy' of not enforcing patent rights against modem chipset competitors. Significantly, this Conduct 1 created a foundation for the OEM-level licensing seen in Conduct 3. Furthermore, the 'no license, no chips' policy in Conduct 2 provided the leverage for Qualcomm to impose various unusual conditions in Conduct 3. Among the triad of elements in Conduct 3, I will briefly touch upon the foreclosure effect of the 'patent umbrella' created by Qualcomm. This umbrella arises from Qualcomm's demands that handset OEMs license their patents to Qualcomm without charge and engage in free cross-licensing arrangements among themselves. This strategy is modeled as a method of Raising Rivals' Costs (RRC). Figure 4.7 illustrates the operation of the patent umbrella.

Q_T and Q_M represent Qualcomm Technology Licensing (QTL), the division handling technology licensing, and Qualcomm CDMA Technologies (QCT), the division responsible for supplying modem chipsets, respectively. Meanwhile, R_M refers to competitors in the modem chipset supply market, such as Intel and MediaTek. A_H and B_H stand for handset OEMs like Samsung and LG. These companies must become licensees of Qualcomm to acquire its chipsets, due to Qualcomm's 'no license, no chip' policy. A_T and B_T denote their respective divisions for mobile communication patent licensing. Q_T levies a royalty fee (r_Q) on A_H and

B_H, regardless of whether the mobile phones they produce are equipped with Qualcomm's modem chipsets or those of its rivals. Q_T does not grant licenses for its chipset-related SEPs to R_M, nor does it collect royalties from R_M. Both Q_M and R_M supply their modem chipsets to A_H and B_H, with Q_M's chipset priced at P_Q and R_M's chipset priced at P_R.

Qualcomm implemented a 'patent umbrella' over its licensees, A_H and B_H, as well as over itself. Under this arrangement, Qualcomm does not enforce patent rights against its licensees operating within the umbrella. This means $A_H(B_H)$ is precluded from charging royalties on its patents to $B_H(A_H)$ and to Qualcomm. However, these licensees do collect royalties, r_A and r_B, from rival modem chip supplier R_M. The patent umbrella increases the chip rival's royalty costs above Qualcomm's by $r_A + r_B$. If the patent umbrella is imposed unilaterally by Qualcomm without the consent of the handset manufacturers, it could be construed as secondary-line injury of price discrimination. In such a scenario, handset manufacturers differentiate royalty charges between Qualcomm and its competitors, thereby influencing competition in the market where their trading partners operate.[103] This imposition by Qualcomm is reminiscent of the 1911 *Standard Oil* case. In that instance, Standard Oil secured rail transportation fares that were lower than those for its competitors' oil transportation and attempted to garner rebates from the railroad companies on payments made by its competitors.

In addition to hindering competition in the modem chipset market through the RRC strategy, the patent umbrella also impairs dynamic competition in the mobile communication technology market. If handset manufacturers are not otherwise compensated by Qualcomm, the relinquishment of royalties from Qualcomm could diminish their incentives for research and development investment and innovation. Furthermore, A_T does not receive royalties from B_H, and B_T does not receive them from A_H. The impact of this arrangement is negligible if the patent portfolios of A_T and B_T are similar. However, if there is an imbalance, the party with the stronger patent portfolio forgoes substantial legitimate royalties. This could further contribute to dynamic inefficiency, particularly in the areas of innovation and investment.

Moving away from the patent umbrella topic, we encounter the so-called "Qualcomm tax." Qualcomm imposes a royalty r_Q on handset manufacturers, even when these manufacturers purchase modem chipsets from Qualcomm's competitors. This practice has sparked heated debates among the US FTC, Qualcomm, and the courts in the United States. It is reported that Qualcomm has been levying a royalty rate equivalent to 5% of the handset's value. Both the KFTC and the US FTC have argued that Qualcomm has been charging excessive royalties that exceed the FRAND level by exploiting the leverage provided by its 'no license, no chip' policy (Conduct 2). The term "Qualcomm tax" refers to the increment above the FRAND level, which is indicative of Qualcomm's monopoly power in the chipset market. Qualcomm has maintained that its royalty scheme is "chip-neutral," asserting that it

[103]The primary-line injury resulting from price discrimination pertains to the negative impact on competition within the market where the discriminator operates.

does not distort competition in the chipset market since it charges royalties to handset makers irrespective of the type of modem chips they install in their mobile phones. The US FTC countered by suggesting that even if Qualcomm's tax might be ostensibly "facially chip-neutral," Qualcomm and its rivals are not on equal footing—Qualcomm acts as a "tax collector," while its competitors are effectively "indirect taxpayers."[104] The implication of Qualcomm's tax is that it increases Qualcomm's revenue and resources for R&D investment, while simultaneously shrinking its competitors' profit margins and diminishing their capacity and incentives for investment and innovation. The crucial point is that the KFTC and US FTC's concerns regarding Qualcomm's tax stem not from its exploitative nature, but from its exclusionary impact on the chipset market.

Qualcomm's licensing and modem chipset supply business model has come under scrutiny from several antitrust enforcement agencies around the world, including those in the United States, Japan, China, Taiwan, and Korea. In 2019, the Seoul High Court largely upheld the decision of the KFTC.[105] The court affirmed the KFTC's decision regarding Conducts 1 and 2 and the associated remedial orders, while it overturned the guilty ruling on Conduct 3 and nullified the related orders. Nonetheless, the court upheld the total surcharge of KR₩1.03 billion, as the sales relevant to the surcharge calculation and the severity of the infringement remained unchanged, even though only Conducts 1 and 2 were adjudged to be violations. In 2013, the Supreme Court concurred with the judgment of the Seoul High Court.[106] In a similar vein, the US FTC filed a lawsuit against Qualcomm on January 17, 2017, echoing the arguments presented in the KFTC's decision of January 20, 2017. The FTC sought a permanent injunction to prohibit the contentious practices of Qualcomm.[107] The US District Court ruled in favor of the FTC on June 26, 2017. However, in an unexpected turn, the US Court of Appeals for the Ninth Circuit, accepting Qualcomm's arguments, reversed this decision on August 11, 2020. The US FTC opted not to petition the Supreme Court for a review of the Qualcomm case, thereby bringing the case to a close.

The Japan Fair Trade Commission (JFTC), on September 28, 2009, was the initial agency to contest Qualcomm's practices. It found only a portion of Conduct 3 to constitute an unfair business practice. Subsequently, on March 15, 2019, the JFTC reversed the prior prohibition order related to this conduct. The China National Development and Reform Commission (NDRC), on February 10, 2015, addressed

[104] A fundamental concept in microeconomics is that the incidence of a tax—referred to in this context as the "Qualcomm tax"—remains unchanged regardless of whether it is imposed on the buyer (handset manufacturers) or the seller (competitor chipset suppliers of Qualcomm).

[105] Seoul High Court 2017nu48, December 4, 2019.

[106] Supreme Court 2020du31897, April 13, 2023.

[107] The US FTC expanded its antitrust litigation against Qualcomm by including the company's exclusive dealing arrangements with Apple, which were facilitated by conditional rebates and payments. In a similar action, the EC fined Qualcomm €997 million on January 24, 2018, for abuse of dominant position linked to these practices. However, in June 2022, the EU General Court ruled against the imposition of this fine.

Conducts 2 and 3, but not Conduct 1. The NDRC ruled that these conducts violated China's Anti-Monopoly Law, ordering their cessation and imposing a fine of approximately CH¥6 billion. Qualcomm proposed a voluntary correction plan, primarily involving the reduction of royalties on handsets sold in China, which the NDRC accepted. The NDRC notably considered Conduct 3 to be both exploitative and exclusionary abuse. The Taiwan Fair Trade Commission (TFTC), on October 20, 2017, charged Qualcomm's business model with violations of the FTC Act, issuing a remedy order and imposing penalty surcharges of NT$ 23.4 billion. The TFTC examined all of Conducts 1, 2, and 3, aligning closely with the positions of the KFTC and the US FTC in their allegations. However, in August 2018, the TFTC reached a settlement with Qualcomm. The settlement was based on Qualcomm's commitment to behavioral changes to address the concerns and its plan to invest an amount equivalent to the surcharges in the development of mobile communications in Taiwan over a period of five years.

Lastly, I will examine the distinctions and parallels between the Seoul High Court decision of December 4, 2019, and the US Court of Appeals for the Ninth Circuit ruling of August 11, 2020. The two verdicts diverge in that the former found Qualcomm guilty of Conducts 1 and 2, while the latter dismissed all allegations related to Conducts 1, 2, and 3. Nevertheless, there are some similar lines of reasoning within the two judgments. In rejecting the claims of anticompetitiveness regarding Conduct 3, the Seoul High Court observed that "the plaintiffs [Qualcomm-related companies] are not competing with handset manufacturers in the market relevant to this case, they are not dominant entities in the handset market, and the KFTC did not base its decision on any exploitative abuse of handset manufacturers." This effectively negates the notion that there is a restraint on competition for handset manufacturers. Moreover, the court indicated that Conduct 3 is seen as "a consequence of Conducts 1 and 2," and it is challenging to discern that "the cross-granting condition has its <u>own separate</u> effect." [underline added for emphasis] The US Appeals Court decision contains similar sentiments. It notes that "the district court characterized Qualcomm's various business practices as "interrelated" and mutually reinforcing, and it described their anticompetitive effects as "compounding" and "cycl[ical]." But even if Qualcomm's practices are interrelated, actual or alleged harms to customers and consumers <u>outside the relevant markets are beyond the scope of antitrust law</u>." (as pp. 30–31) [underline added for emphasis].

As an economist, I find myself at odds with the perspectives taken by the courts in both Korea and the United States regarding two key points: firstly, the notion that the assessment of anticompetitive effects should be limited strictly to the relevant market in which the defendant has a dominant position; and secondly, the belief that the interconnectedness, mutual reinforcement, and cyclical nature of effects within a vertical market structure should not be considered. I contend that to fully comprehend the substantial anticompetitive effects in cases involving multiple levels and several markets, our analysis should not narrowly segment and isolate the markets by rigidly demarcating the boundaries of interrelated markets.

4.4.8 Siemens *(2018): Charging Unreasonable Prices on Maintenance Software for CT/MRI*

In 2018, the KFTC found Siemens guilty under §3-2 (1) of the MRFTA for abuse of dominant position by interfering with competitors' businesses for unfair business practices by discriminating in prices or trade conditions.[108] The KFTC identified the relevant market as the domestic services for maintenance and repair of Siemens CT and MRI equipment, where Siemens held an almost monopolistic position. The abusive conduct in question included: (1) imposing unreasonable conditions, compared to standard business practices, by providing basic level Service Software Keys (SSKs) essential for accessing the software installed on the equipment for maintaining and repairing Siemens CT and MRI machines at abnormally high prices to Independent Service Organizations (ISOs), whereas it was common practice to allow equipment owners free access to such software for basic maintenance and repair, and (2) unfairly discriminating in price, the range of functions and access rights, and the issuance time of SSKs based on whether hospital customers using Siemens equipment conducted business with ISOs or with Siemens directly. The KFTC maintained that such behaviors impeded the business of ISOs and stifled competition in the after-purchase services market. The Seoul High Court, in 2020, disagreed with the KFTC's arguments regarding the interference with competitors' businesses and the alleged harm to competition. Consequently, the court annulled the KFTC's corrective order, which would have required Siemens to provide the basic maintenance software virtually for free irrespective of whether the transactions were with ISOs, and also nullified the surcharges that had been imposed.[109]

Jeon and Nahm (2017), after reviewing the Examiner's Report, provided an economic analysis on behalf of the defendant prior to the commission hearing. They challenged the Examiner's Report on three fundamental issues. (1) Relevant Market Definition: They posited that the pertinent product market for this case should encompass both the primary system market of initial equipment sales and the secondary market of after-service provisions, rather than solely the Siemens-specific after-service market. They argued that the purchasing and selling decisions for CT/MRI equipment are influenced by the Total Cost of Ownership (TCO) or the whole-life cost of acquiring and operating the equipment. They also contended that manufacturers are unlikely to exploit customers with installed equipment through exorbitant post-purchase maintenance and repair costs due to concerns over reputation. (2) Exclusionary Potential of Pricing Policies: Jeon and Nahm evaluated the competitive impact of Siemens' Service Software Key (SSK) pricing policy by

[108] KFTC 2018-094, March 13, 2018. The KFTC charged Siemens with unfair practices aimed at inducing or coercing competitors' customers to engage in transactions with Siemens, constituting an additional violation of §23 (1). However, I will set aside this matter and concentrate solely on the alleged abuse of dominance.

[109] Seoul High Court 2018nu43100, February 6, 2020. The Supreme Court upheld the appellate court judgment. Supreme Court 2020du36892, November 28, 2024.

considering whether it could exclude a hypothetical equally efficient competitor from the Siemens-specific aftermarket, which was identified as the relevant market by the Examiner's Report solely for analytical purposes. They assessed the profitability of Siemens issuing SSKs to itself at the same price charged to Independent Service Organizations (ISOs) and found the exclusionary potential to be highly improbable. (3) Intellectual Property Protection: They argued that the maintenance software for CT/MRI machines and the SSKs required for access constitute intellectual property that merits protection. Restrictions on pricing, particularly the mandate for a virtually free open policy, could inhibit innovation and investment, ultimately diminishing consumer welfare over time. Additionally, they warned of a potential "waterbed" effect, where equipment prices might increase, negating the pricing function of SSKs and undermining the pro-competitive effects of second-degree price discrimination inherent in SSK pricing.

The KFTC addressed most of the defendant's arguments, offering counterpoints to refute them. The appellate court recognized the KFTC's market definition of brand-specific aftermarkets and affirmed the market-dominant position of the defendant. Nonetheless, it concluded that Siemens' policy regarding the pricing of Service Software Keys (SSK) fell within the bounds of legitimate intellectual property rights and did not impede competition in the relevant market, despite potentially causing some harm to competitors.

4.4.9 Naver—Shopping *(2021): Self Preferencing*

The KFTC, in 2021, charged Naver with exploiting its market dominance in the comparison shopping service sector to unfairly benefit its open market service over the period from February 2012 to August 2020. The KFTC delineated two pertinent product markets: the "comparison shopping service," where Naver held a market-dominant position, and the "open market service," into which Naver was accused of attempting to extend its dominance. The contentious practice involved Naver Shopping manipulating its search algorithm to preferentially display stores from its own 'Smart Store', Naver's comparison shopping service, in search results, to the detriment of competing open market stores. This practice, known as "self-preferencing," was claimed to contravene §5 of the Act by unfairly discriminating in trade conditions and thus interfering with competitors' businesses. In response to these allegations, the KFTC levied penalty surcharges amounting to KR₩26.6 billion and issued a cease-and-desist order against Naver.[110]

[110]KFTC 2021-027, January 27, 2021. The KFTC invoked provisions under § 45, such as those concerning unfairly discriminatory trade conditions and unfairly inducing or coercing competitors' customers to conduct business with the dominant firm. However, for the purpose of this discussion, I will omit these issues and concentrate solely on the abuse of market dominance.

Jeon et al. (2020) submitted an expert witness report in support of Naver to the KFTC. Their definition of the market was markedly distinct from that of the KFTC. Considering the dynamic evolution and competition in the online shopping industry, they contended that the relevant market should be characterized as a "shopping platform service," which would include online comparison shopping services as well as online shopping services. Even when adopting a conservative view, Naver Shopping is active in two overlapping markets: "online comparison shopping service" and "online shopping service." It's important to note that online shopping service is an umbrella term that comprises open markets, social commerce, and online shopping malls, all of which have increasingly adopted similar hybrid business models over the past decade. Furthermore, Smart Store provides online sellers with business solutions and tools rather than functioning as an online shopping site like Naver Shopping. Therefore, Naver Shopping operates across two markets: one for online comparison shopping services and another for online shopping services.

If the relevant market is broadly defined as "online platform service," Naver Shopping's market-dominant position may be questionable, as its market share falls below 20%. Jeon et al. supported this broader market definition with the SSNIP test, using survey data. This challenges the KFTC's claims of market expansion, as Smart Store's market share within the online shopping service was only about 8% in 2018. Moreover, even under KFTC's narrower market definition of "open market service," the evidence does not support an anticompetitive effect. During the period in question, there was notable growth in the open market sector as a whole, and also an increase in the transaction volume of open market operators via Naver Shopping. This observation does not align with the patterns typically associated with market exclusion or foreclosure.

In 2022, the Seoul High Court aligned with the KFTC in all aspects concerning market definition, the presence of a dominant position, and the effects of leveraging power. The court notably stated that "if the plaintiff (Naver Shopping) favored sellers within Smart Store by exploiting a market-dominant position in the comparison shopping service, leading to a higher growth rate than competitive open markets in metrics such as market share, transaction volume, and number of sellers, then it could be sufficiently recognized that anticompetitive effects or concerns have arisen. Additionally, the court pointed out that mere increases in the absolute volume of competitive open markets, Naver Shopping's failure to become the top operator in the open market, the overall growth of the open market, and the entry of new operators would not negate concerns regarding the potential to restrain competition."[111] The final judgment from the Supreme Court is still forthcoming.

The issue of self-preferencing by Google was scrutinized in both the United States and the EU, albeit in slightly different contexts. The controversy involved Google altering its search algorithm to favor its own Google Shopping service in the vertical search results, overshadowing those of competitive vertical search websites

[111] Seoul High Court 2021nu36129, December 14, 2023.

and organic search results, an act termed as "search bias."[112] The US FTC, in 2013, concluded that there was no wrongdoing associated with the alleged search bias. The FTC stated, "Product design is an important dimension of competition and condemning legitimate product improvements risks harming consumers. … Although at points in time various vertical websites have experienced demotions, we find that this was a consequence of algorithm changes that also could plausibly be viewed as an improvement in the overall quality of Google's search results."[113] Conversely, the EC raised antitrust concerns regarding Google's practice. In 2017, the EC decided to fine Google €2.42 billion for abusing the market dominance of its search engine by illegally favoring its own comparison shopping service.[114] The EU General Court upheld the EC's decision in this matter.[115]

4.4.10 Google *(2021): Anti-Fragmentation Agreement*

Google established agreements with device manufacturers that included the Play Store license and Android Pre-Release Software License Agreement (APSLA), contingent upon the Anti Fragmentation Agreement (AFA) since 2011. These agreements prohibited device manufacturers from using any version of Android not approved by Google, known as Android forks. To pre-install Google's proprietary applications, such as the Play Store, and to gain early access to new versions of Android software—approximately six months prior to the public release—manufacturers were obliged to pledge not to develop or market any devices operating on an Android fork. In 2021, the KFTC found that Google had breached §5 of the Act by unfairly imposing deal or action that put trading partners at a disadvantage and by unfairly trading with partners under the condition that they do not conduct business with competitors. As a result of these violations, the KFTC levied penalty surcharges of KR₩207.4 billion against Google and issued a cease and desist order.[116]

---

[112] Please note that the self-preferencing in the Google case pertained to the vertical search results of a comparison shopping service conducted by a general search engine, whereas in the Naver case, it involved favoring the sellers in Naver's open market through Naver's comparison shopping service.

[113] The U.S. FTC, "Statement of the Federal Trade Commission Regarding Google's Search Practices In the Matter of Google Inc. FTC File Number 111-0163, January 13, 2013.

[114] EC ("Commission seeks feedback on commitments offered by Google to address competition concerns—questions and answers," April 25, 2013) noted that "The factual and legal environments are different in the US and Europe. In particular, Bing and Yahoo represent a substantial alternative to Google in web search in the USA: there combined market share is around 30%. In contrast, Google has been holding market shares well above 90%."

[115] EU General Court Case T-612/16, Google and Alphabet v Commission (Google Shopping), November 23, 2021.

[116] KFTC 2021-329, Dec. 30, 2021. The KFTC provoked the provisions under §45, related to unfair business conduct, in their case against Google.

Google was accused of holding a dominant position in the "worldwide (excluding China) licensable smart mobile OS market" and the "worldwide (excluding China) Android-based app-market." The company was charged with engaging in the previously mentioned abusive conduct. According to the KFTC's decision, the consequences of Google's actions included the exclusion of Google's competitors in these two pertinent markets, the preservation of its dominance therein, and the extension of its market power into the adjacent "smart non-mobile OS development market." This latter market encompasses operating systems for various smart devices such as watches (Wear OS), televisions (Android TV), cars (Android Auto), speakers, drones, and robots.

There are some significant distinctions between the KFTC decision and the EC decision dated July 18, 2018[117] in the Google case. The EC addressed the issue of Google tying its search and browser apps to Android devices and the conditional payments for the exclusive pre-installation of Google Search, as well as the obstruction of the development and distribution of competing Android operating systems. It is worth noting that in 2013, the KFTC had made a no-guilt decision regarding the pre-installation of Google Search, since Google's market share in Korea was approximately 10% both before and after the pre-installation, while Naver maintained about a 70% share in the search service market. Regarding the AFA issue, while the decisions by the KFTC and EC appear quite similar, there are still some differences. The AFA in the EU pertained to the licensing of the Play Store and the Google Search app, whereas in Korea, it was related to the Play Store license and the Android Pre-Release Software License Agreement (APSLA). This discrepancy might seem minor but could reflect the different market configurations of the search service between the two regions.

However, there are two significant differences between the EU and Korea in the application of corrective measures concerning the Anti-Fragmentation Agreement (AFA): Firstly, the KFTC examined the anticompetitive effect in the "innovation market" of "smart non-mobile OS development," referencing several instances where innovation was impeded. Examples include Samsung Electronics' development of a fork OS for Galaxy Gear 1, LG Electronics' work on a fork OS for smart speakers, Amazon's marketing of Fire OS for smart TVs, and Samsung Electronics' use of fork OS for IoT devices, drones, robots, etc. Secondly, the EC injunction order applies to smart mobile devices imported into the European Economic Area (EEA), whereas the KFTC's cease and desist order extends to all products produced and distributed by Korean companies and their affiliates, including products imported into Korea. This results in a significantly broader coverage than the EC decision. The geographical extent and the stage of development covered by the corrective measures will be a critical point of contention in subsequent appellate cases.

In addition, the KFTC examined Google's potentially anticompetitive conduct within its app market. Google Play held a market share of between 80% and 95% in Korea and 95% to 99% internationally (from 2014 to 2019), excluding China. In

[117] European Commission Case AT.40099—Google Android, 18 July 2018.

2016, three telecom companies and Naver consolidated their individual app markets into 'One Store' to more effectively compete with Google Play. In response, Google offered major mobile game companies app-market "featuring" (placement on the first page) and overseas marketing support, but only on the condition of exclusive dealing with Google Play. As a result, Google's market share increased by approximately 10%, from 80–85% in 2016 to 90–95% in 2018. During the same period, One Store saw its market share decrease by a corresponding amount, from 15–20% (the sum of the individual market shares before integration) in 2016 to 5–10% in 2018. In 2023, the KFTC concluded that Google had breached §5 of the Act by engaging in unfair trade practices that interfered with competitors' businesses, specifically by trading with partners on the condition that they refrain from doing business with competitors. Consequently, the KFTC levied penalty surcharges of KR₩42.1 billion against Google and issued an injunction order.[118]

Cases

KFTC 2001-068, *Posco* Market Dominance Abuse, April 12, 2001.
KFTC 2006-009, *Hite-Jinro* Merger, January, 24, 2006.
KFTC 2006-042, *Microsoft* Market Dominance Abuse, February 24, 2006.
KFTC 2007-555, December 18, 2007.
KFTC 2008-251, *NHN [Naver]* Market Dominance Abuse, August 28, 2008.
KFTC 2008-295, *Intel* Market Dominance Abuse, November 5, 2008.
KFTC 2009-281, *Qualcomm I* Market Dominance Abuse, December 30, 2009.
KFTC 2015-049, *LGU Plus* Market Dominance Abuse, February 23, 2015.
KFTC 2017-025, *Qualcomm II* Market Dominance Abuse, January 20, 2017.
KFTC 2018-094, *Siemens* Market Dominance Abuse, March 13, 2018.
KFTC 2021-027, *Naver - Shopping* Market Dominance Abuse, January 27, 2021.
KFTC 2021-329, *Google* Market Dominance Abuse, December 30, 2021.
KFTC 2023-103, July 20, 2023.
Seoul High Court 2001nu5370, *Posco* Market Dominance Abuse, August 27, 2002.
Seoul High Court 2003nu2252, *Moohak-Daesun* Merger, October 27, 2004.
Seoul High Court 2008nu2851, August 20, 2008.
Seoul High Court 2008nu27102, *NHN [Naver]* Market Dominance Abuse, October 8, 2009.
Seoul High Court 2008nu35462, *Intel* Market Dominance Abuse, June 19, 2013.
Seoul High Court 2010nu3932, *Qualcomm I* Market Dominance Abuse, June 19, 2013.
Seoul High Court 2015nu38278, *LGU Plus* Market Dominance Abuse, January 31, 2018.
Seoul High Court 2017nu48, *Qualcomm II* Market Dominance Abuse, December 4, 2019.
Seoul High Court 2018nu43100, *Siemens* Market Dominance Abuse, February 6, 2020.
Seoul High Court 2021nu36129, *Naver - Shopping* Market Dominance Abuse, December 14, 2023.
Supreme Court 2002du6826, *Posco* Market Dominance Abuse, November 22, 2007.
Supreme Court 2009du1983, May 27, 2010.
Supreme Court 2008du16322, June 10, 2011.
Supreme Court 2009du20366, *NHN [Naver]* Market Dominance Abuse, November 13, 2014.
Supreme Court 2013du14726, *Qualcomm I* Market Dominance Abuse, January 31, 2019.
Supreme Court 2018du3770, *LGU Plus* Market Dominance Abuse, June 30, 2021.

[118] KFTC 2023-103, June 20, 2023.

Supreme Court 2020du31897, *Qualcomm II* Market Dominance Abuse, April 13, 2023.
Alcoa, 148 F.ed 416, 424, 2d Cir. 1945.
American Tobacco, 328 U.S. 781, Supreme 1946.
Archer-Daniels-Midland, 695 F. Supp. 1000, S.D. Iowa 1987.
Archer-Daniels-Midland, 866 F.2rd 242, 8th Cir. 1988.
Brooke Group Ltd. vs. Brown & Williamson Tobacco Corp., 509 U.S. 209, Supreme 1993
China NDRC, *Qualcomm*, 2015.
Concord Boat vs. Brunswick 207 F.3d 1039, 8th Cir. 2000.
du Pont 351, U.S. 377, 76 S.Ct. 994, 100 L.Ed.1263, Supreme 1956.
EC C-3/37.990, *Intel*, May 13, 2009.
EC AT.40099, *Google Android*, June 18, 2018.
EU Court of Justice, *United Brands*, February 14, 1978
EU Court of Justice, *Intel*, September 6, 2017.
EU General Court, *Intel*, June 12, 2014.
EU General Court, *Google Shopping*, November 10, 2021.
FTC v. Morton Salt, 334 U.S. 37, Supreme 1948.
FTC v. Staples, 979 F. Supp. 1066, D.D.C. 1997.
Grinnell Corp., 384 U. 563, Supreme 1966.
Japan FTC, *Intel*, 2005.
Japan FTC, *Qualcomm*, 2009.
Japan FTC, *Qualcomm*, 2019.
LePage's v. 3M, 324 F.3d 141, 3rd Cir. 2003.
MCI v. AT&T, 708 F.2d 1081, 7th Cir. 1983.
Mercy Health Services, 920 F.Supp. 968, N.D. Iowa 1995.
Microsoft, 1995-2 Trade Cases para. 71, D.D.C. 1995.
Microsoft, No. 97-5343, D.C. Cir. 1988.
Microsoft, 253 F.3d 34, D.C. Cir., 2001.
Microsoft, 231 F. Supp. 2e 1443d 34, D.D.C. 2002.
Standard Oil Co. of New Jersey, 221 U.S. 1, Supreme 1911.
Taiwan FTC, *Qualcomm*, 2017.
Taiwan FTC, *Qualcomm*, 2018.
Terminal R.R. Ass'n, 224 U.S. 383, Supreme 1912.
United Mine Workers v. Pennington, 381 U.S. 657, Supreme 1965.

References

Adams WJ, Yellen JL (1976) Commodity bundling and the burden of monopoly. Q J Econ 90(3): 475–498
Amelio A, Jullien B (2012) Tying and freebies in two-sided markets. Int J Ind Org 30(5):436–446
Böckers V, Heimeshoff U (2014) The extent of European power markets. Energy Econ 46(2014): 102–111
Bork RH (1978) The antitrust paradox: a policy at war with itself. Basic Books
Capps CS, Dranove D, Greenstein S, Satterthwaite M (2001) The silent majority fallacy of the Elzinga-Hogarty criteria: a critique and new approach to analyzing hospital mergers. NBER Working Paper 8216
Carlton D, Waldman M (2002) The strategic use of tying to preserve and create market power in evolving industries. RAND J Econ 33:194–220
Choi JP, Stefanadis C (2001) Tying, investment, and the dynamic leverage theory. RAND J Econ 32:52–71
Church J, Ware R (2000) Industrial organization: a strategic approach. Irwin McGraw-Hill

Coate MB, Simons JJ (2009) Models, mathematics, and critical loss. Mimeo

Cowling K, Waterson M (1976) Price-cost margins and market structure. Economica 43:267–274

Danger KL, Frech HE III (2001) Critical thinking about 'critical loss' in antitrust. Antitrust Bull 46(2):339–355

Deaton A, Muellbauer J (1980) An almost ideal demand system. Am Econ Rev 70(3):312–326

Daljord O, Sorgard L, Thomassen O (2007) The SSNIP test and market definition with the aggregate diversion ratio: A reply to Katz and Shapiro. J Comp Law Econ 3:263–270

Dranove D, Sfekas A (2009) The revolution in health care antitrust: new methods and provocative implications. Milbank Q 87:607–632

Elzinga KG, Hogarty TF (1973) The problem of geographic market delineation in. antimerger suits. Antitrust Bull 18(1):45–81

Engle RF, Granger CWJ (1987) Co-integration and error correction: representation, estimation, and testing. Econometrica 55(2):251–276

European Commission (1997) Commission notice on the definition of the relevant market for the purposes of community competition law. Off J Eur Commun C 372

European Commission (2005) DG competition discussion paper on the application of article 82 of the treaty to exclusionary abuses

European Commission (2008) Guidance on the commission's enforcement priorities in applying article 82 EC treaty to abusive exclusionary conduct by dominant undertakings

Farrell J, Shapiro C (2008) Improving critical loss. Antitrust Source

Forni M (2004) Using stationarity tests in antitrust market definition. Am Law Econ Rev 6(2): 441–464

Fumagalli C, Motta M, Calcagno C (2018) Exclusionary practices: the economics of monopolization and abuse of dominance. Cambridge University Press

Gilbert RJ (1999) Networks, standards, and the use of market dominance. In: Kwoka JE, White LJ (eds) The Antitrust Revolution, 3rd edn. Oxford University Press

Gibert RJ, Katz ML (2001) An economist's guide to U.S. v. Microsoft. J Econ Perspect 15(2):25–44

Granger CWJ (1969) Investing causal relations by econometric models and cross-spectral methods. Econometrica 37(3):424–438

Harris R, Jorde T (1983) Market definition in the merger guidelines: implications for antitrust enforcement. Calif Law Rev 71:464–482

Jeon S (2004) Geographic market definition relevant to Moohak-Daesun Merger. Expert Witness Report to Seoul Hight Court. [in Korean]

Jeon S (2007) Economic analysis of competitive effects of Intel's rebates. Expert Witness Report to KFTC. [in Korean]

Jeon S (2008) Complementary economic analysis of competitive effects of Intel's rebates. Expert Witness Report to KFTC. [in Korean]

Jeon S (2016) Anti-competitiveness of, and corrective remedies for, Qualcomm's Business Model. Expert Witness Report to KFTC. [in Korean]

Jeon S (2020) Fair trade cases and economic analyses. Park Young Publishing. [in Korean]

Jeon S, Lee H (2005) Geographic market definition relevant to Posco's refusal of trade. Expert witness report to the Supreme court. [in Korean]

Jeon S, Nahm J (2017) Economic effects of Siemens' policy of pricing CT/MRI SSK. Expert Witness Report to KFTC. [in Korean]

Jeon S, You J (2008) Economic analysis for defining market relevant to video-streaming contents and evaluating the status of market dominance. Expert Witness Report to KFTC. [in Korean]

Jeon S, Kim C, Park S, Yoon K (2005) Product market definition relevant to Hite-Jinro Merger and portfolio effects of the Conglomerate Merger. Expert Witness Report to KFTC. [in Korean]

Jeon S, Han C, Kim S, Chung J (2020) Economic analysis of abuse of market dominance by Naver Shopping. Expert witness report to KFTC. [in Korean]

Katz ML, Shapiro C (2003) Critical loss: let's tell the whole story. Antitrust 17:49–56

Korea Fair Trade Commission (2021) Guidelines for review of the abuses of market dominance position

Korea Presidential Decree (2021) Enforcement Decree of the Monopoly Regulation and Fair Trade Act, No. 32274
Kranttenmaker T, Salop S (1986) Anticompetitive exclusion: raising rivals' costs to achieve power over price. Yale Law J 96:209–295
Kreps DM, Wilson R (1982) Reputation and imperfect information. J Econ Theory 27(2):253–279
Kuhn K-U, Van Reenen J (2009) Interoperability and market foreclolsure in the European Microsoft Case. In: Lyons B (ed) Cases in European Competition Policy. Cambridge Press
Landes W, Posner R (1981) Market power in antitrust cases. Harv Law Rev 94:937–996
Langenfeld J, Li W (2001) Critical loss analysis in evaluating mergers. Antitrust Bull 2001:299–337
Marvel HP (1982) Exclusive dealing. J Law Econ 25(1):1–26
McAfee RP, McMillan J, Whinston MD (1989) Multiproduct monopoly, commodity bundling, and correlation of values. Q J Econ 104(2):371–383
McGee JS (1958) Predatory price cutting: the standard oil (N. J.) case. J Law Econ 1:137–169
Milgrom P, Roberts J (1982) Predation, reputation, and entry deterrence. J Econ Theory 27(2): 280–312
Motta M (2004) Competition policy theory and practice. Cambridge University Press
O'Brien DP, Wickelgren AL (2003) A critical analysis of critical loss analysis. Antitrust Law J 71: 161–184
OECD (2008) Roundtable on bundled rebate and loyalty discounts and rebates. June 10:2008
Pepal L, Richards D, Norman G (2014) Industrial organization: contemporary theory and empirical applications, 5th edn. Wiley
Posner RA (2001) Antitrust Law, 2nd edn. The University of Chicago Press
Rasmussen EB, Ramseyer JM, Wiley JS Jr (1991) Naked exclusion. Am Econ Rev 81(5): 1137–1145
Rodriguez AE, Williams MD (2001) Measuring the intensity of competition across. Geographic markets. Litig Econ Rev 5(1):19–27
Rubinfeld DL (2014) Maintenance of Monopoly: *U.S. v. Microsoft* (2001). In: Kwoka JE Jr, White LJ (eds) The Antitrust Revolution, 6th edn. Oxford University Press
Salop S, Sheffman D (1983) Raising rivals' costs. Am Econ Rev 73(2):267–271
Salop S, Sheffman D (1987) Cost-raising strategies. J Ind Econ 36:19–34
Scheffman D (1992) The application of raising rivals' costs theory to antitrust. Antitrust Bull 37(1): 187–206
Scheffman DT, Simons JJ (2003) The state of critical loss analysis: let's make sure we understand the whole story. Antitrust Source, pp 1–9
Segal I, Whinston JD (2000a) Naked exclusion: comment. Am Econ Rev 90(March):296–309
Segal I, Whinston JD (2000b) Exclusive contracts and protection of investments. RAND J Econ 31 (Winter):603–633
Selton R (1978) The chain store paradox. Theory Decis 9(2):127–159
Stigler GJ (1968) A note on block booking. In: Stigler GJ (ed) The organization of industries. Irwin, Homewood, IL
Stigler GJ, Sherwin RA (1985) The extent of the market. J Law Econ 28(3):555–585
US Antitrust Modernization Commission (2007) Report and recommendations
US DOJ (2008) Competition and monopoly: single-firm conduct under Section 2 of the Sherman Act
US DOJ and FTC (2010) Horizontal merger guidelines
Viscusi WK, Vernon JM, Harrington JE (2000) Economics of regulation and antitrust, 4th edn. MIT Press
Werden GJ (2003) The 1982 Merger guidelines and the ascent of the hypothetical monopolist paradigm. Antitrust Law J 17:259–266
Werden GJ, Froeb LM (1993) Correlation, causality, and all that jazz: the inherent shortcomings of price tests for antitrust market delineation. Rev Ind Org 8(3):329–353
Whinston MD (1990) Tying foreclosure, and exclusion. Am Econ Rev 80(4):837–859

Whinston MD (2006) Lecture on antitrust economics. MIT Press
Williamson O (1968) Wage rates as a barrier to entry: the pennington case in perspective. Q J Econ 82(1):85–116
Wooldridge JM (2006) Introductory econometrics: a modern approach, 3rd edn. Thomson
Wu L, Wu D (1997) Measuring the degree of interindustry competition in U.S. v. Continental Can. Antitrust Bull 4(1):51–84

Chapter 5
Merger Regulation in Korea

One of the fundamental objectives of the Monopoly Regulation and Fair Trade Act (MRFTA) is to prevent "any excessive concentration of economic power," as stated in Sect. 5.1. The concept of economic power concentration can be stratified into three levels within the scope of economic organization: (i) concentration of ownership and control within the governance of a firm or a group of firms, (ii) concentration of a firm's activities within a particular market, and (iii) overall concentration of a firm's activities across the economy. Merger regulation primarily aims to curb market concentration beyond its current state, thereby influencing the overall concentration within the economy. Most countries implement merger regulations based on the same fundamental principle of reasonableness. Conversely, chaebol regulation, addressed in Chap. 2, specifically addresses the unique challenges associated with the concentration of ownership and control and the general economic concentration in Korea that have arisen during periods of rapid economic growth.

In this chapter, we will first explore the primary characteristics of the Korea Fair Trade Commission's (KFTC) approach to enforcing merger regulations. Subsequently, I will provide a detailed examination of the various concepts and analytical tools employed in the assessment of the competitive effects of mergers. This includes traditional methodologies such as market share and concentration indexes, as well as more contemporary approaches like empirical analyses derived from natural experiments, merger simulations, and Upward Pricing Pressure (UPP) metrics for horizontal mergers. Additionally, for the analysis of non-horizontal mergers, I will cover a range of methodologies, including vertical arithmetic, bargaining models, the vertical Gross Upward Pricing Pressure Index (vGUPPI), Cournot effects, and considerations around the elimination of double marginalization. These diverse tools enable a nuanced understanding of the potential competitive impacts across different merger types, ensuring a thorough and sophisticated regulatory review. Lastly, we examine a series of intriguing Korean merger regulation cases, which include *Hyundai Motor—Kia Car* in 1999, *Moohak Soju—Daesun Soju* in 2003, *Hite Beer—Jinro Soju* in 2006, *Eland Outlets—Carrefour* in 2006,

S. Jeon, *Antitrust Policy in Korea*, https://doi.org/10.1007/978-981-95-0632-3_5

eBay—G Market in 2009, *Microsoft—Nokia* in 2015, SK *Telecomm—CJ HelloVision* in 2016, *Delivery Hero—Woowa Brothers* in 2021, and *Korean Air—Asiana Airlines* in 2022. The analysis of these cases employed various economic methodologies, and many experts, including myself, participated in the evaluations. Furthermore, these cases offer an international perspective through which to view Korean merger regulations in comparison with those of other nations.

5.1 Main Features of Merger Regulation in Korea

In this section, I provide a concise overview of the principal components of merger regulation, including the procedure for merger review and the evolution of enforcement practices within the Korean regulatory framework.

5.1.1 Key Elements

The MRFTA §9 prohibits any "combination of enterprises" that may "substantially restrain competition." This encompasses various forms of business combinations, including stock acquisitions, concurrent executive positions, business transfers, and participation in new company establishments. A combination is presumed to significantly impede competition under specific conditions: if the aggregate market shares of the involved companies (i) meet the presumptive requirements of a market-dominant enterprise, (ii) hold the largest share in the relevant market, and (iii) exceed the market share of the second-largest firm by at least 25 percentage points. These presumptive conditions can be summarized as follows: if the combined enterprise's market share, denoted by s_1, is such that (i) $s_1 \geq 50\%$, or s_1 is the largest and CR3 $\geq 75\%$, and (ii) $s_1 \geq 4/3\ s_2$ (where s_2 is the market share of the second-largest company). Furthermore, with the intention of protecting small and medium-sized enterprises (SMEs), a presumption of merger regulation applicability arises if a large company or a person with a special interest merges enterprises in a specific business area where SMEs command at least two-thirds of the market share and the combined entity would possess 5% or more of the market share. This presumption is rebuttable by considering other market factors, such as barriers to entry, foreign competition, adjacent markets, and buyer power. Defenses based on merger-specific efficiencies, cognizable efficiencies, and the failing firm doctrine are also permissible.

The KFTC's merger assessment process commences with the mandatory reporting of a business combination when the aggregate assets or sales of the involved companies surpass a specified threshold, and the degree of consolidation is substantial in terms of ownership and control. In addition to the total assets or sales criteria for reporting obligations, a comprehensive revision of the Act in 2021 introduced the criteria of "transaction value" or "significant activity." Consequently, even if the assets or sales of the partner company do not meet the reporting threshold, the acquiring company must report the merger if the transaction value exceeds a certain amount and the partner company has a significant domestic presence in terms of product or service supply or the use of research resources. (Act §11 Reporting on Combination of Enterprises). This revision aims to close the regulatory gap for platform businesses that may offer services free of charge to certain customers, thus potentially evading merger control.[1]

A report should be filed within 30 days after the date of the combination, as a general rule. However, if the combination involves at least one large company or meets the newly added criteria of transaction value and significant domestic activity, the report must be filed within the timeframe spanning from contract conclusion to combination completion. It is important to note that in Korea, *ex post* merger reporting is the norm, whereas prior reporting is the exception. This stands in contrast to the *ex ante* reporting requirement commonly observed in jurisdictions like the United States and the EU. The KFTC is obligated to notify the parties of the merger review outcome within 30 days from the date of the filing. This review period can be extended by up to an additional 90 days. However, the time taken for the submission of supplementary documents is not counted within this deadline. Therefore, the actual review period can exceed 120 days for cases that are complex or significant.[2] Additionally, there is a provision for a preliminary review process. Parties intending to undertake a combination can request a preliminary review from the KFTC to determine whether the combination is permissible before the specified filing period. The same review period applies to these preliminary review cases as well.

5.1.2 Merger Review Process

The chart below illustrates the merger review process post-filing, as set out in the Korea Fair Trade Commission's merger guidelines (Fig. 5.1).[3]

[1] The issue surfaced in 2014 when Facebook's acquisition of WhatsApp did not trigger a reporting obligation to competition authorities in the EU, despite the platform having millions of users across European countries. In response to this oversight, Germany and Austria amended their merger reporting regulations in 2017, incorporating the size of the transaction volume as a criterion for reporting liability. This move was designed to address such lapses. On the other hand, the European Commission has not yet introduced notification thresholds based on transaction value.

[2] In the case of the *Microsoft-Nokia* merger in 2015, it took approximately 1 year and 9 months from the date of filing to reach a review conclusion by means of a consent decree. Moreover, in 2016, it took nearly 1 year and 8 months to ultimately halt the merger between *SK Telcomm and CJ HelloVision*.

[3] KFTC (2021), "Guidelines for the Merger Review," December 20, 2021. Refer to KFTC (2021, p. 144) *Annual White Report* for the flow chart.

For mergers eligible for a simplified review, the KFTC verifies the accuracy of the information provided in the report. The KFTC then communicates the results of the review within 15 days of the filing date.

For the general review process, the initial step involves defining the relevant market as outlined in Stage 2. This market is a specific business domain characterized by competitive interactions among concerned entities and is distinguished by the nature of the trade object (product market) and the locality (geographic market). The predominant method for determining market definition is the SSNIP test, as detailed in the preceding chapter. That is, the pertinent product (or geographic) market is identified as a collection of products (or areas) where a significant number of consumers are likely to switch their purchases in reaction to a SSNIP (a small but

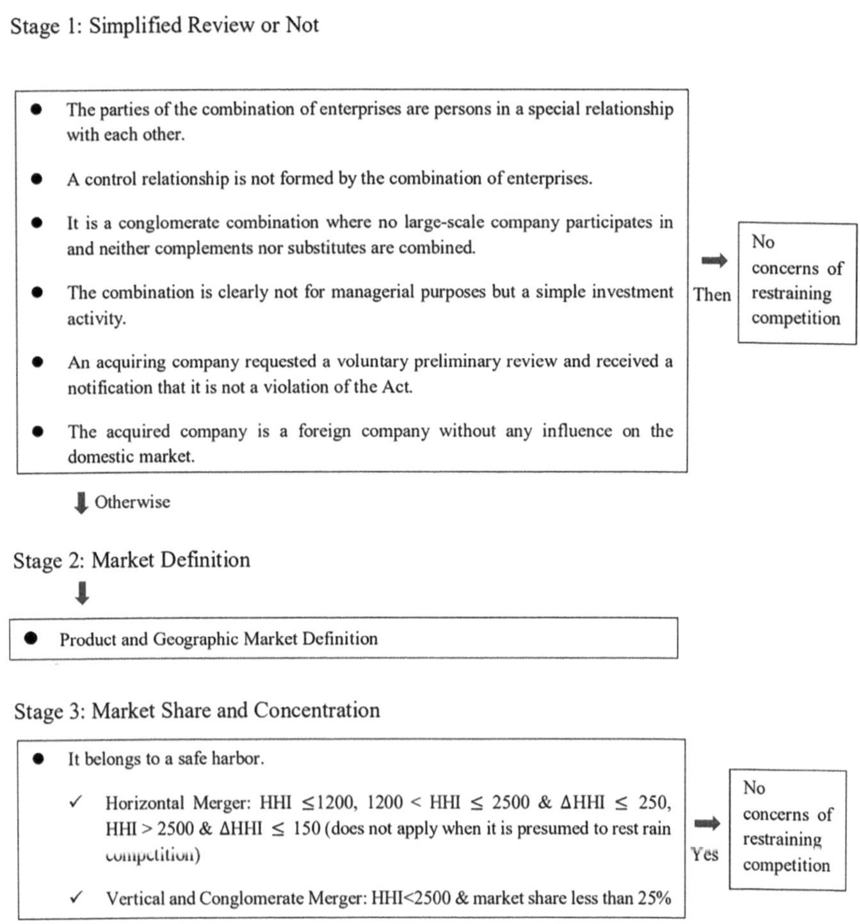

Fig. 5.1 Flow chart of KFTC merger review

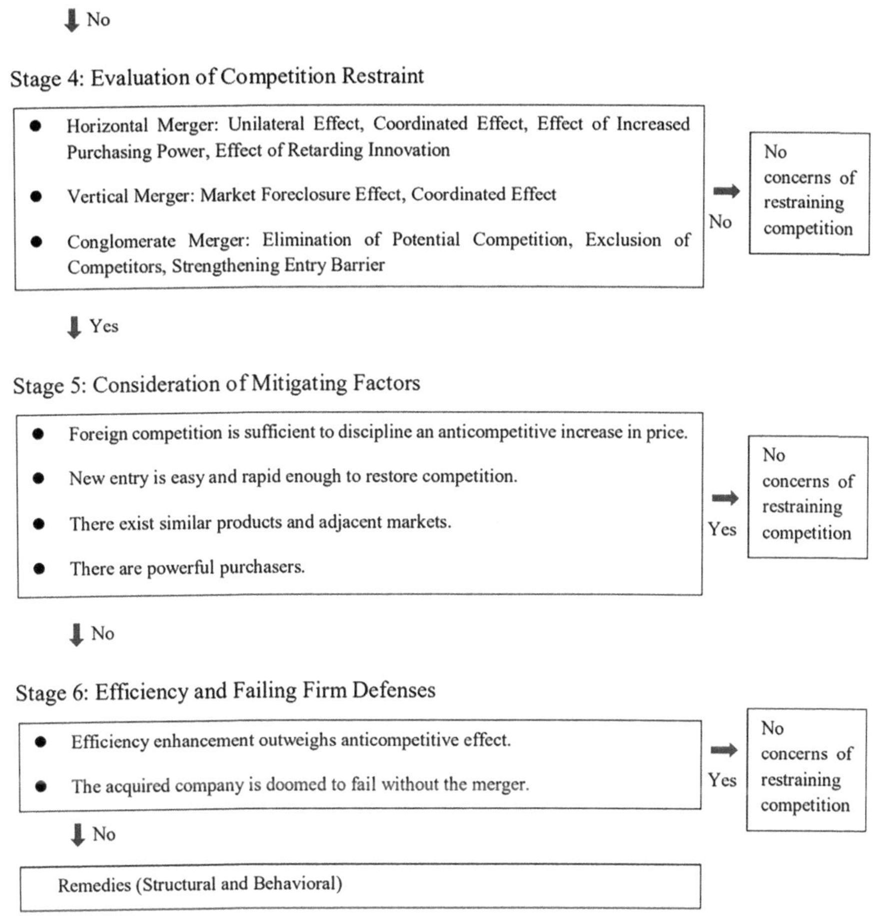

Fig. 5.1 (continued)

significant and non-transitory increase in price) concerning a specific product (or within a specific area). Defining the relevant market is of paramount importance for antitrust enforcement overall, as it pinpoints the competitors capable of competitively constraining the entities involved and preventing them from acting independently of market forces.[4] During merger assessment, this definition serves as the foundation for calculating the market shares of the firms within the market and determining the degree of market concentration, as addressed in Stage 3.

The KFTC's merger guidelines provide safe harbor thresholds for all types of mergers—horizontal, vertical, and conglomerate—by employing the Herfindahl-Hirschman Index (HHI) and its delta (ΔHHI) in the case of horizontal mergers. It's important to note that the MRFTA predetermines the presumption that a merger

[4]Refer to European Commission (1997).

significantly restrains competition based on market share parameters and the combined market share of the top three firms (CR3). This presumption is set forth in the Act itself, presenting a stringent threshold that may be challenging for the enforcement agency to counteract in practice, even though it is theoretically rebuttable. This explicit legislative approach to presumptive conditions is uncommon in the antitrust laws of other nations, where the conditions indicating anti-competitive concerns or establishing safe harbors are typically outlined at the guideline level, rather than in the statute.

The assessment of a horizontal merger that potentially restrains competition involves the evaluation of unilateral effects, coordinated effects, increased purchasing power, and the impact on innovation. The initial evaluation focuses on whether the merged entity can unilaterally alter competitive parameters such as price, output, quality, and innovation. This is assessed with reference to the combined market share, the degree of its increase, and its disparity from competitors' market shares. In markets with differentiated products, the direct competition between the merging firms takes precedence over market share. Therefore, the diversion ratio, which is part of the Upward Pricing Pressure (UPP) analysis, relies less on the traditional market definition and market share calculations. Coordinated effects stem from a reduced number of competitors, which may facilitate implicit collusion through parallel conduct and the monitoring and sanctioning of deviations. Horizontal mergers can also augment monopsony power, adversely affecting competition by diminishing the procurement of inputs or raw materials. The consideration of the impact on innovation is a relatively recent addition to merger analysis, as mergers can dampen the incentives for R&D and reduce competition in innovation.

Vertical mergers often lead to increased efficiencies through the reduction of transaction costs and the resolution of coordination failures between upstream and downstream firms. Nevertheless, they may also restrict competition if they result in market foreclosure. This occurs when the merged entity impedes competitors' access to supplies in the upstream market or to customers in the downstream market, or when it hinders the entry of potential new competitors. Additionally, the merged company could exploit trade information, such as pricing data, to coordinate or facilitate tacit collusion. Prior to a merger, a powerful buyer may have served as a regulator of coordination among upstream competitors; post-merger, this role may be diminished or lost. Conglomerate mergers, which involve companies in adjacent markets, can yield various efficiencies, including synergies from shared resources, risk diversification, and internal financing. However, they may also suppress competition by eliminating potential competitors, excluding rivals with comprehensive business capabilities, and creating barriers to market entry.

Even in the presence of competition concerns following a merger, several factors may alleviate such worries and restore competition. The importation of goods from overseas, the entry of new market participants, the availability of similar products in adjacent markets, and the presence of influential purchasers could all counteract any anticompetitive behavior from the merged entity. These factors may prevent the merged company from successfully raising prices or reducing quality, especially if the response from these countervailing forces is sufficiently swift.

Mergers of all types possess the capacity to increase efficiency; thus, the critical balance between potential anti-competitive effects and efficiency gains is a key aspect of merger regulation. Efficiency defenses are permissible when argued convincingly and verifiably as being specific to the merger, achievable solely through the merger, and not through less anti-competitive means. The KFTC guidelines recognize two categories of merger efficiencies: those related to production, sales, and research and development, and those impacting the national economy at large. The latter seems to be unique in Korean merger policy, taking into account factors such as employment, regional economic impact, influence on related industries, energy provision, and environmental considerations. This approach suggests a broader review criterion based on national or social welfare, as opposed to a narrow focus on consumer welfare. However, recent trends indicate that the KFTC has been aligning more closely with international standards, emphasizing consumer welfare in its merger review processes.

When a merger is assessed as significantly impeding competition, the imposition of corrective measures is necessary to address these concerns. These remedies are categorized as either "structural" or "behavioral." Structural remedies may involve injunctions, divestitures of assets, or restrictions on intellectual property rights. Behavioral remedies, on the other hand, restrict the terms, methods, or scope of the merging companies' sales activities internally for a set period. The KFTC's 2021 guidelines on merger remedies state that structural measures should be the default corrective action. Behavioral measures may accompany structural ones to ensure their effectiveness or may be used exclusively in instances where structural remedies are unfeasible or ineffective. It remains to be seen how this stance in the new guidelines will influence future KFTC policies on merger regulation, especially considering the historical rarity of structural remedies in its enforcement actions.

5.1.3 Enforcement Record

The period between 1981 and 1987 saw a modest application of merger regulation in Korea, with only six remedial corrections imposed. It was not until 1998, following the Asian Financial Crisis and subsequent demand for industrial restructuring, that the KFTC began to actively enforce merger regulations.[5] This period also saw a surge in mergers driven by the establishment of new IT companies. The MRFTA was amended in 1999 to articulate defenses for mergers, including efficiency and failing firm arguments, as well as the introduction of behavioral remedies to mitigate competition concerns. The merger between *Hyundai Motor and Kia Car* in 1999 is a notable example, where KFTC approved the merger while imposing behavioral remedies specific to the truck market. This decision highlighted two contentious issues: whether industrial restructuring demands during a financial crisis could

[5] See KFTC (2011), *30 Years History of Fair Trade Commission*.

override stringent antitrust merger reviews and whether temporary price control as a behavioral remedy is sufficient to address significant competition concerns.

Table 5.1 summarizes the significant merger cases from 2001 onward, as documented in the KFTC *Annual White Paper*. It includes a selection of high-profile cases where the KFTC imposed remedies. Please note that this list is not exhaustive but includes a curated set of instances that required specific corrective measures following an in-depth review by the KFTC.

Between 2001 and 2024, the KFTC reported on 59 cases in its *Annual White Paper*. Out of these, 6 were blocked and 4 were withdrawn. One case was resolved by consent decree, 17 were approved with structural remedies, and 32 with behavioral remedies—accounting for more than 50% of the cases. Notably, of the cases that were approved with behavioral remedies, 9 mergers, constituting 30%, involved telecommunications companies. This reflects the consideration of rapid technological and business model advancements in the telecom industry. A unique case was the 2016 *SK Telecom and CJ HelloVision* merger, which was blocked, contrasting with the 2019 merger of *LGU Plus and CJ HelloVision*, which was allowed with behavioral remedies. Despite the similarity of the telecom operations of the acquiring companies and a 3-year gap, the merger involving SK Telecom was not permitted, potentially due to its more substantial comprehensive business power compared to LGU Plus. As for the structural remedies, they were imposed in 17 cases, roughly 30% of the total. These remedies included divestitures of plants, assets, intellectual property, local stores, and shares associated with the competitive concerns.

Blocked merger cases are relatively infrequent in Korea, with only 6 out of 59 reported cases (approximately 10%) being blocked. Two notable examples include the *Moohak-Daesun* case in 2002 and the *Samick-Youngchang* case in 2004, both involving the complete disposal of stocks post-merger. The four withdrawn cases were international, involving foreign companies with global operations, where coordination with antitrust agencies like the US DOJ, FTC, and the EC took place. In these cases, the companies retracted their merger plans, likely due to a negative outlook on approval. The consent decree in the *Microsoft-Nokia* merger of 2015 stands out especially, marking the first time a merger in Korea was concluded by a consent decree. This case is also notable for the KFTC's unique stance compared to the unconditioned approval by US and EU authorities.

5.2 Methods of Evaluating Competitive Effects of Horizontal Merger

The conventional method of assessing the competitive impact of a horizontal merger involves determining the appropriate market scope, calculating the changes in market shares and concentration following the merger, and using these findings to assess potential harm to competition and determine whether the merger should be

Table 5.1 Summary of KFTC merger regulation since 2001 (Cases highlighted in bold are examined more thoroughly in Sect. 5.4. Cases that are underlined indicate instances that are blocked)

Year	Companies	Merger type (relevant market)	Remedy/Conclusion
2001	SK + Daehan Oil Pipeline	Vertical (domestic oil products + oil transport)	Behavioral
2002	Kolon + Kohap Nylon	Horizontal (domestic nylon film)	Structural (plant divestiture)
	Moohak + Daesun Distilling	Horizontal (local soju)	Blocked (complete stock disposal) approved by the Seoul High Court in 2004
2003	LG Chemical &[a] Honam Petro Chemical + Hyundai Petro Chemical	Horizontal (domestic petro chemical products)	Structural (divided plant takeover)
	Yongsan Chemical + Korea PTG	Vertical (domestic chemical products + material)	Behavioral
2004	Samick + Youngchang Musical Instruments	Horizontal (domestic upright/grand/digital piano)	Blocked (complete stock disposal) approved by the Supreme Court in 2008
	INI Steel & Hyundai Hysco + Hanbo Steel	Horizontal (domestic steel)	Structural (plant divestiture)
2005	Hyundai Motor & Siemens VDO Automotive + Hyundai Autonet	Vertical (domestic car assembler + auto parts)/Horizontal (auto parts)	Behavioral
	Hite Beer + Jinro	Conglomerate (domestic beer + soju)/Horizontal (domestic soju)	Behavioral
	Hyundai Home Shopping + Kwanak Cable TV	Horizontal (local cable TV)/ Vertical (local cable + TV home shopping)	Behavioral
2006	Dongyang Chechul Chemical + Colombian Chemical	Horizontal (domestic carbon black)	Structural (stock disposal or plan divestiture) approved by the Supreme Court in 2009
	Eland Outlets+ Carrefour	Horizontal (local large discount stores)	Structural (local stores divestiture)
	Emart + Walmart	Horizontal (local large discount stores)	Structural (local stores divestiture) partly approved by Seoul High Court in 2008
2007	CJ Cable Net + 2 Cable TVs in Chungnam Province	Horizontal (local cable TV)	Behavioral
	Posco + Hankuk Core	Vertical (domestic steel products + cores)	Behavioral
	Owens Corning + Saint-Gobain Vetrotex	Horizontal (domestic glass reinforced fiber)	Structural (stock disposal or plant divestiture)

(continued)

Table 5.1 (continued)

Year	Companies	Merger type (relevant market)	Remedy/Conclusion
2008	SK Telcom + Hanano Telcom	Horizontal/Vertical/Conglomerate (various local telecom services)	Behavioral
	E Bay + G Market	Horizontal (local open market)	Behavioral
	Home Plus + Home Ever	Horizontal (local large discount stores)	Behavioral
2009	Lotte Hotel + Paradise Global	Horizontal (local tax-free stores)	Blocked
	Digital Medianet + Hankook Cable TV (Kyungki East)	Horizontal (local cable TV)	Behavioral
	Lotte Chilsung Beverage + Haetae Beverage	Horizontal (domestic fruit drink beverage)	Behavioral
2010	CJ O Shopping + On Media	Horizontal (domestic program provider)/Conglomerate (cable system operator)	Behavioral
	BHP Billiton + Rio Tinto	Horizontal (worldwide ironstone)	Withdrawn
2011	T Broad Nakdong + East-West Digital Broadcasting	Horizontal (local cable TV)	Behavioral
	Western Digital + BBT Technology	Horizontal (worldwide hard disk drive)	Structural (asset disposal)
	Lotte Shopping + CS Retail	Horizontal (local super supermarket)	Structural (local stores disposal)
2012	JCN Unsan Broadcasting + CNM Ulsan Cable TV	Horizontal (local cable TV)	Behavioral
	Lotte Incheon Development + Shinsegae Incheon Department Store	Horizontal (local department store)	Structural (local department store disposal)
2013	MediaTek + M Star Semiconductor	Horizontal (worldwide SoC for DTV)	Behavioral
	ASML + Cymer	Vertical (worldwide lithography system + light sources)	Behavioral
	Essilor Amera + Daemyung Optical	Horizontal (domestic single/progress focus glasses)	Blocked
2014	B&M Holdings + Item Bay	Horizontal (domestic game item intermediation)	Behavioral
	Hyundai Steel, etc. + Dongbu Special Steel	Vertical (domestic wire rod + CHQ wire/CD bar)	Behavioral
	Hawha Chemical + Samsung Total	Horizontal/Conglomerate (domestic various petrochemical products)	Behavioral
2015	**Microsoft + Nokia Mobile Handset**		Consent decree

(continued)

Table 5.1 (continued)

Year	Companies	Merger type (relevant market)	Remedy/Conclusion
		Horizontal (worldwide tablet PC)/Vertical (worldwide mobile software + handset)	
	American Materials + Tokyo Electron	Horizontal (worldwide semiconductor manufacturing equipment)	Withdrawn
2016	**SK Telecom + CJ HelloVision**	Horizontal/Vertical/Conglomerate (various domestic telecom services)	Blocked
	LAM Research + KLA Denko	Vertical (worldwide semiconductor manufacturing equipment upstream + downstream)	Withdrawn
	Beringer Engelheim + Sanopy	Horizontal (worldwide veterinary drugs)	Structural ((asset disposal)
2017	Dow + Dupont	Horizontal/Conglomerate (worldwide chemical products)	Structural (asset disposal)
	Esmeralda + DS Power	Vertical (local waste heat vapor + energy)	Behavioral
	Maersk Line + Hamburg Sud	Horizontal (overseas container transportation)	Structural (dropout from some overseas consortia)
	CJ Hellovision + Hana Broadcasting	Horizontal (local cable TV)	Behavioral
2018	Qualcomm + NXP Semiconductor	Conglomerate (worldwide semiconductor products for various uses)	Structural (IPs Disposal) + Behavioral (licensing condition)
	Celanese + Blackstone	Horizontal (worldwide special chemical products)	Withdrawn
	Linde + Flex Air	Horizontal (worldwide industrial gas)	Structural (asset disposal)
2019	LGU Plus + CJ Hellovision	Horizontal/Vertical/Conglomerate (various domestic telecom services)	Behavioral
	Dongbang + Sunkwang + Younjin + Wooryung	Vertical (local car ferry cargo unloading + ferry port operation)	Behavioral
2020	**Delivery Hero + Woowa Bro.**	Horizontal (domestic delivery app/local delivery mediation/local shared kitchen)	Structural (stock disposal)
	Borealis + DYM Solution	Horizontal/Conglomerate/Vertical (various domestic semiconductive shields of power cable and materials)	Behavioral
2021	KT Skylife + Hyundae HCN, Hyundae Media	Horizontal/Conglomerate/Vertical (cable TV, PP, etc.)	Behavioral
2022	**Korean Air+Asiana Air**	Horizontal/Conglomerate/Vertical	Structural (slots and transportation rights) +

(continued)

Table 5.1 (continued)

Year	Companies	Merger type (relevant market)	Remedy/Conclusion
		(passenger and cargo airline, related services)	Behavior (airfares and seat supplies)
	LX Int'l & LX Housis + Hankuk Glass Indus.	Horizontal/Vertical (plain glass, coated glass, construction window)	Behavioral
2023	Hanwha + Daewoo Shipbuilding	Vertical (defense industry, shipbuilding)	Behavioral
	Broadcom + VMware	Conglomerate (Fiber Channel host bust adapter + server virtualization software)	Behavioral
2024	Mega Study + ST Unitas	Horizontal (online class)	Blocked
	Kakao + SM Entertainment	Horizontal/Vertical/Conglomerate (pop music related)	Behavioral
	HD Korea Shipbuilding & Offshore Engineering + STX Heavy Industry	Vertical /Horizontal	Behavioral

[a]"&" denotes a consortium

approved.[6] However, defining the relevant market is often complex and subject to controversy. Consequently, alternative analytical techniques have been developed to assess the competitive effects of a horizontal merger without relying solely on market definition. In this section, I will discuss both the traditional approach and newer methods such as empirical analysis of "natural experiment" data, merger simulation, and Upward Pricing Pressure (UPP).

5.2.1 Traditional Method of Using Market Share and Concentration

The MRFTA specifies the criteria for presuming the anti-competitiveness of a merger based on market shares and concentration ratio. Denoting the market share of the combined entities by s_1, a merger is presumed to raise concerns of restraining competition if (i) $s_1 \geq 50\%$ or s_1 is the largest and CR3 $\geq 75\%$, and (ii) $s_1 \geq 4/3\ s_2$ (s_2 is the market share of the second largest company). Additionally, the KFTC merger guideline proposes a safe harbor for mergers if the Herfindahl-Hirschman Index (HHI), a measure of market concentration, satisfies certain thresholds: HHI $\leq$ 1200,

[6]The concept of a "relevant market" was initially mentioned in the *Columbia Steel* case in 1948. Subsequently, the *Philadelphia National Bank* case in 1963 proposed that mergers resulting in a significant shift in market shares within a well-defined market might be disallowed due to concerns related to anti-competitive practices.

$1200 < \text{HHI} \leq 2500$ & Δ HHI ≤ 250, HHI > 2500 & Δ HHI ≤ 150. However, it is important to note that these conditions for presumption and safe harbor are not definitive. They serve as an initial evaluation and require further examination. One of the challenges with the traditional approach of utilizing market shares and concentration is its dependence on market definition, which is often a subject of controversy.

In evaluating the competitive impact of a hypothetical merger between Coke and Pepsi, the definition of the relevant market is pivotal. If the market is defined as "carbonated drinks," the merger would likely raise significant anticompetitive concerns due to the high combined market share of the two largest market participants. Conversely, if the market is broadly defined as "portable bottled drinks," which includes a wider range of beverages beyond carbonated drinks, the merger may not appear as anticompetitive, with the merged entity facing substantial competition from other types of drinks. The use of market share as a metric can be limiting because it does not necessarily reflect the degree of product substitutability within the market. For example, if Coke, Pepsi, and 7up each have a one-third share of the "carbonated drink" market, a merger between any two of these firms would result in a combined two-thirds market share. However, the actual competitive impact could vary. Coke and Pepsi are direct substitutes, and a merger would likely reduce competition significantly. On the other hand, if 7up occupies a different niche or appeals to different consumer preferences, a merger with Coke may not have the same anticompetitive effect, despite resulting in the same market share change. Therefore, understanding the level of substitutability between products is essential for a more nuanced and accurate competitive analysis.

Intuitively, market shares are indicative of a firm's competitive behavior and market power. A firm with a significant market share may be less inclined to lower prices, as such a decision impacts not only the acquisition of new customers but also the existing customer base. Furthermore, a dominant firm could potentially increase production more substantially in absolute terms compared to a smaller firm.[7] A fundamental hypothesis within traditional industrial organization economics, which follows the Structure-Conduct-Performance (S-C-P) paradigm, suggests that higher market concentration can lead to more collusive behavior among firms, potentially resulting in poorer economic performances.[8] This traditional notion has evolved, leading to the establishment of a theoretical relationship among market structure (S), firm conduct (C), and market performance (P), expressed as: $\frac{P-MC}{P} = \frac{(1+v)H}{E_D}$ where H denotes Herfindahl-Hirschman Index (a measure of market concentration), v measures the degree of collusive behavior among firms in the market, the extent of concerted conduct of firms in the market, and E_D is the price elasticity of market

[7] See US DOJ and FTC (2010, p. 15) Guidelines.

[8] One of the long-standing disagreements between the Harvard School and the Chicago School centers around this particular issue.

demand.[9] This equation suggests that the price-cost margin is directly proportional to the degree of market concentration and the extent of collusive behavior and inversely proportional to the price elasticity of demand.

This passage underscores the theoretical underpinnings for using market shares and concentration as indicators in the assessment of a merger's competitive effects. Although defining the market is often a challenging and contentious process, it remains a crucial step in the majority of antitrust cases, particularly those concerning mergers and market dominance. Even with newer analytical methods that do not commence with a market definition, a diluted form of market definition, such as "identifying competitive alternatives available to customers," is often required at some stage of the analysis.[10] Furthermore, while recently developed tools like merger simulation and Upward Pricing Pressure (UPP) are primarily employed to gauge the unilateral effects of a merger, the analysis of coordinated effects still predominantly depends on the traditional method of utilizing market shares and concentration indices. This reliance is due to the fact that coordinated effects pertain to the behavior of firms within a market, which is intrinsically linked to their market shares and the overall market structure.

5.2.2 Empirical Analysis Based on "Natural Experiments"

In merger analysis, employing the concept of "natural experiments" provides a means to deduce the competitive impact of a merger without relying on market definitions, which are often contentious. Natural experiments are historical occurrences that enable a connection to be drawn between changes in competitive circumstances and market outcomes.[11] This approach can be particularly effective in retail industries, where markets differ regionally and entries and exits of firms occur frequently. The *1997 Staples-Office Depot* merger case is a prime example where economic experts for both the US FTC and the defendant utilized historical data within an econometric model to project the potential effects of the merger on Staples' pricing. In this case, there was a stark contrast in the definition of the relevant product market; the FTC posited a narrow definition limited to the sale of "consumable office supplies through office superstores (OSSs)," whereas the defendant argued for a broader definition encompassing "all" office supplies sales, including those through "non-OSSs" and "durable" goods.[12] The application of

[9]Cowling and Waterson (1976) established this relationship using an oligopolistic framework that encompasses Cournot quantity rivalry. Please refer to Sect. 4.3 in Chap. 4 for further details.

[10]See US DOJ and FTC (2010, p. 7) Guidelines.

[11]In the context of merger analysis, the term "natural experiments" can be described as "historical occurrences that links changes in competitive circumstances and changes in market performance." [Coate (2013)].

[12]For a comprehensive overview of the development and significant aspects of the Staples case, refer to Dalkir and Warren-Boulton (2004).

empirical analysis grounded in natural experiments provided an alternative route to address the contentious issue of market definition.

Professor Ashenfelter, representing the FTC, and Professor Hausman, on behalf of Staples, utilized the widely accepted fixed effects panel model[13] to explain the Staples' price index. Their analysis incorporated the presence and number of different competitors, including Office Depot, although they differed in the details of their respective models.[14] The FTC's proposed model is as follows:

$$\log(p_{it}) = \alpha_i + \sum_{k=1}^{K} [\beta_{1k} D_{kit} + \beta_{2k} \log(N_{kit})] + \gamma_i t + \varepsilon_{it}; \quad i = 1, \ldots, N; t = 1, \ldots, T \tag{5.1}$$

where

p_{it} = price index of Staples' store i in t,[15]

α_i = store i's fixed effects,

D_{kit} = absence dummy which is 0 if competitor k exists in i's local market at period t, and 1 otherwise,

N_{kit} = number of competitor k's stores in i's local market at period t,[16] and

ε_{it} = disturbance term with mean zero.

In this model, the variable $\{\alpha_i : i = 1, \ldots, N\}$ represents the fixed effect for each Staples' store and captures unique characteristics of individual stores that remains constant over periods. These characteristics could include factors like rent costs, utility expenses, store size, and store presentation style, among others, which collectively impact the store's pricing but do not change from one period to another. The log-linear model indicated by Eq. (5.1) suggests a nonlinear relationship between price and the level of competition. This implies that the impact of adding competitors on price reduction diminishes as the number of competitors grows. The FTC model operates under the assumption that geographic markets are delineated by Metropolitan Statistical Areas (MSAs), using these demarcations as the boundaries for assessing competitive effects.

On the other hand, the Staples model deviates from the FTC's approach by not explicitly defining geographic local markets. Instead, it aims to capture the influence on pricing by considering the proximity of competitors to each store, implying that the effect on a store's pricing could vary based on how close or far away its competitors are located. This model allows for a nuanced understanding of

---

[13] The fixed effects model incorporates an explanatory factor that encompasses all hidden, consistent temporal elements that impact the variable being analyzed. In Eq. (5.1) below, α_i denotes these fixed, unobserved effects.

[14] Refer to Ashenfelter et al. (2006) for the common features and differences of the two models.

[15] The price index is constructed in two steps, firstly within a product group and secondly across product groups, where product groups are divided by price sensitivity.

[16] In cases of $N_{kit} = 0$, $\log(N_{kit})$ should be omitted and only $D_{kit} = 1$ be included in explanatory variables.

competitive impact, acknowledging that competition may have a different magnitude of effect on pricing depending on the distance between competing stores.

$$\ln(p_{it}) = \alpha_i + \sum_t^T \gamma_t D_t + \sum_{k=1}^K [\theta_{1k} D5_{kit} + \theta_{2k} D10_{kit} + \theta_{3k} D20_{kit}] + \sum_{k=1}^{K} [\theta_{4k} \ln(N5_{kit}) + \theta_{5k} \ln(N10_{kit}) + \theta_{6k} \ln(N20_{kit})] + \varepsilon_{it} \quad (5.2)$$
$$i = 1, \ldots, N; t = 1, \ldots, T.$$

where

D_t = time dummy[17]

D_{kit} = absence dummy which is 0 if competitor k exists within store i's radius at period t, and 1 otherwise; $D5$, D10, and $D20$ are to take into account the effects on price of competitors with the distance from store i as far as 0~5, 5~10 and 10~20,

N_{kit} = number of competitor k's stores within store i's radius at period t; $N5$, $N10$, and $N20$ are to take into account the effects on price of competitors with the distance from store i as far as 0~5, 5~10 and 10~20, and others are the same as in Eq. (5.1).

The model incorporates a broad spectrum of competitors, which includes not only office supply superstores (OSSs) such as Office Depot and Office Max but also non-OSSs like mass merchandisers (Walmart, Target, Kmart), computer superstores (Best Buy, Computer City, CompUSA), and warehouse clubs (PriceCostco, BJ's, Sam's Club). By factoring in all potential market participants, this model attempts to mitigate reliance on the contentious process of market definition, instead capturing a comprehensive competitive landscape. Thus, two models in Eqs. (5.1) and (5.2) are basically the same but with the differences in the way of addressing how the local market relevant to store i should be delineated; MSA was used in the former, while the local market was not defined explicitly, and the competitive effects are differentiated by distance in the latter.

Another subtle difference between the two approaches lies in the measurement of the merger effect. The FTC suggested the index of after-merger price increase as follows:

$$\Delta p_A = \frac{\sum_{i,t} \left[\beta_{1,OD} - \beta_{2,OD} \ln(N_{OD,i,t})\right]}{n_1} \quad (5.3)$$

which predicts how much the prices of Staples stores in the local market where Office Depot existed over the whole data periods would rise on average if all Office Depot's stores over the whole data periods do not operate anymore after the merger. On the other hand, Staples's index is:

[17] Notice the difference in how to treat the effect of time between Eqs. (5.1) and (5.2).

$$\Delta p_B = \frac{\sum_i [\theta_{1,OD} + \theta_{2,OD} + \theta_{3,OD} - \theta_{4,OD} \ln(N5_{OD,i,T}) - \theta_{5,OD} \ln(N10_{OD,i,T}) - \theta_{6,OD} \ln(N20_{OD,i,T})]}{m} \tag{5.4}$$

which predicts how much the prices of Staples stores in the local market where Office Depot existed <u>at the current moment</u> would rise on average if all Office Depot's stores <u>at the current moment</u> do not operate anymore after the merger.

Determining the superior model and index for accurately predicting post-merger price increases is a challenging task. It is difficult to determine beforehand which combination will provide more accurate results. In order to analyze the competitive impact of mergers in retail industries such as office superstores, large discount stores, and department stores, various combinations can be used. These industries have ample barcode scan data on prices, and their local markets are restricted geographically based on customer proximity. However, it is important to note that the concept of analyzing based on natural experiments extends beyond just econometric modeling and the utilization of extensive data sets. For instance, a simple comparison between the prices in areas where both Staples and Office Depot (and Office Max) were present and areas where only Staples (and Office Max) operated historically can serve as a concise example of how natural experiment analysis can be applied. Nevertheless, it is essential to acknowledge that the findings of such analysis may be influenced by factors other than competitive conditions.

5.2.3 *Merger Simulation*

The FTC and Staples models mentioned earlier are a simplified version that aims to explain pricing based on key factors of competitive conditions while abstracting from the competitive process. On the other hand, merger simulation seeks to comprehend the competitive process by employing a "structural" characteristic of "calibrating quantitative aspects (e.g., demand elasticities) of the industry" in an oligopolistic model and predicting the equilibrium choice of price and quantity before and after a merger.[18] Merger simulation has been utilized since the mid-1990s to assess the competitive impacts of mergers.[19]

---

[18]The horizontal merger guidelines by US DOJ and FTC (2010, pp. 25–26) note: "One type of modeling the Agencies use is "merger simulation," which calibrates a model to match quantitative aspects (e.g., demand elasticities) of the industry in which the merger occurs and uses the calibrated model to predict the outcome of the competitive process after the merger."

[19]For example, the methods were used in evaluating the mergers of 1995 *Interstate Bakeries-Continental Baking*, 2000 *MCI Worldcom-Sprint* in the United States and 2000 *Volvo-Scania* in the EU. In those merger evaluations, the substitutability among relevant differentiated products was regarded as significant.

Merger simulation entails a two-step process: (i) front-end estimation and (ii) back-end simulation. Initially, within an oligopoly framework, firms' profit maximization conditions are established. For industries offering differentiated products, a price (Bertrand) competition model is employed, whereas a quantity (Cournot) competition model is applied to industries with homogeneous products. By utilizing observed prices and quantities, relationships between estimated demand elasticities[20] and profit margins are deduced. These inferred profit margins enable the assessment of each firm's profitability. Subsequently, in the back-end simulation phase, new profit maximization conditions for the merged entity are formulated. The post-merger prices are forecasted by incorporating the demand estimates and profit margins obtained from the initial stage. This simulation approach provides a predictive outlook on the merger's impact on market prices.

Suppose, for the sake of illustration, that there are three companies manufacturing three distinct products and engaging in price competition using the Bertrand approach. Each company's demand function can be represented as follows:

$$q_1 = D_1(p_1, p_2, p_3); \quad q_2 = D_2(p_1, p_2, p_3); \quad q_3 = D_3(p_1, p_2, p_3). \tag{5.5}$$

In the process of conducting front-end estimation, the estimation of demand functions and elasticities involves utilizing suitable methods. This entails determining and quantifying the own elasticities as well as the cross elasticities, totaling nine elasticities in all.

The subsequent equations represent the primary requirements for achieving maximum profit:

$$\begin{aligned} \frac{\partial \pi_1}{\partial p_1} &= q_1 + (p_1 - c_1)\frac{\partial q_1}{\partial p_1} = 0; \\ \frac{\partial \pi_2}{\partial p_2} &= q_2 + (p_2 - c_2)\frac{\partial q_2}{\partial p_2} = 0; \\ \frac{\partial \pi_3}{\partial p_3} &= q_3 + (p_3 - c_3)\frac{\partial q_3}{\partial p_3} = 0, \end{aligned} \tag{5.6}$$

where $\pi_i = (p_i - c_i)q_i \; i = 1, 2, 3$.

[20] Estimating individual demand functions at the firm level is a challenging task. It involves tackling two main obstacles: the "curse of dimensionality" and "endogeneity." These hurdles become even more daunting when faced with limited data, as estimating N^2 coefficients for N products without making bold assumptions becomes nearly impossible. To address these challenges, several estimation methods have been developed, including Logit, Mixed Random Coefficient Logit, Multi-Stage Budget, and PCAIDS. These techniques aim to overcome the dimensionality problem. On the other hand, endogeneity, a common issue in demand estimation, can be addressed by employing suitable instrumental variables. Refer to Epstein and Rubinfeld (2004) and Whinston (2006) for further insights into the problems and solutions related to estimating demand functions for merger simulation.

By inputting the observed prices and quantities into the equations mentioned, we can evaluate the marginal costs or profit margins of each firm. This process is known as front-end estimation.

When firm 1 and firm 2 merge, the profit optimization requirements for the newly formed entity alter. The combined firm seeks to determine p_1 and p_2 that will maximize the total profit, represented by $\tilde{\pi} = \pi_1 + \pi_2$.

$$\begin{aligned}
\frac{\partial \tilde{\pi}}{\partial p_1} &= q_1 + (p_1 - \tilde{c_1})\frac{\partial q_1}{\partial p_1} + (p_2 - \tilde{c_2})\frac{\partial q_2}{\partial p_1} = 0, \\
\frac{\partial \tilde{\pi}}{\partial p_2} &= q_2 + (p_1 - \tilde{c_1})\frac{\partial q_1}{\partial p_2} + (p_2 - \tilde{c_2})\frac{\partial q_2}{\partial p_2} = 0; \\
\frac{\partial \pi_3}{\partial p_3} &= q_3 + (p_3 - c_3)\frac{\partial q_3}{\partial p_3} = 0.
\end{aligned} \tag{5.7}$$

The condition for firm 3 appears to be unchanged, but its price might change as it adapts to the modification in p_1 and p_2 following the merger. By incorporating the demand elasticities and marginal costs, represented by $\tilde{c_1}$ and $\tilde{c_2}$, which reflect the cost efficiency resulting from the merger (if a 10% cost reduction is expected post-merger ($\tilde{c_1} = 0.9\ c_1$ and $\tilde{c_2} = 0.9\ c_2$ with c_1 and c_2 being the estimated values in the first stage), we can predict the prices after the merger. This process is referred to as the back-end simulation.

Observe the modifications in the first two equations in Eq. (5.7) compared to their counterparts in Eq. (5.6). The additional terms of $(p_2 - \tilde{c_2})\frac{\partial q_2}{\partial p_1}$ and $(p_1 - \tilde{c_1})\frac{\partial q_1}{\partial p_2}$ reflect the effect of the merger on prices. That is, an individual firm before the merger considers only the effect on the demand of each own product, whereas the combined firm takes into account the effect on the demand of the other product under its control, in addition to the previous effect, when determining p_1 and p_2. This will induce the "upward pricing pressure" after the merger. In essence, the combined firm "internalizes" the externality between products 1 and 2. As it raises prices p_1 and p_2, the other firm has the incentive to follow suit and increase p_3.

Merger simulation offers several advantages compared to the simplistic approach of using market shares. Firstly, merger simulation enables the consideration of variations in cross elasticities between different products when evaluating the impact of a merger on prices. Let's consider a carbonated drink market with three products: Coke, Pepsi, and 7up. Each product holds an equal market share of 33.3%. If we assess the competitive effect of a merger solely based on market shares, we would not distinguish between a merger of Coke-Pepsi and a merger of Coke-7up. However, it is likely that the cross elasticities between Coke-Pepsi and Coke-7up differ. We expect Coke and Pepsi to be closer substitutes than Coke and 7up, resulting in stronger concerns regarding anti-competitive behavior in the former merger. Merger simulation, which involves a structural analysis, considers the magnitude of cross-price elasticities for products under the control of the merged firm. This becomes particularly important when examining the competitive impact of a merger involving firms that produce differentiated consumer products.

Secondly, merger simulation accounts for strategic interaction among firms within a market both as part of a merger and outside of it. Consider two scenarios reflecting the market share distribution among four firms: (i) firms 1, 2, 3, and 4 each have 25%, and (ii) firms 1 and 2 each have 25%, firm 3 has 45%, and firm 4 has 5%. The strategic significance of firm 3 varies markedly between markets (i) and (ii). Merger simulation can discern the implications of a merger between firms 1 and 2 under the distinct market conditions of (i) and (ii) with a high degree of accuracy. This is true even though the combined market share of the merging firms remains constant in both scenarios, as does the resultant change in the Herfindahl-Hirschman Index.

The third advantage of merger simulation lies in its ability to operate without a rigid definition of the relevant market. It focuses on products included in the merger, accounting for their strategic interactions and subsequent price changes. Prices of products not involved in the merger are assumed to be constant and are not included in these strategic considerations. Consequently, products whose prices are not anticipated to be affected by the merger can be excluded without significant impact. This allows for a targeted analysis, including only those products whose prices may be influenced by the strategic effects of a merger.

Finally, merger simulation offers the capacity to evaluate the dual effects of competition restraint and efficiency enhancement concurrently. With precise estimates of cost efficiencies resulting from a merger, we can incorporate the adjusted cost parameter values derived from initial estimations into subsequent simulations. For instance, anticipating a 10% cost reduction due to a merger allows us to apply the adjusted cost figures, such as multiplying the original costs c_1 and c_2 by 0.9 in Eq. (5.7). Additionally, it enables us to quantitatively determine the extent of efficiency gains or cost reductions needed to counterbalance the price increase resulting from a merger. Enriching the analysis further by modeling consumer preferences allows us to assess the impact on consumer and social welfare attributable to the competitive effects of a merger.[21]

Despite the theoretical advantages outlined above, practical limitations of merger simulation also merit consideration. First, selecting an appropriate model of oligopolistic competition that accurately reflects the market conditions of a merger presents challenges. The common models—Bertrand for differentiated product markets and Cournot for homogeneous product markets—fail to capture the complexities of real-world markets adequately. Second, merger simulations may overlook the potential for collusive behavior that can arise with increased market concentration post-merger. Third, the inherently static nature of merger simulations means they do not account for new market entries or product repositioning, elements that are crucial

[21] Nevo (2000) analyzed an extensive model of merger simulation for evaluating the effects of actual and counterfactual mergers in the cereal market in the United States.

in the dynamic competition of modern IT and online industries, which are characterized by rapidly evolving technology and business models. Fourth, the practical application of merger simulation may be hindered by the limited timeframe for antitrust evaluation and the paucity of readily available data.[22]

5.2.4 UPP (Upward Pricing Pressure)

Merger simulation, despite its numerous advantages in assessing the competitive impacts of mergers, faces a practical challenge when applied to merger regulation. This is due to its complexity and the extensive data requirements involved. Upward Pricing Pressure (UPP) analysis serves as a simplified version of merger simulation, capturing its essential aspects in a more accessible manner. Specifically, the UPP index for product 1, arising from the merger of product 1 and product 2, is defined as follows:[23]

$$\text{UPP}_1 = D_{12}(p_2 - c_2) - Ec_1 \quad \text{where } D_{12} \equiv \Delta q_2/\Delta q_1. \tag{5.8}$$

D_{12} commonly referred to as the diversion ratio, representing the proportion of the decreased sales attributed to a price increase of product 1 that is redirected toward the purchase of product 2. E denotes the efficiency of cost reduction resulting from the merger. For instance, $E = 0.1$ signifies a 10% reduction in costs. It should be noted that UPP_1 in Eq. (5.8) corresponds to $(p_2 - \tilde{c}_2)\frac{\partial q_2}{\partial p_1}$, which is an additional term in the first equation of Eq. (5.7). This demonstrates the concise nature of UPP, which captures the fundamental aspects of merger simulation.

US DOJ and FTC (2010, p. 20) explains UPP succinctly as follows;

> Adverse unilateral price effects can arise when the merger gives the merged entity an incentive to raise the price of a product previously sold by one merging firm and thereby divert sales to products previously sold by the other merging firm, boosting the profits on the latter products. Taking as given other prices and product offerings, that boost to profits is equal to the value to the merged firm of the sales diverted to those products. The value of sales diverted to a product is equal to the number of units diverted to that product multiplied by the margin between price and incremental cost on that product. In some cases, where sufficient information is available, the agencies assess the value of diverted sales, which can serve as an indicator of the upward pricing pressure on the first product resulting from the merger.

"The value of diverted sales" in the above statement is represented by $D_{12}(p_2 - c_2)$ in Eq. (5.8), which quantifies the pressure of price increase resulting additionally

---

[22] Merger evaluation has emerged as a captivating subject in empirical industrial organization, focusing on the assessment of merger effects by analyzing historical data. A notable illustration of this is Nevo's (2000) study.

[23] Farrell and Shapiro (2010) proposed the UPP metric, which was later included in the 2010 US DOJ and FTC Horizontal Merger Guidelines.

from a merger. The cost efficiency, Ec_1, acts as a counteracting force, putting downward pressure on prices. Hence, UPP_1 is a "net" index of upward pricing pressure.

According to Moresi (2010), an index called GUPPI (Gross Upward Pricing Pressure Index) can be used to measure the impact of increasing price while disregarding the influence of decreasing price resulting from cost efficiency.

$$\text{GUPPI}_1 = D_{12}M_2\frac{p_2}{p_1}, \quad \text{where } M_2 = \frac{p_2 - c_2}{p_2}. \tag{5.9}$$

The given expression UPP_1 divided by p_1 is always positive. Roughly, we can interpret the half of GUPPI as the rate of price increase after a merger. Assuming that pass-through rate is 1/2,[24] it can be inferred that the rate of price increase after a merger is likely to be less than 5%.

In contrast, Farrell and Shapiro (2010) propose a measure called the UPP index that calculates the ratio of UPP_1 to p_1, taking into account the impact of efficiency.

$$\frac{\text{UPP}_1}{p_1} = D_{12}M_2\frac{p_2}{p_1} - E(1 - M_1), \quad \text{where } M_1 = \frac{p_1 - c_1}{p_1}. \tag{5.10}$$

In case of $E = 0$, this simplifies into GUPPI. Assuming linear demands or a pass-through rate of 1/2, the UPP/P may be understood as the "net" rate at which prices increase as a result of a merger.

Antitrust law experts have pointed out the bias of GUPPI toward false positive regulation of mergers. For example, Simons and Coate (2010) noted that UPP screening "identifies as potentially problematic far more mergers than would be challenged or even investigated under the enforcement standards that have existed for more than twenty years." Moresi (2010) suggested GUPPI below 10% as a safe harbor in evaluating horizontal mergers to offset the pro-regulation bias intrinsic to GUPPI. Also, in a similar context, Farrell and Shapiro (2010) considered recognizing a certain level of "default marginal-cost efficiencies" or "standard reduction," as much as 10%, which may be regarded as generous, in a preliminary and simple test.

Experts in antitrust law have highlighted the tendency of GUPPI (Gross Upward Pricing Pressure Index) to favor overregulation of mergers, leading to a bias toward false positives. Simons and Coate (2010) observed that UPP screening "identifies as potentially problematic far more mergers than would be challenged or even investigated under the enforcement standards that have existed for more than twenty years." To counterbalance GUPPI's inclination toward regulation, Moresi (2010) recommended a threshold of GUPPI below 10% as a criterion for considering horizontal mergers safe, implying a less stringent approach. Similarly, Farrell and Shapiro (2010) proposed the acknowledgment of certain "default marginal-cost

[24] Pass-through rate refers to the rate at which factors like cost increase or UPP (unit production price) pass through to an increase in price. When dealing with linear demands, the pass-through rate is equivalent to one-half.

efficiencies" or a "standard reduction" of up to 10%, which they considered generous, in their preliminary and straightforward analysis.

In this subsection, I have presented various methodologies for assessing the competitive consequences of horizontal mergers. These range from traditional techniques, such as analyzing market shares and concentration ratios, to contemporary analytical tools, including reduced-form regression based on natural experiments, merger simulation, and Upward Pricing Pressure (UPP) analysis. This evolution highlights a significant shift in merger enforcement strategies, moving from a singular focus to a multifaceted approach. Shapiro (2010) eloquently described this transition as moving "from hedgehog to fox," indicating a move from a simplistic to a more complex and nuanced perspective on merger analysis.

5.3 Methods of Evaluating Competitive Effects of Non-Horizontal Merger

Non-horizontal mergers involve the combination of two firms that do not operate within the same relevant market. These mergers can be either vertical, linking an upstream supplier with a downstream buyer, or conglomerate, uniting firms that produce products closely related to each other, such as complements or weak substitutes. Typically, such mergers promote pro-competitive efficiencies by streamlining previously independent decision-making processes or by reducing transaction costs. However, under certain conditions, they may pose anticompetitive risks, such as the potential for unilateral foreclosure of competitors or the facilitation of collusion. It is crucial for antitrust agencies to carefully weigh these countervailing effects on competition and determine which impact predominates.

5.3.1 Vertical Merger

Vertical mergers can negatively impact competition through mechanisms such as foreclosure and unilateral increases in rivals' costs. For these concerns to be deemed potentially significant, the merged entity must possess market power in the upstream market of a related product, such as an input, granting it the *ability* to either completely foreclose rivals by denying access to a crucial input or to partially foreclose them by disadvantaging them in terms of price or quality. The underlying *incentive* for such actions is to augment the total profits of the merged firm.[25] To

[25] I present the associated product as an input, the corresponding market as downstream, and the relevant practice as input foreclosure for the purpose of clarity. However, we can also apply this explanation similarly to the opposite scenario, where the associated product is distribution, the relevant market is upstream input, and customer foreclosure becomes the focal point.

address these issues, antitrust economists have developed a suite of analytical tools designed to assess the merged firm's incentive to foreclose its downstream competitors. These tools evaluate the likelihood of both complete foreclosure, where access to a critical input is withheld from targeted rivals, and partial foreclosure, where competitors are disadvantaged through price or quality manipulation.

Among the analytical tools for evaluating the incentive for vertical foreclosure are vertical arithmetic, the bargaining model, vGUPPIs (Vertical Gross Upward Pricing Pressure Indices), and merger simulation. Vertical arithmetic assesses the incentive for complete foreclosure by weighing the costs and benefits of withholding crucial inputs from rivals. The remaining tools are designed to measure the incentive for partial foreclosure by assessing the impact on rivals' costs in price-related terms. Implementing merger simulation involves constructing models of competition at both the upstream and downstream levels to simulate vertical mergers. This process, which includes stages of *ex ante* estimation and *ex post* simulation, can be particularly challenging for practical applications. The predictions of merger effects derived from these simulations are highly sensitive to the choice of theoretical model and the accuracy of parameter estimates. Given these complexities, I highlight vertical arithmetic, the bargaining model, and vGUPPIs as being comparatively more manageable for practical application than vertical merger simulation. These tools offer a more straightforward approach to assessing the potential for vertical foreclosure and its impact on competition.

5.3.1.1 Vertical Arithmetic[26]

Vertical arithmetic evaluates whether a vertically merged firm may be motivated to pursue a foreclosure strategy by entirely withholding an input from a specific downstream rival. This strategy aims to boost profits in the downstream segment of the merged entity. However, it must also consider the potential losses incurred by the upstream segment due to the cessation of input sales to the downstream competitor. Vertical arithmetic is the method used to calculate the net effect of this strategy, assessing the incremental losses and gains resulting from complete foreclosure. The analysis confirms the presence of a foreclosure incentive if the calculated profits outweigh the losses.

The incremental losses resulting from foreclosure are characterized as the reduction in sales experienced by the upstream segment of a merged firm, which occurs when the firm decides to withhold input supply from a downstream rival targeted for foreclosure. These losses are quantified using the following formula:

$$\text{Incremental Losses} = (1-\alpha) \times Q_R \times M_U \tag{5.11}$$

where

[26] Refer to Davis and Garces (2010) and Baker et al. (2011) for the exposition of vertical arithmetic.

α (departure rate): the portion of final customers which depart from the target downstream rival and switch to all the other downstream firms, merged or not. [Notice that the upstream merging part can continue to sell inputs to such diverting customers and that that portion should be excluded from incremental losses.]

Q_R: the quantity of sales to a downstream rival targeted for foreclosure

M_U: the margin of the upstream part of a merged firm

However, the combined company has the potential to boost sales in the lower segment by reclaiming a share of customers who were previously diverted elsewhere. Therefore, the additional profits can be determined using the subsequent formula:

$$\text{Incremental Profits} : \alpha \times D \times Q_R \times M_D \tag{5.12}$$

where

D (diversion ratio): the portion of departing customers who switch into the downstream part of a merged firm

M_D: the margin of the downstream part of a merged firm

Comparing the incremental losses of the upstream part with the incremental profits of the downstream part in this way, we can determine the incentive of complete input foreclosure affirmatively if the latter is larger than the former.

5.3.1.2 Bargaining Model[27]

The bargaining model aims to forecast the price increase following a vertical merger, drawing on a straightforward economic theory of bargaining. Utilizing the Nash bargaining solution, which is widely applied in economic contexts, it is anticipated that the buyer and seller will negotiate a price P that falls between the seller's cost of production C and the value of the good to the buyer V. The formula for determining the negotiated price is as follows:

$$P = \mu V + (1 - \mu)C \tag{5.13}$$

where

μ denotes the relative bargaining strength of the seller *vis-à-vis* the buyer.

Notice that the vertical transaction changes the costs of the merged seller in terms of opportunity costs by ΔC, which represents the lost profits that the seller will forgo if the seller serves the original buyer. In conjunction with the incremental profits in Eq. (5.12) above, ΔC can be expressed as follows:

[27] Refer to Rogerson (2014) for the exposition of the bargaining model.

$$\Delta C = \alpha \times D \times M_D \tag{5.14}$$

where

α, D, M_D are the same as in Eqs. (5.11) and (5.12) above.

Combining Eqs. (5.13) with (5.14), we have:

$$\Delta P = (1 - \mu) \times \alpha \times D \times M_D \tag{5.15}$$

The central concept of the bargaining model is that the merged firm now considers the incremental profits from withholding an input as new opportunity costs associated with supplying the good to the original buyer. This change in cost is then utilized as leverage in price negotiations following the vertical transaction.

5.3.1.3 vGUPPIs[28]

vGUPPIs extend the UPP index for analyzing the competitive effect of horizontal merger within the vertical context. Moresi and Salop (2013) suggest the "incentive scoring devices" to measure the upward pricing pressure resulting from unilateral incentives following a vertical merger. They derive three vGUPPI scores: vGUPPu for the pricing incentives of the upstream merging firm in selling inputs to a targeted foreclosed downstream rival, vGUPPIr for the pricing incentives of the targeted downstream rivals, and GUPPId for the pricing incentives for the downstream merger partner. These three vGUPPIs serve to evaluate the incentives of input foreclosure and output reduction concerns. Essentially, a vertical merger between an input supplier and a downstream manufacturer can create unilateral incentives for the supplier to raise the price of its inputs to the targeted competitors of the manufacturer.

Suppose that each input supplier produces a single input, and each output manufacturer purchases inputs from several suppliers. For simplicity, suppose further that the upstream merging firm targets only one downstream rival and that the targeted downstream rival cannot substitute the input away from the upstream merger firm to other suppliers. Applying the same methodology of the horizontal GUPPI as in Eq. (5.9), we have the formula for vGUPPIu as follows:

$$\text{vGUPPIu} = DR_{UD} \times M_D \times \frac{P_D}{W_R} \tag{5.16}$$

where

DR_{UD} denotes the "vertical" diversion ratio from the upstream merging firm U to the downstream merging firm D, following a unilateral increase in the input price charged to the targeted downstream rival R under consideration

[28] Refer to Moresi and Shapiro (2013) for the explanation of vGUPPIs.

M_D denotes the downstream merger partner's percentage incremental profit margin

P_D denotes the price of the output sold by the downstream merging firm

W_R denotes the price of the input (per unit of output) sold by the upstream merging firm to the targeted downstream rival.

From the formula for vGUPPIu, we have the formula for vGUPPIr as follows:

$$\text{vGUPPIr} = \text{vGUPPIu} \times \text{PTR}_U \times \frac{W_R}{P_R} \tag{5.17}$$

where

PTR_U denotes the cost pass-through rate of the upstream merging firm

P_R denotes the price of the output sold by the targeted downstream rival.

The downstream merging partner has two incentives to change the output price in the opposite directions, i.e., the incentive to increase the output price due to the consideration that consumer substitution away from the firm to rivals increases the input sales that the upstream partner makes to rivals and the incentive to reduce its output price below the pre-merger level due to the so-called EDM (elimination of double marginalization) effect. Incorporating the two countervailing effects, the formula for the vGUPPId can be represented as follows:

$$\text{vGUPPId} = DR_{DU} \times M_U \times \frac{W_U}{P_D} - M_{UD} \times \frac{W_D}{P_D} \tag{5.18}$$

where

DR_{DU} denotes the "vertical" diversion ratio from the downstream merging firm to the upstream merging partner,

M_U and W_U denote the upstream merger firm's profit margin and price

M_{UD} and W_D denote the margin and price of the upstream merging firm on input sales to the downstream merging firm.

The former part in Eq. (5.18) represents the upward pricing incentive of the downstream merging partner, attributed to output substitution favoring the upstream partner. Conversely, the latter part indicates the downward pricing incentive resulting from the EDM effect. Consequently, the net effect remains indeterminate, either positive or negative.

Notice that vGUPPIu in Eq. (5.16) could be significantly high if the input's price constitutes a small fraction of the output's price, i.e., if the ratio of $\frac{P_D}{W_R}$ is exceedingly high, while vGUPPIr in Eq. (5.17) would be substantially lower than vGUPPIu due to the multiplication factors of PTR_U, usually less than 1 (e.g., 0.5 in case of linear demand), and the reversed ratio of input and output prices. Moresi and Shapiro (2013) suggest using vGUPPIr rather than vGUPPIu, as vGUPPIr more accurately reflects the potential harm to consumers purchasing the downstream product.

Accounting for input substitution, all vertical gross upward pressure indices (vGUPPIs) will be reduced, as such substitution tends to offset the cost increase and the consequent rise in the price of the targeted firm's output. Consequently, the diversion to the downstream merging firm resulting from the input price increase is also diminished. On the other hand, if the merged firm targets multiple downstream rivals, vGUPPIs will increase because the incentive to elevate the input price for any given targeted rival intensifies if the merged firm concurrently increases prices to other rivals as well.

vGUPPIs suffer from the same drawbacks as horizontal GUPPI, which include a failure to consider the strategic reactions of non-merging companies and a tendency to favor false positive regulation. Furthermore, as Eqs. (5.16), (5.17), and (5.18) show, more information is necessary to use vGUPPIs practically in evaluating the incentives of a vertically merged firm to foreclose its rivals.

Many vertical mergers result in efficiencies that must be considered when evaluating their overall potential impact on effective competition. A vertical merger can enable the involved parties to enhance coordination between production and distribution processes, leading to reductions in inventory costs. More broadly, a vertical merger can align the incentives of the parties concerning pricing, product introduction, and marketing strategies. Specifically, it allows the merged entity to synchronize the pricing strategies of its upstream and downstream divisions and to address the issue of double marginalization that existed prior to the merger, contingent upon market conditions.[29]

5.3.2 *Conglomerate Merger*

Competitive issues can emerge from conglomerate mergers in two primary ways: by removing potential entrants and by leveraging a dominant position from one market to another through tying, bundling, or other exclusionary practices. A non-horizontal merger, whether vertical or conglomerate, involving a firm already present in a market along with a potential entrant, could lead to a reduction in competitive pressure within that market. The US Department of Justice (1984)[30] distinguishes between "perceived" and "actual" potential competition. Although the distinction is nuanced, "actual" potential competition refers to situations where plans for new entry have been disclosed, while "perceived" potential competition pertains to

[29]Refer to EC (2008) Non-Horizontal Merger Guidelines. On the other hand, the US FTC (September 15, 2021), withdrawing the US DOJ and FTC (2020, "Vertical Merger Guidelines"), asserted that there does not exist any statutory basis for permitting a merger due to efficiencies. Especially, the withdrawal statement of the US FTC (2021) regarded the reliance of the 2020 Guidelines on the elimination of double marginalization (EDM) as "theoretically flawed because the economic model predicting EDM is limited to very specific factual scenarios: a merger involves one single-product monopoly buying another single-product monopoly in the same supply chain, where both charge monopoly prices pre-merger and the product from one firm is used as an input by the other in a fixed-proportion production process. Yet outside this limited context, economic theory does not predict that EDM will create downward pricing pressure."

[30]It is the part of the original "Merger Guidelines" relevant to non-horizontal mergers that the US DOJ and FTC issued and revised "Horizontal Merger Guidelines" in 1992, 1997, and 2010.

scenarios where entry is merely possible. The economic theory of limit pricing indicates that dominant firms may avoid price increases as a strategy to deter new entrants.

The traditional perspectives on anti-competitive leverage effects have been challenged by the "single monopoly profit theorem" posited by the Chicago School, which now possesses rigorous theoretical underpinnings. Whinston (1990) demonstrated that a monopolist could induce exits or deter entries in scenarios where tied markets are product-differentiated and feature oligopolistic competition. Following this revelation, numerous iterations of dynamic leverage theory have been developed, including works by Nalebuff (2000, 2004), Carlton and Waldman (2002), and Choi and Stefanadis (2001). These theories support the notion that a monopolist has incentives to employ tying strategies either to safeguard its market power within the tying market or to extend its market power into a tied market. Furthermore, Vergé (2003) applied these dynamic concepts to the practice of full-line forcing in distribution channels. Conversely, leverage effects may bolster competition when a merged entity, starting from a weaker market position, uses leverage as a foothold to challenge the dominance of an incumbent firm.[31]

Although there is no standard definition, the term "portfolio effects" has been referred to in regard to conglomerate mergers that combine weakly substitutable products.[32] According to Neven (2005), portfolio effects may stem from two sources: (i) conditional sales such as bundling, tying, and full-line forcing; (ii) economies of scale and scope. The consequences of the former are the leverage effect discussed above. Economies of scale and scope come from either the supply side or the demand side. Combined firms can reduce costs by integrating production, distribution, marketing, or R&D, while consumers may reduce transaction costs through one-stop shopping of products portfolio. Also, according to Stigler (1968) and Adams and Yellen (1976), tying or bundling may be adopted as a means of price discrimination when consumers' preferences are heterogeneous and result in market enlargement. Moreover, Evans and Salinger (2005) suggest that conglomerate mergers may facilitate market participation of potential entrants by reducing fixed costs of production and distribution. Consequent efficiency gains and price decreases are pro-competitive, enhancing consumer and social welfare.

While there is no universally accepted definition, the term "portfolio effects" is commonly used in the context of conglomerate mergers that amalgamate products which are weakly substitutable. Neven (2005) identifies two primary sources of portfolio effects: (i) conditional sales, including bundling, tying, and full-line forcing; and (ii) economies of scale and scope. The former leads to the leverage effect previously discussed. Economies of scale and scope arise from both the supply side

[31] Ponsoldt and David (2007) remarks that, "A second business justification that renders tying permissible involves a smaller new entrant attempting to a toehold in a market occupied by powerful, larger competitors. Courts may justify casting a blind eye toward otherwise per se illegal tie-ins by evaluating the overall pro-competitive effects of more diverse market."

[32] See Chung and Jeon (2014).

and the demand side. Merged entities can achieve cost reductions by integrating production, distribution, marketing, or R&D activities. Concurrently, consumers may benefit from reduced transaction costs by availing of a diversified product portfolio through one-stop shopping. Furthermore, Stigler (1968) and Adams and Yellen (1976) argue that practices such as tying or bundling can serve as mechanisms for price discrimination in markets with heterogeneous consumer preferences, potentially leading to market expansion. Additionally, Evans and Salinger (2005) propose that conglomerate mergers may lower barriers to market entry for potential competitors by reducing the fixed costs associated with production and distribution. Such efficiency gains and subsequent price reductions are pro-competitive, ultimately enhancing consumer and social welfare.

The varied interpretations of portfolio effects have led to divergent approaches by antitrust enforcement agencies toward conglomerate mergers. The European Commission and National Regulatory Agencies have frequently expressed concerns regarding portfolio effects in several notable cases of conglomerate mergers, such as *Coca-Amalgamated*, *Coca-Carlsberg*, and *Guinness-Grand Metropolitan* during the late 1990s. In contrast, US antitrust authorities have critiqued the potential for overreliance on the theory of portfolio effects, arguing that it could prompt regulatory bodies to obstruct or discourage mergers that are pro-competitive and based on economies of scale and scope. The US DOJ in 2001 pointed out that the theory of portfolio effects might be overly concentrated on conditional sales as a means of leveraging market power through bundling, tying, or full-line forcing, thereby neglecting the possible benefits related to efficiency enhancements. This difference in perspective between European and US competition authorities regarding the impact of portfolio effects in conglomerate mergers reached a peak in the widely discussed case of the 2001 *GE-Honeywell* merger.

One efficiency particularly noteworthy in the context of a conglomerate merger between firms producing complementary goods is the so-called "Cournot effect," which serves as the conglomerate parallel to the elimination of double marginalization (EDM) observed in vertical mergers.[33] Theoretically, the efficiencies arising from both the Cournot effect and EDM originate from the same principle: the internalization of externalities from one party to another. In the Cournot effect, a pre-merger horizontal externality exists in which an independent supplier of one input does not account for the positive impact that reducing its own price would have on the profits of another input supplier. Similarly, in EDM, a pre-merger vertical externality exists where an independent downstream output producer overlooks the beneficial effect of lowering its own price on the upstream input supplier's profits. Depending on market conditions, a merged entity may internalize this externality, potentially incentivizing a price reduction if it leads to higher overall profits following the merger.

[33] Both Cournot effect and EDM were originally suggested by Cournot (1927).

Table 5.2 Market shares in the domestic car industry in 1998 (sales volume) (KFTC 1999-043, April 7, 1999)

	Passenger Car	Bus	Truck
Hyundai	222,771 (39.1%)	43,838 (58.3%)	68,811 (50.3%)
Kia	94,167 (16.5%)	12,000 (15.9%)	60,591 (44.3%)
Daewoo	209,532 (36.8%)	19,347 (25.8%)	6297 (4.6%)
Samsung	41,593 (7.3%)	–	730 (0.5%)
Imports	1993 (0.3%)	–	83 (0.1%)
Others	–	–	228 (0.2%)
Sum	570,056 (100%)	75,185 (100%)	136,739 (100%)

5.4 Cases of Merger Regulation in Korea

In this section, I examine a selection of merger regulation cases in Korea that are significant in terms of legal precedents, economic analyses, and international comparisons. I will introduce the principal rulings made by the KFTC and the courts and discuss their implications for future merger regulation.

5.4.1 Hyundai Motor-Kia Car *(1999):*[34] *Horizontal*[35]

In 1999, Hyundai Car and its affiliates acquired controlling shares of Kia. Prior to the acquisition, both companies held substantial shares in various car market segments in 1998, as detailed below (Table 5.2):

The combined entity was presumed to significantly restrict competition across all relevant markets, as it would command market shares exceeding 50%–56% in passenger cars, 74.2% in buses, and 94.6% in trucks. Moreover, its market shares were more than four-thirds the size of its nearest competitor's, a condition that, according to the Act, indicated a presumption of anti-competitive restraint for a horizontal merger. Despite these considerations, the KFTC approved the merger in the passenger car and bus segments without imposing any conditions. For the truck segment, however, the merger was approved with a behavioral remedy that included restrictions on price increases for a duration of four years.

[34] The year mentioned corresponds to when the KFTC issued its decision on the case. This convention is maintained subsequently.

[35] The case could be involved with other types of mergers. The noted type is one which is primarily focused on.

The KFTC provided two primary justifications for the unconditional approval of the merger in the passenger car and bus segments: the failing firm defense and efficiency gains. Firstly, Kia was identified as a failing firm, in a state of bankruptcy, with no other prospective buyers aside from Hyundai Motor at the time. This context suggested that the merger might be the only viable option to prevent the collapse of Kia. Secondly, the merger was anticipated to facilitate economies of scale in areas such as integrated platform production, parts procurement, and distribution. More crucially, it was expected to significantly enhance the global competitiveness of Hyundai and Kia. This improvement would stem from the promotion of technological development and marketing activities, as well as achieving a management size deemed necessary for sustaining and excelling in international competition.

The *Hyundai-Kia* case must be contextualized within the historical backdrop of the Korean economy's industrial restructuring efforts to surmount the East Asian financial crisis in the late 1990s. Under normal economic conditions and from an antitrust policy standpoint, the merger might not—and arguably should not—have been permitted, given its clear trajectory toward transforming the Korean car market from an oligopoly to a near monopoly. This concern is especially pertinent considering that the Daewoo Group, which owned the next largest car company, was also facing financial difficulties at the time and subsequently collapsed soon after the KFTC's decision.

In hindsight, it can be argued that the Korean car industry enhanced its global competitiveness at the cost of fostering a domestic monopoly through the *Hyundai-Kia* merger. Hyundai Motor Group ascended to third place in global car sales during the January-September period of 2022.[36] Conversely, within the domestic market, Hyundai Motor Group's share reached 74%, with sales totaling 1,241,065 vehicles in 2021. Imported foreign cars and other domestic cars accounted for 16% (267,167 vehicles) and 10% (171,747 vehicles) of the market share, respectively.[37] Despite the significant growth in sales of imported foreign cars over the past two decades, the market dominance of Hyundai-Kia vehicles has notably strengthened.

Meanwhile, the monopolistic dynamics within the Korean car market have incurred substantial costs across various sectors, impacting Korean consumers, the automobile industry, and the economy at large. It has been observed that Korean consumers faced exploitation through "reverse discrimination," evidenced by the price differential between the monopolistically priced domestic cars and competitively priced foreign equivalents. Workers from Hyundai and Kia capitalized on the companies' large monopoly rents to demand higher wages and more favorable working conditions. The Hyundai Motor Group, aiming to avert the risks of strikes or shutdowns, acquiesced to these demands. This situation resulted in a twofold distortion of economic resources within the Korean automobile industry: firstly,

[36] Business Korea, "Hyundai Motor Group Ranked 3rd in Global Auto Sale," http://www.businesskorea.co.kr/news/articleView.html?idxno=80296.

[37] The data sources are KAMA (Korea Automobile Manufacturers Association) and KAIDA (Korea Automobile Importers and Distributors Association).

through capital-intensive input substitution, and secondly, via the diversion of domestic capital abroad. Both consequences have contributed to a decrease in domestic labor employment.

Perhaps the most significant harm inflicted by the monopoly on the overall economy is the promotion of the so-called "labor aristocracy," which prioritizes its interests over the welfare of the general workforce. The rigidity of the Korean labor market, characterized by its inability to adjust employment flexibly in response to economic conditions, along with the duality dividing workers into two categories—those with job security and those temporarily employed—originated, at least in part, from the environment of a strong labor movement sustained by monopoly rents. This scenario represents a variant of the monopoly cost associated with rent-seeking behavior, specifically, rent-extracting.

5.4.2 Moohak Soju-Daesun Soju *(2003):*[38] *Horizontal*

In January 2003, the KFTC issued an order requiring Moohak to divest all shares of Daesun that it had acquired in 2002.[39] The KFTC determined that the acquisition would significantly restrict competition in the local soju markets of the Busan and Kyungnam regions, in violation of MRFTA §9. Daesun, the company being acquired, held a dominant position in the Busan area, commanding an 84.4% market share in 2001, while Jinro, the largest soju producer in the country, had a mere 7.2% share in the region. Conversely, Moohak, the acquiring company, occupied a monopolistic stance in Kyungnam province with an 84.3% market share in 2001. Market shares of other producers were negligible, with the exception of Daesun's 12.9% share in the region.[40]

The KFTC identified the geographic market relevant to the *Moohak-Daesun* merger as the diluted soju market in Busan and Kyungnam.[41] Within this defined market, the combined entity would hold a 91.5% share in Busan and a 97.2% share in Kyungnam, thereby fulfilling the criteria for presumptive competitive concerns under §9 of the MRFTA. Furthermore, the KFTC highlighted the presence of *de*

[38] The introduction of this case is based on Jeon (2016).

[39] Moohak and its owner purchased 41.21% of Daesun's stocks from June 2002 to December 2002. See KFTC 2003-027, January 18, 2013.

[40] Administrative districts of South Korea include a capital city, 6 broad cities, and 9 provinces. Busan and Kyungnam are a broad city and a province, respectively, and both of these regions are located in the southeastern part of the country.

[41] Soju is a popular liquor in Korea, which is a kind of spirit with an alcohol content of about 20%. There are two kinds of soju—distilled and diluted. The popular one in Korea is the diluted one, which are made by diluting alcohol essence extracted from grains—ethanol made from rice, barley, corn, etc. The sales of diluted soju in 2004 were about 2.34 trillion won. Total liquor sales were 6.64 trillion won in 2004. Hence, diluted soju accounts for 35.2% of the total liquor markets. On the other hand, beer, whose sales were 3.45 trillion won in 2004, accounts for 52%.

facto, though not *de jure*, entry barriers in the soju industry. Building brand recognition in the soju market is a lengthy and costly process. Additionally, soju producers are prohibited from engaging in wholesaling activities, complicating new entrants' efforts to establish distribution networks. This is exacerbated by the fact that incumbent distributors have already formed long-term relationships with Moohak and Daesun in these regions. Moohak contested the KFTC's decision by appealing to the Seoul High Court. However, the court upheld the KFTC's ruling. During the proceedings, both parties—Daesun opposing and Moohak supporting the merger—submitted economic analyses concerning the relevant geographic market.[42] The court meticulously reviewed these analyses before making its decision.

To thoroughly understand the *Moohak-Daesun* case, it is crucial to recognize the strong consumer loyalty toward local products in Busan and Kyungnam. Daesun, based in Busan, significantly increased its market share by more than 20% in 1997, while Jinro, a nationally dominant producer, experienced a nearly 20% loss in market share. Subsequently, Daesun solidified its market dominance, maintaining around an 85% share in the 2000s. The enduring preference for local products and the dramatic market share shifts in the late 1990s can be attributed to the historical regulatory landscape of local soju markets and the shifting political power among regions in Korea. A regulation mandating wholesalers to purchase more than 50% of their soju from local producers was introduced in the mid-1970s to protect local soju manufacturers. This regulation was repealed in 1992, reinstated in June 1996, and ultimately declared unconstitutional in December 1996 by the Constitutional Court. Intriguingly, local product loyalty intensified following the definitive abolition of this mandate. Facing increased competitive pressures since the mid-1990s, local producers, particularly Daesun, embarked on aggressive survival strategies, including price reductions and the introduction of new products with lower alcohol content.[43] Additionally, regionalism in Busan and Kyungnam intensified following a political power shift away from these regions. This shift appears to have fostered a stronger sense of regional solidarity among the inhabitants,[44] further reinforcing consumer loyalty to local soju brands amidst a politically charged atmosphere.

To assess whether Busan and Kyungnam constitute the relevant geographic market for diluted soju in the context of the *Moohak-Daesun* merger, Jeon (2004) conducted an analysis comparing the critical and actual loss of regional sales across various levels of Small but significant and non-transitory increase in price (SSNIP). The results, derived from survey data collected from dining/drinking places, are summarized in Table 5.3.[45]

---

[42] See Jeon (2004) and Ryu and Yi (2004).

[43] For example, it introduced a new product of low-alcohol soju with an alcohol content of 23%, which was less than the contemporary standard 25%, and lowered its price by 9.5% in 1996.

[44] The power base of President Park Jung Hee (1961–1978), Chun Doo Hwan (1981–1987), Roh Tai Woo (1988–1992), and Kim Young Sam (1993–1997) was all the Youngnam regions (Busan, Kyungnam, and Kyungbuk). On the other hand, Kim Dae Jung (1998–2002) based his power on the Honam regions (Chonmam and Chonbuk).

[45] Similar results were obtained with data from retail stores.

Table 5.3 Critical loss analyses with data from dining/drinking places

	Actual loss vs. critical loss	Enlarge the geographic market beyond Busan and Kyungnam?
5% increase	14.6% > 13.6%	Yes
10% increase	19.9% < 23.9%	*No*
15% increase	23.2% < 32.0%	*No*
30% increase	34.5% < 48.5%	*No*

The findings indicate that a hypothetical monopolist operating in the Busan and Kyungnam regions would not be able to increase profits with a SSNIP of 5% but could achieve profitability with higher SSNIP levels, such as 10%, 15%, and even 30%. This scenario is attributable to the existence of two distinct consumer groups within the region: a larger cohort of price-insensitive consumers with a strong loyalty to local products and a smaller group of price-sensitive consumers. A monopolist could thus pursue a strategy of high pricing to capitalize on the loyal consumer base, albeit at the risk of losing the price-sensitive segment. These results underscore that the relevant geographic market for diluted soju in the context of the merger is specifically limited to the local areas within Busan and Kyungnam provinces, rather than extending to the entire country.

The Seoul High Court, affirming Jeon (2004)'s analysis, issued a definitive ruling in 2004 that supported the decision made by the KFTC.[46] A key economic issue debated in court was the definition of fixed costs, specifically whether they should be identified as costs that do not vary with the level of operation within a year. Consequently, there was discussion on whether "wages and salaries," "training" expenses, "advertising," and "maintenance costs should be classified as fixed costs, alongside 'rent,' 'depreciation,' 'intangible asset deduction', 'taxes and charges,' 'insurance,' and 'membership fees'." However, the Seoul High Court's 2004 ruling clarified that costs such as labor, advertising, and maintenance should not be easily categorized as fixed over the significant duration in which monopoly power might be exerted, suggesting that the relevant time horizon should extend beyond a single year. This decision established a crucial precedent for calculating margins appropriately for the assessment of critical loss and diversion ratio, which are essential in the economic analysis of market definition and merger evaluation.

[46] Seoul High Court 2003nu2252, October 27, 2004. Moohak chose not to pursue any further appeals, thereby concluding the case.

Table 5.4 "Pub alcoholic drink" market in 2004

	Sales (mil. won)	Share
Hite[a]	837,598	34.0%
Jinro	613,254	24.9%
OB[b]	543,313	22.1%
Others[c]	468,245	19.0%
Total	2,462,410	100.0%

Sales are in terms of net sales amount before taxes
[a]Hite beer + Hitejujo soju
[b]OB beer + Cass beer (both brands belong to the same company)
[c]All others are local soju producers such as Moohak, Daesun, Keumbokju, etc.

5.4.3 Hite Beer-Jinro Soju *(2006):*[47] *Conglomerate*

In August 2005, Hite acquired a 52.1% stake in Jinro. In 2004, Hite's assets were valued at 1,852 billion won, with sales reaching 861 billion won. Its primary product was beer, holding a 60.2% share of the national beer market that year. Conversely, Jinro's assets and sales in 2004 were 923 billion won and 693 billion won, respectively. Jinro's main product was soju, commanding a 55.8% national market share in the soju market for the same year. Hite owned a subsidiary soju company, Hitejujo, which had a modest national market share of 1.5%. Despite Hitejujo's relatively minor presence in the national soju market, it held the largest market share in Chonbuk province at 50.6%, with Jinro being the second largest with a 42.5% market share in 2004.

The competitive concerns surrounding the *Hite-Jinro* merger, along with the issues related to defining the relevant market, were twofold: one concerning the merger between Hite's beer and Jinro's soju, and the other regarding the merger between Hitejujo's soju and Jinro's soju. For the first concern, parties opposing the merger, particularly OB beer—which shared nearly half of the Korean beer market with Hite—argued that beer and soju are such close substitutes that they should be considered a single product market, termed "pub alcoholic drink." Under this classification, the merger would pose significant challenges, as it would effectively be a horizontal merger leading to a substantial increase in market concentration, as demonstrated in the table provided by Ryu and Yi (2005) (Table 5.4).

Conversely, if beer and soju are considered separate products, the merger would primarily be classified as a conglomerate. Even within this framework, some anti-competitive concerns may persist, given that both beer and soju companies utilize the same wholesale distribution channels. However, under this scenario, the strength of anti-competitive allegations is likely to diminish.

The horizontal aspect of the merger involving Hitejujo was not considered a major issue due to the company's relatively small size. However, a notable point of discussion was whether the relevant geographic market should be limited to the local

[47]The introduction of this case is based on Jeon (2016).

province of Chungbuk or extended to a national scope. It's important to remember that the geographic soju market relevant to the *Moohak-Daesun* merger was confined to the local areas of Busan and Kyungnam. If the geographic market in this instance were also defined on a local basis, such as Chungbuk, then the horizontal merger would result in a virtual monopoly within the region; the combined market share of Hitejujo and Jinro in Chungbuk would be 92.8%. Conversely, if the relevant market is considered to be national, the merger would not significantly alter market concentration.

In this particular case, Jeon et al. (2005) conducted economic analyses for Hite and submitted their findings to the KFTC. They delineated the relevant product market for the first conglomerate scenario as two distinct markets: beer and soju. For the second horizontal scenario, they identified the relevant geographic market as the national soju market, with the exclusion of some southern regions. Conversely, Ryu and Yi (2005), representing OB Beer Company, argued that the relevant product market constituted a single market of beer and soju, referred to as "pub alcoholic drinks. Notably, both parties utilized the same methodology for defining the market—critical loss analysis. However, discrepancies in their calculations of actual and critical losses led to divergent conclusions regarding the definition of the relevant product market.

Upon reviewing the economic analyses submitted by both parties, the KFTC aligned with the market definitions proposed by Jeon et al. (2005). The KFTC's final decision in 2006 was to approve the merger, albeit with certain behavioral remedies in place. These remedies included imposing a price cap on Hite and Jinro's beer and soju at the Retail Price Index (RPI) + 5%, separating the marketing workforce and organization of Hite and Jinro for a period of five years, and requiring Hite to implement specific arrangements to prevent future exclusionary practices.[48]

During the application of critical loss analysis in the *Moohak-Daesun* and *Hite-Jinro* cases, several issues emerged. Firstly, the estimation of margins using accounting data requires a certain level of discretionary or *ad hoc* classification between fixed and variable costs. Parties advocating for a broader market definition tend to favor a classification that attributes more costs as fixed, and the reverse is true for those arguing for a narrower market scope. This is because a larger proportion of fixed costs leads to a higher margin rate, thereby reducing the critical loss level required for market definition. As previously mentioned, the Seoul High Court determined that the appropriate time horizon for the SSNIP test should extend over a significant period during which monopoly power could be exercised, and not be limited to just one year. This implies that costs such as labor and advertising should not be automatically classified as fixed. In the *Hite-Jinro* case, the KFTC adhered to this precedent set by the court's decision in *Moohak-Daesun*, acknowledging the nuanced considerations in defining costs and the relevant time horizon for assessing market power.

[48] KFTC 2006-009, January 24, 2006.

Secondly, in estimating price elasticities of consumer demand and actual losses corresponding to various levels of price increases in the SSNIP test, Jeon (2004) and Jeon et al. (2005) utilized survey data. Typically, economists prefer to use actual historical data for demand estimations rather than relying on survey data. However, challenges often arise due to data limitations; the necessary level of disaggregation, adequate time span, and representativeness may not be available. The recent proliferation of barcode scanning systems in retail outlets and the subsequent availability of point-of-sale (POS) data represent a promising advancement that could potentially address these data issues in the future.[49] Nevertheless, in many instances, such as the *Moohak-Daesun* and *Hite-Jinro* cases, POS data may suffer from significant sample selection bias. This occurs when the data represent only a small segment of the population, and the sample characteristics do not accurately reflect those of the broader population. In these scenarios, a well-conducted survey can serve as a valuable alternative data source. Survey data are sometimes criticized for leading questions that could predetermine answers, and respondents may exaggerate or minimize their responses. However, the questions posed in surveys for the SSNIP test are designed to be straightforward, asking consumers how their purchasing behavior would change in response to price increases, thus minimizing the risk of predetermining answers. The issue of respondents' tendency to overstate or understate remains. It is crucial to consider this factor carefully when drawing conclusions. If the survey results display significant margins, the conclusions derived can be considered robust, even after adjusting for such tendencies.

Thirdly, Jeon (2004) expanded the range of price increases considered in the SSNIP test to include substantial hikes of 15% and 30%, in addition to the conventional 5% and 10%, in the *Moohak-Daesun* case. This approach was adopted in response to the presence of two distinct consumer groups in the regions: one that is price-sensitive and another that exhibits strong loyalty to local brands. In such scenarios, there is a concern that a local monopolist might exploit brand-loyal, captive consumers with a high-price strategy, despite being unable to profit from minor price increases. Typically, the standard SSNIP test thresholds of 5% or 10% are adequate for most situations, especially in markets lacking a significant number of brand-loyal consumers. However, the inclusion of higher price increases in the analysis acknowledges the potential for a monopolist to leverage consumer loyalty through elevated pricing strategies in specific market contexts.

The final observation pertains to the case-specific nature and potential asymmetry in market definition within antitrust cases. Specifically, market definition is inherently case-specific, determined by the initial point of analysis from which the need to potentially expand the relevant market is assessed. Consequently, it is entirely plausible for the geographic market relevant to the *Moohak-Daesun* merger to be limited to Busan and Kyungnam, while the market relevant to the *Hitejujo and Jinro* merger could be considered national, encompassing Busan, Kyungnam, and beyond.

[49] POS data have already played an important role in antitrust econometrics in the US merger case of *Staples-Office Depot* in 1997 and a recent Korean retailing merger case of *Eland-Carrefour* in 2006.

Similarly, there is no inconsistency in a situation where a critical loss analysis starting with the soju product categorizes soju as a separate market, whereas an analysis beginning with the beer product suggests that beer and soju belong to the same market, even though this specific outcome did not materialize in the Hite-Jinro case. Such distinctions do not signify any contradiction but rather reflect the varied preferences of consumers across different regions or products, leading to asymmetric cross-elasticities in their consumption behaviors.

5.4.4 Eland Outlets-Carrefour *(2006): Horizontal*

In the late 2000s, the retail industry witnessed a series of mergers among large-scale discount stores, notably *Eland-Carrefour* in 2006,[50] *Emart-Walmart* in 2006,[51] and *Home Plus-Home Ever* in 2008[52] (the entity resulting from the Eland and Carrefour merger was subsequently renamed Home Ever). Of these, the Eland-Carrefour merger stands out as a significant precedent in terms of market definition and economic analysis. This case has influenced the evaluation of subsequent mergers within the retailing industry, including those between department stores, supermarkets, and other retail formats.

The KFTC, in addressing the *Eland-Carrefour* merger, defined the relevant product market as "large-scale general retailers equipped with sales stores exceeding 3,000 m^2, offering consumers a variety of goods including food, household products, and clothing in a one-stop shopping environment." This definition led to the conclusion that Eland's outlets ("New Core Outlet" and "2001 Outlet") and Carrefour's large discount stores were in direct competition within the same market. For the relevant geographic market, the KFTC adopted an approach termed "the union of overlapping circles," described as follows: "initiating from the region within a radius of 5 km (in cases of large cities) or 10 km (in other provinces) from the acquired undertaking, Carrefour, and extending the area by incorporating regions within the same radius from all discount stores in the original region, while excluding any overlapping circles from discount stores in newly included areas." Essentially, this methodology was applied only once. Based on this market definition, the KFTC mandated a structural remedy involving the divestiture of three stores, either from Eland outlets or Carrefour discount stores, in three distinct regions. These stores were to be sold within a specified period to a third party that would not exacerbate competitive restraints.

Economic experts representing Eland, Jeon and Whang (2006) presented dissenting views regarding the KFTC's market definition on two fronts: the product market and the geographic market. Firstly, they argued that an Eland outlet does not closely

[50] KFTC 2006-261, November 6, 2006.

[51] KFTC 2006-264, November 14, 2006.

[52] KFTC 2008-265, October 17, 2008.

resemble a large-scale discount store in its entirety, and the competitive interaction between Eland and Carrefour is limited to hyper products (foods and casual household goods), not extending to non-hyper products (fashion clothing, living furniture, etc.).[53] Therefore, they proposed that the relevant product market should be defined as "a basket of fresh and dry foodstuffs, and non-food consumables sold in a supermarket environment," akin to the EC's 1999 case of *Walmart-ASDA*. This cluster market definition, focusing on a subset of products offered by a retailer, is supported by the notion of one-stop shopping convenience. For instance, the US FTC identified the product market in the *Staples-Office Depot* merger as "consumable office supplies sold through office superstores," accounting for about half of the sales in office superstores like Staples and Office Depot.[54]

Secondly, Jeon and Whang (2006) questioned the rationale behind applying the approach of a union of overlapping circles[55] only once and in a highly restrictive manner. They illustrated the potential issue with the following diagram:

Starting with a Carrefour store (the acquired entity), a circle with a 5 km radius, shaded as A in Fig. 5.2, is drawn. Subsequently, other stores within this circle, such as Emart and Eland, serve as new centers from which circles B and C are delineated. The relevant geographic market is then defined as "the union of overlapping circles," encompassing areas A, B, and C. It is important to note that no additional overlapping circles originating from a Home Plus store in area B or a Lotte Mart store in area C are included, nor is consideration given to a circle from a Walmart store in area D. This method stipulates that the overlapping circles approach is to be applied only once.

The rationale for employing the approach of a union of overlapping circles as a method for defining the geographic market can be found in the concept of "chains of substitution." EC (1997) elucidated this, stating, "In certain cases, the existence of chains of substitution might lead to the definition of a relevant market where products or areas at the extreme of the market are not directly substitutable" (para 57, emphasis added). Therefore, there is fundamentally no reason to limit the number of chains of substitutions to merely one or two occurrences.[56] Furthermore, the starting point need not necessarily be the "acquired" store (Carrefour). It could

[53]Take note that the Eland outlet typically occupies a tall structure situated within the city, rather than being located in rural areas. It closely resembles a department store in terms of the variety and appearance of its merchandise. The distinguishing factor, however, lies in the fact that the Eland outlet offers discounted prices on carryover goods, whereas a department store sells brand-new products.

[54]Refer to the 1977 *Staples* ruling, as well as the research conducted by Dalkir and Warren-Boulton (2004).

[55]The method of a union of overlapping circles was introduced in *Tesco-Carrefour* case by EC (December 22, 2005).

[56]The recent EC (2021) evaluation of EC (1997) basically confirmed that "the Notice provide correct, comprehensive and clear guidance as regards chains of substitution," with the cautionary remark that "this must be carefully considered given the risk of widening the markets excessively." (pp. 53–54).

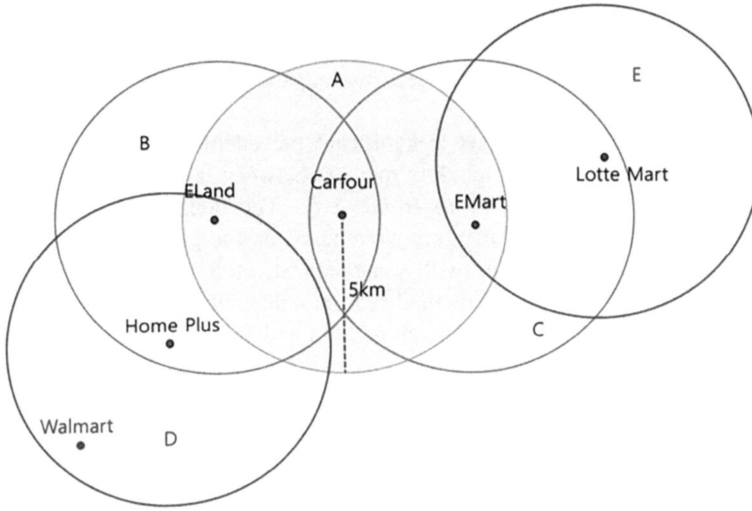

Fig. 5.2 Illustration of a union of overlapping circles

Table 5.5 Effects of Eland-Carrefour merger on price indexes

	ΔP_A	ΔP_B
Effect on Carrefour price index	−1.12% (−1.341)[a]	−0.65% (−1.368)
Effect on Eland price index	2.71% (1.915)	2.35% (1.715)

[a]t-statistics in ( )

equally begin with the "acquiring" entity (Eland); then, applying the method of overlapping circles once could yield a relevant market defined by the union of areas B, A, and D, as opposed to A, B, and C. If both unions are considered together, then the combination of areas A, B, C, and D would represent the relevant geographic market.

Jeon and Whang (2006) conducted an empirical analysis using the method of "natural experiments," as outlined in Sect. 5.2. Their model closely followed the structure of Eq. (5.2). The analysis utilized panel data, including monthly figures from January 2000 to December 2005 for 31 Carrefour stores and from January 2000 to June 2006 for 17 Eland stores. A price index was computed for the category of hyper products commonly sold by both Eland and Carrefour. The analysis considered competitors comprising other large discount stores such as Emart, Lotte Mart, Home Plus, Walmart, Nonghyup Hanaro, GS Mart, and Save Zone, along with department stores like Lotte, Hyundai, and Shinsegae. To estimate the price increases post-merger, variations of Eqs. (5.3) and (5.4) were employed. The results of these estimations are as follows (Table 5.5):

The analysis revealed that all effects were either negative or positive but statistically insignificant. The KFTC chose not to incorporate these findings in assessing the competitive impacts of the merger. Instead, the KFTC utilized the results to support its market definition.

The *Eland-Carrefour* case set a significant precedent for subsequent mergers within the retailing industry, including mergers between large discount stores such as *Emart-Walmart* and *Home Plus-Home Ever*. The definitions of product and geographic markets for these mergers were based on the precedent established by the *Eland-Carrefour* case, albeit with some sophisticated modifications.[57] Furthermore, Lee (2007) employed the method of empirical analysis using "natural experiments," closely mirroring the approach of Jeon and Whang (2006), and presented the findings to the appeal court in the *Emart-Walmart* case. The court dismissed concerns over the merger's anti-competitive effects, referencing the comparative analysis of price index values between monopolistic and competitive regions.

5.4.5 eBay -G Market *(2009): Horizontal*

eBay, a global leader in Internet shopping, made significant strides in the Korean market by acquiring Auction, the pioneer of Internet auction services in Korea, in 2001, and G Market, the country's largest open market operator, in 2008. eBay sought a prior examination of the *eBay-G Market* merger, and after a thorough review in a plenary committee, the KFTC decided to permit the merger, subject to certain behavioral remedies. Consequently, eBay proceeded with the merger, and the KFTC, following the outcome of the preliminary evaluation in 2009, approved the merger with specific conditions. These stipulations required the merged entity to refrain from increasing transaction fees charged to sellers on their Internet open markets for three years, to cap any increase in other fees within the Consumer Price Index (CPI) inflation rate, and to develop policies aimed at protecting SME sellers and ensuring compliance with the Act.[58]

Open market operators facilitate an online marketplace where sellers can directly offer their products to consumers, assuming a minimal role as a platform provider, including site management, transaction settlements, etc. In contrast, general online shopping malls purchase products from suppliers, maintain inventory, and sell to consumers via Internet sites under their own responsibility. Open markets and online shopping malls serve as quintessential examples of a two-sided market, mediating transactions between two distinct customer groups: consumers and sellers. Significantly, the KFTC delineated the relevant product market for each side separately, as illustrated in the following figure.

---

[57] The utilization of a union of intersecting circles has been expanded to incorporate various uses, as in the KFTC decision concerning the merger of department stores.

[58] KFTC 2009-146, June 25, 2009.

The KFTC adopted a broad definition for the consumer side of the market, classifying it as the Internet shopping market. This decision was based on the observation that "consumers of Internet shopping perceive open markets and general shopping malls as equivalent shopping venues and frequently use multiple Internet shopping platforms for price comparison." Conversely, the KFTC delineated the seller side of the market more narrowly, distinguishing open markets from general online shopping malls. This distinction was made by considering factors such as the pricing and functionality of services provided, the similarity of utilities, sellers' perceptions of market boundaries, and substitutability. The geographic market relevant to this analysis was defined as domestic, primarily due to the barriers presented by language differences and transportation costs.

Auction and G Market, when combined, held a market share of 37% in the consumer segment of the Internet shopping market and an impressive 87.5% share in the seller segment of the open market, based on transaction volume in 2008. While the merger did not elicit significant anti-competitive concerns within the consumer side of the market, it was presumed to potentially restrain competition on the seller side according to the relevant legislation. Despite short-term concerns, the KFTC anticipated that dynamic competition, spurred by the entry of new services utilizing IPTV and mobile networks, along with the potential for businesses to reposition their models in adjacent markets, would mitigate these concerns in the medium to long term. Consequently, the merger was approved with certain temporary behavioral remedies imposed on the seller side of the market. These included a prohibition on increasing transaction fees for a period of three years.

I consider the *eBay-G Market* case to be practically the first instance in which the KFTC exercised significant rational discretion to approve a merger that met the legal criteria for presuming anti-competitiveness, albeit with certain conditions attached. The earlier *Hyundai-Kia* merger in 1999, which was cleared despite its presumptive anti-competitive nature as previously mentioned, may not be seen in the same light, since, in my opinion, the KFTC's decision was influenced not solely by antitrust reasoning but also by the need for industrial restructuring during Korea's economic crisis. The *eBay-G Market* case is also noteworthy for its contributions to market definition and economic analysis. First, it raised an intriguing issue regarding market definition in antitrust cases involving two-sided platforms: namely, whether separate markets for each side or a single market encompassing both sides should be considered relevant. Second, Jeon et al. (2008), representing eBay, undertook a merger simulation aimed at assessing the competitive effects, particularly on the seller side. The merger simulation model for the seller side is complex and technical.[59] Therefore, I will focus solely on the issue of market definition in the discussion that follows.

[59] The task involves examining the potential rise in transaction fees for sellers following the merger of the Internet shopping operator. This analysis will be conducted through two stages: ex ante estimation and ex post simulation. A unique aspect of this merger simulation is the consideration of how the increased transaction fees would impact the operator's transaction volume. Sellers have two possible responses to this increase: either switching to alternative operators or passing on the costs to consumers by raising prices. For a detailed model, refer to Jeon (2020, Chap. 3).

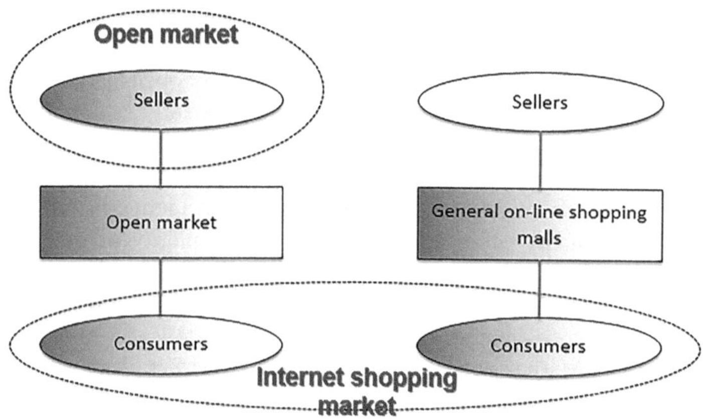

Fig. 5.3 KFTC's definition of relevant product markets

As depicted in Fig. 5.3, the KFTC distinguished between the product markets relevant to each side of the online transaction platform, defining them differently. Conversely, Jeon et al. (2008) and the defendant argued that the market for both sides should be unified under the same Internet shopping market definition. They supported their stance by utilizing the method of critical loss analyses specifically tailored for two-sided platforms. A defining characteristic of two-sided platforms is the interrelation of demand between the two sides' customers, facilitated by an indirect network effect: an increase in demand from customers on one side typically boosts the demand from customers on the other side. Given this positive feedback effect, the critical loss for a two-sided platform is posited to be smaller than the conventional threshold $CL = \frac{X}{M+X}$.[60]

One contentious issue in the antitrust economics of two-sided platforms is whether the relevant market should be treated as a unified single market for both sides or divided into two distinct markets. Filistruchi et al. (2014) and Wismer et al. (2017) suggest that conceptualizing a single market that encompasses both sides may be fitting for *two-sided transaction platforms*, whereas the idea of segregating into two separate markets for each side could be applicable for *two-sided non-transaction platforms*. Two-sided transaction platforms serve as direct intermediaries between two groups of customers. Examples include shopping platforms, which facilitate transactions between buyers and sellers, and credit card platforms, linking cardholders with merchants. For these platforms, both sides are integral to their operations. Conversely, two-sided non-transaction platforms do not inherently

[60] See Evans and Noel (2005) for the critical loss analysis for a two-sided platform.

require the involvement of both sides but rather strategically choose to engage them. For instance, a media platform like a newspaper could theoretically operate solely with paid subscribers. However, it may adopt a two-sided platform model to engage both subscribers and advertisers, optimizing its business strategy.[61]

Even for transaction platforms, the adoption of a single market definition is not always straightforward. The KFTC's decision on the *eBay-G Market* merger exemplifies this complexity. Similarly, the evolution of the American Express (Amex) case in the United States highlights the practical understanding of this issue. Initially, the District Court ruled that Amex's anti-steering clause, which prevents merchants from discouraging customers from using their Amex card, violated the Sherman Act within the separately defined relevant market of credit card services to the merchant side, distinct from the cardholder side.[62] However, the appellate court overturned and remanded the lower court's decision. By considering both the cardholder and merchant sides as a single market, the Appellate Court determined that the plaintiffs failed to demonstrate the clause's net harm to "Amex consumers as a whole," which includes both sides.[63] Ultimately, the Supreme Court upheld the appellate court's decision by a narrow margin of 5-4.[64] The Supreme Court's opinion endorsed the Appellate Court's single market definition and clarified that focusing solely on one side of the market could result in "mistaken inferences" regarding the competitive effects of the conduct in question. Despite the case's complexities and the close final decision, it sets a significant precedent for market definition and the evaluation of competitive effects in future antitrust cases involving two-sided platforms. This is particularly noteworthy as the Supreme Court's opinion was grounded in robust antitrust economics.[65]

5.4.6 Microsoft-Nokia *(2015): Vertical*

Microsoft finalized an agreement on April 16, 2014, to purchase the shares of 38 Nokia subsidiaries and to acquire Nokia's mobile telecommunications devices and services business assets. To address the competitive concerns arising from this merger, Microsoft submitted a consent decree to KFTC, which announced its final

---

[61] A dating platform, like a matching platform, can be considered as a transaction platform. However, an audience-providing or advertising platform such as Internet search engines differs slightly from non-transaction platforms because it necessitates both parties to engage in business. Nevertheless, it shares similarities with media platforms as it does not directly mediate between the two sides.

[62] *US v Am. Exp. Co.*, 88 F. Supp. 3rd 143, E.D.N.Y. (2015).

[63] *US v Am. Exp. Co.*, 838 F. 3rd 179, 2nd Cir. (2016).

[64] *Ohio v Am. Exp. Co.*, 138 S. Ct. 2274, 201 L. Ed. 2d 678 (2018).

[65] The court's opinion referred to several scholarly articles in the field of industrial economics that focused on two-sided markets. These articles included the works of Rochet and Tirole (2003), Evans and Noel (2005), Evans and Schmalensee (2008), and Filistruchi et al. (2014).

decision regarding the consent decree on August 24, 2015.[66] The merger was multifaceted, encompassing various aspects of both vertical and horizontal integrations: (i) a vertical merger between smartphone/tablet operating systems (OS) and devices, (ii) mobile patents and devices, (iii) mobile applications (apps) and devices, and (iv) a horizontal merger involving devices. Among these, the KFTC identified competitive concerns related to potential vertical foreclosure, particularly with respect to the vertical merger of type (ii).

The KFTC determined that Microsoft, holding numerous standard essential patents (SEPs) and non-SEPs implemented in the Android OS, had the potential capability to foreclose the supply of operating systems to competing mobile device original equipment manufacturers (OEMs) by increasing related patent royalties. Microsoft would be incentivized to undertake such actions if the revenue increase from higher sales of Windows devices exceeded the loss in royalties resulting from diminished sales of competing Android devices. Furthermore, Microsoft was perceived to have an incentive to discourage new entrants among Android device OEMs by elevating related royalties. Additionally, the business collaboration agreement (BCA) between Microsoft and mobile device OEMs contained clauses regarding the sharing of information about new product development, sales, and marketing. Such provisions could potentially facilitate cooperation that might adversely affect market competition.

Under the terms of the consent decree, Microsoft committed to licensing its standard essential patents (SEPs) in accordance with fair, reasonable, and non-discriminatory (FRAND) conditions and to licensing its non-SEPs at royalty rates and other non-price terms that are consistent with prevailing market terms. Additionally, Microsoft was prohibited from transferring selected non-SEPs to third parties for five years and was barred from seeking orders of sales or import injunctions based on the infringement of its non-SEPs, unless smartphone/tablet OEMs based in Korea failed to make their best efforts to engage in license negotiations. Regarding the BCA, it was stipulated that the agreement should be amended to remove any clauses involving the exchange of information related to smartphones or tablets that could potentially impact competition. The KFTC deemed that these measures would be sufficient to address the competitive concerns associated with the merger.

Jeon et al. (2014) conducted an economic analysis on behalf of a third party, presenting several arguments concerning the potential for Microsoft to increase the royalties of SEPs and non-SEPs charged to competing Android OS OEMs following the merger. Specifically, they highlighted concerns regarding (i) vertical foreclosure through raising rivals' costs, (ii) the decoupling of Cournot complementary mobile patents between Microsoft and Nokia, and (iii) the potential transformation of Nokia into a patent troll. The KFTC primarily focused on the first argument concerning the raising of rivals' costs. However, the second and third arguments merit attention due to their implications on the merger's strategic outcomes. Microsoft's decision not to

[66]KFTC 2015-316, August 24, 2015.

incorporate Nokia's valuable mobile patents, which were complementary to Microsoft's own, raises notable concerns. According to the theory of Cournot complements, the amalgamation of complementary patents is beneficial for both the merged firm's profitability and consumer welfare. Yet, Microsoft chose to separate all of Nokia's mobile patents from other assets, leaving them with Nokia post-merger. This decision suggests that Microsoft passed up the opportunity for mutual gains in both profit and consumer surplus. Furthermore, with Nokia ceasing to manufacture devices and retaining only its patents, there is a possibility of the company transitioning into a patent troll. While such a strategic choice of non-acquisition cannot be legally condemned as anti-competitive, it should be considered when evaluating the merger's motivations and economic effects.

It is noteworthy that the EC and the United States cleared the *Microsoft-Nokia* merger without conditions,[67] while the KFTC and competition agencies in China and Taiwan imposed restrictions on Microsoft's future patent licensing terms.[68] The variance in the decisions made by different antitrust jurisdictions reflects the mobile device industry's scale and importance across various countries. For East Asian countries, smartphone OEMs constitute a larger portion of their domestic economies compared to the United States or the EU, making the stakes in the *Microsoft-Nokia* merger significantly higher for them. In hindsight, Microsoft's foray into the smartphone industry did not unfold as anticipated.[69] However, it is crucial to recognize that East Asian antitrust agencies were compelled to meticulously examine the merger's potential impact on their domestic mobile industries from an *ex ante* perspective, given the substantial implications for their economies.

5.4.7 SK Telecom-CJ HelloVision *(2016): Horizontal*

SK Telecom (SKT), a leading conglomerate telecommunications company in Korea, endeavored to acquire and merge with CJ HelloVision (CJHV), a cable TV multiple system operator (MSO) and a mobile virtual network operator (MVNO), in November 2015. After an extensive review period, KFTC decided to fully block the merger in July 2016. The KFTC's decision was viewed as somewhat radical, given that many within the telecommunications industry anticipated the merger might be approved subject to certain structural and behavioral remedies.[70]

---

[67] The US FTC and DOJ have been granted early termination approval for a decision they made, although the specifics of the decision have not been disclosed. See "U.S. Approves Microsoft Purchase of Nokia's Mobile Business," *Reuters*, December 2, 2013. In contrast, EC (2013) released a comprehensive and detailed decision on *Microsof-Nokia* approval.

[68] See Chuang and Chao (2020) for the detailed comparison of the approval conditions of the *Microsoft-Nokia* merger in the East Asian countries and the comparative study of the case.

[69] Microsoft eventually sold Nokia's Device and Service Unit to Foxconn and HMD Global.

[70] According to a newspaper article on February 2, 2017, at the time, the opinion in media and industry expected that KFTC would 'approve the merger with conditions,' such as sales of MVNO

Table 5.6 Merger types of *SKT-CJHV* combination

	SK Group				
Relevant market	SK Telecom	SK Broadband	SK Telink	CJ HelloVision	Merger type
Pay TV		O		O	Horizontal
Broadband Internet		O		O	Horizontal
Mobile retail	O (MNO)		O (MVNO)	O (MVNO)	Horizontal
Mobile wholesale	O (MNO)		O (MVNO)	O (MVNO)	Vertical
All telecom markets above					Conglomerate

SKT-CJHV combination involves various forms of mergers, as the following table shows:

The primary focus of the merger between the involved entities was the horizontal integration within the pay TV market, as outlined in Table 5.6. The KFTC raised anti-competitive concerns regarding this aspect of the merger. CJHV was an MSO active in 23 cable TV (CATV) broadcasting areas. The merger of SK Broadband and CJHV would have resulted in the combined entity holding the largest market share in 21 CATV areas. According to legal standards, this consolidation was presumed to potentially restrict competition in 16 of those areas.

Jeon et al. (2016), representing SKT, conducted a detailed economic analysis on the competitive effects encompassing all aspects of the SKT-CJHV merger. Below, I will outline their key arguments concerning the merger within the pay TV market: Firstly, they argued that the geographic market relevant to pay TV should be considered "nationwide" rather than confined to cable TV (CATV) areas, which were demarcated historically for the purpose of CATV operation licensing. This broader market definition reflects the current competitive landscape more accurately than the traditional, localized approach. Secondly, the analysis employed upward pricing pressure (UPP) assessments, which are insightful regardless of the specific market definition used. The results from the UPP analyses indicated that the merger would not lead to significant price increases for pay TV services in the relevant regions. Following these points, I will also discuss the KFTC's responses to these arguments as part of its decision-making process.

In assessing the competitive effects of the merger on the pay TV market, it's important to recognize that a cable TV system operator (CATV SO), despite holding an operational license for a specific broadcasting region, competes against nationwide Internet Protocol Television (IPTV) or satellite broadcasting operators that

business and prohibition of price increase, etc. However, contrary to these expectations, the KFTC ultimately decided to block the merger. This decision came after multiple delays in making public announcements regarding the matter. (http://www.mediatoday.co.kr/?mod=news&act=articleView&idxno=137666).

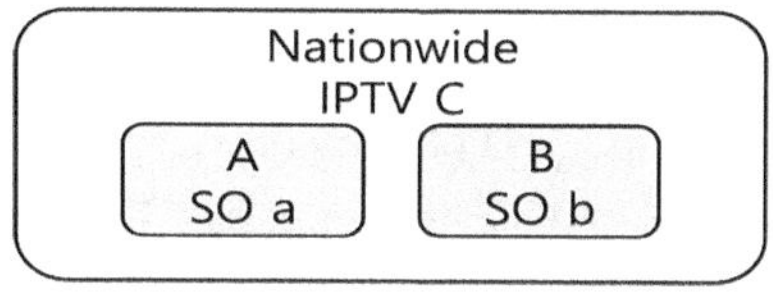

Fig. 5.4 Competitive pressure between local operators through the intermediation of the national operator

offer uniform pricing across the country. At the time of evaluation, the combined market share of these nationwide operators in the pay TV market was nearly 50% and showed a rising trend. Under the "common pricing constraints"[71] faced by these nationwide operators, entities such as IPTV have the capacity to exert competitive pressure across the country onto local CATV operators. This occurs through the mechanism of "chains of substitution,"[72] effectively distributing competitive dynamics from the national to the local level. Figure 5.4 illustrates this concept:

SO *a* and SO *b* in the above figure compete directly with national IPTV *c* within their respective regions A and B. Additionally, SO *a* and SO *b* in competition with each other through the intermediation of the national IPTV provider *c*. If SO *a* decides to reduce its service price, this action directly impacts the competitive pressure on the national IPTV provider *c*, which in turn indirectly affects SO *b* through the national IPTV provider *c*. Essentially, the chains of substitution can be conceptualized as being interconnected in the sequence of $a \leftrightarrow c \leftrightarrow b$.

Despite the arguments presented regarding the competitive dynamics across different broadcasting and service platforms, the KFTC adhered to the traditional market definition when considering the merger.[73] This definition was focused on the merger between SOs within the same CATV broadcasting area. Consequently, the KFTC identified the relevant geographic market as the 23 local CATV areas where CJHV operated its CATV services locally and SK Broadband (SKB) provided IPTV services on a national scale. This approach by the KFTC overlooked the distinct nature of the merger at hand, which involved a national IPTV operator and a large MSO encompassing 23 local cable TV operators, compared to previous mergers between local CATV SOs. Furthermore, the KFTC's decision did not sufficiently consider the structural and technological evolutions within the pay TV industry, such as the expansion of national IPTV services, the rise of large MSOs, and the digitalization of CATV services, which have significantly altered the competitive landscape.

If the geographic market had been defined as "nationwide," the merger between SKT and CJHV would not have significantly raised concerns regarding the

[71] The common price constraint, by which a telecom operator should charge the same price over the nation, has been one of the reasons for nationwide market definition in the regulation of the telecom industries. See Ofcom (2004).

[72] See EC (1997, para. 57) for the concept of chains of substitution.

[73] For instance, KFTC 2013-207, December 12, 2013.

restriction of competition within the pay TV market. As of March 2014, the combined market share of SKT-CJHV in the nationwide pay TV market would have been 24.0% (25.0% in the digital pay TV segment), which is less than the 27.4% (40.3% in digital pay TV) held by KT IPTV, the leading operator in the pay TV market. This indicates that the merged entity would have served as an effective competitor against the dominant player, especially in the increasingly significant digital pay TV sector. However, by defining the geographic market on a narrow basis as local CATV areas, SKT-CJHV emerged as the entity with the largest market share in 21 CATV areas and was, according to the Act, presumed to potentially restrict competition in 16 local areas.

The potential for nationwide competition in the pay TV market can be assessed using UPP analyses, which evaluate the likelihood of unilateral price increases by the merged entity, independent of market definition. According to Jeon et al. (2016), the GUPPI values for CJHV were found to be less than 5% in most areas and below 10% in all areas. When considering a "standard efficiency credit of 10%," the UPP/P values were negative for almost all areas,[74] suggesting that the merger would not likely raise anti-competitive concerns, even if the geographic market were defined as local CATV areas. Conversely, this analysis implies that the market ought to be defined nationwide. However, the KFTC, in its decision to block the merger, did not accept such analyses. The KFTC, estimating diversion ratios and margins to be much higher than those proposed by Jeon et al. (2016), calculated positive UPP values, which supported the KFTC's concerns regarding the merger's potential to restrain competition.[75]

Afterward, the KFTC approved two related mergers—*LGU plus-CJ HelloVision* in December 2019, and *SK Broadband-T Broad* on January 2020—with certain behavioral conditions imposed, such as restrictions on service price increases and reductions in the number of channels.[76] These mergers closely resembled the *SKT-CJHV* merger in terms of their competitive effects within the pay TV market. Each involved a nationwide IPTV operator merging with large CATV MSOs that operated across numerous regional areas, and each was presumed to potentially restrain competition in over 10 CATV areas. It could be argued that structural and technical changes in the relevant market over the three years between the *SKT-CJHV* merger and the subsequent mergers of *LGU plus-CJ HelloVision* and *SK Broadband-T*

[74] Refer to Sect. 5.3 within this chapter for GUPPI and UPP/P analyses. One interesting aspect regarding the SKT-CJHV context is that if a user of CJHV (cable TV) is not already a subscriber of SKB (broadband Internet service), they must sign up for SKB in order to switch from CJHV to SKB. The additional profits obtained from diverting CJHV users into SKB should be considered in the GUPPI or UPP analysis. The margin data were estimated based on the accounting reports of the respective firms. The diversion ratios were estimated using two approaches: one based on the inference from current market shares and the other based on the results of a user survey. For a more detailed analysis, please refer to chapter 4 in Jeon (2020).

[75] KFTC 2016-213, July 18, 2016. See chapter 4 in Jeon (2020) for an evaluation of the KFTC's UPP analyses.

[76] KFTC 2019-284, December 11, 2019, and KFTC 2020-011, January 10, 2020.

Broad were significant enough to mitigate anti-competitive concerns regarding the latter two mergers. However, it might also be contended that such changes were sufficiently foreseeable at the time of the *SKT-CJHV* merger review. This raises a question about the appropriateness of the decision to block the *SKT-CJHV* merger at that time, considering the forward-looking nature of merger evaluations.[77]

5.4.8 Delivery Hero-Woowa Bros. *(2021): Horizontal*

Delivery Hero SE (DH), headquartered in Germany, operates global delivery app services, including in Korea, where it provides online food platform services Yoggiyo (YGY) through Delivery Hero Korea (DHK) and Baedaltong as a separate business. On December 30, 2019, DH announced a contract to acquire an 88% stake in Woowa Brothers, which operates the delivery app service Baedal Minjok (BM).[78,79] BM and YGY are the leading competitors in Korea's delivery app service market, holding market shares of 49.1% and 39.3%, respectively, as of June 2020, based on Google Play Store download counts. Baedaltong, another branch of DH, holds a market share of 4.7%. In 2021, the KFTC mandated the divestiture of DHK by requiring its sale to a third party. Additionally, DH was ordered to implement several behavioral remedies, including operating BM and YGY independently, refraining from increasing various fees charged to restaurants registered with YGY, and maintaining consumer discounts for YGY delivery app users until the completion of DHK's sale.[80]

The KFTC identified the primary product market related to this merger as the food delivery app service. Conversely, the defendant contended that the market definition should be broadened to encompass all food delivery services, including direct call orders and franchise-owned app/web services.[81] The KFTC substantiated its market definition through various methods, including a modified critical loss analysis designed to consider the dual customer groups intermediated by the

[77] It is worth mentioning in passing that LGU plus, which successfully acquired CJHV three years later, was a vocal opponent of the *SKT-CJHV* merger, advocating for a significantly higher UPP as a consequence of the merger. However, it is broadly recognized that complaints from competitors ought to be approached with caution or even disregarded entirely. The rationale behind this perspective is that a competitor is unlikely to raise objections if they genuinely anticipate that a merger would result in a price increase, as such an outcome would be beneficial for them.

[78] 'Baedal' means delivery, and 'Minjok' means nation.

[79] The delivery application is a platform for ordering food that connects customers and restaurants offering home delivery services. There are two types of delivery app services: marketplace (MP), which acts as an intermediary for food orders, and own delivery (OD), which not only facilitates orders but also delivers the food. YGY and BM are examples of MP services, while DHK and Woowa Bros. offer OD services, such as YGY Express and BM Express, respectively. However, both companies primarily focus on providing marketplace services at present.

[80] KFTC 2021-032, February 2, 2021.

[81] Food delivery agencies and shared kitchens are other product markets relevant to this merger.

two-sided platform, as well as focusing on the aggregate diversion ratio between YGY and BM from the consumer perspective. It is important to note that the cost of delivery app services to consumers is represented by discount coupons, which effectively have a negative price, whereas the cost to restaurants encompasses various fees, such as intermediation, advertising, and transaction processing. The geographic market was designated as nationwide, reflecting that YGY and BM make pricing and marketing decisions on a national scale and engage in competition across the country.

The primary concerns regarding competition stem from the horizontal merger of YGY and BM within the food delivery app service market. BM, the firm being acquired, holds the largest market share, while the acquiring firm's apps, YGY and Baedaltong, are the second and third largest, respectively.[82] The combination of the top three companies would essentially create a monopolistic entity with only minor competitors remaining, raising concerns about unilateral price increases on both sides of the market. On the consumer side, the merger could potentially diminish promotional competition and lead to a reduction in discount coupons. To assess the likelihood of a decrease in discount offerings, the KFTC conducted an Upward Pricing Pressure (UPP) analysis, which revealed that the Gross Upward Pricing Pressure Index (GUPPI), adjusted for the two-sided market, exceeded 10%. Additionally, the KFTC observed that BM and YGY offered more discount coupons in regions where their market shares were comparatively lower, suggesting that the increased market concentration post-merger could result in diminished discount promotions. On the restaurant side, the merger could negatively impact the competition between the two companies for enlisting restaurants on their delivery platforms, potentially leading to an increase in various fees and alterations in the fee structure to the detriment of the restaurants.

Concerns about anti-competitive effects were also raised in relation to conglomerate mergers involving the delivery app service with a delivery agency service and the delivery app service with shared kitchens. The merging firms, through their affiliates, provide own delivery (OD) model services, which integrate food intermediation and delivery under the brands BM Express and YGY Express. Post-merger, the entity would become the third-largest player in the delivery agency service market. There exists a plausible scenario where the merged firm might expand its OD business model or bundle delivery services with intermediation, potentially diminishing competition in the delivery agency market by leveraging its monopoly power in the delivery app service. Woowa Brothers has ventured into the shared kitchen market with the brand BM Kitchen, whereas Delivery Hero (DH), despite having established numerous shared kitchens in other countries, has not yet entered this market in Korea, making DH a likely potential competitor. The merger could

[82] The KFTC evaluated the market shares primarily based on the gross food value, which represents the total value of food transactions between consumers and food stores through a specific platform. However, the specific figures pertaining to these market shares were not disclosed in the publicly announced decision.

stifle potential competition and disadvantage other market players by capitalizing on the merged entity's comprehensive business strengths in delivery app services. Furthermore, the merger involves consolidating a vast amount of information related to consumers, restaurants, transactions, and deliveries. This consolidation might reduce the merged firm's need to invest in and effort toward providing food stores with valuable marketing information, thereby dampening non-price competition in the realm of information provision.

The defendant posited that the dynamic nature of the delivery app market, characterized by easy entry and the active repositioning of business models by players in adjacent markets, would adequately address any anti-competitive concerns. This argument held sway in the 2009 *eBay-G Market* case, where competition from contiguous markets was effective and the repositioning and convergence of Internet shopping business models were ongoing. However, the KFTC assessed the current case differently. It observed that all new entrants, despite their origins in Internet portals and online shopping, failed to evolve into effective competitors against the merging entities, whose dominance has not only persisted but also intensified. It's noteworthy that the UK Competition and Markets Authority (CMA) unconditionally approved the merger between Just Eat (based in the UK) and Hungryhouse (a wholly owned subsidiary of DH) in 2017. In that scenario, the market share of the acquired company (Hungryhouse) was less than 10%, even though the combined entity's market share exceeded 80%. Furthermore, other competitors like Deliveroo and UberEATS were gaining market shares and imposing a stronger competitive pressure on Just Eat than Hungryhouse.[83] Additionally, the efficiency defenses proposed by the defendant were not well-received by the KFTC, which deemed that most of these efficiencies were not specific to the merger.

5.4.9 Korean Air-Asiana Airlines *(2022): Horizontal*

Korean Air finalized an agreement to acquire a 63.88% stake in Asiana Airlines on November 17, 2000, with the state-run Korea Industry Bank providing a loan of 0.8 trillion won for the deal, which was valued at 1.5 trillion won. This transaction marks the first attempt at a merger between full-service carriers (FSCs).[84] In 2022, the KFTC conditionally approved the *Korean Air-Asiana Airlines* merger, stipulating both structural and behavioral remedies.[85] The KFTC's examination identified anti-competitive concerns for 26 international passenger airline routes out of 65 duplicative routes and 14 domestic routes out of 22 duplicative routes, where "duplicative" refers to routes currently operated by both airlines. To mitigate these concerns, the

[83] According to the UK CMA (November 16, 2017), an econometric analysis revealed that Hungryhouse was imposing a limited competitive constraint on Just Eat in reality.

[84] FSCs can be distinguished from LCCs, which are airlines that offer lower ticket prices.

[85] KFTC 2022-107, May 9, 2022, and KFTC press release on the decision.

merger conditions required the transfer of slots and transportation rights for new entrants on the concerned routes for a duration of 10 years. Additionally, measures such as airfare restrictions, a prohibition on reducing seat supplies, and the maintenance of service quality were implemented. It is important to note that the structural remedy involving the transfer of slots and rights would only be effective if new entrants requested such transfers on the relevant routes. The merger also attracted scrutiny from antitrust agencies in other countries, given its potential competitive effects on their jurisdictions. The KFTC conducted an in-depth review of the case for one year, basing its decision on an economic analysis of the potential anti-competitive effects across various passenger airline routes.

The merger between Korean Air and Asiana Airlines encompassed a variety of combinations, including vertical, conglomerate, and horizontal mergers, spanning services such as airline passenger, cargo, repair, and maintenance, among others. Of these, only the horizontal merger within the passenger airline markets was identified as potentially harmful to competition. For international passenger airlines, each round-trip route between origin and destination (O&D) city pairs was considered a separate relevant market. Conversely, for domestic routes, a one-way route constituted the relevant market, with express rail services included for inland routes to accurately reflect consumer purchasing patterns. As of 2019,[86] the combined entities were projected to hold approximately 48.9% of the market share for all international passengers and 62% for domestic Seoul-Jeju passengers. For those passenger airline routes identified with anti-competitive concerns—26 international and 14 domestic—the combined market shares ranged from 60% to 100%, leading to the presumption of anti-competitive effects. In addition to calculating changes in market shares and concentration ratios, the KFTC also assessed potential price increases on these routes post-merger, based on economic analyses.

The KFTC conducted an econometric analysis using a reduced-form estimation model, detailed as follows:

$$\ln\left(\text{Fare}_{ijt}\right) = \alpha + \beta_1 \ln(\text{HHI}_{it}) + \beta_2 \ln(\text{Dist}_i) + Z_{ijt}{}'\delta + \mu_j + \tau_t + \varepsilon_{ijt}. \tag{5.19}$$

where

Fare_{ijt} is the average fare of O&D route i from Korea to destination country j in period t

HHI_{it} is Herfindahl-Hirschman of O&D route i in t

Dist_i is the freight distance of O&D route i

Z_{ijt} denotes other explanatory variables

μ_j is a dummy for destination country j

τ_t is a time dummy

ε_{ijt} is an error term.

[86] Instead of analyzing the merger's impact using data from 2020, the KFTC investigated the effects in 2019 due to the abnormal influence of the Covid pandemic on the airline industry in the following year.

By applying the coefficient β_1 to interpret the effect of the change in HHI post-merger, the impact of the merger on airfares was predicted. The analysis indicated that the merger would lead to an increase in average airfare by 26.3% for routes to North America, 11.5% for Europe, 2.9% for Japan, 7.6% for China, and 4.9% for Southeast Asia. The KFTC also examined the merger's effects on fares for domestic airlines operating to and from Jeju, using a model analogous to Eq. (5.19), and forecasted an average price increase of 12.4% for flights originating from Jeju and 9.9% for flights destined for Jeju.

On the contrary, Carlton et al. (2021), serving as economic experts for the defendant, proposed an alternative regression model that utilized the number of competing airlines as a proxy for competitive pressure instead of relying on the HHI. However, the KFTC criticized this approach for failing to adequately capture the essence of the merger, specifically the combination of the top two airlines originating from Korea. The KFTC argued that in scenarios where more than two competing companies exist, using merely the decrease in the number of firms would likely underestimate the merger's effect. Furthermore, in practical terms, Korean Air and Asiana Airlines consider their market shares, rather than the mere number of competitors, when setting airfares.[87]

All competition agencies in the world have approved the KAL-Asiana merger. These approvals were given by Turkey (February 2021), Taiwan (May 2021), Thailand (May 2021), the Philippines (May 2021), Malaysia (September 2021), Vietnam (November 2021), Korea (February 2022), Singapore (February 2022), Australia (September 2022), China (December 2022), the UK (February 2023), Japan (January 2024), EU (February 2024), and the United States. (October 2024). The approvals were granted with conditions, such as divesting certain international airline routes for passengers or cargo to competitive third parties, to address anti-competitive concerns.

Cases

KFTC 1999-043, *Hyundai-Kia* Merger, April 7, 1999.
KFTC 2003-027, *Moohak-Daesun* Merger, January 28, 2003.
KFTC 2006-009, *Hite-Jinro* Merger, January, 24, 2006.
KFTC 2006-261, *Eland-Carrefour* Merger, November 6, 2006.
KFTC 2006-264, November 14, 2006.
KFTC 2008-265, October 17, 2008.
KFTC 2009-146, *eBay-G Market* Merger, June 25, 2009.
KFTC 2013-207, December 12, 2013.
KFTC 2015-316, *Microsoft-Nokia* Merger, August 24, 2015.
KFTC 2016-213, *SK Telecom-CJ Hello Vision* Merger, July 18, 2016.

[87] Korean Air, for instance, evaluates the airfares of rival companies in the following manner: if its market share exceeds 70%, it adds 150 thousand won to its prices; if it hovers around 50%, it maintains a similar pricing level; and if it falls below 20%, it reduces its fares by 50 thousand won.

KFTC 2019-284, December 11, 2019.
KFTC 2020-011, January 10, 2020.
KFTC 2021-032, *Delivery Hero-Woowa Brothers* Merger, February 2, 2021.
KFTC 2022-107, *Korean Air-Asiana Air* Merger, May 9, 2022.
Seoul High Court 2003nu2252, *Moohak-Daesun* Merger, October 27, 2004.
Am. Exp. Co., 88 F. Supp. 3rd 143, E.D.N.Y., D.C. 2015.
Am. Exp. Co., 838 F. 3rd 179, 2nd Cir. 2016.
Colombia Steel Co., 334 U.S. 495, Supreme 1948.
EC M.3905, *Tesco/Carrefour (Czech Republic and Slovakia)*, December 22, 2005
EC M.7074, *Microsoft/Nokia*, October 29, 2013
FTC v. Staples, 979 F. Supp. 1066, D.D.C. 1997.
Ohio v Am. Exp. Co., 138 S. Ct. 2274, 201 L. Ed. 2d 678, Supreme 2018.
Philadelphia Nat'l Bank, 374 U.S. 321, Supreme 1963.
U.K. CMA, *Just Eat/Hungryhouse*, November 16, 2017.

References

Adams WJ, Yellen JL (1976) Commodity bundling and the burden of monopoly. Q J Econ 90(3): 475–498

Ashenfelter O, Ashmore D, Baker JB, Gleason S, Hosken DS (2006) Empirical methods in merger analysis: econometric analysis of pricing in FTC vs. staples. Int J Econ Bus 13:265–279

Baker JB, Bykowsky M, DeGraba P, LaFontaine P, Ralph E, Sharkey W (2011) The yea in economics at the FCC, 2010-11: protecting competition online. Rev Ind Org 39:297–309

Carlton D, Waldman M (2002) The strategic use of tying to preserve and create market power in evolving industries. RAND J Econ 33:194–220

Carlton D, Hore J, Keating B (2021) An economic analysis of the merger between Korean Air and Asiana Airlines. Expert Witness Report, June 21

Choi JP, Stefanadis C (2001) Tying, investment, and the dynamic leverage theory. RAND J Econ 32:52–71

Chuang L, Chao S (2020) Microsoft-Nokia merger control in East Asia. Santa Clara Technol Law J 36(5):449–479

Chung J, Jeon S (2014) Portfolio effects in conglomerate mergers: the empirical evidence of leverage effects in Korean Liquor Market. Appl Econ 43:4345–4359

Coate MB (2013) The use of natural experiments in merger analysis. J Antitrust Enforc 1(2): 437–467

Cournot AA (1927) Research into the mathematical principle of the theory of wealth. Macmillan

Cowling K, Waterson M (1976) Price-cost margins and market structure. Economica 43:267–274

Dalkir S, Warren-Boulton FR (2004) Prices, market definition, and the effects of merger: Staples-Office Depot (1997), Case 2. In: Kwoka JE Jr, White LJ (eds) The antitrust revolution: economics, competition, and policy, 4th edn. Oxford University Press

Davis P, Garces E (2010) Quantitative techniques for competition and antitrust analysis. Princeton University Press

Epstein JR, Rubinfeld DL (2004) Effects of mergers involving differentiated products. Technical Report for EC Commission, COMP/B1/2003/07, 7 October 2004

European Commission (1997) Commission notice on the definition of the relevant market for the purposes of community competition law. Off J Eur Commun C 372, 9 December 1997

European Commission (2008) Guidelines on the assessment of non-horizontal mergers under the Council Regulation on the control of concentrations between undertaking. Off J Eur Union C 265/07, December 18, 2008

European Commission (2021) Evaluation of the Commission notice on the definition of the relevant market for the purposes of Community Competition Law of 9 December 1997. Commission Staff Working Document, July 12, 2021

Evans D, Noel M (2005) Defining antitrust markets when firms operate two-sided platforms. Colum Bus Law Rev 2005:102–134

Evans D, Salinger M (2005) Why do firms bundle and tie? Evidence from competitive markets and implications for tying law. Yale J Regul 22:149–163

Evans D, Schmalensee R (2008, February 19) Markets with two-sided platforms. Competition Law and Policy (ABA Section of Antitrust Law), 1, Chapter 28

Farrell J, Shapiro C (2010) Antitrust evaluation of horizontal mergers: an economic alternative to market definition. B.E. J Theor Econ 10(1):1–39

Filistruchi L, Geradin D, van Damme E, Affeldt P (2014) Market definition in two-sided markets: theory and practice. J Comp Law Econ 10(2):293–339

Jeon S (2004) Geographic market definition relevant to Moohak-Daesun merger. Expert Witness Report to Seoul Hight Court. [in Korean]

Jeon S (2016) Critical loss analyses in Korean liquor mergers, Chapter 5. In: Habib M (ed) Empirical modeling and its application. InTech, pp 87–110

Jeon S (2020) Fair trade cases and economic analyses. Park Young Publishing. [in Korean]

Jeon S, Nahm J, Shin I, Ahn H (2008) Competitive effects of Auction-G Market merger. Expert witness report to KFTC. [in Korean]

Jeon S, Whang Y (2006) Economic analysis on the competitive effects of Eland-Carrefour merger. Expert Witness Report to KFTC. [in Korean]

Jeon S, Kim C, Park S, Yoon K (2005) Product market definition relevant to Hite-Jinro Merger and portfolio effects of the Conglomerate Merger. Expert Witness Report to KFTC. [in Korean]

Jeon S, Kwon N, Chung J (2014) Anti-competitiveness of Microsoft-Nokia Merger. Expert Witness Report to KFTC. [in Korean]

Jeon S, Kwon N, Kim S, Lee S, Nahm J (2016) Competitive effects of SK Telecom-CJ HelloVision merger. Expert Witness Report. [in Korean]

Ofcom (2004) Review of the wholesale broadband access market: Identification and analysis of markets, determination of market power, and setting of SMP Conditions. Final Explanatory Statement and Notification

Korean Fair Trade Commission (2011) Thirty years history of Korea Fair Trade Commission: trace of advocating market economy (1981~2010). [in Korean]

Korea Fair Trade Commission (2021) Annual White Paper. [in Korean]

Korea Fair Trade Commission (2021) Guidelines for the merger review. December 20, 2021. [in Korean]

Lee H (2007) Empirical analysis on the competitive effects of Emart-Walmart merger. Expert Witness Report

Moresi S (2010) The use of price pressure indices in merger analysis. Antitrust Source, February 2010

Moresi S, Salop SC (2013) vGUPPI: scoring unilateral pricing incentives in vertical mergers. Antitrust Law J 79(1):185–214

Nalebuff B (2000) Competing against bundling. In: Hammond P, Myles G (eds) Incentives, organization and public economics. Oxford University Press, Oxford

Nalebuff B (2004) Bundling as an entry barrier. Q J Econ 119:159–187

Neven DJ (2005) The analysis of conglomerate effects in EU merger control. In: Handbook of Antitrust economics. MIT Press

Nevo A (2000) Mergers with differentiated products: the case of the ready-to-eat cereal industry. Rand J Econ 31(3):395–421

Ponsoldt JF, David CD (2007) Comparison between U.S. and E.U. antitrust treatment of tying claims against Microsoft: when should the bundling of computer software be permitted. Northwest J Int Law Bus 422:421–451

Rochet J-C, Tirole J (2003) Platform competition in two-sided markets. J Euro Econ Ass 1(4):990–1029
Rogerson W (2014) A vertical merger in the video programming industry: the case of Comcast-NBCU. In: Kwoka JE, White LJ (eds) The antitrust revolution, 6th edn. Oxford University Press, pp 534–575
Ryu K, Yi S (2004) Economic analysis on the geographic market definition relevant to Moohak-Daesun merger. Expert Witness Report. [in Korean]
Ryu K, Yi S (2005) Competitive effects on liquor market of hite's acquisition of Jinro. Expert Witness Report. [in Korean]
Shapiro C (2010) The 2010 horizontal merger guidelines: from Hedgehog to Fox in forty years. Antitrust Law J 77(1):49–107
Simons JJ, Coate MB (2010) Upward Pressure on Price (UPP) Analysis: issues and implications for merger policy. Eur Compet J 6(2):377–396
Stigler GJ (1968) A note on block booking. In: Stigler GJ (ed) The organization of industries. Irwin, Homewood, IL
U.S. DOJ (1984) Non-horizontal merger guidelines
U.S. DOJ and FTC (2010) Horizontal merger guidelines, August 19, 2010
U.S. DOJ and FTC (2020) Vertical merger guidelines, June 30, 2020
U.S. FTC (2021) Federal trade commission withdraws vertical merger guidelines and commentary. Press release, September 15, 2021
Vergé T (2003) Portfolio effects and merger control: full-line forcing as an entry deterrence strategy. CMPO Working Paper Series No. 02/046
Whinston MD (1990) Tying foreclosure, and exclusion. Am Econ Rev. 80(4):837–859
Whinston MD (2006) Lectures on antitrust economics. The MIT Press
Wismer S, Bongard C, Rasek A (2017) Multi-sided market economics in competition law enforcement. J Eur Compet Law Pract 8(4):257–262

Chapter 6
Cartel Regulation in Korea

A universal consensus among antitrust experts posits that cartels engaging in price-fixing and quantity reduction significantly impair consumer surplus. Consequently, cartel regulation occupies the forefront of antitrust enforcement priorities for competition agencies globally, with the KFTC being no exception.

This chapter begins by addressing the principal aspects of cartel regulation in Korea. Next, I discuss the economic logic underpinning leniency programs. These programs are implemented globally to incentivize cartel members to disclose evidence to competition authorities. Subsequently, the discussion extends to the challenges associated with estimating cartel damages, focusing on the price overcharges and the pass-through of costs. The chapter concludes by highlighting several notable cases of cartel regulation in Korea, which include cartels involving: *Military Oil Procurement* in 2000, *Graphite Electrodes* in 2002, *Flour* in 2006, *Credit Card/VAN* in 2006, *BMW/Lexus Dealers* in 2008, *Ramen* in 2008, *Industrial Explosives* in 2015, *Compound Feed* in 2015, *LNG Tank* in 2016, *Iron Scrap Purchase* in 2021, and *Public Procurement of Reinforcing Bar* in 2022. These instances are significant for their influence on subsequent cartel regulation efforts and the integration of economic analyses in decisions made by the KFTC or the courts, with a particular emphasis on cartel damage estimation.

6.1 Main Features of Cartel Regulation in Korea

In this section, I will provide a summary of the key elements, significant revisions, and performance outcomes of cartel regulation in Korea.

S. Jeon, *Antitrust Policy in Korea*, https://doi.org/10.1007/978-981-95-0632-3_6

6.1.1 Key Elements

Article 40 (1) of the Korea Monopoly Regulation and Fair Trade Act (MRFTA) prohibits unfair collaborative acts, stipulating: "No enterprise shall, through contract, agreement, resolution, or any other means, agree with other enterprises to jointly engage in activities that fall under any of the following sub-paragraphs, which unfairly restrict competition (hereinafter referred to as 'unfair collaborative act') or permit another enterprise to engage in such an unfair collaborative act." The criteria for constituting an unfair collaborative act include: (i) the involvement of two or more enterprise entities, (ii) an agreement among them, and (iii) the act results in competitive restraints. Residents of an apartment complex who may collude on housing prices are not subject to liability under this provision, as they do not qualify as business enterprises. Notably, under the MRFTA, an agreement in principle, even if not enacted, is considered an unfair collaboration. The KFTC bears the burden of proving that the collaborative act in question unfairly restricts competition, implying that not all cartels are inherently illegal.

Nine types of unfair collaborative acts are specified as follows: (i) Fixing, maintaining, or altering prices; (ii) Establishing terms and conditions for the trade of goods or services, including the payment thereof; (iii) Limiting the production, supply, transportation, or trade of goods, or limiting the provision of services; (iv) Restricting the geographical region of a transaction or the choice of trading partners; (v) Obstructing or limiting the establishment or expansion of facilities, or the installation of equipment necessary for producing goods or delivering services; (vi) Imposing restrictions on the types and specifications of goods or services that are produced or traded; (vii) Collaboratively undertaking, managing critical aspects of a business, or forming a company for the joint execution and management thereof; (viii) Determining the winner of bids or auctions, bid amounts, maximum prices, contract prices, and other aspects as defined by Presidential Decree; (ix) Effectively limiting competition within a specific business domain through interference or restriction of other enterprises' business activities or content, including the exchange of information regarding prices, production, and other matters beyond those described in items (i) through (viii), as specified by Presidential Decree. These provisions aim to comprehensively address and prevent a wide array of collaborative behaviors that unfairly restrict competition within the market.

The above-mentioned unfair collaborative acts can be categorized into two distinct groups: "hardcore" and "softcore" cartels. Hardcore cartels encompass activities such as (i) price fixing, (iii) production reduction, (iv) market division, and (viii) bid rigging. According to the KFTC (2021) cartel guideline, these cartels are characterized as inherently restricting competition due to the nature of the collaborative act itself. Such cartels are identified as unfair collaborative acts without the need for detailed evaluation of the specific competitive restraint, except under extraordinary circumstances. However, even in these instances, a preliminary analysis of the market structure, trading practices, and market competition is required.[1] Conversely, other collaborative acts, namely (ii), (v), (vi), (vii), and (ix), are classified as softcore cartels. These are viewed as potentially able to both restrict competition and enhance efficiency. For these cases, the "rule of reason" is applied, similar to situations involving abuses of market dominance and mergers, requiring a more nuanced assessment of their impact on competition and efficiency.

In response to cartel involvement, the KFTC is authorized not only to mandate the cessation and public announcement of such activities but also to levy a penalty surcharge on each enterprise found in breach of cartel prohibitions. This surcharge can amount to as much as 20% of the relevant turnover, defined as the sales of goods or services in the pertinent market during the period of infringement. A significant amendment to the MRFTA on December 28, 2021, has seen the maximum penalty surcharge for cartel participants increase from 10% to 20% of the relevant turnover, marking a substantial escalation in punitive measures. The determination of the penalty surcharge, as outlined in public notifications, takes into account several factors including the severity of the violation, any previous infractions, the degree of cooperation with the KFTC investigation, and any financial hardships faced by the enterprise. This approach ensures that penalties are not only punitive but also considerate of the broader circumstances influencing the enterprise's involvement in cartel activities.

In the EU, the basic fines for violations of competition law generally can reach up to 30% of the relevant turnover, calculated as the annual relevant sales multiplied by the duration of the infringement. Specifically, for cartel offenses, an additional deterrent is applied, amounting to a one-time fee of 15–25% of the annual relevant sales. However, there is a cap on these fines: they cannot exceed 10% of the company's total annual turnover, or of the group to which the company belongs, particularly if the parent company exerted decisive influence over the subsidiary involved in the infringement during the period in question. The determination of the actual fines may either increase or decrease from the base level, taking into account both aggravating and mitigating factors.[2] Comparing the basic framework of cartel fines between Korea and the EU does not yield a clear-cut conclusion as to which jurisdiction imposes larger fines in principle. If the infringement involves all products of the company or its affiliated group, then the overall 10% limit may render the EU's cartel fines less severe than those in Korea. Conversely, the fines in the EU could be considerably more substantial than those in Korea if they amount to up to 30% of relevant turnover, coupled with the additional deterrent fines specific to cartel cases.

The penalty surcharges or fines imposed in Korea and the EU, as previously discussed, are of an administrative nature. The MRFTA mandates that any individual involved in a cartel may face criminal penalties, including imprisonment for up to three years or a fine not exceeding 200 million won. Conversely, the EU does not

[1] Supreme Court 2010du18703, April 26, 2012, and KFTC (2021) cartel guidelines.

[2] EC (2011), "Fines for breaking EU Competition Law." November 2011.

have criminal prosecution for violations of competition law, with such prosecutions occurring only within some Member States. In contrast, the US Sherman Act enforces criminal sanctions for all types of infringements under Section 1, although the DOJ Antitrust Division primarily prosecutes hardcore cartels. According to Section 1, entities found in violation can incur fines up to $10 million for corporations and $350,000 for individuals, alongside possible imprisonment for up to ten years. Furthermore, Section 6 of the subsequently enacted Criminal Fine Improvement Act stipulates that criminal fines may exceed these amounts, allowing for penalties up to twice the gross profits or losses resulting from the infringement.[3]

Due to the near *per se* illegality and severe penalties associated with hardcore cartels, participants often endeavor to collude covertly, striving to leave no evidence of their activities. This secretive nature significantly challenges antitrust agencies in detecting such cartels. To address this difficulty, leniency or amnesty programs have been implemented as strategic measures to facilitate the detection of cartels and thus deter their formation. These programs offer exemptions or reductions in penalty surcharges and criminal prosecution to individuals or entities that voluntarily report unfair collaborative acts or cooperate with investigations by providing evidence or other assistance. Specifically, complete immunity from all penalties is granted to the first party to report, while a reduction of up to half of the surcharges may be applied to subsequent cooperators. The United States pioneered the adoption of an amnesty program in 1978, followed by the EU and Korea in 1996. Both the United States and Korea have further refined this approach with the introduction of the "Amnesty Plus" program. Under this scheme, if a participant in an ongoing investigation voluntarily discloses involvement in additional cartel activities, antitrust authorities may reduce sanctions not only for the case under scrutiny but also for the newly reported offenses.

Civil damage recovery serves as an additional deterrent against cartels. The MRFTA establishes provisions for liability in cases of damage: if an enterprise or an organization of enterprises breaches the Act, thereby causing harm, they are held liable for compensating the affected parties. For an accused entity to be exempt from liability, it must demonstrate that the Act was not violated through either deliberate action or negligence. This liability applies to all breaches of the Act, although civil damage lawsuits are predominantly filed in relation to cartels, particularly those involving public procurement. Traditionally, in accordance with civil law principles, the scope of damage recovery in Korea is compensatory. However, in 2019, the approach toward calculating damages for cartel offenses was revised to include a punitive element, allowing for damages up to three times the losses incurred from the cartel activities. This modification introduces a punitive aspect to damage liability for cartel cases, aligning with the concept of treble damages found in US antitrust law, albeit the actual amount awarded may be less than threefold the incurred losses, taking into account various mitigating factors. It's important to note that similar provisions for punitive damages exist under the KFTC's jurisdiction for special acts,

[3]Refer to Reims (2022).

such as the Subcontracting Act, Large Retail Business Act, and Franchise Business Act.[4]

6.1.2 Major Revisions

The regulatory framework governing cartels in Korea has undergone numerous revisions since the initial enactment of the Act in 1980. One significant amendment occurred in 1986, marking the transition from an *ex ante* to an *ex post* regulatory approach for cartels. Initially, cartels were required to register with and obtain approval from the precursor to the KFTC if they met certain criteria. However, this *ex ante* regulatory system was deemed incompatible with the fundamentally retrospective nature of antitrust policy, leading to its abolition in 1986. Despite this change, remnants of the previous system persist, notably in the provision allowing for the exemption of cartels under special circumstances, such as economic depression or industrial restructuring. Nonetheless, such exemptions have not been commonly granted in recent times.

A more significant amendment occurred in 1992, altering the definition of an unfair collaborative act to focus on the existence of an agreement itself, rather than on actions taken pursuant to an agreement. This change marked a pivotal strengthening in the enforcement of cartel regulations. In a subsequent revision in 1999, the criterion for determining "unfairness" shifted from "substantially restraining competition in the relevant market" to "unfairly restraining competition." This modification appears to be an effort to incorporate the principle of *per se* illegality into cartel regulation. However, as previously mentioned, this principle has not been consistently upheld in subsequent court decisions.[5] As highlighted earlier, the judiciary has mandated the assessment of the relevant market structure, trade practices, and market competition, even in cases involving hardcore cartels. This approach indicates a nuanced consideration of cartel activities, requiring a detailed examination beyond the mere existence of an agreement to determine their impact on market competition.

The leniency program in Korea was introduced in 1997 and underwent significant enhancements in 2005. Initially, the program was seldom utilized, primarily because the legislation lacked clarity regarding penalty exemptions and failed to guarantee the confidentiality of informants. The 2005 amendment addressed these issues by automating the exemption of penalty surcharges—a full 100% for the first reporting party and initially 30%, later increased to 50%, for the second reporting party—provided the exemption criteria were met. Additionally, the "Amnesty Plus" program was introduced, and the confidentiality protections for leniency applicants were significantly strengthened. These revisions led to a marked increase in the

[4] See Chap. 3, Sect. 3.3.

[5] Lim and Cho (2023, pp. 229–231).

frequency of leniency applications, subsequently facilitating the easier detection of cartels.

The MRFTA underwent a comprehensive revision in 2020. This revision involved a structural overhaul, streamlining provisions that had been added incrementally through successive amendments. More importantly, in the context of cartel regulation, the revision introduced several measures to strengthen enforcement.[6] A significant addition was the explicit inclusion of "the conduct of practically restraining competition by exchanging information about price, production, etc., among enterprises" within the list of unfair collaborative acts. Previously, the exchange of such information was considered circumstantial evidence in establishing an agreement among parties. However, courts have historically demanded rigorous proof of an explicit agreement in cases where information exchange constituted the primary evidence. A notable instance is the Supreme Court's 2012 decision in the *Ramen* case, where it was determined that "the conduct of information exchange cannot straightforwardly be recognized as an agreement on the act of determining and maintaining prices."[7] The intent of this revision was to facilitate the KFTC's enforcement efforts regarding the regulation of cartels, particularly in cases involving information exchange. The impact of this revision on future court decisions remains to be seen, indicating a cautious approach to evaluating its effectiveness in strengthening cartel regulation.

Another notable change in the 2020 amendment of the Act is the increase of the maximum penalty surcharges on cartel participation from 10% to 20% of the relevant sales.[8] This revision effectively doubled the cap on penalty surcharges across various infringements, including an increase from 3% to 6% for abuse of market dominance, from 2% to 4% for general unfair trade practices, and from 5% to 10% for unfair subsidization involving owner families or affiliate firms. Despite these across-the-board increases, the impact of raising the ceiling for penalty surcharges in cartel cases is likely to be the most profound, both in terms of the absolute increment in penalty surcharges and in enhancing the overall punitive and deterrent effect. This move underscores a deliberate effort to strengthen the regulatory framework against cartels, reflecting the heightened seriousness with which such violations are viewed and the intent to curb anti-competitive practices more effectively.

[6] See Chap. 1 for the comprehensive revision in other aspects.

[7] Supreme Court 2013du25924, December 24, 2015. See *Ramen* case in Sect. 6.5.5.

[8] Penalty surcharges for cartel violations were initially implemented in the revised legislation of 1986, with a maximum punishment set at 5%. However, this level was subsequently increased to 10% in the revised legislation of 2005.

6.1.3 Enforcement Record

Cartel regulation has been the primary focus of antitrust enforcement in Korea. The majority of cartels involve price fixing (45%) and bid rigging (40%). Since the enactment of the MRFTA up to 2021, 838 cartel cases have had penalty surcharges imposed on them, constituting 26% of the total 3224 antitrust cases where such penalties were applied. The significance of cartel enforcement becomes even more apparent when considering the proportion of penalty surcharges by amount; cartel-related penalties account for approximately 65% of the total, equating to 6.5 trillion won out of 10 trillion won. The KFTC has taken legal action against individuals involved in approximately 15% of the cartel cases it has regulated. Despite this, instances of imprisonment have been exceedingly rare, a trend consistent across all antitrust cases in Korea. This disparity underscores the primary focus on financial penalties as the primary deterrent and punitive measure against anti-competitive practices, highlighting the challenges and priorities within Korea's approach to antitrust enforcement.[9]

The leniency program has played a pivotal role in detecting cartels, particularly following the implementation of the enhanced program in 2015. Table 6.1 presents the annual data on the imposition of penalty surcharges, the application of the leniency program, and the corresponding relative ratios over the years.

During the period from 1991 to 2024, a total of 958 cartel cases were subject to penalty surcharges. Among these, 561 cases, or 60.1%, were detected through the leniency program. Particularly noteworthy is the period from 2005 to 2024, which saw a marked increase in the utilization of the leniency program. During this time, out of 881 cartel cases where penalty surcharges were imposed, 557 were identified via the leniency program, translating to a leniency application rate of 63.2% relative to total cartel detections. This data underscores the significant impact of the leniency program in uncovering cartel activities, especially in the years following the enhancement of the program.

6.2 Economics of Leniency Program

The leniency program is recognized as the most effective tool for detecting and deterring cartels across most antitrust enforcement agencies. The program's success in uncovering and preventing cartel activities is well substantiated by economic theories, which also provide a framework for its strategic design. The principles of economics not only elucidate the program's impact on detection and deterrence but also offer guidance on optimizing its structure to ensure maximum efficacy in combating anti-competitive behaviors.

[9] Refer to Lee (2019) for the criminal enforcement of antitrust cases in Korea, such as imprisonment, probation, etc.

Table 6.1 Leniency application trend

Year	# of penalty surcharge imposed (A)	# of leniency applied (B)	% of leniency application (B/A)
1999	15	1	6.7
2000	15	1	6.7
2001	8	0	0
2002	14	1	7.1
2003	11	1	9.1
2004	14	0	0
2005	23	6	26.1
2006	27	6	22.2
2007	24	10	41.7
2008	43	20	46.5
2009	21	13	61.9
2010	26	18	69.2
2011	35	30	85.7
2012	24	12	50.0
2013	29	23	79.3
2014	58	45	77.6
2015	63	48	76.2
2016	44	29	65.9
2017	53	42	79.2
2018	97	41	42.3
2019	50	34	68.0
2020	68	48	70.6
2021	52	34	65.4
2022	45	28	62.2
2023	47	24	51.1
2024	52	46	88.5
Total	958	561	60.1

KFTC (2025), *Annual White Paper*

6.2.1 Detection and Deterrence Effects of Leniency Program

The prisoner's dilemma provides a clear justification for the leniency program. Imagine two firms involved in collusion, each independently deciding whether to report the cartel to the KFTC. If found guilty of collusion, the firms face penalty surcharges estimated at 100 billion won. Under the leniency program, if one firm reports the cartel while the other does not, the informant is exempted from all penalties, whereas the non-reporting firm incurs the full 100 billion won penalty. If both firms opt to report simultaneously, each has a 50% chance of being acknowledged as the first reporter. In such a scenario, the expected penalty for each firm is calculated as 25 billion won, derived from 0.5 (the probability of being the first to report) times 0 (complete exemption) plus 0.5 (the probability of being the second

Table 6.2 A simple example of leniency game

		Firm B	
		Leniency	No report
Firm A	Leniency	−25, −25	0, −100
	No report	−100, 0	−10, −10

reporter) times 50 billion won (half exemption). On the other hand, if both firms decide to remain silent, the likelihood of the KFTC detecting the cartel on its own is 10%, with each firm then facing potential penalties of 100 billion won, leading to an expected penalty of 10 billion won for each. This scenario illustrates the strategic dilemma cartel participants face under the leniency program, effectively captured in a game matrix where outcomes are expressed in terms of the expected penalty surcharges.

As demonstrated by the prisoner's dilemma game, the dominant strategy for each participant is to opt for the leniency report, irrespective of the other's decision. This characteristic underscores the effectiveness of the leniency program in detecting cartels. The strategic incentive to report first, encouraged by the potential for exemption or reduced penalties, ensures that participants are more likely to disclose information about the cartel, thereby enhancing the program's capacity to uncover and dismantle such anti-competitive arrangements.

The simplistic framework presented in Table 6.2 fails to fully incorporate the dynamic nature of the leniency program's deterrent effect. Harrington (2008) develops a more nuanced oligopoly model, wherein each firm evaluates the decision to either sustain the cartel or report it through the leniency program in each period. This decision-making process is influenced by the anticipated benefits of leniency and the probability of detection and subsequent conviction by the competition agency. Harrington delineates three effects impacting the decision to maintain or deviate from cartel behavior. Firstly, the *Deviator Amnesty Effect*, which posits that a firm's incentive to defect from the cartel and seek leniency amnesty intensifies with the increase in leniency benefits. The prospect of obtaining amnesty serves as a significant motivator for firms to abandon cartel agreements. Secondly, the *Cartel Amnesty Effect*, which suggests that the potential for reduced penalty surcharges, facilitated by the leniency program in the event of a KFTC investigation, might inadvertently bolster the incentive to form or continue cartels. The interplay between this effect and the Deviator Amnesty Effect creates a counterbalancing dynamic. Thirdly, the *Race to the Courthouse Effect*, the impact of which varies based on the magnitude of leniency amnesty. When leniency benefits are substantial, as illustrated in Table 6.2, firms are incentivized to preemptively report to antitrust authorities to secure leniency, effectively making it a dominant strategy. In contrast, with smaller leniency benefits, the situation resembles a coordination game characterized by two potential equilibria: one where all firms report to the agency, and another where all firms remain within the cartel. Such a possibility can be seen through the following game matrix (Table 6.3):

The revised game model is predicated on a scenario where the benefits of leniency are diminished. For instance, consider that the penalty surcharges for the first firm to

Table 6.3 A modified example of leniency game

		Firm B	
		Leniency	No report
Firm A	Leniency	−75, −75[a]	−50, −100
	No report	−100, −50	−10, −10

[a]In scenarios where two firms simultaneously apply for leniency, the expected penalty surcharges for each firm amount to 75 billion won. This calculation is derived as follows: 0.5 (the probability of being the first to report, which grants a half exemption) multiplied by 50 billion won (representing the reduced penalty for the first reporter) plus 0.5 (the probability of being the second reporter, who receives no exemption) multiplied by 100 billion won (the full penalty surcharge)

report are halved to 50 billion won, while the second reporting firm receives no exemption. Under these conditions, we observe two Nash equilibria:[10] one where both firms choose to report (Leniency, Leniency) and another where neither firm reports (No Report, No Report).

Harrington (2008) elaborates that the dynamic equilibrium of this game is defined by optimal strategies that hinge on the threshold values for the probability of independent detection by the agency. Specifically, firms are incentivized to remain within the cartel when the likelihood of agency detection is low. Conversely, as the probability of detection increases, firms are more likely to defect from the cartel, either to engage in competition or to report the cartel in hopes of receiving leniency benefits. This strategic calculation illustrates the complex interplay between the incentives provided by the leniency program and the firms' assessments of the risks and benefits of remaining in or departing from a cartel arrangement.[11]

6.2.2 *Optimal Design of Leniency Program*

Leniency programs differ slightly from country to country. Table 6.4 shows a variety of such programs.

Economic research offers insights into the optimal design of leniency programs among the various models discussed.[12] Harrington (2008) posits that, from a theoretical standpoint, granting a 100% exemption exclusively to the first reporter is optimal. Providing an exemption to the second reporter does not significantly increase the likelihood of dismantling a cartel initially and may, in fact, reduce the expected penalty surcharges associated with cartel participation. Nevertheless, subsequent leniency applications can bolster the evidence and improve the chances of

[10]A Nash equilibrium represents a set of strategies chosen by players in which each player's selection is the optimal response to the choices of the others.

[11]Refer to Harrington (2008) for a comprehensive examination of the dynamic game.

[12]I heavily relied on Kim and Nahm (2010) to introduce the pertinent literature.

Table 6.4 Leniency programs in countries

	US	EU	Germany	UK	Japan	Korea
Exemption to the second and the later	100% exemption to only 1st reporter	– 1st: 100% – 2nd: 30~50% – 3rd: 20~30% – 4th or later: ~20%	– 1st: 100% – 2nd or later: ~50%	– 1st: 100% – 2nd or later: ~50%	[a]Before investigation – 1st: 100% – 2nd: 20% (+40%) – 3rd to 5th: 10% (+40%) – 6th and after 5% (+40%) [a]After investigation – 1st–3rd: 10% (+20%) – 4th and after: 4% (+20%)	– 1st: 100% – 2nd: 50%
Exemption after investigation	O (automatic exemption)	O (automatic exemption)	O (automatic exemption)	O (discretionary reduction)	O (discretionary reduction)	O (automatic exemption)
Complete exemption to originator	X	O	X	O	O	O
Exemption to individuals	O	X	X	O	X	X
Reward to individual reporters	X	X	X	O	X	O

Kim and Nahm (2010). [a]Japan's leniency program underwent significant updates with the 2019 amendment, which specified the maximum additional reduction for cooperation, as indicated in the details provided above successful cartel prosecution. Motta and Polo (2003) argue that offering exemption benefits after the commencement of an agency investigation could enhance the leniency program's effectiveness. This approach boosts a firm's incentive to report under the leniency program as soon as an investigation is underway, indirectly amplifying the program's deterrent effect. The willingness to grant leniency exemptions even to the originator or instigator of a cartel reflects a pragmatic trade-off between enhancing detection and deterrence and upholding social justice or equity principles. Allowing even the cartel's originator to benefit from leniency exemptions could deter other firms from participating in cartel activities, anticipating such possibilities. Biogoni et al. (2009) support the hypothesis that excluding the cartel originator from leniency exemptions might diminish the program's deterrent effect and lead to higher price overcharges due to cartels. The impact of individual amnesty programs is closely linked to the threat of criminal sanctions. Aubert et al. (2006) find that criminal penalties and individual amnesty programs have been effective in deterring cartels in the United States. Notably, Korea pioneered the initiative to reward individual whistleblowers in 2002, with the UK following suit in 2008. Aubert et al. (2006) also provide a theoretical foundation for the effectiveness of reward programs in enhancing cartel deterrence.

6.3 Cartel Damage Estimation

The empirical evidence of price increases resulting from cartel activities can significantly influence both competition agencies and courts in determining the illegality of a cartel. The magnitude and statistical significance of the price increase are crucial factors in assessing the existence of a cartel, especially when the evidence is ambiguous, and in determining the amount of penalty surcharges, even in the presence of concrete evidence. Furthermore, the accurate estimation of price overcharges due to cartel activities is of paramount importance during civil court trials. In recent years, there has been a notable increase in civil lawsuits seeking damages for cartel activities in Korea, particularly regarding cases of bid-rigging in public procurement. This trend underscores the growing importance of empirical analyses in both the enforcement of competition law and the adjudication of related civil disputes.

The price overcharge attributable to a cartel is defined as the difference between the collusive price and the but-for price. Cartel damages are then calculated by multiplying the price overcharge by the actual purchases made during the period of collusion.[13] While collusive prices are the actual prices charged during the collusion,

[13]In theory, the decline in consumer satisfaction caused by a rise in prices should be considered when calculating the damages resulting from collusion. However, this requires us to assess the demand function, adding complexity to the analysis. Moreover, identifying the rightful claimants of the lost consumer satisfaction is practically challenging, as the affected consumers remain unidentified.

Table 6.5 Estimation methods of counterfactual price

Type	But-for or counter-factual competitive prices
Before and after	Non-collusive prices before or after collusion
Yardstick	Prices in other markets similar to collusive market
Dummy variable	Estimating the relationship among prices, demand/supply factors for all periods (or markets) and collusion dummy statistically and excluding the effects of collusive dummy variable
Forecasting or residual	Forecasting non-collusive prices during collusion by estimating the relationship among prices and demand/supply factors for non-collusive periods (or markets) and inserting the values of explanatory variables for collusive periods (or markets)
Difference-in-difference	Introducing two dummy variables of collusive periods and markets and considering the difference between collusive and non-collusive periods (before and after) and the difference between collusive and non-collusive markets (yardstick)
Cost-based	Adding margins of non-collusive periods (or markets) into the costs of collusive periods (or markets)
Theoretical modeling	Estimating theoretical competitive prices based on the oligopolistic competition model

but-for prices represent hypothetical competitive prices that would have prevailed in the absence of collusion. Therefore, it is necessary to estimate these but-for prices, or counter-factual competitive prices, to accurately assess the extent of the overcharge and subsequently calculate cartel damages.

6.3.1 *Methods of Estimating Counterfactual Competitive Price*

Ashurst (2004) provides a comprehensive overview of different approaches employed to determine counterfactual competitive prices (Table 6.5).[14]

The Before-and-After (Yardstick) method simplifies the comparison between prices during collusive periods (or markets) and prices during non-collusive periods (or markets). The Dummy Variable Model advances this concept econometrically, isolating the impact of collusion on prices by controlling for other influencing factors through multiple regression analysis and introducing a collusion dummy variable to specifically identify the effect of collusion. The Forecasting or Residual Model also employs multiple regression analysis but relies solely on data from non-collusive periods (or markets) to estimate the relationship between prices and demand/supply

[14] Oxera (2009) presents various approaches which are conceptually similar to the ones introduced in Table 6.3. However, there are differences in the terminology used. The before-and-after method is referred to as "time-series analysis," the yardstick method is described as "cross-sectional analysis," the cost-based method is labeled as "financial-analysis-based approach," and the theoretical modeling is denoted as the "market-structure based approach."

factors. It then forecasts competitive prices for the collusive periods (or markets) by applying the explanatory variables' values from these periods (or markets) to the established price-explanatory variable relationship. The difference between the actual collusive prices and the forecasted prices reflects the effect of the cartel. The Difference-in-Difference (DID) Model further refines the multiple regression analysis used in the Dummy Variable Model by incorporating both the Before-and-After and Yardstick concepts through two dummy variables for collusive periods and markets. DID is a more sophisticated approach that necessitates panel data encompassing both non-collusive periods (time series) and markets (cross-section). The Cost-based Method uses accounting data to calculate non-collusive prices by applying margins from non-collusive periods (or markets) to the costs of the collusive periods (or markets). Finally, the Theoretical Modelling Approach constructs a theoretical framework of oligopoly competition to estimate competitive prices, offering a more theoretical approach to understanding and quantifying the impact of collusion on pricing.

The Cost-based Method, while straightforward, presents several challenges inherent to accounting data, making it overly simplistic for complex analyses. Conversely, the Theoretical Modelling Approach, despite its theoretical sophistication, proves difficult to apply in practical settings due to its abstract nature. Among the methodologies outlined, the econometric approaches—specifically the Dummy Variable, Forecasting, and Difference-in-Difference (DID) Models—stand out for their incorporation of both Before-and-After and Yardstick concepts. These methods have gained considerable acceptance among antitrust experts, provided that the necessary data are available. These econometric models offer a balanced blend of empirical rigor and practical applicability, making them particularly valuable for analyzing cartel effects when comprehensive and reliable data sets are accessible.

6.3.2 *Dummy Variable vs. Forecasting*

Both the Dummy Variable and Forecasting models employ multiple regression analysis, incorporating the principles of either the before-and-after or yardstick method. The Dummy Variable Model utilizes data from both collusive and non-collusive periods, whereas the Forecasting Model relies exclusively on non-collusive data to estimate the relationship between the dependent variable (prices) and the explanatory variables, which include demand and supply factors, among others. The estimation equation for the Dummy Variable Model can be articulated as follows:[15]

---

[15]Typically, in multiple regression models, all variables, with the exception of the dummy variable, are subjected to the natural logarithm transformation (ln). This transformation allows for the interpretation of the β estimates as elasticities. The estimate of the dummy variable, on the other hand, remains as not transformed by the natural logarithm and can be understood as the percentage rate of price overcharge resulting from a cartel.

$$p_t = \alpha + \beta X_t + \delta D_t + u_t \tag{6.1}$$

where

p_t = prices observed in period t
X_t = explanatory variables that affect demand or supply in period t
D_t = dummy variable with 1 if t is collusive and 0 otherwise
u_t = disturbance term in t.

On the other hand, the forecasting model lacks a dummy variable:

$$p_t = \alpha + \beta X_t + u_t \tag{6.2}$$

where t covers only collusive periods (or markets) in the forecasting model of Eq. (6.2), while t covers both collusive and non-collusive periods (or markets) in the dummy variable model of Eq. (6.1). The forecasted values of counter-factual competitive prices in t during collusion are calculated as follows:

$$\widehat{p_t} = \widehat{\alpha} + \widehat{\beta} X_t. \tag{6.3}$$

where $\widehat{\alpha}$ and $\widehat{\beta}$ are the estimates of α and β in Eq. (6.2) by using non-collusive data. $\widehat{p_t}$ is calculated by plugging the values of X_t in period t during collusion into Eq. (6.3). The difference between the actual collusive price and the forecasted counter-factual price is the residual at period t during collusion:

$$R_t = p_t - \widehat{p_t} \tag{6.4}$$

which represents the price overcharge resulting from a cartel. Both equations can be interpreted in terms of time-series if they incorporate the idea of before-and-after or in terms of cross-section if they incorporate the idea of yardstick.[16]

The Dummy Variable Model and Forecasting Model each offer distinct advantages and limitations. Often, the availability of relevant data during collusive periods (or markets) is insufficient, making it challenging to achieve statistically significant estimates using only non-collusive data. A principal benefit of the Dummy Variable Model is its ability to incorporate data from collusive periods, thereby enhancing the statistical significance of the results. Additionally, this model presents a nuanced advantage by treating the effects of collusion and other explanatory variables in a balanced manner, a point that will be further discussed. However, the Dummy Variable Model faces a significant challenge due to the potential regime shift

[16] In estimating Eqs. (6.1) and (6.2), we should be careful to avoid the well-known problem of endogeneity in estimating a reduced-form demand equation. That is, the omitted variables captured in the disturbance term may affect the dependent variable of prices or the explanatory variables in X_t and hence, the disturbance term u_t may not independent. If that is the case, OLS estimates may be biased. Then it is necessary to employ 2-stage OLS estimation by using appropriate instrumental variables.

between collusion and competition phases. This shift can alter the impact of explanatory variables on prices during periods of collusion. One way to partially address this issue is by introducing interaction terms between the dummy variable and other explanatory variables, which can help account for changes in the relationship between these variables and prices during collusive periods.[17] Another concern is the assumption that the effect of collusion is constant, represented as δ in Eq. (6.1). This simplification may not accurately capture the dynamic nature of collusion's impact on prices over time.[18]

The Forecasting or Residual Model also presents its own set of strengths and weaknesses. If there is a sufficient length of non-collusive data to statistically significantly estimate the relationship in Eq. (6.2), then the forecasting method can circumvent the issue of regime shifts between collusive and non-collusive periods. Additionally, it allows for the accommodation of cartel effects that vary across different periods, with the effect of collusion being reflected in the residuals in Eq. (6.4), which change with each period during collusion. However, a primary limitation of the forecasting method is the potential for data scarcity, which can hinder the model's ability to produce statistically significant estimates. Moreover, this approach might underestimate the effect of collusion. This underestimation occurs because the model attributes price effects primarily to demand and supply factors, treating residuals as indicative of collusion. This contrasts with the Dummy Variable Method, which equitably considers the impact of both collusion and other explanatory variables, assigning them comparable significance in the analysis.[19]

The choice between the Dummy and Forecasting Methods is not inherently clear-cut. However, in practice, the Dummy Variable Model may be utilized more frequently due to the challenges associated with securing sufficient data length for the Forecasting Method. Additionally, the Dummy Variable Model offers the flexibility to be expanded into a Difference-in-Differences Model when panel data, encompassing both time-series and cross-sectional information for collusive/non-collusive periods and markets, are available. This adaptability further underscores the practical utility of the Dummy Variable Model in antitrust analysis.

[17] See White et al. (2006).

[18] If there are some changes in collusive periods in terms of concerted behavior, e.g., cheating by some member or variation in the number of participants, then we may introduce several dummy variables by partitioning collusive periods. Furthermore, in cases where non-collusive periods exist before and after collusion, then we may introduce another dummy for the periods after collusion, which captures the inertia of pricing behavior or the lingering effect of the cartel.

[19] Finkelstein and Levenbach (1983) noted the potential for downplaying the impact of collusion when using forecasting models.

Table 6.6 Numerical example of DID

	Collusive market	Non-collusive market	Difference
Collusive period	110	80	30 Difference between collusive and non-collusive markets in collusive periods (Yardstick)
Non-collusive period	90	75	15 Difference between collusive and non-collusive markets in non-collusive periods
Difference	20 Difference between collusive and non-collusive periods in collusive markets (before-and-after)	5 Difference between collusive and non-collusive periods in non-collusive markets	15 (Difference-in-Difference)

6.3.3 *Difference-in-Differences (DID)*

The idea of DID can be explained with the following simple numerical example (Table 6.6).

Suppose the price in collusive markets during collusive periods is 110, while in non-collusive markets during the same periods, it is 80. Conversely, during non-collusive periods, the price in collusive markets is 90, and in non-collusive markets, it is 75. The initial difference observed in collusive periods between collusive and non-collusive markets is 30, embodying the Yardstick Method's principle. However, of this 30, a 15-point difference may not be attributable to collusion but rather to inherent differences between collusive and non-collusive markets. Therefore, the Difference-in-Differences (DID), calculated as 30 minus 15, equals 15, representing the net effect of collusion on prices by isolating the impact from market characteristics. This DID concept is further validated when reversing the order of differencing. Subtracting the price difference between collusive and non-collusive periods in non-collusive markets (5) from the price difference in collusive markets over the same periods (20), which aligns with the Before-and-After approach, yields the same DID outcome of 15. This calculation demonstrates the DID method's robustness in isolating and quantifying the true effect of collusion on market prices.

We can formulate the DID idea with a multiple regression model by extending the dummy variable model in Eq. (6.1) as follows:[20]

[20]Refer to Wooldridge (2006) for the general introduction of the DID model and estimation. In the DID literature, the collusive markets and periods are called the "treatment group," whereas the non-collusive markets and periods are called "control group."

Table 6.7 DID in multiple regression

	Collusive market $\text{DCM}_i = 1$	Non-collusive market $\text{DCM}_i = 0$	Difference
Collusive period $\text{DCT}_t = 1$	$\alpha + \beta' X_{it} + \delta_M + \delta_T + \delta_{MT}$	$\alpha + \beta' X_{it} + \delta_T$	$\delta_M + \delta_{MT}$ Difference between collusive and non-collusive markets in collusive periods
Non-collusive period $\text{DCT}_t = 0$	$\alpha + \beta' X_{it} + \delta_M$	$\alpha + \beta' X_{it}$	δ_M difference between collusive and non-collusive markets in non-collusive periods
Difference	$\delta_T + \delta_{MT}$ Difference between collusive and non-collusive periods in collusive markets	δ_T Difference between collusive and non-collusive periods in non-collusive markets	δ_{MT} DID (Difference-in-Difference)

$$p_{it} = \alpha + \beta X_{it} + \delta_M \text{DCM}_i + \delta_T \text{DCT}_t + \delta_{MT} \text{DCM}_i \cdot \text{DCT}_t + u_{it} \quad (6.5)$$

where

p_{it} = prices observed in market i and period t
X_{it} = explanatory variables that affect demand or supply in market i and period t
DCM_i = dummy variable with 1 if market i is collusive and 0 otherwise
DCM_t = dummy variable with 1 if period t is collusive and 0 otherwise
u_{it} = disturbance term in market i and period t.

Table 6.7 in the following explains DID in the multiple regression model in Eq. (6.5).

Notice that the coefficient δ_{MT}, representing the interaction effect of two dummies $\text{DCM}_i \cdot \text{DCT}_t$, incorporates the difference-in-difference in the general multiple regression model.

6.4 Intermediate Goods Cartels and Cost Pass-Through

The estimation of damages resulting from a cartel in the market for a final consumption good typically involves calculating the price overcharge attributed to the cartel's activities. However, in civil damage litigation concerning intermediate goods cartels, the plaintiffs can be either direct purchasers (i.e., producers of final goods that utilize the intermediate goods as inputs) or indirect purchasers (i.e., consumers of the final goods). In such cases, it is essential to estimate the damages to direct purchasers by accounting for the pass-through of cost increases from the intermediate goods cartel to the prices of final goods. Similarly, the damages to indirect purchasers should be assessed based on the extent of cost pass-through. Nonetheless, determining the level of cost pass-through involves complex economic considerations and is not a straightforward task. Additionally, legal debates persist regarding whether and how cost pass-through should be factored into the calculation of damages in civil lawsuits involving intermediate goods cartels. These controversies highlight the challenges in aligning economic principles with legal frameworks to ensure fair and accurate compensation for cartel-induced harm.

6.4.1 Legal Disputes Over Cost Pass-Through

The US Supreme Court, in the 1968 *Hanover Shoe* case, rejected the defendant's defense on the ground that direct purchasers passed on the price increase in intermediate goods due to the cartel. As a consequence, the entitlement of indirect purchasers to claim cartel damages was also denied in the 1977 Supreme Court decision of *Illinois Brick*.[21] These two decisions operate in conjunction, establishing a legal framework that avoids the risk of over-compensation by precluding not only the passing-on defense but also denying indirect purchasers the right to recover cartel damages. Allowing both direct and indirect purchasers to claim damages without permitting the passing-on defense could lead to excessive compensation claims against defendants. Conversely, restricting damage recovery exclusively to indirect purchasers while allowing the passing-on defense might result in under-compensation. Therefore, the combined effect of the *Hanover Shoe* and *Illinois Brick* decisions—prohibiting the passing-on defense and limiting damage recovery to direct purchasers—has sparked legal debates around the issues of cost pass-through and eligibility for damages in cases involving intermediate goods cartels. These decisions underscore the complex interplay between economic principles and legal standards in addressing cartel-induced harm.

At first glance, the decisions in *Hanover Shoe* and *Illinois Brick* may appear counterintuitive or not aligned with standards of equity, especially considering the practical likelihood that direct purchasers often pass on at least part of the cost increase from a cartel to indirect purchasers, who ultimately bear the burden of higher prices for final consumption goods. However, the US Supreme Court's rulings were based on practical considerations and policy objectives rather than a straightforward application of economic theory. Firstly, the Court recognized the difficulty in separately quantifying the damages incurred by direct purchasers and those suffered by indirect purchasers, given the complex interrelation between these two groups. The task of disentangling and accurately attributing the specific portion of overcharge passed through to each level in the supply chain was deemed impractical. Secondly, the Court anticipated that limiting the right to recover damages exclusively to direct purchasers would bolster cartel deterrence. Direct purchasers,

[21] *Hanover Shoe, Inc. v. United Shoe Machinery Corp.*, 392 US 481, Supreme 1968, and *Illinois Brick Co. v. Illinois*, 431 US 720, Supreme 1977.

being closer to the source of the anticompetitive behavior and more directly affected by it, are presumed to have a greater incentive and capacity to initiate legal action against cartels. This strategic limitation aims to simplify the litigation process and enhance the effectiveness of antitrust enforcement by concentrating legal recourse in the hands of those most capable of pursuing it.

As anticipated, the *Hanover Shoe* and *Illinois Brick* decisions have sparked considerable controversy and backlash in the United States. In response, several states, including California and the District of Columbia, have moved to repeal the *Illinois Brick* decision, recognizing the right of indirect purchasers to recover damages. These jurisdictions challenge the notion that the practical difficulties of estimating cost pass-through are insurmountable. Furthermore, they argue that direct purchasers might possess a diminished incentive to sue for damages, thereby contributing less to the deterrence of cartels, especially in scenarios where cost pass-through to indirect purchasers is significant. The core concern among these states is that prohibiting the passing-on defense for defendants and denying indirect purchasers the right to recover damages could compromise distributive equity. This is based on the perspective that such legal constraints might enable direct purchasers to reap undue gains, while indirect purchasers bear the losses unjustly. In light of these ongoing disputes, the US Antitrust Modernization Commission (2007) recommended allowing both direct and indirect purchasers the entitlement to recover cartel damages, effectively calling for the repeal of the principles established by the *Hanover Shoe* and *Illinois Brick* decisions. This recommendation reflects a shift toward a more inclusive approach to damage recovery in antitrust law, aiming to address concerns over fairness and the effectiveness of cartel deterrence.

According to Ashurst (2004), EU member countries generally grant both direct and indirect purchasers the right to recover antitrust damages, recognizing the passing-on defense under the condition that defendants bear the burden of proof. EC (2008) White Paper on antitrust damage actions, reinforcing the 2006 *Manfredi* decision by the Court of Justice, affirms that "any individual" may claim antitrust damages in the court of the relevant country. A notable proposal in the EC White Paper is the introduction of a "rebuttable presumption" that allows indirect purchasers to assume that the illegal price increase resulting from a cartel has been wholly passed on to them, aiming to reduce their burden of proof for damages. However, there are concerns that defendants might struggle to effectively counter this presumption of complete pass-through. This difficulty arises because rebutting the presumption necessitates access to comprehensive information on competition, demand, and costs in the direct purchasers' market, much of which is proprietary to direct purchasers. Thus, there's a risk that the presumption of complete pass-through may stand in many cases, potentially skewing the fairness of proceedings. In Korea, the courts have been accommodating both the passing-on defense and the entitlement of direct purchasers to cartel damages recovery in practice. This approach will be further discussed in the subsequent subsection on case studies, highlighting the practical application and implications of these legal principles in the Korean context.

6.4.2 Economics on Cost Pass-Through

For an expositional purpose, I denote as follows:

w_0, x_0: price and quantity of an intermediate good but for collusion
w_1, x_1: actual price and quantity of an intermediate good in collusion
p_0, q_0: price and quantity of a final good but for collusion
p_1, q_1: actual price and quantity of a final good in collusion
$\pi(p, w)$: profit of a direct purchaser who produces the final good using the intermediate good

The price overcharge of the intermediate good resulting from a cartel, the cost pass-through to the final good, and the subsequent profit loss experienced by the direct purchaser can be represented by Δw, Δp and $\Delta \pi$, respectively.

Estimating Δw and of Δp is conceptually straightforward. To estimate Δw, one can apply Eq. (6.1) within the context of a cartel in the market for an intermediate good. For estimating Δp, a modified model of Eq. (6.1), which omits the collusion dummy, can be used. This approach utilizes the coefficient of the intermediate good as a cost factor to calculate Δp. The initial estimate of $\Delta \pi$ might be based on the following considerations:

$$\Delta \pi = -x_1 \Delta w + q_1 \Delta p \tag{6.6}$$

However, the economic interplay among Δw, Δp and $\Delta \pi$ is complex and influenced by various factors, including the competitive conditions in the intermediate goods market and the demand and supply dynamics of the final goods market. Despite this complexity, I will demonstrate how Eq. (6.6) can serve as a useful approximation under the assumption of oligopolistic competition in the intermediate goods market, a condition that is characteristic of most cartels.[22]

According to microeconomic theory, the impact of a price overcharge in an intermediate goods market on the profit of a direct purchaser can be expressed as follows:[23]

$$\begin{aligned}\frac{d\pi}{dw} &= \frac{\partial \pi}{\partial w} + \frac{\partial \pi}{\partial p}\frac{dp}{dw} + \frac{\partial \pi}{\partial r}\frac{dr}{dw} \\ &= \frac{\partial \pi}{\partial w} + \frac{\partial \pi}{\partial r}\frac{dr}{dw} \\ &= -x + \frac{\partial \pi}{\partial r}\frac{dr}{dw}\end{aligned}$$

Hence, the following relationship holds true:

[22] There are many studies conducted to assess the damage caused by cartels in the intermediate good cartel, for example, Brander and Ross (2005), Ashurst (2004), Cotterill et al. (2001), Cotterill (1998), and Harris and Sullivan (1979). However, these studies primarily examine the impact of cost pass-through on estimating damages when the plaintiffs are indirect purchasers.

[23] This is an application of envelope theorem and Hotelling's Lemma in microeconomic theory. See Mas-Colell et al. (1995).

$$\begin{aligned}\Delta\pi &= \frac{d\pi}{dw}\Delta w \\ &= -x\Delta w + \frac{\partial\pi}{\partial r}\frac{dr}{dw}\Delta w,\end{aligned} \tag{6.7}$$

where r denotes the price set by rivals of a direct purchaser in the supply of intermediate goods. The first part of Eq. (6.7) represents the direct effect of profit losses due to the cartel's price overcharge, whereas the second part details a countervailing indirect effect, which captures the increase in rival firms' prices $\frac{dr}{dw}$ (>0) as a response to the cartel price overcharge and the subsequent impact on the profit of the direct purchaser $\frac{\partial\pi}{\partial r}$ (<0). This indicates that rivals are likely to adjust their prices upward in reaction to the cartel price overcharge, allowing the direct purchaser the possibility to increase its own price to mitigate the losses incurred from the cartel's actions.

The accurate estimation of $\frac{\partial\pi}{\partial r}\frac{dr}{dw}\Delta w$ poses significant practical challenges, as it necessitates advanced theoretical modeling of oligopolistic competition alongside complex empirical analysis using firm-level supply and demand data. As an alternative, I suggest approximating $\frac{\partial\pi}{\partial r}\frac{dr}{dw}\Delta w$ as $q_1\Delta p$. That is, the direct purchaser can benefit from the price increase in the final goods market, reflecting the oligopolistic competition in the intermediate good market, which may offset profit losses due to cartel price overcharge. Then, Eq. (6.7) can be approximately reformulated as follows:

$$\begin{aligned}\Delta\pi &= -x\Delta w + \frac{\partial\pi}{\partial r}\frac{dr}{dw}\Delta w \\ &\cong -x_1\Delta w + q_1\Delta p\end{aligned} \tag{6.8}$$

In other words, the direct purchasers have the right to seek compensation for the damages caused by the cartel as much as $-x_1\Delta w$. On the other hand, the defendants have the opportunity to present their passing-on defenses with $q_1\Delta p$.

6.5 Cases of Cartel Regulation in Korea

In this section, I examine a selection of cartel regulation cases that are significant in terms of legal precedents, economic analyses, and international comparisons. I will outline the main decisions made by the KFTC and the courts, and discuss their implications for subsequent cartel regulation. This analysis aims to shed light on the evolving nature of antitrust enforcement, highlighting key legal and economic considerations that have shaped the approach to regulating anti-competitive practices both within Korea and in a broader international context.

6.5.1 Military Oil Procurement *(2000)*

In 2000, the KFTC ruled that five oil companies had colluded in bidding for military oil procurements over the three years, 1998, 1999, and 2000, resulting in substantial penalty surcharges and criminal charges against them.[24] This decision was followed by an administrative lawsuit filed by the defendants seeking to overturn the KFTC's decision, a criminal lawsuit initiated by the prosecutor, and a civil lawsuit for damage recovery filed by the military defense minister. The case concluded in 2013 with a determination of damages. This case is noteworthy for its emphasis on the economic analysis of cartel damage estimation and the judicial assessment thereof. It sparked intense and prolonged debates among the plaintiff, defendants, and economic experts regarding the appropriate application of the difference-in-difference method for estimating damages. Furthermore, there was a divergence in opinion between the first trial court and the appellate court regarding the correct method for damage estimation. Ultimately, the Supreme Court set the precedent for estimating cartel damages, marking a significant moment in the legal and economic approaches to addressing cartels. This case highlights the complexities and challenges of quantifying the economic impact of anti-competitive behavior and establishes a critical benchmark for future cartel damage estimations.

The military defense minister filed a civil lawsuit for damage recovery, claiming approximately 160 billion won. This figure represented the discrepancy between the actual procurement payments and the competitive prices, which were benchmarked against MOPS (Mean of Platt's Singapore), an international spot market price, in 2001. In contrast, the defendants, relying on the analysis of economic experts who utilized the Difference-in-Differences (DID) methodology,[25] contended that the damages amounted to approximately 30 billion won. The trial court enlisted a team of appraisers, comprising economists from Seoul National University, to provide a reasoned estimate of the damages. The appraisers submitted a valuation of damages at 114 billion won.[26] Notably, both the economic experts representing the defendants and the appointed appraisers applied the DID method. However, a significant discrepancy between the appraisers' estimate and that of the defendants' economic experts led to vigorous debates. These disputes centered on the appropriate selection of explanatory variables, estimation techniques, and other methodological considerations within the framework of the DID approach.

The utilization of the DID methodology in this case was feasible due to the availability of data for both before-and-after (collusive vs. non-collusive periods) and yardstick (collusive vs. non-collusive markets) comparisons. In Eq. (6.5), the collusive markets, denoted by $\mathrm{DCM}_i = 1$, referred to military oil procurements, whereas the non-collusive markets, where $\mathrm{DCM}_i = 0$, involved private oil

[24] KFTC 2000-158, October 17, 2000. The adjusted final sum amounted to approximately 100 billion won, making it the most significant amount recorded during that period.

[25] Seong et al. (2002).

[26] Kim et al. (2004).

procurements by airline companies, electricity providers, etc. The collusive periods, indicated by $DCM_t = 1$, spanned the years 1998, 1999, and 2000, while the non-collusive periods, with $DCM_t = 0$, included the years 1995, 1996, 1997, 2001, and 2002. Differences between the appraiser team and the economic experts representing the defendants emerged in detail regarding the selection and implementation of explanatory variables in X_{it}. Notably, the appraiser team chose to separate the collusion dummy for each of the years 1998, 1999, and 2000, in contrast to the defendants' expert team, which aggregated it into a single dummy for the three-year span. Furthermore, the appraisers opted for the Weighted Least Squares (WLS) estimation technique, whereas the defendants' experts applied the Ordinary Least Squares (OLS) method. The choice between WLS and OLS became a technical point of contention among econometricians, with the rationale for using WLS in this context not being widely understood by most economists. The appraiser team argued that WLS could more accurately estimate damages by assigning greater weight to larger procurements. However, it is well-known among economists that WLS is primarily suited for addressing heteroscedasticity in error terms, which can render OLS estimates biased or inefficient, rather than for the reasons proposed by the appraiser team.[27] The modeling of explanatory variables in Eq. (6.5) encompassed numerous additional differences, which are not discussed here, further illustrating the complexity and nuance involved in applying econometric methods to legal disputes over cartel damages.

The defendants enlisted a new team of economic experts from Sogang University (the Sogang team) to assess the validity of the appraisal report conducted by economists from Seoul National University (the SNU appraisal team). The Sogang team meticulously reviewed the SNU appraisal report, focusing on aspects such as data treatment, the validity of the WLS estimation technique, the use of individual collusion dummies, and the selection of explanatory variables.[28] Notably, the Sogang team recommended employing a model with varying coefficients, wherein the effect of collusion varies with procurement size. This approach aimed to assign greater weight to larger procurements, as the SNU appraisal team had insisted, but without resorting to the WLS estimation technique. Furthermore, the Sogang team introduced two separate collusion dummies: one for 1998 and 1999, and another for 2000, to account for the price adjustment mechanism implemented by the military defense department in 2000, which considered changes in international oil prices. The Sogang team also identified several errors in the SNU appraisal team's data treatment, including duplication, omission, and inconsistencies when handling private contracts following unsuccessful bids during both collusive and non-collusive periods. In response to these critiques, the SNU appraisal team submitted a

[27] Heteroscedasticity refers to a situation where the error terms in the estimation equation exhibit unequal variances, thereby violating the assumption of individually identical distribution (i.i.d). This undermines the ability of OLS estimation to meet the criteria of superior estimators like the Best Linear Unbiased Estimator (BLUE).

[28] Jeon (2020, Chap. 10) explains the difference in detail.

supplementary report, revising the estimated damages to 112 billion won—a slight reduction of two billion won from their initial estimate. This adjustment addressed some errors in data treatment and incorporated a few of the Sogang team's suggestions, such as the model with varying coefficients. However, the SNU team maintained their use of the WLS estimation method, demonstrating a selective integration of the feedback provided by the Sogang team.

The First Trial Court dismissed the use of international spot market prices from MOPS as the benchmark suggested by the plaintiff, reasoning that it was inappropriate to directly compare two markets without taking into account the specific characteristics of buyers and the various variables that influence prices in these markets. The court endorsed the DID method and recommended that the appraisal team re-estimate the damages. Specifically, the court advised using the OLS rather than the WLS estimation technique, consolidating the collusion effects of 1998 and 1999 under a single dummy and treating 2000 with a separate dummy, and consistently excluding all private contracts following unsuccessful bids, among other recommendations. This directive reflects the court's adherence to the conventional econometric theory that WLS is warranted primarily under specific conditions of heteroscedasticity in error terms.[29] Regarding the segregation of yearly collusion dummies, the court found no compelling rationale for distinguishing between the years 1998 and 1999, while it acknowledged that the extent of collusion in 2000 could have been influenced by a congressional audit concerning high procurement prices toward the end of 1999.[30] Following these guidelines, the revised estimate of the damages was approximately 81 billion won, significantly adjusting the compensation figure based on the court's recommendations and the orthodox principles of econometric analysis.

The Appellate Court witnessed continued disputes over the correct application of the DID model for estimating damages from the procurement cartel, with no signs of resolution. In response to the escalating disagreement among economists and the widening gap in their damage estimates, the court decided to abandon the DID estimation model in favor of a simpler method based on MOPS as a yardstick. The Appellate Court remarked that "the multiple regression analysis must be a scientific method in itself, but the difficulty in the normative control of economic arguments, the substantial divergence—exceeding a factor 5.5 times—between the damage estimates produced by each model, no allowance of triple damage recovery in our system of damage compensation, etc. restrict us in many ways from adopting the above method for estimating damages in this case."[31] Furthermore, the court acknowledged the considerable accuracy of MOPS in predicting successful bid prices over an extended period following the collusion. With some adjustments based on MOPS, the Appellate Court ultimately determined the damages to be approximately 141 billion won. This decision reflects a pragmatic shift toward a

[29] Jeon et al. (2004).

[30] Seoul District Court 2002gahap16982, January 23, 2007.

[31] Seoul High Court 2007na25137, December 20, 2009.

more straightforward and ostensibly objective method of estimating cartel damages, underscoring the challenges inherent in balancing scientific rigor with legal and practical considerations in antitrust litigation.

The Supreme Court overturned the Appellate Court's decision, critiquing its reliance on MOPS as a yardstick for determining damages in the case of military oil procurement. The Supreme Court argued that "the domestic market of military oil procurement, characterized by its oligopolistic structure differs significantly from the spot markets, which are closer to perfect competition in terms of market structure, trade conditions, etc. … Thus, we may not determine the prices obtained by adding subsidiary costs according government accounting guidelines into MOPS during cartel periods ("MOPS reference prices") as counter-factual competitive prices." Further, the Supreme Court set forth a basic standard for estimating cartel damages, or antitrust damages more broadly, as follows: "the counter-factual competitive prices should be identified by isolating price overcharges attributable solely to collusion, while keeping all other price-determining factors in the market where the collusive conduct arises as they are. … In estimating these counterfactual competitive prices, … we should not include the price changes affected by the price-determining factors irrelevant to collusive conduct in the range of damages."[32] This approach aligns with the main purpose of multiple regression in econometrics, which is to distinguish the price overcharges solely attributable to collusion from the impacts of various factors that affect prices apart from collusion. By controlling for all other changes in commodity, market, and economic conditions, multiple regression allows for the separation of collusion-induced price changes from other influences.

The case concluded with a settlement between the plaintiff and the defendants, based on the damage estimate from the First Trial Court, as recommended by the Supreme Court upon remanding the case. This legal proceeding is now considered a landmark precedent for several reasons. Firstly, it established a rational guideline for estimating antitrust damages, endorsed by the Supreme Court's decision, aligning with the scientific principles of multiple regression analysis in economics. This guideline underscores the importance of isolating the effects of collusion from other price-determining factors in the market, offering a methodical approach to damage calculation that is both rigorous and grounded in economic theory. Secondly, the Court demonstrated its ability to judiciously interpret and apply complex economic concepts, such as multiple regression, difference-in-difference, Ordinary Least Squares (OLS), heteroscedasticity, and Weighted Least Squares (WLS), within the legal framework. This proficiency indicates a sophisticated understanding of the intricate economic arguments at play, reflecting the Court's respect for the expertise of appraisers while balancing the arguments presented by both the plaintiff and the defendants in a fair manner. This case exemplifies the judiciary's capacity to navigate sophisticated economic analyses, integrating scientific methods into legal

[32] Supreme Court 2010da18850, June 28, 2011.

decision-making processes to achieve reasonable and just outcomes in antitrust litigation.

6.5.2 Graphite Electrodes *(2002)*

The KFTC issued an injunction and levied penalty surcharges against six foreign companies for their participation in an international graphite electrode cartel from 1992 to 1998. The appellate court's decision underscored the application of the "effects doctrine" in the extraterritorial enforcement of the MRFTA. Furthermore, the decision addressed a procedural issue of the appropriate methods for notifying and serving foreign companies, as well as the fairness of imposing penalty surcharges on these entities. This ruling marks a significant moment in the enforcement of antitrust laws, emphasizing the global reach of national regulations when domestic markets are affected by international cartels.[33]

Graphite electrodes are crucial components for steel production in electric arc furnaces, serving as large rods that generate high temperatures of approximately 3000 °C to melt scrap steel. During the collusive period from May 1992 to February 1998, the accused companies—UCAR International Corp. (UCAR), SGL Carbon Aktiengesellschaft (SGL), Showa Denko K.K. (Showa Denko), Tokai Carbon Corporation Ltd. (Tokai), Nippon Carbon Corporation Ltd. (Nippon), and SEC Corp. (SEC)—are all foreign entities that collectively held about 91% of the Korean import market for graphite electrodes. South Korea does not have domestic production of graphite electrodes; the remainder of the market demand is met by imports from non-major companies based in Russia, India, and other countries. This context underscores the significant market influence wielded by the accused companies within the Korean steel industry.

Article 19 (now Article 40) of the MRFTA prohibits "agreements intended to unfairly restrain competition in collaboration with other undertakings." It is widely recognized that antitrust laws in various countries categorize price-fixing agreements as virtually *per se* illegal. However, for prosecuting agreements among foreign companies established under foreign laws, especially those that have effects abroad, the proof of anti-competitive "effects" as well as "agreements" is generally required. This principle is known as the effect doctrine in the extraterritorial application of antitrust laws, a concept that was referenced in the KFTC's decision regarding the international graphite electrodes cartel. The KFTC invoked the effect doctrine to justify its jurisdiction over the case, emphasizing the significant impact of these foreign agreements on the Korean market. In the United Sates, the effect doctrine is articulated more explicitly. In 1995, the US DOJ and the FTC published the "Antitrust Enforcement Guidelines for International Operations." These guidelines specify that the Foreign Trade Antitrust Improvements Act (FTAIA) of 1982 applies

[33] Seoul High Court Judgment 2002nu61110, August 19, 2004.

to foreign commerce, excluding imports, only if the foreign firms' actions have a "direct, substantial, and reasonably foreseeable effect on US commerce."

It is noteworthy that the international cartel involving graphite electrode producers faced convictions in the United States, the EU, and Canada. In these jurisdictions, the extraterritorial application of antitrust laws did not pose a significant issue, as some members of the cartel were either domestic companies or foreign subsidiaries with established local bases. Conversely, in the case of Korea, all the accused companies exported graphite electrodes from their respective home countries without maintaining any local bases within Korea. The KFTC detailed in its decision that these foreign companies convened multiple times at locations abroad and agreed to raise and maintain prices in the Korean market during the identified collusive period.

According to KFTC's ruling, the implicated foreign companies held several meetings at different international venues and came to a mutual understanding to raise and maintain prices in the Korean market throughout the alleged period of collusion. The KFTC concluded that the agreement on price increases among the accused companies was effectively implemented in, and had significant effects on, the Korean market. Consequently, this agreement warranted evaluation for legality under the jurisdiction of the MRFTA. In substantiating the anti-competitive effects of the international graphite electrodes cartel on the Korean import market, the KFTC highlighted three key pieces of evidence: Firstly, the collective market share of the accused companies accounted for 91% of the Korean graphite electrodes market, which is composed exclusively of imports. Secondly, there was a 48.9% increase in the average price of sales by the accused companies in Korea during the period from 1992 to 1997. Thirdly, following their last meeting in 1998, there was a noticeable decrease in prices. These points of evidence presented by the KFTC establish the international graphite electrodes cartel as a *prima facie* case, wherein the anti-competitive effects on the Korean market appear to be self-evident.

Jeon (2004) conducted an economic analysis on behalf of Showa Denko to argue that special circumstances regarding the structure and performance of the market should be considered when evaluating the domestic effects of the international graphite electrodes cartel. Key points from this analysis include: Firstly, the market share among the accused firms was relatively evenly distributed: Showa Denko (24%), UCAR (18.5%), Nippon (15.7%), Tokai (15.6%), SGL (13%), and SEC (4.6%). This distribution contrasts with the market structures in the US, EU, and Canada, where one or two firms typically hold dominant market shares. Secondly, unlike the situations in the US, EU, and Canada, there is no dominant or domestic firm in Korea that could lead a price-fixing collusion, leveraging influence, and/or local information. Thirdly, the importers of graphite electrodes in Korea are large-scale steel producers such as POSCO and INI Steel. Additionally, the period identified as potentially collusive coincided with a surge in demand in the import market. These structural characteristics of the market suggest potential barriers to effective collusion. Given that participants in collusion stand to gain significantly from secret price cuts and may be tempted to undercut the market, the market structure analysis casts doubt on the efficacy of the international cartel's impact on the Korean import market for graphite electrodes. This perspective challenges the assumption of the cartel's effectiveness and underscores the need for a nuanced understanding of market dynamics when assessing the implications of alleged anti-competitive behaviors.

Jeon also conducted an evaluation of competitive performances in the Korean import market for graphite electrodes. The KFTC cited a 48.9% price increase during the presumed collusive period as evidence of anti-competitive performance. However, Jeon argued that price increases in oligopolistic markets can also stem from changes in demand and supply conditions. Notably, steel production in electric arc furnaces experienced a 116% surge during the same period, indicating that the demand for graphite electrodes, which is closely tied to steel production in electric arc furnaces, likely saw a comparable increase. The ratio of the price rise to the demand increase in Korea was 0.43, which is significantly lower compared to ratios in other countries where the cartel's activities were deemed illegal. For instance, during the relevant period in the EU, prices increased by 50% while demand only grew by 12%, resulting in a price rise to demand increase ratio of 4.17—nearly ten times higher than Korea's ratio. This disparity suggests that the predominant factor driving the price increase during this period in Korea was the exceptionally high demand for graphite electrodes, rather than anti-competitive practices. This analysis challenges the notion that the price increase was primarily due to collusive behavior and highlights the importance of considering market dynamics when assessing competition in oligopolistic markets.

Furthermore, Jeon conducted a multiple regression analysis using a dummy variable model, as outlined in Eq. (6.1). The KFTC pointed to the price decline following the last verified meeting of the accused firms in 1998 as the third piece of evidence indicating the anti-competitive effect of the alleged collusion. However, Jeon argued that the price decrease observed since the end of the presumed collusive period could be attributed to factors other than collusion, such as a demand boom. Significantly, the Korean import markets experienced a severe downturn during the foreign exchange crisis of 1998 and 1999. The price index of imported manufactured goods in dollar terms fell by more than 10%; the index dropped from 105.7 in 1997 to 95.7 in 1998, and further to 93.8 in 1999. This decline was primarily due to importers demanding lower dollar prices to partially offset the substantial cost increases caused by the devaluation of the won. To isolate the individual effects of various factors influencing price movements, Jeon's regression analysis included domestic import prices of graphite electrodes, steel production in electric arc furnaces, the price index of imported manufactured goods, and a collusion dummy. The analysis revealed that the collusion dummy was not statistically significant. This finding suggests that the price movements during and after the presumed collusive period were more likely influenced by broader economic factors, such as the foreign exchange crisis and changes in demand, rather than by any collusive behavior among the accused firms.

The courts recognized the evidences presented by the KFTC in assessing the impact of the cartel on the relevant Korean market. However, they reduced the amount of penalty surcharges levied on Showa Denko, reasoning that the initial amount was unfairly excessive in comparison to the penalties imposed on other companies involved.[34]

6.5.3 Flour *(2006) and* Credit Card/VAN *(2008)*

In 2006, KFTC levied penalty surcharges totaling 43 billion won against eight flour manufacturers for colluding on supply quantities and prices starting from the year 2000.[35] SPC Samlip, a bakery and food company, subsequently pursued damages against CJ and Samyang, two of the cartel participants, in civil court. This damage recovery suit revolved around two primary issues: One is to estimate the price overcharge resulting from the cartel. The plaintiff, SPC Samlip, calculated its damages as the multiplication of the price overcharge by its volume of purchases. The other is the potential for a passing-on defense, which is particularly relevant in cases involving intermediate goods cartels, such as this one, where "flour" serves as an intermediate good in the production of "bakery and food," the final product. The defendants contended that damages should be calculated by considering the cost pass-through, essentially arguing that damages should be the price overcharge minus any amount passed on, as depicted in Eq. (6.6). These issues highlight the complex dynamics of assessing damages in cases involving intermediate goods and the implications of pass-through costs on the calculation of such damages.

In response to the requests from both the plaintiff, SPC Samlip, and the defendants, CJ and Samyang, the district court appointed an appraiser to estimate the price overcharge and the extent of pass-through. Utilizing a dummy variable model as outlined in Eq. (6.1), the appraiser calculated the price overcharge and the resultant damages to SPC Samlip, for which CJ and Samyang were found liable, at 7.54 billion won and 2.98 billion won, respectively. Furthermore, through an additional multiple regression analysis, the appraiser determined the amounts that SPC Samlip passed on to final consumers as a result of the damages inflicted by CJ and Samyang to be 1.36 billion won and 0.31 billion won, respectively.[36]

The first court recognized the appraisal's legitimacy, stating that "the damages were estimated legitimately based on a scientific and reasonable method, supported by both theory and data," and accordingly determined the damages. However, regarding the passing-on defenses, the court did not accept them as a given. It expressed skepticism about the direct causality between the defendants' collusion-induced flour price increase and any revenue gains the plaintiff might have achieved through price adjustments in independent contracts. The court noted, "There may not be a considerable causality between the increase in flour price resulting from

[34]Seoul High Court 2002nu61110, August 19, 2004, and Supreme Court 2004du11275, March 24, 2006.

[35]KFTC 2006-079, March 24, 2006.

[36]Whang (2008). I served as an advisor during the appraisal process.

collusion by the defendants and the revenues of the plaintiff by increasing prices through independent contracts." Nevertheless, the court acknowledged that "in light of the idea of damages compensation as equitable distribution of damages, we can limit the compensation of damages on the plaintiff as a direct purchaser by taking the fact of damages passing-on and the extent into account." Essentially, the court factored in all of the appraiser's estimates regarding pass-through at the stage of determining "the limit of damages." Therefore, after taking into account the pass-on by the plaintiff and the incentive payments received from the defendants, the first court "limited" the damages for which the defendants were liable to 1.24 billion won for CJ and 0.23 billion won for Samyang.[37]

The decision of the first court was upheld by both the appellate and the supreme courts. The Supreme Court validated the appraisal conducted in the first court, which "using the regression analysis of econometric method, regressed a dependent variable of flour price with the explanatory variables such as post-collusion dummy, price of original vein 3 month prior, real GDP, etc., estimated the competitive flour price thereof, and determined the damages of the plaintiff accordingly." However, the Supreme Court also noted the complexity of establishing a direct causal link between the increase in product prices and the subsequent rise in goods prices, or the degree to which the product price increase is mirrored in the goods price increase. The court stated, "It is not clear whether there exists a direct causality between the price increase of products and the price increase of goods, or whether the extent of the price increase of products reflects in that of goods to that extent." Despite this uncertainty, the Supreme Court suggested that "the principle of equity may make it legitimate to consider the possibility that the price increase of products as such might reduce the damages in determining damages if it exists." Consequently, the Supreme Court endorsed the lower courts' decisions, emphasizing a balanced approach that acknowledges potential complexities in the causation and effect relationship while adhering to principles of fairness in the assessment of damages.[38]

Thus, the Korean courts have recognized the passing-on defense and considered cost pass-through in estimating damages for indirect purchasers, aligning with the EU tradition. This approach contrasts with the precedents set by the US *Hanover Shoe* and *Illinois Brick* decisions, as discussed in the previous section. The stance of Korean courts toward accommodating the passing-on defense and acknowledging cost pass-through in damage estimation is further evidenced in the case involving a successive cartel of credit card and VAN (Value-Added Network) companies.[39] This case presents notable differences from the earlier case of the flour cartel. Firstly, the damage recovery suit was initiated by a cartel of credit card companies acting as

[37] Seoul District Court 2006gahap99567, May 27, 2009.

[38] Supreme Court 2010da93790, November 29, 2012. In the citation above, the "products" are interpreted as final consumer products, such as breads, and the "goods" as intermediate goods, such as flour.

[39] KFTC 2008-080, March 4, 2008. Seoul District Court 2008gahap19596, 2984 combined, November 4, 2011. The first court decision was maintained in the later court decisions.

Table 6.8 Damages in *Flour* Case vs. *Credit Card/VAN* Case

	Flour cartel	Credit card/VAN cartels
Nature of cartel	Cartel of flour sellers → price increase (X) Bread com.'s passing-on (Y)	Cartel of credit card com.'s as VAN service buyers/cartel of VAN companies as resellers → service fee decrease (X′)/agency fee decrease (Y′)
Direct damages	Bread companies' damages (X − Y)	VAN companies' damages (X′ − Y′)
Indirect damages	Bread consumers' damages (Y)	VAN agencies' damages (Y′)

"buyers" of VAN services, whereas the previous case involved a cartel of flour manufacturers as "sellers" to bread makers. Secondly, the direct sellers of VAN services colluded to reduce service fees for their agents, effectively passing on the decrease in service fees to downstream agencies. The following table compares the two cases (Table 6.8).

Notice that the direct sellers, VAN companies, were the defendants in the latter damage suit as well, as they participated in a successive cartel, and that the indirect sellers, VAN agencies, became the plaintiffs. VAN companies had repaid the fees for VAN agencies completely in practice.[40] That is, the passing-on was complete, i.e., X' = Y'. The court-appointed appraiser estimated but-for VAN service fees according to a model in Eq. (6.1),[41] and the court determined the damages to VAN agencies accordingly.

A distinctive aspect of the court's decision in the *Credit Card/VAN* case, building upon the *Flour* case, is its explicit acknowledgment of the rights of indirect victims to recover damages in antitrust cases. The court emphasized the compensatory over the deterrent function of the damage compensation system, stating: "the system of damage compensation in our country emphasizes the function of compensation more than that of deterrence. ... Fair Trade Act §56 (1) (new §109 (1)) does not differentiate between direct and indirect victims by stipulating 'those who are harmed by an enterprise's or enterprise association's violating this act.'"

Given that the passing-on defense is recognized, ensuring damage recovery for indirect victims is crucial to hold cartel participants accountable for the damages caused and to fulfill the dual objectives of *ex ante* deterrence and *ex post* compensatory equity. In cases where the indirect victims are a few large, well-identified enterprises, they may collectively claim damages, as seen in the *Credit Card/VAN* case. However, when the victims are numerous consumers dispersed across a wide area, it becomes challenging for them to individually come forward and claim their damages without the mechanism of a class action lawsuit. EC (2008) recommended the adoption of class action lawsuits in the EU, similar to the system in place in the

[40] VAN companies received the fees for Data & Draft Capture services from credit companies, and they consigned Draft Capture services to agencies.

[41] Yi and Whang (2011).

United States, to facilitate the process for consumers seeking redress for antitrust violations. Similarly, the importance of class action lawsuits in the context of antitrust damage recovery should be earnestly considered in Korea as well. This approach would not only streamline the process for widespread, indirect victims to claim compensation but also enhance the deterrent effect against engaging in anti-competitive practices, thereby contributing to a more equitable and just market environment.

6.5.4 BMW/Lexus Dealer *(2008)*

The BMW-Lexus dealer cartels present a complex narrative of interactions between the KFTC and the courts, characterized by concurrent beginnings, diverging paths, and eventual convergence in outcomes. In 2008, the KFTC discovered that seven BMW dealers and nine Lexus dealers had reached agreements to restrict discounts, leading to the imposition of penalty surcharges amounting to 145 billion won for the former group and 74 billion won for the latter. Both groups appealed the KFTC's decision to the administrative courts, resulting in markedly different outcomes in 2010: the court upheld the KFTC's decision in the BMW case but reversed it in the Lexus case. Subsequent appeals by the BMW dealers (in the former case) and the KFTC (in the latter case) brought both matters before the Supreme Court, which in 2012 issued decisions to reverse and remand to the lower administrative courts. By 2014, the courts that received the cases on remand reached conclusions that, while somewhat unified, exhibited distinct nuances. Central to the discussions at every stage of these cases was the issue of relevant market definition—specifically, whether the market should be narrowly defined to a specific brand of car, broadly encompassed to include a range of luxury imported cars, or even further extended to all high-end vehicles, including those from domestic manufacturers like Hyundai and Kia. Throughout the various phases of the case, several economic analyses were submitted to argue the positions of both the KFTC and the defendants concerning the definition of the relevant market. The following discussion will dissect each decision in detail, highlighting the pivotal role of market definition in antitrust proceedings and the intricate legal and economic considerations that underpin such cases.

In 2008, the KFTC charged BMW and Lexus dealers with engaging in unfair collaboration by prohibiting price discounts and colluding on other trade terms during the periods of September 2004 to July 2007 and June 2006 to May 2007, respectively.[42] The relevant market in each case was defined as the domestic sales market of BMW and Lexus cars, respectively. The KFTC did not elaborate on the rationale behind this brand-specific market definition, other than noting that "in this collaborative conduct, the entities were domestic BMW (or Lexus) dealers and the

[42] KFTC 2008-323 and 324, December 15, 2008.

effects were limited only to the domestic sales prices of BMW (or Lexus)."[43] With the market share of the cartel participants nearing 100% in each respective case, the KFTC contended that the anti-competitive effects of their actions were beyond dispute. Furthermore, the commission argued that any potential benefits from promoting competition between different brands were speculative and unlikely to compensate for the detrimental impact on competition within the same brand.

The dealer groups challenged the KFTC decisions by filing appeals with the Seoul High Court, the administrative court responsible for antitrust appellate suits. The Lexus appellate court contested the KFTC's market definition, opting to expand the market boundaries to include not only Lexus cars but also the broader category of imported cars and domestic high-end cars that could serve as substitutes for Lexus vehicles. The court highlighted the high price elasticities relative to domestic small and medium cars, suggesting that a SSNIP would likely cause consumers to switch to other alternatives within the expanded market group. Consequently, the market share of the plaintiffs (Lexus dealers) within this broader market was determined to be less than 15%, insufficient to exert market control. Therefore, the KFTC's decision was reversed.[44] Conversely, the BMW appellate court upheld the KFTC's decision by endorsing the narrow market definition focused on domestic BMW sales. The court derived justification for this brand-specific market delineation from the characteristics inherent to the collusive conduct, including the objectives, intentions of the participating companies, the scope of collusive activities, the methods employed, and the direct and indirect effects of the collusion. In rejecting the plaintiffs' argument for a broad market definition encompassing all luxury brand cars, both imported and domestic, based on the SSNIP test—without directly addressing the test—the court argued that competition among BMW dealers (intra-brand competition) should be evaluated distinctly from the competition among various luxury brands (inter-brand competition).[45]

In response to the appellate court decisions, the KFTC appealed to the Supreme Court in the Lexus case, while the BMW dealers filed an appeal in the BMW case. In the Lexus case, the Supreme Court emphasized that the KFTC, bearing the burden of proof for defining the relevant market, needed to present more substantial evidence to justify limiting the relevant market to brand-specific cars. This required considering the substitutability between imported and domestic luxury cars more thoroughly. In the BMW case, the Supreme Court critiqued the market definition adopted by the appellate court, pointing out that the characteristics related to collusive behavior and its participants, which the appellate court had considered, were pertinent to assessing the anti-competitive effects within a predefined relevant market rather than defining the market itself. The Supreme Court highlighted a

---

[43]The KFTC believed that it might be possible to overlook the rigorous determination of the relevant market when substantiating unfair collaboration practices. However, this notion was refuted by subsequent court rulings.

[44]Seoul High Court 2009nu1930, May 9, 2010.

[45]Seoul High Court 2009nu9873, June 22, 2010.

circular reasoning flaw in the appellate court's rationale, essentially identifying the scope within which anti-competitive effects occur as the relevant market itself. Consequently, the Supreme Court reversed and remanded both cases to the lower courts for reconsideration. These Supreme Court directives underscored the necessity for a more rigorous and evidence-based approach to market definition in antitrust cases, clarifying the distinction between evaluating the scope of the market and assessing the behavior and effects within that market.[46]

The decisions made by the courts upon remand were fundamentally aligned: they upheld the finding of unfairness in the collusive behaviors, supporting the KFTC's decisions, while also mandating a reduction in penalty surcharges by excluding certain taxes (special consumption tax and education tax) from the relevant sales calculations. However, there was a nuanced difference in defining the relevant markets: the BMW case was confined to a single-brand market, whereas the Lexus case encompassed a broader market of imported luxury cars, including brands such as BMW, Mercedes-Benz, Audi, Lexus, and Volvo. In defining these relevant markets, the courts considered the KFTC's critical loss analyses and accepted its conclusions despite acknowledging some limitations in sample selection.[47] The courts deemed these shortcomings insufficient to undermine the credibility of the KFTC's findings. The variance in market definitions between the two cases did not impact the ultimate assessment of unfairness, as the combined market share of the cartel participants—25.6% in the imported luxury car market—was deemed adequate to adversely affect consumer welfare through a price cartel. Both courts concurred that the negative impact of restraining intra-brand competition surpassed any potential benefits from fostering inter-brand competition in these instances.[48] The culmination of these cases was marked by the Supreme Court's confirmation of the decisions and the KFTC's imposition of recalculated penalty surcharges.

During the reverse-remand litigation phase, economic experts presented several analyses concerning market definition. Kim and Kim (2013), representing the KFTC, conducted a critical loss analysis based on a consumer survey, which supported the KFTC's stance on a narrow market definition. Conversely, Whang (2013), on behalf of BMW dealers, utilized a random coefficient logit model, famously known as the BLP model (Berry et al. 1995), with actual purchase data to estimate the demand for individual brand cars. Whang's findings suggested that the relevant market should be broadly defined to include all luxury cars, both imported and domestic, according to the SSNIP test. Yi and Oh (2014), advocating for Lexus, critiqued the KFTC's critical loss analysis, particularly highlighting the inherent issues with using consumer surveys to estimate actual losses resulting from

[46] Supreme Court 2010du11757, April 26, 2012, and Supreme Court 2010du18703, April 26, 2012.

[47] Interestingly, the Lexus court remarked that "there does not exist any empirical evidence which shows that endowment effect (the phenomenon which leads people to overestimate their possessions) might underestimate actual losses" in critical loss analysis.

[48] Seoul High Court 2012nu15385, April 28, 2014, and Seoul High Court 2012nu11241, May 7, 2015.

SSNIP, as well as significant sampling errors in the KFTC's analysis. These diverse analyses underscore the complexities involved in defining relevant markets in antitrust cases, with varying methodologies leading to different interpretations of market boundaries and the impact of competitive behaviors.[49]

6.5.5 Ramen *(2012)*

In 2012, the KFTC charged four ramen companies with unfair collaboration in setting prices from 2001 to 2010, resulting in total penalty surcharges of 136 billion won.[50] Nongshim held a dominant position in the Korean ramen industry, commanding approximately 70% of the market share, while the other three companies—Samyang Foods, Ottogi, and Hy—shared the remainder. According to the KFTC's findings, these companies entered into a basic agreement on price coordination and maintenance around December 2000 or January 2001. As part of this agreement, Nongshim was responsible for initiating price increases, disseminating relevant information to the other companies, who then proceeded to adjust their prices accordingly. This coordinated approach led to a total of six price increases by 2010. The continuous exchange of management information among these companies was identified as a crucial factor in facilitating their collusive behavior. Additionally, the practice of "old price support"—whereby companies continued to supply products at the previous price for a certain period following a price hike—was alleged to support collusion. This practice provided a mechanism to manage and control any deviations from the agreed-upon pricing strategy, further entrenching the collusive arrangement.

Three defendants appealed to the Seoul High Court, challenging the KFTC's decision.[51] However, the appellate court upheld the KFTC's ruling, agreeing with the majority of its factual findings and arguments.[52] Notably, while the appellate court considered the collusion as a singular entity, it distinguished the nature of the collusion into two distinct parts: the first price increase in 2001, which was based on the basic agreement and categorized as explicit collusion, and the subsequent second

[49]For more information about the BMW-Lexus cases and the economic analyses, Refer to Kwon et al. (2015).

[50]KFTC 2012-107, July 12, 2012. The KFTC applied penalty surcharges at a relatively low basic rate, 2% of the total relevant sales, which is significantly lower than the maximum limit of 10%. Several factors were taken into consideration when determining this rate, including the cost increments that occurred during the period of collusion, the primary method of collusion through the exchange of information, and the requirement of prior consultation with the government before any price increase.

[51]One company was exempted from penalties due to a leniency report. The remaining three companies each filed separate appeals. In this discussion, I will focus on the court decision pertaining to Nongshim's case, as the outcomes in the other cases were similar.

[52]Seoul High 2012nu24223, November 8, 2013.

to sixth price increases, which were primarily facilitated through information exchanges and classified as implicit collusion.

The decision, however, was reversed by the Supreme Court.[53] Firstly, the explicit collusion related to the first price increase in 2001 was discredited due to the absence of direct evidence, with the only support coming from inconsistent hearsay statements made by a late director of one of the defendant companies. Secondly, regarding the implicit collusion associated with the subsequent five price increases, the Supreme Court found that mere exchanges of information did not adequately demonstrate "the interconnection of minds among enterprises," a necessary condition for establishing an agreement. The Supreme Court highlighted several market characteristics and practices that could raise suspicions of implicit collusion in this case, as follows.

Firstly, the market had an established practice wherein a leading company would initiate a price increase, followed by its competitors, even before 2001. This suggests that a separate agreement on this sequential price increase mechanism may not have been necessary. Additionally, given the government's role in negotiating with Nongshim, which holds a 70% market share, regarding the pricing of ramen—an essential food item—it could naturally occur that competing companies would adjust their prices in response to Nongshim's changes due to cost pressures, even in the absence of a formal agreement. Thirdly, Samyang Foods, having previously ceded the number one position to Nongshim, would likely resist entering into a prolonged period of collusion that could potentially solidify the market share distribution as it stood at that time. Fourthly, the ramen market features a wide array of products, making it challenging to reach a consensus on leading or following the price adjustments for each specific product. Fifthly, while the practice of old price support could theoretically serve as a tool to facilitate collusion by penalizing those who deviate from agreed prices, it could also be employed as a strategy for aggressive competition, potentially undermining the stability of any collusive arrangement. These factors collectively suggest a complex market dynamic where explicit or implicit collusion is not the only plausible explanation for observed price movements and behaviors.

As a consequence of this judgment, the defendants were entitled to reimbursement for the penalty surcharges they had paid to the KFTC, along with interest at the legally prescribed rate. The KFTC's failure to prove the existence of collusion through evidence of information exchanges in the Supreme Court prompted an effort to address this loophole.[54] A new subparagraph was added to Paragraph 1 of Article 40 (which lists unfair collaborative conducts) in the comprehensive revision of the

[53] Supreme Court 2013du25924, December 24, 2015.

[54] There have been several instances prior to this, such as the soju collusion case (Supreme Court 2011du16049, February 13, 2014, and the life insurance collusion case (Supreme Court 2013du25924, July 24, 2014), where the Supreme Court did not acknowledge price collusion based on information exchange, and consequently overturned the decision made by the KFTC. Furthermore, in a recent ruling, in the case of compound feed collusion (Supreme Court Judgment 2017du56346, June 22, 2022), the Supreme Court reached a similar verdict.

MRFTA on December 29, 2020: "9. ... the conduct in actual restraint of competition by exchanging information as stipulated by Presidential Decree (such as cost, shipment, inventory, sales, trade terms, or payment condition)." This addition aims to specifically address collusion through information exchange, setting a guideline for how such cases might be approached and adjudicated in the future. It remains to be seen how this explicit stipulation regarding information-exchange collusion will influence court decisions moving forward. The Supreme Court's decision also had international repercussions. Retailers and consumers in the United States and Canada initiated class action lawsuits seeking damage recovery. However, these efforts ultimately lost momentum in light of the no-guilt judgment issued by the court in Korea, illustrating the wide-reaching impact of national court decisions on related legal actions in other jurisdictions.

6.5.6 Industrial Explosives *(2015)*

In 2015, the KFTC imposed penalty surcharges totaling 65.5 billion won on two industrial explosives manufacturers/sellers, identified here as A and B. These entities were also referred to the prosecutor for colluding on prices and quantities and for hindering new market entry by a third party, C.[55] The period of collusion in this case sparked debate during the KFTC investigation and committee discussions, ultimately being designated as two distinct phases: the first from March 1999 to September 2002, and the second from March 2005 to May 2012. The KFTC's decision was upheld through to the final court ruling.[56] A noteworthy aspect of this case is the serious consideration given to the economic analysis by Jeon et al. (2014) concerning evidence of the cartel's breakdown in the KFTC's decision-making process. This emphasis on economic analysis highlights the increasing reliance on detailed, data-driven investigations to substantiate claims of anti-competitive behavior and to inform regulatory and judicial outcomes.[57]

The industrial explosives market has traditionally been a duopoly, with the dominant company A holding a market share of more than 70%. An attempt at new market entry occurred in January 2004 but ultimately failed by December 2006. The defendants were accused of obstructing the new entrant, C, and were alleged to have played a significant role in its failure. Notably, the period of this attempted entry (January 2004 to December 2006) coincided with both the disrupted period of competition (October 2002 to February 2005) and the second collusion period (March 2005 to May 2012). The expert witness report highlighted the transactions of ANFO (a commonly used explosive) between the two companies as a mechanism for enforcing the cartel agreement, wherein company A purchased ANFO from

[55] KFTC 2015-100, April 8, 2015.

[56] Supreme Court 2017du30788, July 20, 2018.

[57] Jeon et al. (2014) presented an economic expert report on behalf of one defendant to the KFTC.

company B to adhere to the predetermined market shares *ex post*. It was observed that ANFO transactions ceased during the cartel breakdown period, whereas significant transactions were recorded during the two periods of collusion. Furthermore, economic experts conducted three complementary econometric analyses demonstrating the presence of significant price-discounting competition during the cartel breakdown period, in stark contrast to the collusive behavior observed in the other periods.

The first regression model employed is a conventional time-series model, which incorporates a dummy variable as a variant of Eq. (6.1):

$$\log(P_t) = \alpha + \sum_{j=1}^{m} \beta_j \log(P_{t-j}) + \gamma' X_t + \delta \mathrm{DCOM}_t + \lambda \mathrm{DENT}_t + u_t \tag{6.9}$$

where t (July 2001~May 2012) covers all three phases: the first collusion (July 2001~October 2002), the cartel breakdown (November 2002~February 2005), and the second collusion (March 2005~May 2012.5). In this mode, P_t represents A's discounted price, X_t includes explanatory variables related to costs and demands of industrial exploitive, DCOM_t is a dummy (Dummy of COMpetition period, November 2002~February 2005) indicating the competition phase due to cartel breakdown, and DENT_t is a dummy variable (Dummy of ENTry period, January 2004~December 2006) representing the new entry period. The analysis revealed that δ was negative (-0.06) and statistically significant, suggesting that prices were reduced during the cartel breakdown period.[58] Conversely, the coefficient λ, linked to the entry dummy, was also negative (-0.01) but not statistically significant. These findings are consistent with the hypothesis that prices decreased during the period of cartel disruption, providing quantitative support for the argument that competitive forces were at play during the breakdown of collusive arrangements.

The second regression model represents a panel data extension of Eq. (6.9), incorporating a twist by utilizing the Difference-in-Differences (DID) methodology to analyze the impact of company C's new entry.

$$\begin{aligned} \ln(P_{it}) = \alpha_i + \sum_{j=1}^{m} \beta_j \log(P_{i,t-j}) + \gamma' X_t + \delta \mathrm{DCOM}_t + \lambda_1 \mathrm{DENTP}_t \\ + \lambda_2 \mathrm{DENTR}_i + \lambda_3 \mathrm{DENTP}_t \cdot \mathrm{DENTP}_i + u_{it} \end{aligned} \tag{6.10}$$

where i represents a dealer of company A and t denotes time as before. The geographic market is delineated by a circle with a radius of 50 km from a dealer's

[58] During the period when the cartel disintegrated, the price witnessed a decline of 6% when compared to the two previous periods under the cartel.

location.[59] New explanatory variables introduced in Eq. (6.10) beyond those included in Eq. (6.9) comprise: α_i, which captures dealer-specific effect not explained by other variables, $DENTR_i$ is a Dummy variable for C's ENTry Region (assigned a value of 0 for A's dealer located within 50 km from C's dealer). Notice that λ_3 is interpreted as the genuine effect of C's entry as per the DID model framework as explained in Sect. 6.3.3 in this chapter. The regression results indicate that both δ (−0.06) and λ_3 (−0.02) were negative and statistically significant. This suggests that the market experienced a competitive effect during the breakdown period and an entrance effect during the entry period, aligning with expectation.[60]

The third regression model employs a reduced-form estimation approach, similar to the one introduced in the 1997 *Staples-Office Depot* case, to analyze the competition dynamics among companies A, B, and C.

$$\log(P_{it}) = \alpha_i + \sum_m \beta_{1m} D_{mit} + \sum_m \beta_{2m} \log(\text{Store}_{mit}) + \gamma_t + u_{it} \tag{6.11}$$

where

m represents a competitor of A's dealer i, which may be a dealer of B, C, or both of A and B,

D_{mit} is an absence dummy which is 1 if competitor m was not present within the radius of 50 km from A's dealer i,

Store_{mit} is the number of competitors if competitor m was present there, γ_t is time dummy.

The model is structured analogously to Eq. (5.1) presented in Chap. 5, Sect. 5.2.2, and aims to ascertain whether companies A and B engaged in competition during the cartel the breakdown period. The primary outcomes of the estimation, conducted for the three distinct periods separately, revealed that that the coefficient β_{1B} was negative (−0.01) and not statistically significant during the first collusion period, turned positive (0.05) and statistically significant in the period of cartel breakdown, and remained positive (0.04) and statistically significant during the second collusion period.[61] These findings suggest that the competitive interaction between A and B was more pronounced during the cartel breakdown period. The change in the

---

[59] The following safety regulation pertains to the proper handling of explosives, specifically emphasizing the practice of "one-day delivery and return." This regulation mandates that a dealer must ensure the delivery of industrial explosives to the designated usage location in precisely the required quantity for that day. Furthermore, the dealer is responsible for promptly returning any unused explosives to their designated storage area once they have been utilized.

[60] The price experienced a decline of 6% due to the breakdown of the cartel and an additional 2% due to the entry of new competitors into the market.

[61] The nonexistence of B's dealer significantly raises the price of A's dealer by 5% during the competition period and by 4% during the second collusion period, but it has no significant impact during the first collusion period. I will not delve into the estimation of other coefficients as they are not materially relevant to the primary concern.

significance and direction of β_{1B} across the different periods indicates variations in the competitive dynamics, with the breakdown period exhibiting a noticeable increase in competitive behavior between the two companies.

The empirical findings regarding the price effects of the cartel breakdown were pivotal in this case, particularly because direct evidence of the cartel's dissolution, such as a formal termination of agreements, was absent. Consequently, circumstantial evidence, including ANFO transactions, alongside the economic insights drawn from regression results, proved instrumental in deducing the actual cessation of collusive activities and the revival of competitive dynamics. This is the reason why economic analyses were thoroughly deliberated during the KFTC's plenary session and factored significantly into its decision regarding the cartel breakdown. Moreover, the question of whether the cartel was intermittently disrupted and segmented into two distinct periods carries substantial practical implications for the defendants. This distinction directly influenced the calculation of penalty surcharges, impacting not only the period during which the cartel was deemed inactive but also the period of the initial collusion. When a cartel is recognized as having been discontinued, as in this instance, the two phases are treated as separate entities rather than as a continuous operation. Consequently, in the case of the first cartel, the statute of limitations had expired, resulting in the waiver of substantial penalty surcharges for that period.[62] Therefore, the defendants had a significant financial interest in establishing the occurrence of a cartel breakdown, beyond the intrinsic concerns of cartel participation.

6.5.7 Compound Feed *(2015)*

In 2015, the KFTC determined that eleven compound feed manufacturers, including Cargill Agripurina, engaged in collusion and imposed penalties totaling 77.3 billion won.[63] A key piece of evidence in this case was the "apparent conformity," also referred to as "parallel behavior," observed as the participating firms adjusted their prices in a similar manner, both in extent and timing. The appellate courts examined whether this apparent conformity could be considered substantial evidence of collusion, as asserted by the KFTC. Expert witnesses representing the defendants contested the interpretation of this apparent conformity, arguing that the similarity in price changes, at first glance, stemmed from an artificially constructed analysis. Furthermore, they suggested that the timing of these price adjustments could be attributed to factors unrelated to collusion, such as significant fluctuations in the costs of common materials during the periods in question. Ultimately, both the

---

[62] During the time of the case, the statute of limitations stipulated a period of "5 years after the termination of violation." However, it was later modified to encompass either "5 years after the termination of violation" or "7 years after investigation."

[63] KFTC 2015-319, September 14, 2015.

appeal Seoul High Court and the final Supreme Court concluded that the KFTC had not sufficiently proven a "circumstantial evidence of meeting of minds" to support the allegation of collusion. Moreover, they found that the existence of "apparent conformity" as a result of collusion was not convincingly demonstrated.

An expert witness representing the KFTC argued that there was a notable difference in the magnitude of price changes by cartel participants during the alleged collusive period (October 2006 to January 2011) compared to the non-collusive period (February 2011 to March 2014). Specifically, both the deviation and the maximum-minimum difference in prices were smaller during the collusive period than in the subsequent non-collusive period, suggesting that such uniformity should be considered significant evidence of collusive behavior.[64] The expert measured the width of price changes using a unit period defined as one month, from the 16th of the previous month to the 15th of the next month. Conversely, the expert witness for the plaintiffs (compound feed companies) challenged the arbitrariness of this unit period definition, indicating that the deviation and the maximum-minimum difference between the two periods could vary substantially if the unit period were defined differently. They proposed a more rational alternative, "unit period," based on the "cluster cycle," a period within which most companies adjusted their prices. Under this alternative definition, they discovered that the extent of price changes—namely, the deviation and the maximum-minimum difference—between the collusive and non-collusive periods did not exhibit a statistically significant difference.[65]

The appellate courts found the cluster approach to defining the unit period reasonable and concluded that "the magnitude of price changes between the collusive and non-collusive periods does not exhibit statistical significance when the timeframe in which most compound feed companies adjusted their prices is identified as a distinct period (cluster)."[66] This judgment underscores the importance of contextually appropriate methodologies in analyzing price movements. Furthermore, one appellate court highlighted the necessity for a comparative analysis of price changes beyond the 11 companies, including the plaintiff, stating, "without a comparative analysis of price changes by entities other than the 11 companies, including the plaintiff, it is challenging to substantiate the existence of a concurrence of intent among them based solely on the KFTC's economic analysis, especially given the inevitable similarity in price changes within the compound feed market."[67] Another appellate court remarked on the correlation coefficients, noting, "if the difference in the correlation coefficient during the alleged collusive period and that in the subsequent period for Daeju (a company not involved in the collusion) is

[64]Lee (2016) submitted the report to the appellate court.

[65]Kim and Kim (2017) submitted the report to the appellate court.

[66]Seoul High Court 2015nu60758, March 9, 2017, Seoul High Court 2015nu61827, May 18, 2017, and Seoul High Court 2015nu62134, June 7, 2017. Three appellate courts made the decisions on this case following several compound feed manufacturers appealing the Seoul High Court against the KFTC's decision.

[67]Seoul High Court 2015nu61827, May 18, 2017.

similar to the difference observed for the 11 companies, including the plaintiff, the high correlation observed for the plaintiff and its associates during the alleged collusive period could be attributable to factors other than collusion."[68] These observations are insightful as they effectively incorporate the Difference-in-Differences (DID) methodology within the analysis of parallel behavior, demonstrating a sophisticated understanding of the complexities involved in distinguishing collusion from other market-driven price adjustments.[69]

Following the appellate courts' dismissal of the KFTC's argument regarding the uniformity in the extent of price changes during the collusive period, the KFTC's expert shifted the analysis toward the synchronization of price changes, focusing on the timing rather than the magnitude of these changes.[70] By defining the timeframe in which price adjustments were notably clustered as the "price change cycle," she presented evidence that a considerable number of firms altered their prices in sync during the collusive period. In contrast, during the non-collusive period, fewer firms engaged in the price change cycle, and the timing of price adjustments was more scattered. While the observed relative uniformity in the timing of price changes during the collusive period was established, such an observation only compellingly suggests an underlying agreement if this apparent conformity cannot be attributed to factors other than collusion.

Jeon and Chung (2017) proposed a significant factor unrelated to collusion that could account for the observed uniformity in the timing of price changes during the collusive period: the fluctuation in import prices of raw materials used in producing compound feed. It is important to note that raw materials, such as limestone and byproducts from grain and slaughter, constitute approximately 80–90% of the composition, with the majority being imported. Consequently, compound feed companies are exposed to similar cost changes. Rapid changes in these common costs can naturally prompt competitors to quickly align with the price adjustments of a leading firm. Conversely, when common costs stabilize, a price change by one firm might be indicative of its unique situation or strategic decision, prompting other firms to consider their own market share and margin policies before responding. The table below illustrates the relationship between the variation in common costs and the lag in price adjustments during both the alleged collusive and non-collusive periods, highlighting how external economic factors can influence pricing behavior independently of collusive agreements (Table 6.9).

This implies that firms synchronized their price changes to reflect the rapid shifts in costs during the period in question, whereas they allowed more time for price adjustments in response to slower cost changes in the subsequent period. As an ancillary observation, this contrast underscores the rationale for using the "cluster"—rather than an arbitrary month—as the unit of time when measuring the

---

[68] Seoul High Court 2015nu62134, June 7, 2017.

[69] Section 6.3 in this chapter explained the idea of DID in the context of price overcharge.

[70] Lee (2017) submitted the report to the appellate courts while the hearings were still ongoing and had not concluded.

Table 6.9 Relationship between the rate of change in raw material cost and the lag of price adjustment

	Collusive period (average)	Non-collusive period (average)
Rate of cost change (monthly %, absolute value)	4.96	2.16
Lag of price adjustment (days)	5.4	21.4

magnitude of price changes, as discussed previously. This approach more accurately captures the market dynamics and the firms' responsive behaviors to external cost influences.[71]

This case concluded with the Supreme Court upholding the appellate courts' not-guilty verdicts.[72] My discussion focused exclusively on the issue of "apparent conformity" or "parallel behavior" as evidence of an agreement in this case. However, in overturning the KFTC's guilty verdicts, the courts took into account a multitude of other factors, including the nature of the agreement and information exchange, incentives to collude, and structural characteristics of the compound feed market. These aspects were not covered in my analysis to maintain a focus on an issue of particular interest from an economist's perspective.

6.5.8 LNG Tank *(2016)*

Thirteen construction companies were found to have manipulated the bidding process for LNG tank construction projects ordered by Korea Gas Corporation across 12 projects from 2005 to 2013. They colluded to predetermine the successful bidders, the bridesmaids (firms that submit bids but do not expect to win), and the bid rates or prices. In 2016, the KFTC levied a total penalty surcharge of approximately 320 billion won against these companies for their involvement in unfair bidding collusion.[73] In pursuit of damage recovery, Korea Gas Corporation approached the civil court, which recommended me for appraising the damages resulting from the cartel through econometric regression to calculate the counter-factual (but-for) competitive price. Conversely, the defendants suggested the appointment of construction engineers to estimate the competitive price by deducing construction costs using engineering techniques and incorporating competitive margins. The court,

[71] The court decisions did not address the arguments put forth by Lee (2017), representing the KFTC, and Jeon and Chung (2017), representing a plaintiff company. This omission occurred because the case was subsequently closed due to the withdrawal of both parties involved.

[72] Supreme Court 2017du47144, May 26, 2022, Supreme Court 2017du47229, May 26, 2022, and Supreme Court 2017du56346, June 22, 2022.

[73] KFTC 2016-161, June 20, 2016.

recognizing the value of both approaches, approved both sets of appraisers and instructed them to impartially estimate the damages incurred by the plaintiff.

The model presented below is the dummy variable estimation model in Eq. (6.1), which I and a co-appraiser proposed to the court for the purpose of the appraisal:[74]

$$p_t = \alpha + \beta X_t + \delta D_t + u_t \tag{6.12}$$

where

p_t = winning bid price over reserved price
X_t = explanatory variables that affect the winning bid ratio
D_t = collusion dummy
u_t = disturbance term in t.

The reserve price for each bid was determined randomly within a range of 95% to 100% of the expected price, which the procuring company calculated based on the anticipated construction costs.[75] A significant challenge encountered during the estimation process in this case was the limited availability of data. Specifically, there were twelve instances of collusive bidding and five instances of non-collusive bidding in LNG tank construction that could be directly compared before and after the collusive period. To address this data scarcity, the appraiser expanded the dataset by including other construction projects that were similar in scale and bidding method to the LNG tank constructions. This supplementary data comprised bids for main conduits (19 biddings) and vaporization facilities (5 biddings) related to LNG gas, as well as electricity power generating facilities (26 biddings) that the plaintiff had previously listed as relevant construction experiences in the pre-qualification (PQ) test for LNG tank construction.[76] Therefore, a total of 67 comparable bidding instances were utilized in the estimation process for Eq. (6.12), ensuring a more comprehensive analysis despite the initial constraints posed by the scarcity of direct bidding data.

The procurement auction format chosen by the plaintiff was initially a sealed bid, lowest price bidding system. However, this system underwent several changes with the incorporation of tests to assess the appropriateness of bid prices. The sample encompassed four auction mechanisms for winner selection: lowest price without an

---

[74] Jeon and Han (2019, 2021) provided two reports—an initial report and a subsequent supplementary one. The latter included various alternative models and their estimated results, which were put forward by both the plaintiff and the defendants for the court's review. The model and its results discussed here are the fundamental ones that were ultimately accepted by the court.

[75] The pricing structure for these projects consists of two components: a predetermined part established at the time of bidding and contracting, and an approximated part that is finalized during the contract period. The predetermined portion is used specifically for the bidding process, while the approximated part is later defined by proportionally applying the winning bid rate.

[76] There was a dispute between the plaintiff and the defendants regarding the inclusion of certain construction projects in the comparison set, aside from the LNG tanks. The plaintiff contended that electricity power-generating facilities might not be suitable for comparison in the bidding process. On the other hand, the defendants challenged the appropriateness of including main conduicts and vaporization facilities as comparable bids.

appropriateness test, lowest price with a simple appropriateness test, and lowest price with appropriateness tests I and II. These appropriateness tests aimed to enhance the lowest price auction mechanism by preventing abnormally low bids that could compromise quality, through evaluating the suitability of prices for various construction processes.[77] The explanatory variables X_t in the model included the logarithm of the reserved price, the natural logarithm of the portion of the determined part in the reserved price, dummies for the simple test, test I, and test II, the percentage increase in the Producer Price Index (PPI), indicators for the financial crisis, the logarithm of the construction business cycle index, the number of bidding participants, an indicator for being among the top 15 in industrial equipment construction capability, and dummies for construction locations. The estimated coefficients for most explanatory variables exhibited reasonable signs. For instance, the number of bidding participants was found to have a negative effect on the winning bid ratio, indicating that increased competition among bidders leads to lower winning bids. Significantly, the key estimate for the collusion dummy coefficient was 0.0581 and was statistically significant, suggesting that collusion led to a 5.81% increase in the winning bid ratio.

The district court expressed a preference for the econometric analysis method for estimating damages in this case over the cost-based approach utilizing engineering techniques. The court highlighted that econometric analysis "can relatively accurately isolate the effect of collusion by controlling for factors other than collusion that influence bidding prices through regression analysis." Furthermore, the court provided detailed justification for the choices of sample, model, and explanatory variables outlined in the appraisal report by Jeon and Han (2021). However, due to the expiration of the statute of limitations for several cases of collusion and the limitation of liability as determined by the court's reasonable discretion, the final damages were assessed at a total of 58.23 billion won.[78] The outcomes of subsequent judgments by the appellate and supreme courts remain to be seen.

6.5.9 Iron Scrap Purchase *(2021)*

Iron scrap, serving as the primary raw material and constituting approximately 70% of the costs for steel products like reinforcing bars and H beams produced in electric furnaces, is not produced but rather collected from post-use scrap. In 2021, the KFTC reported that eleven steel companies had engaged in collusion over an 18-year period, from June 2010 to April 2018. These companies coordinated to set, maintain, and adjust the reference price range and timing for iron scrap purchases and exchanged internally confidential information relevant to the pricing of iron scrap. The KFTC concluded that these actions breached §40 of the Act, which pertains to

[77] The specifics of the test methods are complex and are not elaborated upon in this context.

[78] Daegu District Court 2017gahap201266, December 8, 2022.

unfair collaboration. Consequently, the commission issued a cease-and-desist order against such practices and levied total penalty surcharges of 300 billion won on the involved companies.[79] Despite the extensive duration of the collusion and the significant volume of purchases affected, the penalty surcharges imposed were notably smaller than those anticipated based on the KFTC's preliminary examination report.

Jeon and Whang (2020) submitted an expert report conducting an economic analysis on behalf of the defendants in the iron scrap purchase collusion case. The report tackled three key issues: the structural and behavioral factors influencing collusion in the iron scrap purchase market, the definition of the relevant geographic market, and the econometric estimation of the cartel's impact on purchase prices. This summary focuses on the issue of defining the relevant geographic market. The KFTC examiner initially defined the geographic market as nationwide, while also recognizing evidence of agreement and collusion implementation by distinguishing between the Young-Nam and Kyung-In regions. To evaluate whether these two regions should be considered as a single market or separate markets, we applied the SSNIP test, utilizing critical loss and diversion ratio analyses. It is important to note that the benchmark price in the SSNIP test refers not to the "retail price" of iron scrap but to the "retail margin," reflecting the value added by retail services rather than the final product price. The findings from the SSNIP test indicated that the two regions should be treated as separate markets, largely due to significant transportation costs. Additionally, a supplementary Elzinga-Hogarty (E-H) test was employed. The LIFO (Little In From Outside) index estimates, which measure the proportion of trade inflow from outside the region relative to total consumption within each region, were approximately 75%. Considering the "Silent Majority Fallacy," as suggested by Capps et al. (2001), which posits that a LIFO-LOFI ratio of around 60% might suffice for a hypothetical monopolist to profitably impose a SSNIP, and acknowledging the inherent market expansion bias in the E-H test, this evidence supports the conclusion that the relevant geographic market should be delineated for each region separately.[80]

The KFTC upheld the "nationwide" market definition in its decision, but opted to exclude the Kyung-In region when calculating the relevant purchase amount, citing the relatively weak effect of the cartel in that area. Additionally, the KFTC imposed a notably low penalty surcharge of 2%,[81] reflecting its assessment that the collusion was "relatively loose, allowing for individual actions by participants according to

[79]KFTC 2021-016, January 18, 2021.

[80]Refer to Chap. 4, Sect. 4.3 for the LIFO index and the silent majority paradox. Notice that the paradox is originally described in the context of hospital mergers, where it is attributed to a form of 'psychic' transportation costs, which stem from patients' preference for hospitals in specific regions. In contrast, in the context of the iron scrap market, the paradox is related to the 'physical' transportation costs of moving iron scrap.

[81]At the time of the decision, the maximum rate for penalty surcharges was set at 10% of the relevant sales. However, this ceiling was increased to 20% following a comprehensive revision of the Act in 2022.

their circumstances within a broader framework aimed at stabilizing the iron scrap market." As of January 2024, the case is under review by the Seoul High Court, serving as the administrative court of appeal for the defendants.

6.5.10 Public Procurement of Reinforcing Bar *(2022)*

In 2022, the KFTC determined that eleven steel companies had colluded by allocating winning bids among themselves and agreeing on their bidding prices for the annual price contract bidding of reinforcing bars conducted by the Public Procurement Service (PPS)[82] during the period from 2012 to 2018. As a result, the KFTC imposed total penalty surcharges amounting to 256.5 billion won and issued a cease-and-desist order against these practices. Furthermore, the KFTC brought charges against seven companies and nine of their former and current employees, referring them for prosecution.[83]

The procurement method utilized in this case is known as "desired-quantity competitive bidding (DQCB)," a mechanism where each seller submits a bid comprising both a supply quantity and a unit price. The buyer then selects the winning suppliers based on the lowest bid prices, continuing until the cumulative supply quantity matches the specified demand amount. The last winning bidder may only supply the remaining required quantity. In Korea, this auction mechanism is commonly applied in the public procurement of raw materials such as reinforcing bars, ready-mixed concrete, and asphalt concrete, especially in situations where a single company is unable to meet the large quantity demanded by the buyer.[84] It is important to note that the auctioned item in desired-quantity competitive bidding is categorized as "single product-multiple units," contrasting with the "single product-single unit" model, which has been the focus of extensive theoretical research.[85]

In typical DQCB processes used in public procurement, the winning bidder is compensated based on the bid price they submitted, a payment approach called as the "your own price" method. Alternatively, in some instances, all winning bidders are paid at the market-clearing price, which is the price at which the total supply offered by all winners matches the demand, referred to as the "market-clearing price" method. However, in the auction case under discussion, the buyer mandated all participants to agree to a contract stipulating that all winners receive the lowest

[82]The PPS is a governmental administrative agency responsible for the procurement, contracting, and management of goods and assets on behalf of the government and the nation.

[83]KFTC 2022-265, November 8, 2022.

[84]Another significant application of DQCB is the auctioning of national and public bonds, a practice employed by central banks in numerous countries.

[85]Refer to Klemperer (2004), Krishna (2010), and Ausubel et al. (2014) for the auction theory in general.

winning bid price, a method I will refer to as the "lowest price" payment method. Uniquely, this "lowest price" requirement was not specified in the auction's official terms but was imposed by the PPS, compelling all private participating companies to acquiesce. This practice is unusual, as it has been seldom employed in auctions beyond those for public procurement of raw materials in Korea. Moreover, the PPS's insistence that bidders accept this payment method, which was not part of the pre-announced auction rules, leveraging governmental authority, marks a significant departure from standard auction procedures.

In the ensuing discussion, I will first examine how the revenue of each winning supplier and the total expenditure of the buyer vary under different payment methods: (i) market-clearing price, (ii) your own price, and (iii) the lowest price, assuming that all participants adhere to uniform bidding strategies irrespective of the chosen payment method. It's important to acknowledge that this assumption is unrealistic, as the incentives and strategies of bidders are likely to be influenced by the specific rules governing the auction. Given this, I will subsequently explore how bidding strategies might adapt in response to the different payment methods. My aim is to identify the equilibrium outcome for each payment method, grounded in assumptions that are plausible within the context of this case, specifically the industrial dynamics of public procurement for reinforcing bar. This analysis seeks to shed light on the strategic considerations bidders must navigate and how these strategies influence the financial outcomes for both the suppliers and the buyer in the auction process.

The following exposition of a theoretical exercise draws upon Jeon and Whang (2023).[86] The auctioneer is the Public Procurement Service (PBS), and the bidders are suppliers of reinforcing bar. The total demand specified by PBS is Q, and each bidder i submits (q_i, p_i), $i = 1, \ldots, N$. The bids are organized in an ascending order such that $p_1 < p_2 < \ldots. < p_N$. The winners are determined as the first K bidders for which the cumulative supply meets or exceeds the total demand, i.e., $Q \leq q_1 + q_2 \ldots. + q_K$. The winning supply amount will be q_i for $i < K$ and $Q - (q_1 + q_2 \ldots. + q_{K-1})$ for the Kth bidder. To illustrate, consider a scenario where $Q > q_1 + q_2 + q_3$, $Q < q_1 + q_2 + q_3 + q_4$, implying that $K = 4$ as in the following figure.

In the scenario depicted in Fig. 6.1, bidder 1, 2, and 3 are awarded quantities, q_1, q_2, q_3, respectively, while bidder 4 secures the remaining quantity, $Q - (q_1 + q_2 + q_3)$. Under the "market-clearing price" payment method, all winning winners (1, 2, 3, and 4) are compensated at the same unit price, p^*, which aligns the step-like supply curve—represented by the horizontal real lines at prices, p_1, p_2, p_3, and p_4, with the vertical demand curve at quantity Q. Conversely, with the "your own price" payment method, each i is paid at their individual bid price, p_i ($i = 1, 2, 3$, and 4). Finally, under the "lowest price" payment method, all winners receive the lowest winning price, p_1, irrespective of their individual bid prices. The following provides

[86] Jeon and Whang (2023) submitted the expert witness report to the criminal court subsequent to the KFTC's accusation against the involved companies and their employees. The forthcoming exposition, while maintaining a degree of formality, does not delve into theoretical rigor.

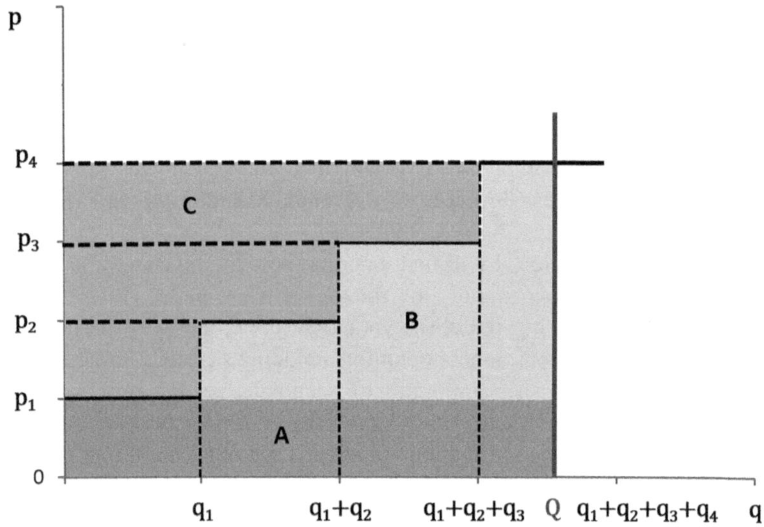

Fig. 6.1 DQCB in case of $K = 4$

Table 6.10 Unit prices and expenditure according to the payment method of DQCB

	Unit prices for bidders	Expenditure of auctioneer
Market-clearing price	$p^* = p_4$ for all	A + B + C = p_4Q
Your own price	p_1, p_2, p_3, p_4, respectively	A + B = $p_1q_1 + p_2q_2 + p_3q_3 + p_4(Q - q_1 - q_2 - q_3)$
The lowest price	p_1 for all	A = p_1Q

a summary of the final unit price awarded for each bidder and the total expenditure incurred by the auctioneer, the PPS (Table 6.10).

The results in Fig. 6.1 look quite different depending upon the payment price method of DQCB. It may hold only if all bidders choose the same strategies regardless of the payment method. Of course, this is not true. An auction is a game in which bidders choose their best response strategies by interacting with other players and expecting others' strategies, given the rule of the game, which is determined by the auction mechanism. We can show that the equilibrium results of the three payment methods in DQCB may be the same in the special circumstances which correspond to the public procurement of reinforcing bar.

The outcomes illustrated in Fig. 6.1 varies significantly based on the payment price method utilized in the DQCB process. This variation presumes that all bidders adopt identical strategies, irrespective of the chosen payment method—a scenario that is, realistically, improbable. An auction functions as a strategic game where bidders determine their optimal response strategies through interaction with other participants, taking into account the anticipated strategies of others within the framework established by the auction mechanism. It is possible to demonstrate that the equilibrium outcomes for the three payment methods in DQCB—market-clearing price, your own price, and lowest price—can converge under specific conditions that mirror those found in the public procurement of reinforcing bar.

We will adopt two basic assumptions that are deemed reasonable in this case. Firstly, bidders determine their bid based solely on the unit price p_i, treating the quantity q_i as a given parameter. This simplification reflects the long-standing practice among companies of allocating approximately 10% of their production capacity to public procurement. This assumption substantially simplifies the bidding game, focusing the strategic decisions of bidders on price rather than quantity. Secondly, bidders accurately anticipate the reservation prices of all participants, denoted as c_1, c_2 .... c_N, which represent the unit costs including normal profit margin, as well as the auctioneer's reservation price. The cost structure for reinforcing bar is characterized by simplicity and stability, and the auctioneer's reservation price is typically derived from the cost estimates submitted by the bidders themselves. Under this framework, the number of participants N will equal the number of winners K whose unit cost is below the auctioneer's reservation price. This is because companies with higher cost are aware that they stand no chance of being selected as winners. In the following, consider the case where $K = 4$ as before.

I will describe the equilibrium outcomes in DQCB across the three price payment methods. Under the "market clearing" price payment, the dominant bidding strategy for each bid is to bid its own unit cost.[87] The rationale behind this strategy is that the payment price is independent of their bidding prices and is instead determined by the market clearing price, which aligns with the unit cost of the last winning bidder, $p_4 = c_4$. Conversely, under the payment methods of "your own price" and "the lowest price," each participant is incentivized to bid at $p_i = c_4$ $(i = 1, 2, 3, 4)$. This strategy ensures that a bidder does not get paid less by bidding below this price, and avoids losing the bid by quoting a higher price. Notice that under all three payment systems, the equilibrium outcomes for the winning bid price of bidders and the auctioneer's total expenditure are identical: $p^* = c_4$ and c_4Q, respectively. This uniformity in expenditure, despite different payment methods, may seem surprising at first glance. However, it can be seen as a derivative of the "revenue equivalence theorem," which is a fundamental principle in auction theory associated with auctions selling "single product-single unit." It is important to note that the equivalence theorem typically does not hold in general for the auction of "single product-multiple units" such as DQCB, where bids comprise both a unit price and a specified quantity.[88] Nevertheless, by adopting the simplification that bidders, considering the quantity as given, submit bids based solely on price, we can extend the applicability of the equivalence theorem to resemble that of "single product-single unit" auctions.

Jeon and Whang (2023) demonstrated that, in the context of public procurement auctions for reinforcing bar, bidders may be incentivized to submit bids that closely approach the reservation price, even in the absence of collusion. This case is

[87] In auction theory, this phenomenon is known as "truthful revelation."

[88] For a comprehensive overview of multi-unit auctions, refer to Ausubel et al. (2014).

currently in the preliminary stages of the judicial process. To date, only the initial criminal court ruling has been issued,[89] following the KFTC's allegations against the involved companies and individuals. The defendants have contested the KFTC's decision, filing an appeal with the Seoul High Court. Concurrently, the PPS is pursuing damages through litigation in the first trial civil court. Given the complexity of the case and the multiple legal avenues being pursued, it is anticipated that reaching final judgments across all related courts will require a considerable amount of time.

Cases

KFTC 2000-158, *Military Oil Procurement* Cartel, October 17, 2000.
KFTC 2006-079, *Flour* Cartel, March 24, 2006.
KFTC 2008-080, *Credit Card/VAN* Cartel, March 4, 2008.
KFTC 2008-323 and 324, *BMW/Lexus Dealers* Cartels, December 15, 2008.
KFTC 2012-107, *Ramen* Cartel, July 12, 2012.
KFTC 2015-100, *Industrial Explosives* Cartel, April 8, 2015.
KFTC 2015-319, *Compound Feed* Cartel, September 14, 2015.
KFTC 2016-161, *LNG Tank* Cartel, June 20, 2016.
KFTC 2021-016, *Iron Scrap Purchase* Cartel, January 18, 2021.
KFTC 2022-265, *Public Procurement of Reinforcing Bar* Cartel, November 8, 2022.
Daegu District Court 2017gahap201266, *LNG Tank* Cartel, December 8, 2022.
Seoul District Court 2006gahap99567, *Flour* Cartel, May 27, 2009.
Seoul District Court 2008gahap19596, 2984 combined, *Credit Card/VAN* Cartel, November 4, 2011.
Seoul District Court 2022gohap1044, *Public Procurement of Reinforcing Bar* Cartel, June 19, 2023.
Seoul High Court 2002nu61110, *Graphite* Cartel, August 19, 2004.
Seoul District Court 2002gahap16982, *Military Oil Procurement* Cartel, January 23, 2007.
Seoul High Court 2007na25137, *Military Oil Procurement* Cartel, December 20, 2009.
Seoul High Court 2009nu1930, *Lexus Dealer* Cartel, May 9, 2010.
Seoul High Court 2009nu9873, *BMW Dealer* Cartel, July 22, 2010.
Seoul High Court 2012nu24223, *Ramen* Cartel, November 8, 2013.
Seoul High Court 2012nu15385, *BMW Dealer* Cartel, April 28, 2014.
Seoul High Court 2012nu11241, *Lexus Dealer* Cartel, May 7, 2015.
Seoul High Court 2015nu60758, *Compound Feed* Cartel, March 9, 2017.
Seoul High Court 2015nu61827, *Compound Feed* Cartel, May 18, 2017.
Seoul High Court 2015nu62134, *Compound Feed* Cartel, June 7, 2017.
Supreme Court 2004du11275, *Graphite* Cartel, March 24, 2006.
Supreme Court 2010da1885, *Military Oil Procurement* Cartel, June 28, 2011.
Supreme Court 2010du11757, *Lexus Dealer* Cartel, April 26, 2012.
Supreme Court 2010du18703, BMW Dealer Cartel, April 26, 2012.
Supreme Court 2010da93790, *Flour* Cartel, November 29, 2012.
Supreme Court 2011du16049, February 13, 2014.

[89] Seoul District Court 2022gohap1044 (June 19, 2023) handed down suspended prison sentences of less than one year to these individuals. Additionally, fines were also imposed on both the companies and the individuals involved.

Supreme Court 2013du25924, July 24, 2014.
Supreme Court 2013du25924, *Ramen* Cartel, December 24, 2015.
Supreme Court 2017du30788, *Industrial Explosives* Cartel, July 20, 2018.
Supreme Court 2017du47144, *Compound Feed* Cartel, May 26, 2022.
Supreme Court 2017du47229, *Compound Feed* Cartel, May 26, 2022.
Supreme Court 2017du56346, *Compound Feed* Cartel, June 22, 2022.
Hanover Shoe, Inc. v. United Shoe Machinery Corp, 392 U.S. 481, Supreme 1968.
Illinois Brick Co. v. Illinois, 431. U.S. 720, Supreme 1977.

References

Ashurst (2004) Study on the conditions of claims for damages in case of infringement of EC competition rules: analysis of economic models for the calculation of damages prepared by Emily Clack, Mat Hughes and David Wirth

Aubert C, Rey P, Kovacic WE (2006) The impact of Leniency and Whistle-Blowing programs on cartels. Int J Ind Org 24(6):1241–1266

Ausubel LM, Cramton P, Pycia M, Rostek M, Weretka M (2014) Demand reduction and inefficiency in multi-unit auctions. Rev Econ Stud 81:1366–1400

Berry S, Levinsohn J, Pakes A (1995) Automobile prices in market equilibrium. Econometrica 63(4):841–890

Biogoni M, Fridolfsson S-O, Coq CL, Spanolo C (2009) Fines, Leniency and rewards in Antitrust: an experiment. IFN Working Paper No. 738, Research Institute of Industrial Economics

Brander JA, Ross TW (2005) Estimation damages from price-fixing. Working Paper 2005-03, Phelps Centre for the Study of Government and Business, Sauder School of Business, University of British Columbia

Capps CS, Dranove D, Greenstein S, Satterthwaite M (2001) The silent majority fallacy of the Elzinga-Hogarty criteria: a critique and new approach to analyzing hospital mergers. NBER Working Paper 8216

Cotterill B (1998) Estimation of cost pass through to Michigan consumers in the ADM price fixing case. In: Cotterill RW (ed) Food marketing policy Center Research Report, 39. University of Connecticut

Cotterill B, Egan L, Buckhold W (2001) Beyond Illinois Brick: the law and economics of cost pass-through in the ADM price fixing case. Rev Ind Org 18:45–52

European Commission (2008) White paper on damage actions for breach of the EC Antitrust Rules, Brussels, 2.4.2008, COM (2008) 165 final

European Commission (2011) Fines for breaking EU Competition Law

Finkelstein MO, Levenbach H (1983) Regression estimates of damages in price-fixing cases. Law Contemp Prob 46:145–169

Harrington JE Jr (2008) Optimal corporate leniency programs. J Ind Econ 56(1):215–246

Harris GR, Sullivan LA (1979) Passing on the monopoly overcharge: a comprehensive policy analysis. Univ Pennsylvania Law Rev 128(2):269–360

Jeon S (2004) Economic analysis of competitive effects of international graphite electrodes cartel on domestic import market. Expert Witness Report. [in Korean]

Jeon S (2020) Fair trade cases and economic analyses. Park Young Publishing. [in Korean]

Jeon S, Chung J (2017) Economic analysis of the possibility of collusion by 11 compound feed companies (case 2015nu61636). Expert Witness Report to Seoul High Court. [in Korean]

Jeon S, Han C (2019, 2021) Econometric estimation of damages in LNG tank construction bid-rigging, Appraisal Report to Court. [in Korean]

Jeon S, Whang W (2020) Economic analyis on the anti-competitiveness of iron scrap purchase collusion. Expert Witness Report to KFTC [in Korean]

Jeon S, Whang Y (2023) Economic analysis on the effect of bidding collusion in public procurement of reinforcing bar. Expert Witness Report to District Court. [in Korean]
Jeon S, Jeong J, Chung J (2014) Economic analysis of collusion and competition in industrial explosives market. Expert Witness Report to KFTC. [in Korean]
Jeon S, Lee H, Wang G (2004) Review of SNU appraisal report on econometric analysis of damage estimation in the civil suit on military oil procurement bid-rigging. Expert Witness Report to District Court. [in Korean]
Kim D, Kim J (2013) Economic analysis of market definition relevant to BMW and Lexus. Expert Witness Report. [in Korean]
Kim D, Kim J (2017) Economic analysis of the possibility of unfair collaboration by compound feed companies. Expert Witness Report. [in Korean]
Kim H, Nahm J (2010) Several topics in Cartel Leniency Program implementation. Appl Econ 12(2):21–48. [in Korean]
Kim S, Ryu K, Yi S, Lee I (2004) Econometric analysis of damage estimation in the civil suit on military oil procurement bid-rigging. Appraisal Project Report, Seoul National University. [in Korean]
Klemperer P (2004) Auctions: theory and practices. Princeton University Press
Korea Fair Trade Commission (2021) Guidelines for evaluating collaborative acts [in Korean]
Korea Fair Trade Commission (2025) Annual White Paper. [in Korean]
Krishna V (2010) Auction theory. Elsevier Academic Press
Kwon D, Kim N, Oh S, Yi S (2015) Market definition in Lexus dealer case: methodology and analytical issues. Comp Law Stud 32:75–115. [in Korean]
Lee H-R (2016) Economic analysis of the case of compound feed collusion. Expert Witness Report. [in Korean]
Lee H-R (2017) An opinion on "economic analysis of the case of compound feed collusion." Expert Witness Report. [in Korean]
Lee S (2019) Does criminal enforcement ensure more effective cartel deterrence? – Some questions on the 2018 amendment proposal to Korea's Competition Law. Korea Law Stud 95:173–221. [in Korean]
Lim Y, Cho S (2023) Fair trade law: theory and practice, 3rd edn. Park Young Publisher. [in Korean]
Mas-Colell A, Whinston M, Green J (1995) Microeconomic theory. Oxford University Press
Motta M, Polo M (2003) Leniency programs and cartel prosecution. Int J Ind Org 21(3):347–379
Oxera (2009) Quantifying antitrust damages: towards non-binding guidance for courts. Study prepared for European Commission
Reims R (2022) The criminal prosecution of hardcore cartels in the USA and the EU – a backdoor criminalization in the EU by the USA? CPI Columns Cartel
Seong S, Sohn Y, Jeong J, Kim I (2002) An economic analysis of damage estimation in civil suit related to bid-rigging. Expert Witness Report. [in Korean]
US Antitrust Modernization Commission (2007) Report and recommendations
Whang Y (2008) Econometric analysis of damage estimation for a civil suit in relation to flour collusion. Expert Appraisal Report. [in Korean]
Whang Y (2013) Economic analysis of market definition relevant to BMW. Expert Witness Report. [in Korean]
White H, Marshall R, Kennedy P (2006) The measurement of economic damages in antitrust civil litigation. Antitrust Law Econ Committee Newsl 6(1):17–22
Wooldridge JM (2006) Introductory econometrics: a modern approach, 3rd edn. Thomson
Yi S, Oh S (2014) Economic analysis of market definition for the analysis of competitive effects of Lexus Dealer collusion. Expert Witness Report. [in Korean]
Yi S, Whang Y (2011) Estimation of competitive fees of collecting sales slip in credit card/VAN collusion. Appraisal Report. [in Korean]

Chapter 7
Conclusion

The Fourth Industrial Revolution, propelled by digital technologies, has fundamentally transformed the competitive dynamics of online platform economies. Consequently, modern antitrust enforcement faces unprecedented challenges. In response, a wide range of new ideas and proposals have emerged regarding how competition law should adapt to the evolving digital landscape.

This concluding chapter is structured in two parts. First, it reviews recent global trends in antitrust thinking and regulatory reform. Second, it examines key insights from contemporary competition policy debates, alongside Korea's historical experience with antitrust enforcement. Drawing on these perspectives, the chapter proposes strategic directions for advancing Korea's antitrust policy to foster competition and innovation for the benefit of both consumers and businesses.

7.1 Recent Developments in Antitrust Thought and Regulatory Reform in the Digital Economy

In light of the growing dominance of major technology firms and concerns over their ability to entrench and expand market power through novel strategies and structural combinations, there has been a noticeable shift among antitrust scholars and practitioners toward more assertive enforcement. This includes heightened scrutiny of exclusionary conduct and mergers that may harm actual or potential competition. In response, a wave of proposals and regulatory reforms aimed at strengthening antitrust oversight has emerged across key jurisdictions, including the European Union, the United States, and Korea.

S. Jeon, *Antitrust Policy in Korea*, https://doi.org/10.1007/978-981-95-0632-3_7

7.1.1 Economic Perspectives on Strengthening Antitrust Enforcement for Digital Platforms

From the 1970s through the early 2000s, antitrust thinking was heavily influenced by the Chicago School, which advocated a restrained approach to regulating exclusionary conduct and mergers. Central to this perspective was the belief that *Type I errors*—false positives, such as wrongly condemning pro-competitive behavior—posed greater risks than *Type II errors*, where anti-competitive practices might go unpunished. The rationale was that government intervention could stifle efficiency-enhancing behavior, with long-lasting effects due to the absence of a subsequent market test.[1] In contrast, markets were seen as self-correcting: over time, new entrants would be incentivized to challenge monopolistic incumbents, thereby restoring competition and mitigating the harm of under-enforcement.

The rise of the digital economy and the increasing dominance of large platform enterprises have prompted a fundamental shift in antitrust thinking. The assumption that new, efficient competitors will emerge to discipline the market behavior of dominant firms is becoming less tenable. At the same time, the capacity of these dominant platforms to entrench and expand their market power—through novel strategies and acquisitions—appears to be growing. This shift is largely driven by structural features of the digital economy that inherently favor large incumbents, including network externalities, economies of scale and scope, and the strategic value of accumulated user data. These characteristics create high entry barriers and reinforce incumbency advantages, thereby weakening the corrective power of market forces. As a result, the risks and long-term costs associated with entrenched dominance are increasing, and the likelihood of spontaneous market correction is diminishing. Consequently, the expected costs of Type II errors—under-enforcement or false negatives—now warrant greater attention in the design and application of antitrust policy.

Lina Khan's (2017) article, "Amazon's Antitrust Paradox," published in the *Yale Law Journal*, and her subsequent appointment as Chair of the US Federal Trade Commission in 2021 at the age of 32, brought significant public and academic attention to emerging antitrust perspectives. In her work, Khan offered a provocative critique of the prevailing Chicago School framework that has long shaped US antitrust enforcement. She challenged its heavy reliance on the consumer welfare standard, particularly in assessing exclusionary conduct and mergers, arguing that this approach has led to systematic under-enforcement and an excessive focus on avoiding Type I errors. Khan used Amazon as a case study to illustrate how dominant digital platforms can engage in predatory practices and vertically integrate

[1] Judge Frank Easterbrook (1984) articulated a foundational argument for the Chicago School's cautious approach to antitrust enforcement. In his words: *"If the court errs by condemning a beneficial practice, the benefits may be lost for good. Any other firm that uses the condemned practices faces sanctions in the name of stare decisis, no matter the benefits. If the court errs by permitting a deleterious practice, though, the welfare loss decreases over time."*

across distinct markets in ways that escape traditional antitrust scrutiny. She contended that the current framework fails to capture the full scope of competitive harm in the digital economy. Her approach draws intellectual inspiration from Justice Louis Brandeis and is often referred to as the New Brandeis School. This school of thought critiques the narrow economic focus of modern antitrust and emphasizes the broader socio-political dimensions of market power. It advocates for antitrust policy that not only protects consumers but also promotes fairness, safeguards small businesses, and supports the welfare of workers, suppliers, innovators, and independent entrepreneurs. Moreover, it calls for a renewed focus on market structure and competitive processes, rather than solely on outcomes such as price or output.[2]

The emergence of the neo-Brandeis movement and the broader leftward shift in antitrust thinking reflect growing concerns over the recent and sustained rise in market power, both in the United States and globally. Over the past few decades, price-cost margins and corporate profits have increased significantly, while the labor share of income has declined.[3] These developments suggest that the problem of market power may extend beyond individual markets, potentially undermining overall economic efficiency and exacerbating economic inequality.[4] This evolving perspective is not confined to progressive or so-called "hipster antitrust" advocates, who are often skeptical of the self-correcting nature of markets. Increasingly, mainstream antitrust scholars are also re-evaluating the traditional Chicago School framework.[5] For instance, Herbert Hovenkamp (2019), in his article "Is Antitrust's Consumer Welfare Principle Imperiled?", defended the core of the consumer welfare standard but argued for a broader interpretation of the term "consumer." He proposed that it should include umbrella consumers (those purchasing from competitors of the defendant), indirect purchasers, trading partners, and even workers in monopsonistic labor markets. While Hovenkamp criticized the neo-Brandeis school for not fully incorporating modern economic insights, he acknowledged the need for more vigilant antitrust enforcement, particularly regarding anticompetitive mergers, such as acquisitions of smaller innovative firms by dominant tech platforms. He also emphasized the importance of scrutinizing predatory pricing strategies used to weaken rivals prior to acquisition, as well as vertical mergers that may foreclose competition.

[2] See Khan (2018).

[3] According to De Loecker et al. (2020), aggregate markups have risen significantly since 1980, increasing from approximately 21% above cost to 61% above cost by 2016. Over the same period, the aggregate profit rate climbed from 1% to around 8%, indicating a substantial rise in firm profitability. This trend has coincided with a decline in labor's share of income, suggesting a redistribution of economic gains away from workers toward capital owners. Further supporting this view, De Loecker and Eeckhout (2018) documented similar global patterns of rising market power since 1980, reinforcing concerns that increasing concentration and pricing power are not confined to the United States but represent a broader international phenomenon.

[4] See Baker (2017).

[5] See Hovenkamp and Morton (2020).

Alongside the broader shift in antitrust thinking toward more progressive and proactive regulatory enforcement[6]—particularly in response to the growing dominance and potentially abusive practices of large digital platforms—numerous expert groups have emerged globally to propose reforms tailored to the unique challenges of the digital economy. These groups comprise economists, legal scholars, technologists, and business practitioners, and their collective efforts have significantly shaped the evolving discourse on competition policy. A prominent example is the European Commission's Competition Report authored by Cremer et al. (2019).[7] This influential report aligns closely with the recent developments in antitrust thought and offers a comprehensive set of recommendations. While not exhaustive, the following are key highlights from their findings:

- Strong incumbency advantages and market tipping driven by platform-specific features, digital ecosystems, and the centrality of data.
- Reconsideration of the consumer welfare standard, emphasizing a longer-term perspective on competitive harm.
- Reduced reliance on market definition, with greater focus on theories of harm and identifying anti-competitive strategies.
- Rebalancing the error-cost framework, placing more weight on the risks of false negatives (under-enforcement).
- Promoting competition for the market by scrutinizing most-favored-nation (MFN) clauses and enabling multihoming and user switching.
- Encouraging complementary services through data portability and interoperability.
- Regulating platform conduct, particularly leveraging and self-preferencing, to ensure fair competition.
- Facilitating access to personal data and promoting data sharing to level the playing field.
- Addressing killer acquisitions, where dominant platforms acquire small, fast-growing startups with significant competitive potential to eliminate emerging threats.

Across the Atlantic, in the United States, the Stigler Center at the University of Chicago commissioned a group of antitrust experts led by Morton Scott to examine the competitive challenges posed by the scale, scope, and data practice by digital platforms. The resulting report of Morton Scott Morton et al. (2019, referred to as the Stigler Center Report) is particularly symbolic given its origin at the University of Chicago, a traditional bastion of the Chicago School of antitrust thought. In a notable departure from that tradition, the report advocated for vigorous antitrust enforcement

[6]Kwaka Jr et al. (2023) characterized the recent transition of antitrust economic thinking as "upheaval."

[7]There are several concurrent and purpose-aligned policy reports in other countries, such as the UK. Competition Report by Furman et al. (2018), the Australia Competition Report by Australia Competition and Consumer Commission (2018), and the German Competition Report by Schweitzer et al. (2018).

and regulatory reform to address the growing market power of digital platforms. The Stigler Center Report echoed many of the findings and recommendations in the European Commission's Competition Report, highlighting a growing transatlantic consensus. While there is considerable overlap in the policy proposals across jurisdictions, the Stigler Center Report introduced several distinctive recommendations. They suggest the creation of a new regulatory institution, referred to as the Digital Authority,[8] designed to complement existing antitrust agencies. This authority would oversee two tiers of regulation: a general framework applicable to most market participants (less interventionist) and a targeted regime for firms with bottleneck power or gatekeeper status (more interventionist). Moreover, they propose the establishment of a specialized competition court with the expertise and institutional capacity to adjudicate antitrust laws and promote market entry, competition, and consumer welfare in digital platform industries.

7.1.2 Regulatory Reforms to Enhance Competition in the Digital Economy

In many jurisdictions, antitrust policy reforms are being proposed and actively debated to address the competitive challenges posed by the digital economy. These discussions focus on issues such as the scope, intensity, and legislative implementation of regulatory measures. The EU is at the forefront of this movement, having enacted the Digital Markets Act (DMA) in 2022—a comprehensive, assertive, and preemptive framework for regulating major digital platform companies.[9] In the United States, several antitrust bills aimed at curving anti-competitive practices by large technology firms were introduced in both the Senate and the House of Representatives in 2021, but these bills have yet to pass through Congress.[10] Nevertheless, US DOJ and FTC (2023) released new "Merger Guidelines," replacing the 2010 Horizontal Merger Guidelines. These updates reflected a more aggressive stance aligned with the Biden administration's broader antitrust agenda. In Korea, the KFTC is considering new legislative measures to address competition concerns arising from the dominance of large online platform operators, both domestic and international.

[8]Unlike the EC Competition Report, which does not propose the creation of a new regulatory institution dedicated to the digital sector, the UK Competition Report explicitly recommends the establishment of "a digital markets unit." This proposed body would be endowed with new legislative powers and tasked with developing a code of competitive conduct specifically for particularly powerful companies, enabling greater personal data mobility and open standard, and promoting data openness—all aimed at overcoming key barriers to entry in digital markets.

[9]The Digital Services Act (DSA) was introduced alongside the DMA. The DSA focuses on user protection (not directly related to market power) and imposes content curation duties on platforms.

[10]The American Innovation and Choice Act is still under consideration in the Senate as of now.

The DMA addresses two core concerns within the EU's digital internal market: contestability (the ability of more efficient and innovative firms to enter and compete in core platform markets) and fairness (ensuring that both consumers and business users receive a proportionate share of the value they help create and are granted equal access to the core market). The DMA targets large digital firms designated as "gatekeepers," which provide "core platform services," including online intermediation services, online search engines, online social networking services, video-sharing platform services, number-independent interpersonal communication services, operating systems, web browsers, virtual assistants, cloud computing services, and online advertising services. A company is designated as a gatekeeper if it has a significant impact on the internal market, serves as an important gateway for business users to reach end users, and enjoys (or is expected to enjoy) an entrenched and durable position. The DMA presumes that a company meets these criteria if it:

(i) Achieves an annual turnover of at least €7.5 billion in the EU in each of the last three financial years, or has a market valuation of at least €75 billion.
(ii) Provides a core platform service in at least three EU Member States.
(iii) Has more than 45 million monthly active end users and more than 10,000 yearly active business users in the EU.

It is noteworthy that the designation of gatekeepers under the DMA is *ex ante*—that is, it is not based on possessing the market power in the relevant market as defined in traditional *ex post* antitrust enforcement. Once a company meets the presumptive thresholds, it may submit rebuttal evidence, which the European Commission reviews through a market investigation process. Following this process, the EC officially designated six companies as gatekeepers in September 2023: Alphabet, Amazon, Apple, ByteDance, Meta, Microsoft. Collectively, these firms were found to provide 22 core platform services subject to DMA obligations. Incidentally, all six designated gatekeepers are headquartered in the United States, underscoring the global reach of US-based tech giants and the EU's stance in regulating their operations within its internal market.

The new EC rules will establish obligations for gatekeepers, outlining the "do's" and "don'ts" they must comply with in their daily operations. Examples of the *"do's"* include:

- Allowing third parties to interoperate with the gatekeeper's own services in certain specific situations.
- Allowing their business users to access the data generated through their use of the gatekeeper's platform.
- Providing companies advertising on their platform with the tools and information necessary for advertisers and publishers to independently verify their advertisements hosted by the gatekeeper.
- Allowing their business users to promote their offerings and conclude contracts with customers outside the gatekeeper's platform.

Examples of the *"don'ts"* include:

- No longer treating services and products offered by the gatekeeper itself more favorably in ranking than similar services or products offered by third parties on the gatekeeper's platform.
- Not preventing consumers from linking to businesses outside their platforms.
- Not preventing users from uninstalling any pre-installed software or app if they wish to do so.
- Not tracking end users outside of the gatekeepers' core platform service for the purpose of targeted advertising without effective consent having been granted.[11]

The purpose of these obligations is to foster "contestability" and to ensure "fairness." The DMA's list above aimed at fostering the contestability of a potential or actual rival platform competing with the incumbent one includes:

- Facilitating consumer switching between platforms by "interoperability."
- Allowing business users to take advantage of their own data through "data access."
- Banning most-favored-nation (MFN) clauses and other exclusivity contracts.
- Allowing business users to indicate other channels of interaction to their users (disintermediation).
- Reducing the so-called "application barrier to entry" by prohibiting the tying of core services with other services.

On the other hand, the DMA's list of violations related to fairness includes:

- "Self-preferencing."
- Using nonpublic data obtained from third-party business users to offer the platform's own products.
- Restrict the uninstallation of pre-installed software applications.[12]

In addition, a designated gatekeeper is required to notify acquisitions in which the merging parties or the target provide core platform services or any other services in the digital sector, or enable the collection of data. This obligation applies regardless of whether the transaction meets the turnover thresholds set out in existing EU merger regulations. The aim is to enhance regulatory oversight and may serve as a *proactive measure to prevent so-called "killer acquisitions"*—where dominant firms acquire emerging rivals to neutralize future competition.

The penalties for non-compliance with the DMA are substantial. A gatekeeper found in breach of its obligations may face fines of up to 10% of its total worldwide annual turnover, and up to 20% in cases of repeated infringements. Beyond financial sanctions, the DMA also provides for *non-financial remedies* in instances of *systematic non-compliance*, following a market investigation. These remedies may include both *behavioral* and *structural measures*, such as the *divestiture of parts*

[11] I referred to the EC's document, "The Digital Markets Act: Ensuring Fair and Open Digital Markets," for this summary of the gatekeepers' "do's" and "don'ts" obligations.

[12] I referred to Tirole (2023, p.577) for this classification of the DMA's list of gatekeepers' obligations according to the two key concepts of contestability and fairness.

of the business, if deemed necessary to restore contestability and fairness in the digital market.

The EU Digital Markets Act marks a significant departure from traditional antitrust policy in several key respects: First, the DMA is a *sector-specific* regulatory framework that targets the digital economy and focuses exclusively on gatekeepers—large online platforms that serve as critical intermediaries. In contrast, conventional antitrust laws apply broadly to all enterprises *across all sectors*. Second, the DMA adopts an *ex ante* approach, meaning that obligations are imposed before any anti-competitive conduct occurs. Gatekeepers are designated based on quantitative criteria, such as turnover and user base, rather than on a demonstrated abuse of market power. Although firms may submit rebuttals during the market investigation phase, the designation is not contingent on defining a relevant market or proving dominance. The obligations and prohibited practices for gatekeepers are predefined, whereas traditional competition enforcement follows an *ex post* model—intervening only after problematic conduct is identified, a relevant market is defined, and dominance is established. Third, the DMA includes mechanisms for updating its rules in response to evolving market and technological developments. In contrast, competition laws are typically framed in broad and flexible terms, allowing them to be interpreted and applied to new circumstances without frequent legislative amendments. Finally, violations of the DMA's specified obligations are treated as *per se* illegal, meaning they are presumed to harm competition without requiring a detailed effects-based analysis. This stands in contrast to the *rule-of-reason* approach in traditional antitrust enforcement, where authorities must assess whether the anti-competitive effects of a practice outweigh any efficiency gains.

The German Competition Authority, the *Bundeskartellamt* (Federal Cartel Office, FCO), played an active role in shaping the EU Digital Markets Act (DMA) from its early stages. In parallel, Germany pursued its own domestic reforms to address the challenges of the digital economy by amending its national competition law, the *Gesetz gegen Wettbewerbsbeschränkungen* (GWB)—the Act Against Restraints of Competition.[13] The ninth Amendment to the GWB, which came into force in 2017, introduced new criteria for assessing market power in digital markets. These included considerations such as the provision of free-of-charge services, the presence of network effects, and access to data—factors increasingly relevant in the digital age. The most significant reform came with the tenth Amendment,[14] enacted in January 2021, which introduced Section 19a, titled *"Abusive Conduct of Undertakings of Paramount Significance for Competition Across Markets."* This provision empowers the FCO to intervene proactively against large digital platforms through a two-step approach:

---

[13]Refer to OECD (2021) for recent developments of German Competition Law.

[14]The latest update is the 11th Amendment in October 2023, which comprehensively revised the law in several other aspects as well.

(i) Designation Phase: The FCO may declare a company to be of paramount significance for competition across markets, based on qualitative factors such as its strategic position, financial strength, and access to data.[15]
(ii) Intervention Phase: Once designated, the FCO can prohibit certain types of conduct,even in markets where the company is not yet dominant. Prohibited behaviors include: self-preferencing, impediment of competitors through data processing, refusal to ensure interoperability, and restrictions on data portability.[16]

While Section 19a and the EU DMA share similarities—particularly in their *ex ante* designation of powerful digital firms and the types of conduct they prohibit—there are important distinctions. First, in terms of designation criteria, Section 19a relies on qualitative assessments, whereas the DMA uses quantitative thresholds (e.g., turnover and user base). Second, in terms of legal effect, under the DMA, obligations apply automatically upon designation, without the need for a separate prohibition decision. In contrast, Section 19a requires the FCO to issue an individual decision before enforcement actions can be taken.

In the United States, several legislative efforts aimed at strengthening antitrust enforcement against large technology firms in the digital economy have not yet succeeded. However, in 2023, the DOJ and the FTC took a significant step by issuing revised Merger Guidelines, applicable to both horizontal and vertical mergers.[17] These guidelines reflect a more aggressive and expansive approach to merger enforcement, consistent with the interventionist stance of the current leadership at both agencies. The revised guidelines articulate 11 specific principles that guide merger analysis, signaling a commitment to proactive scrutiny of mergers and acquisitions. Among the most notable changes is the strengthening of the structural presumption of illegality. Under Guideline 1, a merger is presumed to substantially lessen competition or tend to create a monopoly if:

- The Herfindahl-Hirschman Index (HHI) exceeds 1800, indicating a highly concentrated market;
- The merged firm's market share exceeds 30%; and.
- The HHI increases by more than 100 points as a result of the merger.[18]

[15] The FCO first designated Alphabet/Google in December 2021, followed by Meta/Facebook and Amazon in 2022.

[16] It is also noteworthy that appeals against decisions by the FCO under Section 19a will be brought directly to the Federal Court of Justice, serving as both the first and last instance for all related disputes. This procedural design aims to expediate the enforcement of regulations targeting the conduct of large digital platforms, whose practices often lead to market tipping—a phenomenon that, once it occurs, is difficult to reverse and can entrench dominant positions.

[17] The previous 2010 guidelines focused on horizontal mergers. In contrast, guidelines for vertical merger were issued separately in 2020, but were withdrawn shortly after their release.

[18] Under the previous 2010 guidelines, if the post-merger HHI exceeds 2,500 (indicating a highly concentrated market), the merger "potentially raises significant competitive concerns" if the HHI

These revisions broaden the scope of anticompetitive concerns by lowering the HHI threshold and introducing market share condition. The new guidelines place greater emphasis on the elimination of potential entrants or nascent competitors, particularly in the context of non-horizontal mergers. This concern is addressed across multiple sections, most notably in Guideline 4, which highlights the risks associated with removing actual or perceived potential entrants. The guidelines introduce a novel focus on "ecosystem" competition in Guideline 6. This concept applies to mergers involving firms that offer a broad portfolio of products or services. The guidelines caution that acquisitions by large incumbents—even of small, non-competing niche firms—can harm competition by reducing the diversity of the ecosystem that collectively constrains the dominant players. The loss of such nascent competitive threats may weaken the overall competitive landscape, even if the merging firms do not directly overlap in their operations.

The new guidelines identify "foreclosure" as a key concern in vertical mergers. Foreclosure refers to a merged firm's ability to limit rivals' access to a product, service, or route to market—referred to as a "related product"—that competitors rely on to compete. The agencies define a "foreclosure share" as the portion of the related market that the merged firm could restrict. A foreclosure share exceeding 50% is considered a threshold for a general inference of harm, absent of compelling countervailing evidence (Guideline 5). Moreover, the guidelines emphasize the importance of industry consolidation trend. A "trend toward consolidation" is treated as a highly relevant factor that may amplify competition concerns. The agencies will assess the proposed merger not in isolation, but in the broader context of ongoing or anticipated industry consolidation activity, including its potential to accelerate future consolidation[19] (Guideline 7). Lastly, when a merger involves a multi-sided platform, the agencies will scrutinize competition between platforms, on a platform, or to displace a platform. A central concern is the conflict of interest that arises when a platform operator also competes on its own platform. This dual role can distort competition, as the operator may have an incentive to favor its own products or services—a practice known as self-preferencing. This can manifest in ranking, placement, or promotional advantages, undermining the platform's role as a neutral facilitator of competition (Guideline 9).

The response to the 2023 Merger Guidelines issued by the US DOJ and FTC has been deeply polarized, reflecting broader philosophical divisions within the antitrust community. Proponents of a more interventionist approach—particularly those

increase is between 100 and 200. Additionally, it is "presumed to be likely to enhance market power" if the HHHI increase is more than 200 points.

[19]The guidelines also introduce the concept of an "arms race for bargaining leverage" as potential competitive harm. This dynamics occurs when the merging parties consolidate to gain bargaining leverage over other firms that they transact with, such as suppliers, distributors, or customers. In response, those other firms may pursue their own mergers to countervailing leverage, triggering a cascade of consolidation across the industry. The result, as described in the guidelines (p. 22), may be "an industry where a few powerful firms have a leverage against one another and market power over would-be entrants or over trading partners in various parts of value chain."

concerned with the growing power of big tech firms—have generally welcomed the guidelines as a necessary recalibration of enforcement tools to address modern market dynamics. In contrast, advocates of a more traditional, cautious approach to competition policy have criticized the guidelines, arguing that they reflect ideological bias rather than neutral, evidence-based policymaking. The controversial nature of the new guidelines may itself pose challenges. Unlike previous iterations, which emphasized methodological neutrality and focused on tools for interpreting evidence, the 2023 guidelines are seen by some as philosophically interventionist. This shift raises concerns about their durability and legal effectiveness. Even if the agencies pursue more aggressive merger challenges under the new framework, success in court is not guaranteed, as judges are not bound by the guidelines and may apply different standards. Moreover, the lack of bipartisan support could undermine the guidelines' longevity. A change in political leadership could result in the issuance of new guidelines, potentially reversing or revising the current enforcement direction.[20]

In Korea, no regulation has been enacted, nor has there been any drastic revision of the merger guidelines to address the challenges of enforcing competition policy in the digital economy. However, the KFTC introduced "the Guidelines in Examining the Market Dominance Abuse by Online Platform Enterprises" in January 2023. As discussed in Chaps. 3 and 4, the KFTC has pursued several notable cases involving unfair business conduct and market dominance abuses. These include *Delivery Hero Korea–Yoggiyo*'s Best Price Guarantee in 2020, *Naver–Video Contents and Shopping*'s Self-Preferencing in 2021, *Google*'s Anti-Fragmentation Agreement in 2021, and *Google Play*'s Exclusive Dealing in 2023. The guidelines reflect the current understanding of potentially harmful conduct of platform enterprises and incorporate insights from past experiences. They outline the key characteristics of online platforms, such as network effects, scale economies, the importance of data, and nominally free services. Additionally, the guidelines provide the foundational principles of market definition that account for the multi-sided platform nature. They also propose standards for assessing anticompetitive concerns and potential efficiencies related to common platform practices, including restrictions on multihoming, most favored nation (MFN) clauses, self-preferencing, and tying.

Since late 2022, several legislators have proposed laws to regulate the monopolistic abuses of large platform enterprises, but these proposals are still pending in the National Assembly. The KFTC announced plans to introduce the "Platform Competition Promotion Act" in December 2023, modeled in part after the EU DMA. The

[20]Carlton (2024), a leading antitrust economist, has been critical of the 2023 Merger Guideline, raising concerns about their legal and economic underpinning. He argues that the guidelines rely heavily on outdated case law and interpretations, which may lead to disagreements with the legal community regarding the current status of antitrust jurisprudence. Carlton also contends that the guidelines exhibit a hostile stance toward mergers and efficiencies, potentially discourage transactions that could yield pro-competitive benefits. He expresses skepticism about the long-term viability of the guidelines, cynically remarking: "I expect that the next revision of the Guidelines will be sooner than the 13 years that have elapsed since the 2010 Guidelines."

proposed legislation sought to designates certain firms as “dominant platform enterprises” and prohibit anti-competitive practices such as self-preferencing and restrictions on multihoming.[21] However, faced with strong resistance from both domestic and foreign platform firms, as well as their business partners, the KFTC has abandoned the plan to enact the standalone “Platform Competition Promotion Act” and instead opted to amend the existing Monopoly Regulation and Fair Trade Act (MRFTA) to address concerns about monopolistic practices in the digital economy. As of now, the KFTC plans to regulate platforms *ex post*—evaluating dominance after an incident occurs, based on criteria like: i) market share over 60%, ii) annual sales exceeding 4 trillion KRW, and iii) more than 10 million users. If a company is found to be dominant and engages in unfair practices, stricter sanctions will apply, including potential temporary suspension orders. This shift reflects a more cautious and flexible regulatory stance, aiming to balance enforcement with concerns about overregulation and innovation stifling.

I am not convinced that the KFTC should rush to introduce a new “Platform Competition Promotion” act. The competitive dynamics of Korea’s digital sector differ significantly from those of the EU, where the most dominant tech firms are US-based. In contrast, Korea is home to strong domestic platform enterprises—such as Naver (search), Kakao (social networking), and Coupang (e-commerce)—that compete effectively with both local and global players. Introducing *ex ante* regulatory framework—such as designating gatekeepers without a clear market definition and preemptively listing prohibited conducts—could provoke strong resistance from both domestic and international firms likely to be subject to such rules. Moreover, the effectiveness of an *ex post* enforcement agency like the KFTC implementing *ex ante* regulation remains unproven. The KFTC already has the reputation for proactive and robust antitrust enforcement, often ahead of its global counterparts. Given this, it might be more prudent to adopt a wait-and-see approach—observing how the EU’s DMA and similar regulatory experiments unfold—before committing to a comparable regulatory model in Korea.

7.2 Principles of Antitrust Policy Enforcement and Lessons from the Korean Experience

There is a well-established consensus among legal and economic scholars, as well as practitioners in the antitrust community—developed over more than 130 years—regarding the fundamental principles of how competition policy should be enforced. I believe some of these shared understandings include the following:

[21] KFTC, “Pushing Forward the Platform Monopoly and Oligopoly Polices to Vitalize People’s Livelihood,” Press Release, December 19, 2023.

7.2.1 Principles of Antitrust Policy Enforcement

First, competition policy has traditionally aimed to enhance "primarily" consumer welfare. However, this should not be interpreted to mean that promoting consumer welfare is the sole objective of competition policy, nor that the term "consumer" should be narrowly defined to include only end users. Across jurisdictions and over time, competition policy has served multiple purposes—some complementary to, and others potentially in contention with, consumer interests. For example, Korea's MRFTA explicitly states in Article 1 that its objectives include not only "protecting consumers" but also "striving for the balanced development of the national economy." This broader mandate is grounded in constitutional principles, such as Article 119 of the Korean Constitution, which calls for the "democratization of the economy through harmony among economic agents." The focus of antitrust enforcement has also evolved in response to changing economic conditions and technological developments. In the United States, for instance, the aftermath of the Great Depression led to a permissive stance in the early 1930s, allowing cartels and granting exemptions from antitrust laws. In contrast, the recent rise of dominant digital platforms has prompted renewed calls for more interventionist antitrust policies across many jurisdictions. Despite these shifts, the consumer welfare standard has remained a central—though not exclusive—benchmark in antitrust enforcement. Importantly, the concept of "consumer" should be included broadly to include all parties affected by a transaction, such as indirect customers, workers, consumers of rival firms, and minority shareholders, in addition to end users.

Second, it is widely emphasized that competition policy is designed to protect *competition*—that is the *competitive process itself*—rather than shield "weak" or "inefficient" competitors from market forces. This principle is particularly relevant in cases involving price-related exclusionary conduct, such as predatory pricing, royalty rebates, and margin squeezes. Many economists advocate for the use of "as-if-efficient competitor" standard when assessing the anticompetitive nature of such practices. Under this approach, only competitors that are as efficient as the dominant firm should be protected, thereby preserving the incentive for price competition and innovation. Accordingly, the dominant firm's own costs are often used as a benchmark in applying relevant legal and economic tests. However, this framework may overlook the structural disadvantages faced by new entrants or less mature firms, especially in digital platform markets. Incumbent firms often benefit from significant economies of scale, strong network effects, and privileged access to vast amounts of user data—advantages that are not easily replicable by newcomers. These asymmetries are inherent to the digital economy and can make it difficult for even potentially efficient entrants to compete on equal footing. Therefore, while the "as efficient competitor" test remains a valuable tool, it should be applied with caution in digital markets. Policy makers and enforcers should consider the potential for new entrants to evolve into effective competitors, particularly when their current inefficiencies stem from industry specific barriers rather than firm-specific shortcomings

Third, competition policy should be applied equally to both domestic and foreign companies. Most jurisdictions adopt the "effect doctrine" in the extraterritorial application of antitrust laws, asserting jurisdiction over foreign conduct that has a significant impact on domestic markets. For example, under the US Foreign Trade Antitrust Improvements Act (FTAIA) of 1982, antitrust laws apply to foreign commerce—excluding imports—only when the conduct has a "direct, substantial, and reasonably foreseeable effect" on US commerce. Korea has similarly applied the effects doctrine in numerous cases involving foreign firms. Notable cases, addressed in this book, include: *Microsoft* in 2006, *Intel* in 2008, *Qualcomm* in 2010 and 2017, *Siemens* in 2018 for market dominance abuse; *Microsoft and Nokia* in 2015 and *Delivery Hero and Woowa Brothers* in 2021 for mergers; and *Graphite Electrodes* in 2002 for cartels. There is a broad consensus that antitrust regulations and enforcement standards should be applied consistently, regardless of a firm's national origin. However, concerns may arise that competition authorities could be tempted to use regulation to favor domestic firms over foreign competitors. Conversely, regulatory measures designed to address domestic market concerns may inadvertently result in "reverse" discrimination against domestic firms. To maintain credibility and fairness, competition agencies must remain vigilant in ensuring neutrality with respect to the nationality of the firms involved—both to avoid protectionism and to prevent unintended disadvantages to domestic enterprises.

Fourth, antitrust regulation should remain independent from policy objectives unrelated to competition. Industrial policies, by their nature, are often selective—aimed at promoting "national champions" or restructuring industries by phasing out underperforming firms. While the effectiveness of such policies—often summarized by the quip, "the state picks winners, and losers pick the state"—they are typically not competitively neutral. When competition policy is used to support industrial policy goals, it risks distorting market dynamics and reinforcing monopolistic structures, thereby undermining the very nature of antitrust enforcement. Similarly, competition policy should not be repurposed as a tool for price control. The predecessor to Korea's MRFTA—"Price Stabilization and Fair Trade Act" of 1976—is not considered the starting point of Korean antitrust law precisely because it primarily focused on curbing inflation following the oil shocks of the late 1970s. While robust competition can contribute to lower prices, improved quality, and innovation—thereby helping to moderate inflation over the long run—competition policy is ill-suited to address short-term inflationary pressures. Using antitrust enforcement to suppress price increases during inflationary periods not only risks ineffectiveness but may also damage the credibility and long-term integrity of the competition agency.

Lastly, antitrust law and competition policy have historically been enforced with flexibility, adapting to an evolving competitive landscape, technological advancements, and shifting political priorities. The legal language of antitrust statutes is often deliberately broad, allowing for interpretive adaptability. For example, the US Sherman Act of 1890 prohibits "every contract, combination, or constraint and conspiracy in restraint of trade," as well as "monopolization, attempted monopolization, or conspiracy or combination to monopolize." Although subsequent statues, such as the Federal Trade Commission Act and the Clayton Act, both enacted in 1914, were introduced to address gaps, they too refrain from offering a definitive list of prohibitive conduct. Much of the interpretation is left to enforcement agencies and courts. The legal ambiguity is rooted in the US antitrust laws, which stem from the Common Law tradition, which heavily relies on case-by-case adjudication. However, even in civil law jurisdictions like Korea and Germany, where statutes are more codified, competition laws are applied with a degree of discretion. Enforcement outcomes often depend on the willingness of agencies to pursue cases and the interpretive stance of the judiciary. This flexibility reflects the reality that many antitrust issues exist in a legal and economic "grey area," where distinguishing between pro-competitive and anti-competitive behavior requires nuanced judgment. As a result, the intensity and direction of antitrust enforcement tend to fluctuate over time, responding to prevailing economic conditions and societal values. While this discretion introduces a degree of uncertainty, it also enables competition policy to remain responsive and relevant—particularly in times of rapid technological change. In today's digital economy, where new business models and market dynamics emerge quickly, the adaptability of antitrust enforcement is not just a feature but a necessity.

7.2.2 *Lessons from the Korean Experience*

Korean antitrust law and policy have made substantial progress since the enactment of the MRFTA in 1981, both in terms of scope and depth. The Act has been amended more than 30 times to date and underwent a comprehensive restructuring in December 2021. A particularly notable development has been the introduction of numerous regulations targeting *chaebols* (large business conglomerates) since 1986. These reforms were driven by the need to address systemic risks associated with the concentrated power of chaebols—risks that became especially apparent during the Asian Financial Crisis in the late 1990s—as well as by political momentum toward "economic democratization." In parallel, Korea introduced a series of special laws aimed at curbing unfair business practices in specific sectors, including subcontracting, large-scale retailing, franchising, and agency relationship. This expansion of antitrust policy to address both the dominance of chaebols and the protection of small and medium-sized enterprises (SMEs) has shaped the distinctive character of Korean competition policy.

Beyond the external expansion of enforcement jurisdiction to address Korea-specific issues—such as large business groups and the widening gap between large and small enterprises—Korean antitrust policy has also advanced significantly in the application of conventional competition laws in the area of market dominance abuse, merger, and cartel regulation. A key development has been the shift from a formalistic, rule-based approach—relying heavily on literal interpretation of statutes and decrees—to a more nuanced, *effect-based* and *rule-of-reason* framework. This modern approach evaluates both the anticompetitive effects and potential efficiencies of business practices, allowing for more balanced and economically grounded enforcement. Over the past two decades, this evolution has been marked by the increasing use of economic analysis in antitrust investigations. While industrial organization theory and antitrust economics have long influenced policy thinking, it was not until the early 2000s that economists began to participate directly in enforcement cases, providing expert analysis on behalf of the KFTC or defendants. Many of these contributions are illustrated in the case studies discussed in previous chapters.

Notwithstanding the overall trend toward the broadening and deepening of Korean antitrust policy, there remains considerable room for further rationalization and refinement. In the following section, I offer several recommendations on how antitrust enforcement in Korea can be improved moving forward. These suggestions are grounded in widely accepted antitrust principles, informed by Korea's past regulatory experiences, responsive to the challenges posed by recent industrial and technological developments, and aligned with current economic thinking and understanding of competition policy.

Suggestions for Chaebol Antitrust Policy

Chaebol regulations in Korea have undergone numerous revisions over the past four decades, shaped by shifts in the country's economic and political landscape. A wide range of rules governing ownership structures and control—particularly those aimed at curbing the concentration of power within chaebol families and preventing opportunistic behavior—have been introduced and progressively strengthened. These regulatory efforts were often prompted by economic crises, such as the foreign exchange crisis of the late 1990s, which exposed structural vulnerabilities in the chaebol system, as well as by growing political demands for "economic democratization." While the current regulatory framework is relatively robust, there remains room for streamlining and adapting Korean antitrust policy to better meet future challenges.

Many aspects of chaebol regulation extend beyond the traditional boundaries of antitrust policy. Some are designed to protect minority shareholders from exploitation by controlling families; others aim to separate industrial enterprises from financial capital, or to prevent improper wealth transfers during leadership succession. While comprehensive oversight by the KFTC could be effective, this would require a unified regulatory purpose and consistent criteria—something difficult to achieve given the diversity of policy goals. A one-size-fits-all approach is not feasible. Certain chaebol-related issues fall outside the KFTC's effective jurisdiction and should be addressed through complementary legal frameworks, including corporate, financial, and tax law. For example, the incentive to confer unfair benefits on related parties—particularly successors to group leadership—often stems from Korea's exceptionally high inheritance tax burden. With rates reaching up to 60% (including additional charges for business succession), Korea has one of the highest inheritance tax rates in the OECD. Without easing this burden to a more reasonable level, business group leaders may be tempted to exploit regulatory loopholes to transfer assets to heirs, undermining the effectiveness of existing regulations.

Korea's experience with chaebol regulation offers valuable insights for addressing the growing influence of large digital platform enterprises. Just as chaebol policy evolved to address the excessive concentration of economic power, the global push for stricter oversight of big tech platforms reflects similar concerns. The EU's DMA is a prominent example of this trend. Rather than introducing entirely new legislation, Korea could consider integrating platform-specific regulations into its existing business group oversight framework. The KFTC already has experience with both *ex ante* regulation of business groups and *ex post* enforcement against unfair practices such as cross-subsidization and self-preferencing. This institutional expertise could be leveraged to regulate dominant platform enterprises more effectively. However, a key concern is that current chaebol regulations apply only to domestic business groups and their affiliates. This raises the risk of "*reverse discrimination*" against Korean firms, especially if foreign platform companies operating in Korea are not subject to equivalent scrutiny. Ensuring a level playing field—where all firms, domestic or foreign, compete under the same rules—is essential for maintaining fairness and credibility in enforcement.

Finally, the concept of the *chaebol* itself warrants reconsideration—both in regulatory frameworks and public discourse. While the official term used in the MRFTA is "large business group," this book intentionally uses "chaebol" to highlight the distinctive governance, ownership, and control structures historically associated with Korean conglomerates. However, the landscape has changed significantly: (i) generational transitions have occurred—often two or three times—within major business groups; (ii) new conglomerates, particularly in the digital sector, have emerged; (iii) regulatory reforms have curbed many of the opportunistic behaviors once associated with the chaebol system; (iv) intense global competition now discourages inefficient management practices. While the KFTC has played a vital role in correcting structural failures within the chaebol system, the need for such intervention may be diminishing. This does not suggest that all existing regulations should be dismantled, but rather that the regulatory framework should evolve to reflect current realities—focusing on promoting fair competition, supporting innovation, and ensuring that enforcement remains targeted, proportionate, and forward-looking.

Suggestions for SMEs Antitrust Policy

The term *SMEs antitrust policy* may be unfamiliar to many competition law experts. In this context, it refers to policies designed to protect small and medium-sized enterprises (SMEs) from abusive practices by larger firms in superior bargaining positions, such as restricting competition, employing unfair methods of competition, or imposing unjust trading terms. This concept should be clearly distinguished from *SMEs subsidization policy*, which supports SMEs and startups through financial assistance and other non-competitive means.

Numerous business practices may be classified as unfair trade practices under Article 45 of the MRFTA (see Table 3.4 in Chap. 3). The criteria for assessing unfairness and illegality are diverse, encompassing *restrictions on competition, unfair methods of competition, and unfair terms of trade.* To reduce the administrative burden on the KFTC and better allocate its expertise and resources, enforcement of unfair trade practices should be streamlined to focus on those that directly restrict competition. Specifically, the KFTC should prioritize cases involving: Refusal to deal, Discriminatory practices, Exclusion of competitors, Tie-in sales, Binding and conditional transactions, and Resale price maintenance. Other types of unfair trade practices could be delegated to the Fair Trade Mediation Agency (a subsidiary of the KFTC), the Ministry of SMEs and Startups, or resolved through civil litigation. These cases—typically involving unfair methods or terms of trade—can often be adjudicated without complex economic analysis of competitive effects or efficiency justifications. This approach should also apply to the four special acts governing subcontracting, large-scale retailing, franchising, and agency relationships. These laws are rooted in the concept of "abuse of superior bargaining position" and should be evaluated primarily based on the fairness of trade terms. Article 45(6) of the MRFTA, which addresses abuses of superior position, is often regarded as the "grandfather clause" for these sector-specific statutes.

Even within the category of competition-restricting practices, enforcement should focus on cases involving firms with *superior bargaining power*. Currently, most unfair trade practices under Article 45 do not require a finding of market dominance—except for those involving abuse of superior position. Introducing a requirement of "transactional dominance" or "relative bargaing power" for KFTC intervention could help concentrate enforcement on more significant cases. In this regard, Section 20 of the German Competition Act offers a useful model. It targets firms with "relative or superior bargaining power," even if they do not meet the threshold for market dominance. The KFTC has often applied Article 45 in conjunction with Article 5 (abuse of market-dominant position), typically using Article 45 as a secondary claim when proving dominance under Article 5 is difficult—especially in cases involving contested market definitions or ambiguous concentration levels. If penalty surcharges were calibrated based on the degree of transactional dominance or power imbalance,[22] the need for concurrent application of Articles 5 and 45 could be reduced. Article 5 would then apply to clear-cut cases of dominance, while Article 45 would address cases where dominance is less certain but relative power is evident.

This proposed reformulation—focusing on competition-restricting practices by firms with relative bargaining power rather than strict market dominance—is particularly relevant in the digital economy. The EU's DMA of 2022, for example, allows for the designation of "gatekeepers" subject to *ex ante* obligations, even if they do not hold conventional market dominance. In digital markets, it is often difficult to establish dominance in the traditional sense. Practices such as best price clauses (MFNs) or self-preferencing by platform incumbents may arise from the

[22]The current maximum of penalty surcharges is set at 6% of relevant sales for market dominance cases and at 4% for unfair trade practice cases. However, the KFTC determines the actual penalty level within these limits based on the guideline of imposing penalty surcharges, considering various relevant factors.

conglomerate power of platform ecosystems rather than from dominance in a narrowly defined market. In such cases, the KFTC may find it challenging to apply Article 5 effectively. Instead, the KFTC could rely on a reformed Article 45 framework—focused on unfair trade practices by firms with superior bargaining positions—and impose enhanced penalty surcharges where appropriate. This would allow the agency to address harmful conduct in digital markets more flexibly and effectively, without being constrained by rigid dominance thresholds.

Suggestions for Market Dominance Abuse Regulation

The maturity of a country's competition policy enforcement can often be gauged by the soundness of its approach to regulating abuse of market dominance—particularly the appropriateness of market definition and the rigor of competitive effects analysis. The depth and quality of economic analysis applied in such cases are critical to ensuring a high standard of reasonableness in enforcement. This is equally true for merger control. Over the past two decades, the KFTC has made steady progress in this area. A pivotal moment came with the Supreme Court's 2007 decision in the *Posco* case, which emphasized the importance of assessing both the intent and effect of conduct aimed at maintaining or enhancing market dominance. This ruling catalyzed the KFTC's adoption of more sophisticated analytical tools and methodologies, laying the groundwork for more robust economic analysis in enforcement.

Despite these advancements, the KFTC still lags behind leading competition authorities in jurisdictions such as the United States, UK, and EU—particularly in terms of in-house economic expertise. The number of Ph.D.-level economists within the KFTC's economic analysis division remains limited. To close this gap, the KFTC should increase its budget for economic analysis, recruit more in-house economists with advanced training, and appoint a high-ranking, well-compensated Chief Economist to lead the analytical function. More importantly, the economic analysis team should be involved from the outset of investigations. Currently, it appears that investigative teams often lead cases and later seek support from economists to validate their findings. For the sake of objectivity and analytical integrity, economists should participate in the early stages of case development—helping to define relevant markets and assess competitive effects before stances are finalized.

As illustrated in Chap. 4, many of Korea's most prominent market dominance cases have involved multinational enterprises, such as Microsoft, Intel, Qualcomm, and Google. These cases have provided the KFTC with valuable opportunities to benchmark its enforcement practices against those of more established agencies. In earlier cases, such as *Microsoft*'s tying practices in 2006 and *Intel*'s conditional rebates in 2008, the KFTC closely referenced precedents set by the European Commission. However, more recent cases—such as *Qualcomm*'s licensing and chip supply model in 2017 and *Google*'s anti-fragmentation agreement in 2021—demonstrate the KFTC's growing confidence in raising novel issues and independently managing complex investigations. This evolution marks a promising shift toward greater institutional maturity.

In multinational cases, enforcement priorities may diverge depending on whether the dominant firms are domestic or foreign. For example, the EU's DMA designates gatekeepers—such as Alphabet, Amazon, Apple, ByteDance, Meta, and Microsoft—all of which are based in the United States. or China. European firms often compete with these giants as new entrants. Korea's platform economy presents a unique landscape. Domestic firms such as Naver (search), Coupang (e-commerce), and Kakao (social networking) hold strong positions and often compete directly with US-based multinationals. In this context, the KFTC must maintain an independent and balanced stance—distinct from both US and EU approaches. To ensure that enforcement is perceived as impartial and not protectionist, the KFTC must apply rigorous economic analysis when defining relevant markets, establishing dominance, and evaluating the competitive effects of alleged abuses. This analytical rigor is essential not only for credibility but also for ensuring that enforcement promotes competition without favoring inefficient domestic or foreign firms.

Suggestions for Merger Regulation

The importance of economic analysis in merger review cannot be overstated. The KFTC has increasingly employed sophisticated tools—such as critical loss analysis, diversion ratios, natural experiments, merger simulations, and upward pricing pressure (UPP)—to define relevant markets and assess competitive effects, as discussed in Chap. 5. While the KFTC has made commendable progress, there remains room for improvement. Enhancing the capacity of the economic analysis team and involving them more proactively at the early stages of merger investigations would significantly strengthen the agency's analytical rigor. In particular, the KFTC should prepare to evaluate *non-horizontal mergers* more systematically, especially in the context of the digital platform economy. This may require updating merger guidelines to provide clearer expectations for firms and to ensure consistent enforcement of non-horizontal merger rules.

A key lesson from Korea's experience is that merger regulation must remain focused on promoting competition and should not be subordinated to broader industrial policy objectives. As illustrated in the 1999 *Hyundai Motor–Kia Car* merger (discussed in Chap. 5), merger decisions can be influenced by government priorities such as industrial restructuring. During the East Asian financial crisis, Hyundai Motor was arguably the only viable acquirer for the financially distressed Kia. Concerns over creditor losses and potential job cuts likely influenced the government's support for the merger. This was not an isolated case. In 2000, the horizontal merger between *SK Telecom and Shinsegi Telecom* significantly increased market concentration (HHI = 2669; ΔHHI = 1213), reinforcing SK Telecom's dominance with a 56.9% market share—38.6 percentage points ahead of its nearest competitor.[23] Despite serious anticompetitive concerns, the merger was approved with a behavioral remedy requiring SK Telecom to reduce its market share below 50% within a year—a condition widely criticized for its ineffectiveness.

[23] KFTC 2000–76, SK Telecom—Shinsegi Mobile Telecom Merger, May 16 2000.

A deviation from the core objectives of competition policy to serve other policy agendas inevitably leads to adverse consequences. As discussed in Chap. 5, the *Hyundai Motor–Kia* merger and the resulting monopoly in Korea's passenger automobile industry significantly strengthened workers' bargaining power. The substantial monopoly rents earned by the merged entity provided a strong basis for labor demands. While these demands may have been legitimate from the workers' perspective, they contributed to a distortion in Korea's labor market—exacerbating the dual structure between high-paid and low-paid sectors. Some may argue that the *Hyundai Motor–Kia* merger had a silver lining: the creation of a globally competitive firm, supported by economies of scale and the financial cushion afforded by domestic monopoly rents. However, in the case of the SK Telecom–Shinsegi merger, no such positive trade-off is evident. Instead, the merger imposed a long-term burden on the telecommunications regulator, which was tasked with maintaining a semblance of competition through "asymmetric regulation." This approach favored weaker competitors by restricting SK Telecom—the dominant carrier—from engaging in competitive strategies such as price reductions and aggressive marketing. Ultimately, this regulatory compromise hindered market dynamics without delivering clear benefits. Unlike Hyundai Motor, SK Telecom has not demonstrated notable success in international markets, raising further questions about the justification for allowing such a concentration of market power.

The conflict between competition policy and industrial policy is not merely a relic of the past—it remains highly relevant today, as demonstrated by the recent merger between *Korean Air and Asiana Airlines*, initiated in 2022 and concluded now in all relevant jurisdictions. The Korea Development Bank (KDB), a major creditor of Asiana Airlines, provided substantial public funds to rescue the airline from financial distress and subsequently led the effort to sell the company to recover its loans. Initially, Hyundai Development Company (HDC) agreed to acquire Asiana in 2019, but the deal collapsed due to the economic uncertainty caused by the COVID-19 pandemic. KDB then selected Korean Air as the alternative acquirer. This background sets the stage for a merger that differs significantly from the *Hyundai–Kia* merger of 1999, particularly in terms of international scrutiny. The KFTC imposed significant structural remedies to address anticompetitive concerns, while other global competition authorities have demanded even stricter conditions—ironically, measures that may weaken the competitive strength of the merged entity, contrary to the objectives stated by KDB and Korean Air. Ultimately, the merger may result in Korean Air monopolizing Korea's two flag carriers and enable KDB to recover its loans to Asiana. However, it may not fulfill the ambition of transforming Korean Air into a "global top 10 airline," as claimed. Unlike the Hyundai Motor–Kia merger, where monopolization was arguably accepted as a trade-off for achieving global competitiveness, the *Korean Air–Asiana Airlines* merger does not appear to offer a similarly compelling justification.

Suggestions for Cartel Regulation

Competition naturally drives price reductions and improvements in quality and service, all else being equal. However, this should not be misconstrued to suggest that competition policy ought to be used as a direct tool to curb price increases. Inflationary pressures are primarily driven by macroeconomic factors—whether on the demand or supply side—and cannot be effectively addressed through microeconomic instruments such as competition policy or industry regulation. During periods of inflation, governments may be tempted to suppress price increases in essential goods by aggressively enforcing competition laws,[24] particularly through the threat of cartel investigations. It has been suggested that the KFTC has, at times, used the threat of such investigations in industries producing staple foods—such as kimchi, ramen, and soju—to deter price hikes that are politically sensitive and of concern to the general public. While such measures may yield short-term results, they are ultimately unsustainable. They risk distorting market signals and leading to inefficient resource allocation over the long term. Therefore, antitrust enforcement—especially in the area of cartel regulation—should not be used as a tool to suppress prices in response to transient populist pressures. Instead, competition policy should remain focused on preserving market dynamics and ensuring long-term consumer welfare through fair and open competition.

Imprisonment represents the most severe form of competition law enforcement. Among global jurisdictions, Korea, Japan, and the United States are notable for allowing criminal prosecution—particularly for cartel offenses—while most other countries rely solely on administrative or civil sanctions.[25] In Korea, the MRFTA grants the KFTC the exclusive authority to initiate criminal proceedings. Under this provision, criminal prosecution for violations specified in the Act can only proceed if the KFTC files a formal complaint. This exclusivity is intended to prevent excessive or inappropriate criminal indictments by entities lacking the KFTC's specialized expertise in competition matters. However, the KFTC's exclusive right to accuse has long been a subject of controversy. Prosecutors have argued that this arrangement may lead to under-enforcement, particularly in serious cases involving hardcore cartels such as price-fixing, market allocation, market-share agreements, and bid rigging. In 2018, an agreement was reached between the KFTC and the Prosecutors' Office to abolish the KFTC's exclusive right to accuse in cases involving hardcore cartels. This would have allowed prosecutors to independently initiate investigations and file criminal charges in such cases. Despite this agreement, the proposed change

[24] The "Price Stabilization and Fair Trade Act" enacted in 1976, which preceded the "Monopoly Regulation and Fair Trade Act" in 1981, seems to suggest a potential misunderstanding of competition policy as being aimed at price stabilization.

[25] Among the 34 OECD countries, only 13 provide for criminal penalties for violations of competition laws. Of these, five countries (Canada, the UK, Austria, Demark, and Ireland) impose criminal penalties exclusively for cartel offenses; two countries (France and Iceland) extend criminal liability to both cartels and abuses of market dominance; and five countries (the United States, Japan, Greece, Norway, and Israel) apply criminal penalties to broader range of violations, including cartels, market-dominance abuses, and anticompetitive mergers. In contrast, Korea imposes criminal penalties for all violations of the MRFTA, making its enforcement regime one of the most comprehensive among OECD countries (see Ji 2021).

was ultimately excluded from the comprehensive amendment of the MRFTA in 2020, reportedly due to political considerations.[26]

Many antitrust experts, myself included, believe that the KFTC's exclusive right to file criminal charges should be maintained in principle for several important reasons. First, allowing unrestricted criminal indictments in antitrust cases could lead to over-enforcement, potentially stifling legitimate economic activity. Antitrust violations often involve complex economic assessments, and criminal prosecution without the KFTC's specialized expertise could result in misjudgments that deter pro-competitive behavior. Second, the exclusivity of this right has already been moderated in practice. The MRFTA requires the KFTC to file a criminal complaint with the Prosecutor General in cases involving serious violations. Moreover, the Prosecutor General may request the KFTC to initiate a criminal charge in other cases. Additionally, high-ranking officials such as the Chairperson of the Board of Audit and Inspection, the Minister of SMEs and Startups, and the Administrator of the Public Procurement Service may also request the KFTC to file a criminal complaint if they deem it necessary from their respective policy perspectives. Finally, the criminal prosecution of antitrust violations should remain insulated from political ideologies and inter-agency interests. Preserving the KFTC's gatekeeping role helps ensure that enforcement decisions are grounded in economic reasoning and legal standards, rather than influenced by shifting political or bureaucratic agendas.

Penalties for cartel participants have been progressively strengthened over time. In 2020, the KFTC raised the maximum surcharge from 10% to 20% of relevant sales. In 2019, punitive damages of up to three times the losses incurred from cartel activities were introduced. Additionally, the KFTC has recently increased the frequency of criminal accusations against cartel participants. Collectively, these measures enhance the deterrent effect against cartel behavior. To further improve both the *ex ante* deterrence of cartels and the *ex post* distribution of damages, I propose the introduction of Anglo-American–style class action lawsuits in antitrust cases, particularly those involving cartels. In such lawsuits, a representative plaintiff files a claim on behalf of a group with shared interests, and the outcome applies to all members unless individuals choose to opt out. Korea took a similar step in 2004 with the enactment of the Securities-Related Class Action Act, aimed at addressing collective injuries in securities trading. A comparable class action mechanism should be introduced for civil litigation seeking redress for collective harm caused by cartel conduct.

Currently, plaintiffs in civil damage recovery cases related to cartels are primarily government agencies or public corporations, which are mandated to seek redress for harm caused by illegal conduct, as well as large firms that purchase intermediary goods from cartel participants and sell final products to consumers. These entities

[26] Ji (2021) examines how interdepartmental conflicts of interest within the government, along with the partisan agendas of various political parties, shaped the process leading to the agreement and ultimately contributed to its abolishment.

typically possess both the incentive and the resources to pursue such claims. In contrast, final consumers—who are numerous, geographically dispersed, and individually affected to a relatively minor extent—often lack the financial and legal capacity to initiate lawsuits. As a result, their injuries frequently go uncompensated. Introducing a class action mechanism would empower groups of final consumers to collectively seek damages from cartels. This would not only strengthen deterrence against anti-competitive behavior but also promote distributive justice by ensuring that compensation is more equitably shared between direct and indirect purchasers.

Cases

KFTC 2000–76, May 16, 2000

References

Australia Competition and Consumer Commission (2018) Digital platforms inquiry: preliminary report. December 2018

Baker J (2017) Market power in the U.S. economy today. Washington Center for Equitable Growth

Carlton, D. (2024) The 2023 merger guidelines: a critical assessment. Working Paper in SSRN

Cremer J, de Montjoye Y-A, Schweitzer H (2019) Competition policy for the digital era, European commission directorate-general competition, April 4, 2019.of cash holdings. Sustainability 13(2):699–721

De Loecker J, Eeckhout J (2018) Global market power. NBER Working Paper

De Loecker J, Eeckhout J, Unger G (2020) The rise of market power and the macroeconomic implications. Quart J Econ 135:561–644

Easterbrook FH (1984) The limits of antitrust. Texas Law Rev 63:1–41

Furman J, Coyle D, Fletcher A, MacAuley D, Marsden P (2018) Unlocking digital competition: report of digital competition expert panel. March 13, 2019

Hovenkamp H (2019) Is antitrust's consumer welfare principle imperiled? J Comp Law 45:65–94

Hovenkamp H, Morton FS (2020) Framing the chicago school of antitrust analysis. Univ Pennsylvania Law Rev 168:1843–1878

Ji CH (2021) Exclusive right to accuse: the age of passion. Holliday Books. [in Korean]

Khan L (2017) Amazon's antitrust paradox. Yale Law Review 126:710–805

Khan L (2018) The new Brandeis movement: America's antimonopoly debate. J Euro Compet Law Pract 9:131–132

Kwaka J Jr, Valletti T, White L (2023) Antitrust economics at a time of upheaval: recent competition policy cases of two continents, edited volume. Competition Policy International

OECD (2021) Ex-Ante regulation and competition in digital markets–Note by Germany. DAF/COMP/WD(2021)61, December 2, 2021

Scott Morton F, Bouvier P, Ezrachi A, Jullien B, Katz K, Kimmelman G, Melamed A, and Morgenstern A (2019) Committee for the study of digital platforms: Market structure and antitrust subcommittee. Stigler Center for the Study of the Economy and the State in Booth Business School at Chicago University, May 15, 2019.

Schweitzer H, Houcap H, Kerber W, Welker R (2018) Modernizing the law on abuse of market power: report for the federal ministry for economic affairs and energy. April 9, 2018

Tirole J (2023) Competition and the industrial challenge for the digital age. Ann Rev Econ 15: 573–605

U.S. DOJ and FTC (2023) Merger guidelines. December 18, 2023

Index

S. Jeon, *Antitrust Policy in Korea*, https://doi.org/10.1007/978-981-95-0632-3

GPSR Compliance

The European Union's (EU) General Product Safety Regulation (GPSR) is a set of rules that requires consumer products to be safe and our obligations to ensure this.

If you have any concerns about our products, you can contact us on ProductSafety@springernature.com

In case Publisher is established outside the EU, the EU authorized representative is:

Springer Nature Customer Service Center GmbH
Europaplatz 3
69115 Heidelberg, Germany

Batch number: 09025099

Printed by Printforce, the Netherlands